W9-ADW-144

The Human Tradition around the World

Series Editors

WILLIAM H. BEEZLEY, Professor of History, University of Arizona
COLIN M. MACLACHLAN, John Christy Barr Distinguished
Professor of History, Tulane University

Each volume in this series is devoted to providing minibiographies of "real people" who, with their idiosyncratic behavior, personalize the collective experience of grand themes, national myths, ethnic stereotypes, and gender relationships. In some cases, their stories reveal the irrelevance of national events, global processes, and cultural encounters for men and women engaged in everyday life. The personal dimension gives perspective to history, which of necessity is a sketch of past experience.

The authors of each volume in this historical series are determined to make the past literal. They write accounts that identify the essential character of everyday lives of individuals. In doing so, these historians allow us to share the human traditions that find expression in these lives.

Volumes in The Human Tradition around the World Series

THE HUMAN TRADITION IN
MODERN BRAZIL

THE HUMAN TRADITION IN
MODERN BRAZIL

EDITED BY
PETER M. BEATTIE

NUMBER 7

A Scholarly Resources Inc. Imprint
Wilmington, Delaware

© 2004 by Scholarly Resources Inc.
All rights reserved
First published 2004
Printed and bound in the United States of America

Scholarly Resources Inc.
104 Greenhill Avenue
Wilmington, DE 19805-1897
www.scholarly.com

Library of Congress Cataloging-in-Publication Data

The human tradition in modern Brazil / edited by Peter M. Beattie.
    p. cm. — (The human tradition around the world ; no. 7)
   Includes bibliographical references and index.
   ISBN 0-8420-5038-8 (alk. paper) — ISBN 0-8420-5039-6 (pbk. :
alk. paper)
   1. Brazil—History—1763–1821—Biography. 2. Brazil—History—
1822—Biography. 3. Brazil—Biography. I. Beattie, Peter M., 1963–
II. Series.

F2534.H86 2003
981'.04'0922—dc21
                                                 2003008943

∞ The paper used in this publication meets the minimum requirements
of the American National Standard for permanence of paper for printed
library materials, Z39.48, 1984.

To the memory of
Professor Robert M. Levine
mentor and friend

About the Editor

Peter M. Beattie is the author of *The Tribute of Blood: Army, Honor, Race, and Nation in Brazil, 1864–1945* (2001), and associate professor of history at Michigan State University. He is currently pursuing research on crime and punishment for a book that is tentatively titled *Penal Institutions and Penology in Slavery and Emancipation: Pernambuco, Brazil, 1830–1930.*

I believe in aristocracy, though—if that is the right word, and if a democrat may use it. Not an aristocracy of power, based upon rank and influence, but an aristocracy of the sensitive, the considerate and the plucky. Its members are to be found in all nations and classes, and all through the ages, and there is a secret understanding between them when they meet. They represent the true human tradition, the one permanent victory of our queer race over cruelty and chaos. Thousands of them perish in obscurity, a few are great names. They are sensitive for others as well as for themselves, they are considerate without being fussy, their pluck is not swankiness but the power to endure, and they can take a joke.

E. M. Forster, *Two Cheers for Democracy* (1951)

Acknowledgments

The contributing authors to this lively collection of biographical essays made the work of bringing them together a pleasurable and stimulating experience. Our frank and amicable exchanges and their patience with my queries nourished the project from the outset, and I feasted on their bountiful repast of collegial enthusiasm. This volume represents the contributors' generosity and commitment as scholars and teachers of Brazilian history, and I feel fortunate to have been able to work with each of them. What a wonderful community of historians of Brazil! I also thank Bill Beezley for inviting me to edit this collection and for his crucial guidance as it took shape. The editorial team at Scholarly Resources, especially Rick Hopper, Eileen M. Schultz, Ann M. Aydelotte, and Michelle M. Slavin gave unstinting support with good cheer.

This book is dedicated to one of the remarkable authors in this volume, Robert M. Levine, Gabelli Senior Scholar in the Arts and Sciences in the History Department at the University of Miami, Coral Gables. Over the last four decades, Professor Levine's contributions to the history of Brazil and Latin America in the form of teaching, mentoring, and service to the profession as well as a host of publications constitute an inspiring and towering edifice of achievement. Regrettably, Bob lost his battle with cancer on April 1, 2003. He will be missed by his many students, colleagues, and friends. *Saudades e abraços*, Bob!

Contents

Introduction: The Individual and the Collective Community in the Human Tradition of Modern Brazil

PETER M. BEATTIE

This volume of life stories explores how individuals with nonclite origins experienced historical continuities and changes related to the rise of national identity and the subsequent emergence of a national state after Brazil won its independence from Portugal in 1822. Biography provides a privileged means to explore how individuals related to their community through their words, silences, actions, and inactions. Humans are a gregarious species, and our survival as individuals has and continues to depend on the collective community. One of the advantages of collective living is the ability to share experiences and memories with others across and within generations. From this sharing arose first oral and later written history, powerful tools in shaping how individuals would come to identify themselves in relation to collectivities. The relative weight of individual versus communal rights and obligations is perhaps the most basic and enduring tension in the human tradition and condition. Philosophers, lawyers, religious leaders, politicians, economists, historians, and others have spilled oceans of ink in their attempts to set the proper limits of individual freedom and communal responsibilities.

Few humans ever lived like the "noble savage," a concept whose power in European consciousness augmented with the drive to colonize the Americas and "civilize" its peoples. For the Swiss philosopher Jean-Jacques Rousseau, the noble savage was a true individual who lived isolated from others in a supposedly "natural" and "uncorrupted" state. Rousseau argued in the late 1700s that it was "civilization" that debased and enslaved the individual. He proposed that to perfect human society and institutions a new "social contract" was needed whereby educated adult males would chose leaders whose authority derived from the consent of the majority. Thus, Rousseau critiqued the institution of monarchy that drew its legitimacy from royal bloodlines and ultimately the idea that the legitimacy of kings and queens derived from divine consent. The idea of the noble savage (for some, the ultimate individual) was key to modern European critiques of traditional ideas about how to organize just government, economy, and community.[1] Enlightenment thinkers such as Rousseau praised leadership and recognition based on talent and effort rather than on birth, and they sought to reorganize their societies in accordance with the "natural laws" that drew much of their inspiration and legitimacy from empirical science rather than from divinity. The French dictator Napoleon saw himself as the embodiment of this new ideology of meritocracy and portrayed himself as the liberator of the peoples of Europe. Most of Spain's and Portugal's populations did not desire French liberation, however, and many resisted or fled before Napoleon's conquering armies, which entered Spain in 1807 and Portugal late that same year. These invasions ultimately sparked the struggles for independence in most of Latin America and led to the precocious development of new nations in most of the Americas by the 1820s.

When Brazil became an independent nation in 1822, the battles did not stop after its relatively quick and painless victory over the armed resistance of Portuguese loyalists. Conflict continued over how to represent the national community, how to form a legitimate government, who would be allowed to participate in public life, and how individuals understood their place in relation to the new national community. The contours of Brazilian society took on hybrid forms. The modern and traditional, the popular and erudite, and the public and private came to interpenetrate one another and to coexist in unique combinations that were not fixed but fluid.[2] Brazilian modernist writers in the 1920s and 1930s espoused this sense of hybridity by embracing the image of the Tupi Indian cannibal as a creative noble savage who consumed European captives as well as European goods, ideas, and culture. But in the process of digesting these European consumables, the cannibal internalized and refashioned them. European cultural influences were thus transformed into uniquely hybrid and original "Brazilian" cultural products, practices, and ideas that were far more than pale imitations of European models.[3]

How did most Brazilians understand evolving ideas and symbols of *brasilidade*, or Brazilianness? How did they invoke or reject this idea of a national community? And how did they respond to state authorities and others who claimed to speak for it? The authors of the essays in this volume explore the conflicting expressions and definitions of national, local, and self-identity that were often mediated by a variety of factors such as one's birthplace, race, gender, class, ethnicity, domicile, legal status, religion, political affiliation, age cohort, occupation, and era. Each essay addresses some aspects of these categories, but each author brings a different approach and a fresh perspective to varying combinations of these factors. The wonderful group of historians who contributed chapters to this volume anchor their essays in historical context to illuminate broader economic, sociological, and political circumstances that shaped the lives, views, and actions of their subjects. They also skillfully demonstrate the force of the individual in shaping historical events and trends. Borrowing from the phrase of the historical sociologist Charles Tilly, this volume is intended to give the reader a better sense of how a wide range of "ordinary people lived the big historical changes" that swept through Brazil after Independence. This viewpoint is the essence of what historians call the new social history, a subfield that emerged from the political ferment of the 1960s and 1970s that emphasizes history from the bottom up rather than from the top down.[4]

What is an individual? This question may seem a naive one, but it is much more complicated to answer when we try to pin down the concept for historical analysis. In the 1990s a new subfield began to emerge that is broadly referred to as the "new cultural history." The passion of new social historians for statistical and quantitative methods ceded ground to the new cultural history's "literary turn" that is more concerned with representation. Many of its practitioners borrow from the new social history and vice versa, but there are some conflicting impulses in these approaches that are not always made explicit, especially in terms of how they conceive of the individual. Social history from below implies the notion of an agent that is often reduced to the modern idea of the individual, whereas the new cultural history's analysis emphasizes the way that all social actors are continually culturally constructed. While social historians emphasize a concept of the individual as more easily distinguishable from the society that surrounds them, cultural history suggests that pulling apart these concepts is difficult because individuals are constantly being remolded by themselves, by circumstances, and by others around them.[5]

While social history emphasized history from the bottom up, the new cultural historians have used some of the same tools developed to study the less powerful instead to analyze the weapons of the powerful.[6] Until recently, studies of race, gender, and class were assumed to focus on nonwhites, women, and the working class, but now scholars have begun to historicize changing concepts of whiteness, masculinity, and elite status among many other categories of analysis. This volume does not try to resolve the tension between the more static concept of the individual present in the new social history and the much less stable conception of the individual in the new cultural history. However, the reader will see influences of both these historiographic traditions in the vignettes presented here. Biography is a refined approach for historians who desire to tease out the tensions between individual identity and action to explore their relationship to the collective community and the material world. These are rich and complex questions that the reader may fruitfully ponder from different perspectives in each chapter.

The contributors use the lives of less than privileged Brazilians to illuminate how different historical actors experienced, thought about, and responded to historical moments of broad importance. Traditionally, historians lavished much more attention on those people who held power and influence than on those who are thought of as "ordinary," unimportant, deviant, or even frivolous. Indeed, those who are wealthy, mighty, and influential tend to leave more documentation about their lives, hopes, and desires than do ordinary folks, who are much more likely to be illiterate. Written documents are the traditional raw materials that historians depend on for their craft, and thus they play a powerful role in shaping interpretations of the past. Since the 1970s, historians have turned more attention to the lives of those who were less fortunate and less influential—individuals and groups who were, as Eric Wolfe described them, "people without history." But is it not more important to understand how the powerful thought, behaved, and lived? Are not the powerful and most talented individuals of history inherently more interesting than those who were less so? As a student once admonished me, there is a good reason why *People* magazine is for sale on the newsstand and not "Ordinary People" magazine.

The most important reason to pay attention to the lives, hopes, and ambitions of nonelite persons is that our understanding of the past is limited and distorted without them. Sometimes a seemingly humble individual will spontaneously choose a course of action that unleashes forces of broad social transformation. For instance, when a tired Rosa Parks sat down in the segregated white section of a Montgomery, Alabama, bus and refused to move when told to do so, could she have anticipated that this act of defiance would spark a citywide transportation strike that electrified the civil rights movement across the United States?

Is the history of famous persons inherently more interesting and significant than that of those who are less so? I would answer an unqualified "no" to this question, and the essays in this volume eloquently support this assertion. Interesting and gifted individuals are born into all social classes and groups. The creativity and courage that less privileged actors demonstrate in the face of adversity can be even more inspiring because they have fewer resources and are more vulnerable. Still, one should not romanticize the poor or the petty bourgeoisie as simply heroic victims of human inequalities and injustices. They, too, were capable of deception, exploitation, and cruelty. Like most of us, they made mistakes they regretted, but they also experienced the elation of achievement. The life stories here beckon the reader to imagine the satisfaction that Carolina Maria de Jesus and Adolfo Ferreira Caminha felt when they saw their first book in print, or when Geraldo Pereira heard on the radio a samba song he had composed. We can ponder the different ecstasies of spiritual revelation and communal solidarity experienced by Agostinho José Pereira, Juca Rosa, Jacobina Maurer, and Dom Hélder Câmara in their religious lives and compare them to the sense of awe that Norma Fraga felt when she took part in massive patriotic rallies. We can imagine the pride that swelled in Domingos da Guia when reporters praised his soccer prowess, and the thrill that stirred the swaggering Jôfre Corrêa Netto when he made international headlines as the charismatic leader of a peasants' strike. We can discern the patriotic fervor that inspired Daniel Gomes de Freitas to participate in conspiratorial plots, and Vicente Racioppi to dedicate himself to the preservation of artifacts and buildings significant to Brazilian history. We can also picture Cândido Rondon's surprise when he was ordered to guide Theodore Roosevelt on a hunting expedition through the Amazon frontier, and Xavante Indian Mario Juruna's amazement when he won election to Brazil's national congress. We can feel the adrenaline rush that Madame Satã must have felt when he won a cross-dressing costume contest or bested a fellow street tough in a barroom brawl.

To say that many historians have recently been more interested in the lives of ordinary people is not to suggest that we can ignore the initiatives and ideas of the rich and powerful in history. Rather, it is to suggest that an understanding of one without the other can lead to misconceptions and erroneous conclusions. For example, historians traditionally explained a popular politician's power and influence in terms of charisma or the ability to manipulate and inspire supporters. In this conception, great men and women forged major historical transformations. More recently, historians have reversed this approach by exploring why followers found certain leaders so compelling that they were willing to take incredible risks to support them.[7] This reversal takes us back to the basic question of the relationship between the individual and the collective. To what extent do followers make or find their leaders and vice versa?

While the contributors to this volume seek to shed light on how ordinary people fared in Brazilian society, the reader should be forewarned that most of the individuals featured here were unusual in one way or another. If they had not been different, there likely would have been little available documentation for the historian. This gap is a dilemma for the social historian because there are often too few sources from which to write a biography. Some life stories in this volume came to light because they caught the attention of authorities for one reason or another and thus became part of a written historical record. Even these biographies are sometimes partial because, after a time, the individual in question disappears from the record. Conversely, some of the vignettes illuminate the lives of individuals of relatively modest backgrounds who became figures of such national importance that they later might be characterized as belonging to the political or cultural elite. Here, more complete information is available and the challenge for the historian is different: How does one select the most significant events, actions, and words to convey a vivid sense of the individual's place in his or her era?

One way to appreciate how Brazilians view individuals and the place of individuality in their culture and history is to consider the Portuguese word commonly used to describe an unusual or striking person: *figura*, someone who is seen as a "character" or a person who is larger than life. As a North American who initially came to know Brazil as a visiting university student, I often puzzled over the meaning of *figura* as I struggled to learn Portuguese and to make my own sense of Brazilian society. I first heard the word in Rio de Janeiro when I was riding a bus through the noisy, humid, and exhaust-filled streets of Copacabana (one of the most densely populated boroughs in the world). Suddenly, a well-dressed, portly, but robust young man a few seats in front of me began to sing an opera aria at the top of his lungs. The other passengers, some sitting, others standing, at first turned in astonishment to see who was singing as if he were on stage. The singer took no notice of the perplexed stares and continued to bellow in Italian most of the way down clamorous Nossa Senhora de Copacabana avenue. He sang beautifully but loudly. When he finished, most of the passengers erupted in applause. An older lady seated next to me leaned over to share her assessment in a bemused mix of admiration and consternation, "Que figura!" "What a character!" Likely assuming that I was a foreigner, she added with a smile, "Only in Brazil, my son!"

Right or wrong, I concluded that a U.S. driver would have stopped the bus and asked the young man to pipe down, or that other passengers would have intervened. This tolerant bus driver in Rio, however, was not alarmed. He smoked, despite the prominent "No Smoking" sign displayed above his head, while weaving through heavy traffic in fits and starts. He also stopped to let passengers on and off at undesignated stops. I later came to learn that these practices were not unusual in Rio, but they were much less common in other parts of Brazil. Without knowing it at the time, I was learning an important lesson about what a *figura* was and how other Brazilians identified with and related to him or her with different mixtures of tolerance, admiration, and unease. Over the years that I spent in Brazil, I heard about a lot of *figuras*, some prominent, others humble, some contemporary, others historical, some men, others women. (At times, my Brazilian acquaintances and friends even called me a *figura*.) In truth, almost everyone will be referred to as a *figura* at some point in his life, but there are those elect few who are much more consistently identified in this way. To call someone a *figura* not ony can be a compliment, but it can also be a slight. It is a complex term, and I finally decided that rather than trying to nail down its exact meaning, I had discovered a rich question that is never definitively answered. Once again, I had returned via a Brazilian bus ride to the basic humanistic question of the relationship between the individual and the collective community.

An important part of learning about another culture and period is to examine this relationship between the individual, the family, and the community. For a variety of historical, socioeconomic, and cultural reasons, family bonds and ties of friendship are generally given a high priority in Brazilian society, while an individual's identification with the broader local and national communities is often more tenuous. These generalizations admittedly are broad and can border on stereotypes, but the life stories that are found here both confirm these assertions and negate them. They help us to see broad patterns and traits from the perspective of individuals who at times not only confirmed but also defied general trends and stereotypes.

In the end, our experience of life and our understanding of our history and identity are intensely personal and colored by myths and interpretations. These interpretations help us to make sense of ourselves as individuals and to present ourselves to others in a more coherent fashion. Humans are wont to embellish their own life history, and this exaggeration may be healthy if it is not taken too far. I hope that this volume will stimulate the reader to ponder these issues. Even though the individuals featured in this volume are very different or distant from us in time, place, and background, as humans we all share a similar struggle to make sense of ourselves and our lives.

∽

As editor of this volume, I sought out a wide variety of life stories to capture some of the diversity of Brazil's regions, economies, climates, peoples, cultures, and eras. No group of fifteen biographies would be entirely able to represent the rich heterogeneity of the country's society and history. Indeed, as Judith Ewell and William H. Beezley sagaciously put it, "No one can 'truly' stand for his or her group."[8] With these caveats in mind, I strove to solicit an interesting mix of vignettes, most of which came out of larger social history research projects that the contributors were still conducting or had recently completed. It is worth noting what the reader will and will not find in the following chapters.

All of Brazil's five major geographical regions are represented at least briefly, but the sparsely settled north gets the shortest shrift (a small part of Cândido Rondon's biography). Conversely, the city of Rio is overrepresented, with six chapters dealing with individuals who led the larger portion of their lives there. The reader should note, however, that four of these six had migrated to Rio from other regions, so these chapters are not exclusively about Brazil's best-known urban center and one-time national capital. On the whole, the urban experience is better represented in the volume, but one-quarter of the chapters feature individuals who lived primarily in rural areas.

Ideally, I would have liked more biographies of women. Only three essays focus on women, far out of proportion to their importance and share in Brazil's population. Still, most of the life stories based on male subjects note the prominent roles that women played in a variety of settings, and gender is a central concern to most chapters whether they focus on men or women. Approximately one-half of the chapters feature persons of African descent, although the racial identity of Daniel Gomes de Freitas is not certain. There is also one *indigene*, and seven individuals whom most Brazilians would likely class as "white," even though some of them claimed a mixed racial heritage. While Afro-Brazilians are well represented, there is no slave biography, but bondspeople and their descendants appear in many of the vignettes. Three essays deal with European immigrants or their Brazilian-born children in Brazil, but immigrants from the eastern Mediterranean and Asia are not treated here.

The variety of occupations held by those featured in the chapters include tailor, housewife, teacher, preacher, priest, military officer, composer, apprentice, museum curator, soccer player, lawyer, labor organizer, sergeant, author, ragpicker, street hustler, garbageman, and politician. Many of these people held a number of jobs over the course of their lives. Interestingly, while there are faith healers and others who dabbled in folk medicine, there are also women and men of science who placed their faith in empiricism and modern northern European styles and thought. Although Brazil was and remains overwhelmingly Catholic, two Protestants are featured in the volume along with one Afro-Brazilian spiritist. A number of the chapters address the commingling of the religious and the political in the lives of many Brazilians. While some identified strongly with a political party or social movement, others had less strongly defined views of formal politics. Dom Hélder Câmara's vignette reveals how an individual's political views and identity can change profoundly over the course of a lifetime. This brief and far from comprehensive overview should give the reader a better sense of the volume's coverage in relation to the broad sweep of the last two hundred years of Brazilian history.

∽

The challenge and pleasure of reading and writing microhistory often involves honing an ability to imagine what the world looks like from a perspective very different from our own. This exercise makes a human connection to the historical actor(s) under analysis, and there is no better vehicle than biography for such an imaginary voyage. The empathy and antipathy that we experience in reading biography is an important part of what connects us to the human tradition—a tradition whose boundaries are much wider than that of our local, ethnic, national, or linguistic community. In a world where globalization is an overused watch word, the ability to understand varying cultural perspectives becomes an important skill that needs to be cultivated not only for humanistic ends but also for commerce as well as for domestic and international politics.

The men and women featured in this volume led lives that were very different from those of most contemporary middle class citizens of North Atlantic nations, and in many ways this difference is what makes their vignettes compelling. Explorations of the events, trends, and conditions that surrounded historical actors give the reader a better sense of how and why they carried themselves through their time and space in history the way that they did. It helps us to understand why some of these people embraced ideas of progress and modernization emanating mostly from North Atlantic nations and why others steadfastly rejected these ideals. In this sense, globalization is far from a new trend, even though modern technology seems to be accelerating it exponentially and fears of the homogenization of world culture modeled along the lines of the United States become even more palpable in the twenty-first century. In these biographies of nonelite Brazilians, we can hear echoes of the current debates over whether globalization and less restrained international trade are beneficial or detrimental to the interests of the majority of the world's population and Earth's environment. There is much that can be learned from the lives of these Brazilian *figuras* who connect us to a global human tradition.

NOTES

1. Afonso Arinos de Melo Franco, *O Indio brasileiro e a Revolução Francesa: As origens brasileiras de teoria de bondade natural* (Rio de Janeiro: Topbooks, 2001 [1937]).

See Jean-Jacques Rousseau, *The Social Contract*, trans. Maurice Cranston (New York: Penguin Books, 1988).

2. Here I borrow from the vocabulary and ideas of Néstor García Canclini, *Hybrid Cultures: Strategies for Entering and Leaving Modernity*, trans. Christopher L. Chiappari and Silvia L. Lopez (Minneapolis: University of Minnesota Press, 1995).

3. Oswaldo de Andrade, *Do Pau-Brasil à antropofagia e às utopias: Manifestos, teses de concurso e ensaios*, 2d ed. (Rio de Janeiro: Civilização Brasileira, 1978).

4. Charles Tilly, "Retrieving European Lives," in *Reliving the Past: The Worlds of Social History*, ed. Oliver Zunz (Chapel Hill: University of North Carolina Press, 1985), 11–52.

5. See Claudio Lomnitz's discussion of this difference in "Barbarians at the Gate? A Few Remarks on the Politics of the 'New Cultural History of Mexico,' " *HAHR* 79:2 (May 1999): 367–83. For an analysis by a variety of authors of the state of debate among Brazilian historians in relation to the new cultural history, see Ciro Flamirion Cardoso and Ronaldo Vainfas, eds., *Domínios da história: Ensaios de teoria e metodologia* (Rio de Janeiro: Editora Campus, 1997).

6. Here the title of James Scott's *Weapons of the Weak: Everyday Forms of Peasant Resistance* (New Haven: Yale University Press, 1985) is paraphrased.

7. See, for example, John C. Chasteen's book that focuses on the "gaze of the followers," *Heroes on Horseback: A Life and Times of the Last Gaucho Caudillos* (Albuquerque: University of New Mexico Press, 1995).

8. Judith Ewell and William H. Beezley, eds., "Introduction," in *The Human Tradition in Modern Latin America* (Wilmington, DE: Scholarly Resources, 1997).

PART I

THE INDEPENDENCE AND
EARLY IMPERIAL GENERATIONS (1800–1869)

Napoleon's threats and eventual moves to invade Portugal in 1808 prompted Dom João VI to relocate his court to Rio de Janeiro with the British navy's assistance. To please his allies in London, the king opened Brazil's ports to international trade, a great boon to British merchants whose access to many European markets had been cut off by the French emperor's blockade. Even after Napoleon's final defeat in 1815, João VI continued to rule from Rio. Powerful merchants and leaders in Portugal, however, wanted their king back in Lisbon where they would have his ear. They also hoped to restrict Brazilian trade to Portuguese ports to reestablish Lisbon's control over the empire's most profitable colonial commerce. In 1820 the Parliament (Cortes) called on João VI to return, and he reluctantly agreed. He left his son, Prince Pedro, behind in Brazil, and he warned his son that it might be necessary to establish Brazil as an independent nation if the political climate in Portugal did not change. Pedro heeded his father's advice in 1822 when reactionary forces in Portugal continued to threaten the rights of merchants in Brazil to trade directly with other nations.

Traditionally, historians have portrayed Brazil's transition from a colonial to a national government in 1822 as one where continuities triumphed over transitions. The relatively peaceful secession from the mother country pleased most major landholders and merchants because plantation agriculture did not tolerate political instability well. The cultivation of sugarcane, coffee, and cotton were highly specialized capital- and labor-intensive enterprises that depended heavily on foreign markets, goods, and credit. The slave labor that worked the plantations constituted about one-third of Brazil's population at the time of Independence. It is hard to exaggerate the importance of African slavery to the development of Brazilian society. Two in every five blacks in the Atlantic slave trade went to Brazil; and today, according to some estimates, only Nigeria has a larger population of people of African descent than Brazil. While slavery was certainly concentrated in some regions more than others, it was a ubiquitous institution in Brazil that was found in every province. Fears of slave rebellion made most members of the master class cautious about resolving factional disputes with their peers through the force of arms.

1

Monarchy also survived Independence in Brazil, unlike in most of Spanish America, where republics and political instability predominated. While many supporters of Independence had been inspired by republican ideals, the fact that the central government's leader was of royal blood lent his rule legitimacy in the eyes of most Brazilians, rich and poor. Pedro oversaw the writing of a charter that guaranteed the emperor the preponderance of power within the framework of a constitutional monarchy. Although a variety of regional rebellions threatened to undermine the central government and to divide Brazilian territory into separate nations in the 1830s and 1840s, none succeeded. Still, the monarch himself was not immune to challenges. Popular protests and parliamentary pressure forced the heavy-handed Pedro to abdicate his throne in 1831 in favor of his five-year-old son. Pedro II became emperor in 1840, and his forty-nine-year rule would see the consolidation of imperial power in Rio. During his reign, two mature political parties emerged: the Conservatives and the Liberals. Most politicians came from the privileged landowning and merchant families, but members of both parties knew that the success of their political careers depended on the emperor's patronage.

The Roman Catholic faith continued to be the official religion of Brazil, even though national law gave Protestant merchants and settlers the right to practice their beliefs discreetly. Brazil's emperors retained the right claimed by Portugal's kings to name clerics to the highest posts in the Church hierarchy within the national territory. Thus, there was no separation of Church and state, and the Brazilian Catholic hierarchy was not nearly as independent or powerful as its counterpart in Mexico.

Pedro I took a keen interest in military matters, and he strove to develop a national military loyal to his rule. After his abdication in 1831, however, Parliament cut the size of the army's ranks in half and established a more decentralized National Guard as a means of counterbalancing the military might of the army and navy. Local political bosses across Brazil sought out officer posts in the National Guard in order to enhance their prestige and their local autonomy and to facilitate the mobilization of clients for elections. So many political bosses came to hold the rank of *coronel* (colonel) in the National Guard that the most basic unit of local political organization came to be called *coronelismo*. The merchants and landowners linked to the agro-export plantation system along with the institutions of slavery, the monarchy, the Catholic Church, and the military formed the pillars that supported Brazil's imperial order.

The largest part of Brazil's population was neither master nor slave, but free poor men and women of all races. Since colonial times, Indians,

Africans, and Europeans (mostly Portuguese men) coupled and formed a population characterized by race mixture. Indeed, most of Brazil's free poor were people of mixed race. A mostly "white" minority negotiated a wary rule over a nonwhite majority of slaves and free people. This white elite envisioned themselves at the top of a natural racial hierarchy. At the bottom of the ladder, they placed African-born slaves and located Brazilian-born slaves one rung above them. Free people of mixed race occupied a middle rung, but the idea of hierarchy tended to privilege those of lighter skin. Visible traces of African lineage implied that one's ancestors had been slaves whom the master class stereotyped as degraded, debauched, and dangerous individuals who lived outside the moralizing Christian influence of the nuclear family. Although rife with contradictions and exceptions, this idea of racial hierarchy attempted to divide the nonwhite majority along lines of color and ethnicity by giving some non whites privileges and status over others. Some nonwhites endowed with talent and favored with elite patronage became respected and wealthy members of Brazilian society to the point that they came to be considered "white." Prejudiced attitudes and practices related to Brazilian pragmatism and ideas of racial hierarchy encouraged individuals to think not only in terms of black and white but also in terms of black and brown with myriad gradations. We should not assume that all Brazilians accepted this racial hierarchy uncritically, but most came to associate "whiteness" with prestige and influence.

Regardless of their race, Brazil's free poor continued to depend on powerful patrons for protection and support after Independence. At election time or in periods of factional disputes they were expected to demonstrate their loyalty and deference to their patrons. While the constitution granted most poor free men suffrage and rights, their ability to take advantage of these legal guarantees freely and independently remained limited.

∽

The two chapters in Part I challenge in different ways the traditional emphasis on continuities outlined above in the half-century after Independence. Daniel Gomes de Freitas conspired and fought to implement liberal ideals that would expand opportunities for Brazilian-born free men, but he and many of his co-conspirators balked at expanding these rights to slaves and former slaves, especially those born in Africa. Conceptions of racial hierarchy proved difficult for most Brazilians to jettison. The black free man Agostinho José Pereira combined education with Protestant religious revelation to promote an alternative view of liberation and independence for his followers, mostly black women in the city of Recife. Authorities feared that his activities were part of a broader conspiracy among Brazilians of color to overthrow white rule. The life stories of Daniel and Agostinho reveal the racial tensions that continued to permeate Brazilian society after Independence.

CHAPTER I

Daniel Gomes de Freitas

Liberal Conspiracy in the Early National Period

HENDRIK KRAAY

In part because of Portuguese military weakness and British diplomatic support for an independent Brazilian state, the battles to liberate Brazil from Portuguese rule were not nearly as bloody or as drawn out as those fought in Spanish America for independence. But as Professor Hendrik Kraay argues, battles and conspiracies to shape the nature of Brazil's independence continued for decades after 1822. The preservation of the monarchy certainly helped to smooth the transition, and the monarchy lent legitimacy to the authority of the central government, but this authority was strenuously contested by Brazilians influenced by liberal ideals that called for greater equality, at least for respectable free men. Still, no regional revolt succeeded in toppling the central government in Rio de Janeiro, although Pedro I was impelled to abdicate his throne in favor of his young son in 1831. Only an army coup in 1889 brought an end to the Brazilian Empire and the monarchy by promulgating the Republic. The relative stability of Brazil's government contrasts starkly to most Spanish American nations, where rebel factions succeeded in toppling regimes repeatedly in the decades after Independence. But as Professor Kraay points out, historians too often overlook the many changes that independence wrought in Brazilian society by stressing instead continuities with the colonial period.

Brazil's separation from Portugal in 1822 meant different things to different participants and onlookers, and many conflicting visions of what society in an independent Brazil would be like. Professor Kraay explores these different perspectives by focusing on the life story of Daniel Gomes de Freitas, a man of middling social status who made his career as an army officer in Bahia's provincial capital, Salvador. Like some other men of his times and his background, Daniel was inspired by leveling liberal ideals that sought to guarantee advancement based on merit rather than on birth or connections. For Daniel and others, they wanted equal access with the landed elite to government jobs and political posts. They also sought to limit the rights of the Portuguese-born living in Brazil to participate in retail and overseas commerce (sectors of the economy that they dominated) as well as in government jobs. Still, the vision of how inclusive the new Brazilian national community would be was limited in the minds of Daniel and many others like him, who sought to distinguish themselves from freedmen and slaves. The type of leveling that Daniel envisioned excluded these members of Brazilian society, but many freedmen and slaves had found inspiration in the news of the successful slave revolt that founded the first black republic of Haiti in 1804 and abolished slavery. Also, the liberating rhetoric of Brazil's rebel conspirators encouraged their active participation in the conspiracies and insurgencies that occurred from the 1820s through the 1840s. Daniel Gomes de Freitas's life demonstrates the many contradictions that rebels with limited views of liberation faced in the slave society of postcolonial Brazil.

Hendrik Kraay, an associate professor of history at the University of Calgary, is a specialist on the history of nineteenth-century Bahia. His book, Race, State, and Armed Forces in Independence-Era Brazil: Bahia, 1790s–1840s *(2001), explores the changing role of military institutions in this important province from colonial times through the early decades of Independence. He is currently working on an analysis of the annual commemorative parades and celebrations of Bahian Independence Day in the nineteenth century.*

𝐵razilian independence is often presented as a peaceful process, in sharp contrast to the violent struggles that wracked Spanish America, and many historians stress that very little changed as a result. Brazil remained a monarchy—the son of the king of Portugal proclaimed independence on September 7, 1822—and major features of the colonial regime persisted long after Independence. Slavery lasted until 1888, while racial discrimination, latifundia, and economic dependence still endure. However, people who lived through the independence years in Brazil would likely have perceived many changes in their lives, although some felt that the changes did not go far enough. Certainly this must have been the case for Daniel Gomes de Freitas, who, as a young army cadet, played a part in the fighting for independence in the province of Bahia and deeply embroiled himself in the violent struggle for liberal reform after Independence.

Daniel Gomes de Freitas was born on September 15, 1806, in Santana, a downtown parish of Salvador. A city of perhaps 50,000 people, it was then one of the largest in the Americas. It was a bustling commercial and bureaucratic center, the capital of the Portuguese captaincy (colonial province) of Bahia, the seat of the archbishop and the appeals court, and the principal entrepôt for trade with its sugar-plantation hinterland, the Recôncavo. There, tens of thousands of mostly African slaves cut and processed sugarcane, as they had done for 250 years, to supply sugar to European markets. Their owners, the *senhores de engenho* (literally, "lords of the sugar mills" but more commonly translated as "sugar planters"), constituted Bahia's aristocracy. The Recôncavo also produced to-bacco, which found a ready market in West Africa, where it was traded for the 6,000 or so slaves brought each year to Salvador. Somewhat more than one-third of the city's population consisted of slaves, who worked in every conceivable occupation. In the year after Daniel's birth, African slaves led the first of dozens of rebellions that wracked Salvador and its hinterland until 1835, when African Muslims staged the largest urban slave revolt in the Americas.

The existence of slavery profoundly shaped the rest of the society into which Daniel was born. Complex racial hierarchies structured this society, with the minority of creole (American-born) slaves generally having privileges over Africans. By 1800, the number of free Afro-Brazilians almost equalled the number of slaves, and only a minority of the population was classed as "white" in the scattered censuses taken during these years. The latter dominated Bahian society, but some of them were becoming concerned about the rise of the "classes of color," as they sometimes put it. Not only did the slave revolts threaten to turn Bahia into another Haiti, the French sugar plantation colony devastated by a slave rebellion in the 1790s, but free blacks and mulattoes also had been involved in a 1798 conspiracy whose stated goals included the end-ing of racial discrimination among the free. (The plotters did not actu-ally call for an end to slavery.) Moreover, in 1808, Britain ended the slave trade to its colonies and began putting pressure on other countries, in-cluding Portugal, to end the trade, which would have devastated Brazil's economy. Living and working conditions on sugar plantations were so harsh that slave populations failed to reproduce themselves and had to be sustained by imports.

Less than two years after Daniel's birth, the city of Salvador hosted Queen Maria I (by then completely insane) and João, her son and the prince regent, along with the entire court. They had fled from Lisbon in late 1807, just ahead of the French invaders. During his stay in Salvador, João issued an important decree opening Brazil's trade to all friendly nations, which effectively ended the Portuguese commercial monopoly (and a key element of Brazil's colonial status). Unfortunately for the Bahian elite, João resolved to move on to the viceregal capital of Rio de Janeiro, where he established a full government apparatus for the entire Portu-guese Empire. In 1815 he raised Brazil to a political status equal to that of Portugal. On the death of his mother in 1816, he finally became King João VI.

Little Daniel knew nothing about these larger changes taking place around him, and his parents were probably more preoccupied with his poor health. Fearing for his life, Luiz José Gomes and Rosa Maria do Espírito Santo had the boy baptized at home, rather than in the parish church. They were unmarried, which meant that Daniel was a "natural" child, a condition halfway between legitimate and bastard. That he bore neither his mother's nor his father's surname is not surprising, for Brazilian naming practices were highly flexible. His parents probably married subsequently, by which he became "legitimated." This status can be inferred from the fact that he later became an army cadet, for which legitimacy or legitimation was required. We know little else about his father or mother, except that they had many children. In 1826, for example, Daniel referred to two sisters and three brothers whom he helped support, along with his mother, grandmother, and by then elderly father. The copy of his baptismal certificate in the army archive omits one piece of information usually included in such documents: an indication of his race. He may well have had some African ancestry, for the custom of using devotional surnames (his mother's last name means "Holy Spirit") was common among Afro-Brazilians, but the army never kept racial information on its officers and treated them all as unmarked white men.

On August 1, 1821, claiming to be fifteen years old, Daniel volunteered to join the army. He enlisted in Salvador's artillery regiment; sometime in September he was recognized as a second cadet. This clue tells us about his father because, according to the law that revised the requirements for cadetship in 1820, the rank of second cadet was awarded to sons of militia officers or army officers up to the rank of major. (Sons of nobles and more senior army officers became first cadets.) Unfortunately, I have located no army or militia officer by the name of Luiz José Gomes in Salvador during this time, but he may have held a commission in the suburban militia. That Daniel became a cadet also indicates that he had learned to read and write and that he had mastered basic arithmetic. Few children received primary schooling at the time, and his literacy suggests that Daniel's family might be classed as members of Salvador's small middle class (although they probably ranked near the bottom of it).

Daniel likely chose the artillery because of its educational opportunities. Since the mideighteenth century, engineering (fortifications) and mathematics courses were offered in that regiment so that its cadets and noncommissioned officers could acquire the technical training needed to operate artillery. Some historians thus see the artillery as a branch of the army that facilitated upward social mobility. Daniel probably did not have much time to study in the 1820s, but he did attend class in the mid-1830s, and he claims in his memoir to have taken the qualifying examination for promotion to first lieutenant. Having enlisted in the local garrison, Daniel expected to stay close to his family. In the previous 150 years, Salvador's troops had only left Bahia once, for a brief stint in Rio de Janeiro to reinforce the viceregal capital during a war scare with Spain. In many ways, regular officers and enlisted men were, for lack of a better word, part-time soldiers. They worked in artisanal trades during their spare time, while officers often had business ventures on the side. Indeed, Daniel probably lived at home and only stayed in the barracks when he was assigned to specific duties.

When Daniel joined the army, dramatic political changes were sweeping through the Luso-Brazilian world. In late 1820 a liberal revolution in the city of Porto, Portugal, ended the absolute rule of João VI. The liberals' ideals of constitutional rule, press freedom, and equality of rights (for free men) appealed to many in Brazil, and in February 1821 artillery officers led a rebellion that overthrew the governor and the garrison commander, proclaiming Bahia's loyalty to the Portuguese liberal regime. The new junta pledged to send deputies to the parliament, or Cortes, that would write a new constitution for the Portuguese nation, seen as consisting of all of the king's subjects, whether they lived in Portugal, Brazil, or any of the colonies in Africa and Asia. Both the locally raised troops (which included the artillery) and a Portuguese infantry regiment stationed in Salvador since 1819 strongly supported the liberal regime, but by the time that Daniel enlisted, relations between Bahians and Portuguese were deteriorating rapidly.

The larger context for this state of affairs was set by the many interests in Portugal who thought that the mother country had been reduced to the status of a colony of Brazil. The liberals ordered João to return to Lisbon, which he did, and they envisaged a unitary government for the entire Portuguese Empire, which meant that many of the institutions of government established in Brazil since 1808 would be dismantled. Because most of these were in Rio de Janeiro (and not Salvador), those Bahians who sought local autonomy were not initially concerned. But relations between Bahian and Portuguese troops, the latter reinforced by contingents from Lisbon during 1821, were increasingly tense. Portuguese troops snubbed their Brazilian counterparts, often insulting them with racial slurs, which Brazilians reciprocated by mocking the Portuguese soldiers' high opinion of their whiteness. A key figure in the garrison's politics at this time was Lieutenant Colonel Manoel Pedro de Freitas Guimarães. He had been the artillery's second-in-command in February 1821, but because of his key role in the coup, he was catapulted into the post of garrison commander by popular acclamation. Freitas Guimarães (no relation to Daniel) was a charismatic figure who reportedly encouraged enlistments into the artillery from men who shared his political views, particularly his dislike of the Portuguese and his advocacy of greater autonomy for Bahia (or Brazil). But Freitas Guimarães suffered from periodic bouts of mental illness (he was in fact declared legally insane in the 1820s), and this handicap hampered his political activism.

Matters came to a head in February 1822, when the liberal government in Lisbon, consistent with its goal of establishing a single government for the Portuguese world, exercised its power to name garrison commanders and ordered Freitas Guimarães to be replaced by the commander of the Portuguese regiment, Inácio Luiz Madeira de Melo. The many supporters of Freitas Guimarães would have none of this, and efforts to conciliate the two parties failed. On February 19, 1822, fighting broke out between Bahian and Portuguese troops in Salvador. Civilian patriots joined the artillery regiment, quartered in Fort São Pedro, where they held out for two days. Before the fort capitulated, most of the patriots, Daniel included, escaped into the Recôncavo. Freitas Guimarães was captured and shipped in chains to Lisbon.

Little is known about what happened during the next five months. The patriots carried their anti-Portuguese struggle to the countryside, while Madeira fortified himself in Salvador. For sugar planters, this conflict was deeply worrisome, given the potential for disorder. In late June and early July 1822 a group of planters organized a provisional Council of Government, pledged their loyalty to Pedro I (who by then was about to turn himself into emperor of Brazil), and organized what they called the Pacification Army to besiege Salvador and, judging by the name, to bring order to the countryside. The soldiers and officers who had dispersed in February soon congregated in Cachoeira, where the Council met, and Daniel reported there on July 7. The creation of the Pacification Army was a difficult task because the patriots had few arms and equipment, for which no amount of enthusiasm could compensate. They won an early victory by preventing a Portuguese naval force from landing at Cachoeira and gradually tightened the siege lines around Salvador. Pedro I sent weapons, a contingent of troops, and a French general, Pierre Labatut, to command the patriots. Shortly after Labatut and the Rio de Janeiro troops took up their position outside of Salvador, Madeira launched an attack. The Battle of Pirajá (November 8, 1821) was a close-run affair, and the tide only turned, according to a widely repeated story, when a bugler on the patriot side incorrectly played the signal for a cavalry charge. The Portuguese, fearing the worst, hastily retreated to their fortifications. About 300 men died in the battle—insignificant casualties by European standards, but a shocking loss of life to Brazilians who had never experienced war on this scale. Daniel must have distinguished himself that day because eight days later, he was commissioned a second lieutenant by Labatut, who liberally handed out promotions in late November.

For the rest of the war, Daniel dropped out of sight, but he must have witnessed all of the changes that the conflict brought. It involved a popular mobilization on a scale hitherto unknown in Bahia, as some

15,000 men came under arms by July 1823. There was much talk of fighting for freedom, which, of course, meant different things to different people. Numerous slaves took advantage of the confusion to flee from their masters, and some found their way into the patriot forces. Labatut took it upon himself to draft slaves confiscated from Portuguese owners into the army (much to the annoyance of the Council, which considered this highly dangerous); after the war, the Brazilian government arranged for the freeing of these men by paying compensation to their masters. Anti-Portuguese rhetoric reached extreme levels during the war, and there was much loose talk of radical reform in the patriot camps, focusing on buzzwords of equality before the law and the rights of citizenship. For the sugar planters who dominated the Council, all of this wrangling was worrisome, and occasionally they ordered the arrest of whomever they perceived to be troublemakers, including an army surgeon, Francisco Sabino Álvares da Rocha Vieira. Labatut's imperiousness and his failure to respect the prerogatives of Bahia's sugar planters led to his overthrow at the hands of senior officers in May 1823, and he was replaced by the commander of troops from Rio de Janeiro

On July 2, 1823, the Portuguese were down to just enough food to stock their ships for the voyage to Lisbon, and they evacuated Salvador. The bedraggled patriots marched into the city that afternoon, and in September, officials demobilized the Pacification Army and organized a peacetime force. Daniel was assigned to the artillery where, as a second lieutenant, he must have busied himself with the routine tasks of running his company and overseeing garrison duties, which mostly involved manning guard posts throughout the city. By many measures, the seventeen-year-old Daniel had done well for himself. He had survived the war and had won an officer's commission, which meant that he would be paid a salary for the rest of his life. Back in the 1810s, it had taken an average of seven to ten years to rise through the noncommissioned ranks to second lieutenant. But Daniel and many of the other officers in the garrison who had received battlefield promotions were not satisfied with their relative good fortune.

To be sure, independence had been won, but this success marked only the beginning of a struggle to define the nature of the new state and the new society that many envisaged. Most of the important issues had not been addressed in 1822 and 1823. What, for example, would be the nature of Emperor Pedro I's relationship to the Brazilian people? Who should be part of the nation? And what rights should citizens have? Pedro convened a constitutional convention but abruptly closed it in late 1823 when it appeared to be producing a draft not to his liking. In March 1824 he granted his own constitution, a document that upheld many of his prerogatives, including a so-called moderating power that gave the monarch the right to close the parliament and call new elections. But the charter also contained an extensive bill of rights for the country's free citizens, including provisions for equality before the law and equal access to government posts on the basis of merit alone—two provisions that were extremely rare in contemporary constitutions elsewhere. Of course, such provisions did not apply to slaves, and the document almost entirely ignored the existence of slavery, except in a few clauses that restricted the political rights of freedmen. Despite having granted the constitution, Pedro proved himself to be a poor constitutional monarch and continually squabbled with the parliament.

Many of the more arcane details of the constitution mattered little to ordinary Brazilians, but the clauses granting equality before the law and equal access to government jobs became something of a touchstone for a sector of upwardly mobile free nonwhite men who used these clauses to challenge the discrimination that they faced. Other issues addressed by the constitution also figured in popular politics. The charter granted Brazilian citizenship to all Portuguese who had not fought against independence, but many Brazilian patriots wanted to rid the country of residents of the former mother country. In the army, many of Daniel's junior-officer cohort, most of whom had been promoted during the war, wanted to remove Portuguese-born officers from the corporation, which would have made promotion more rapid.

Anti-Portuguese feeling also had a more mundane but very important source: natives of Portugal dominated the retail trades and they gained a reputation as gouging shopkeepers, becoming the targets of food rioters during periods of unrest. The constitution had established a centralized system of government, but many people believed that a more decentralized or, as Brazilians called it, federal system of government would be more responsive to local interests, not to mention offer greater opportunities for Bahians not connected to court elites. Complaints about taxation that only served to support courtiers in Rio de Janeiro also figured in radical liberal discourse. After Independence, slave unrest continued in Bahia, with periodic major rebellions led by Africans. Many observers reported that all of the talk about gaining freedom from Portuguese rule had been interpreted by slaves to mean that they should be free of their masters. A worried Spaniard calculated that within three years, "the white race will be finished off at the hands of the other castes and the province of Bahia will disappear from the civilized world."[1]

Where Daniel stood in the political ferment of the early 1820s is difficult to determine. His name does not turn up in the principal chronicles of the political events of these years; perhaps because of his youth, he was more a follower than a leader at this time. He avoided the fate of about a half-dozen lieutenants who were expelled from the army in 1824 on the grounds that they were too undisciplined and too politicized. The garrison commander, Colonel Felisberto Gomes Caldeira, made himself unpopular by such measures, and on October 25, 1824, the soldiers and junior officers of one infantry battalion mutinied. This battalion, the so-called Periquitos ("Parakeets," after the yellow and green trim on their uniforms), included a significant number of the slaves who had been freed after the war for their military service. Their principal demand was for the return of a popular commander, a man who had a reputation for radical political ideas, but the brutal murder of Caldeira may have unnerved the conspirators, and the mutiny degenerated into a standoff between the Periquitos and a growing contingent of regulars who retreated from Salvador. After about a month, the mutineers gave up and the government quickly removed the troublesome soldiers from Bahia.

Daniel was sufficiently associated with the mutineers that military authorities had him court-martialed, but he claimed that the charges were due mostly to the dislike that some officers and cadets nurtured for him. Two infantry officers—a major and a second lieutenant—served as scapegoats and were publicly executed in early 1825. Daniel avoided their fate but his case dragged on through military and civilian courts until February 29, 1828, when he was finally acquitted, as were most of those officers arrested. At this time, Brazil was at war with the Argentine Confederation over control of what eventually became the independent republic of Uruguay. Daniel hastened to join his unit, now designated the Seventh Artillery, but he did not see combat (much later, another officer insulted Daniel by saying that he had only served in "prison ships [*presigangas*] and fortress dungeons [*abóbadas*]" during the war).[2] Judging by his personnel file, Daniel had other pressing professional concerns. Back in 1826, while he had been in prison, Emperor Pedro I had visited Bahia where he issued a general promotion of one-half grade to all of the province's officers (except those who were in jail). Because of his acquittal, Daniel judged that he also deserved this promotion, with the appropriate retroactive seniority. Without it, he would rank behind his entire cohort when it came to promotion, given the importance of seniority in the Brazilian army. Some officers received retroactive promotions in the 1820s, but Daniel's case dragged on until 1831, when a special commission charged with investigating all such outstanding cases ruled that he should get the promotion.

Meanwhile, the war went badly for Brazil, and late in 1828 the British government brokered a peace that resulted in the creation of Uruguay. The Bahian troops likely looked forward to returning home, but

Pedro I retained them in Rio de Janeiro and other garrisons in the south of the country, while Salvador received contingents of troops from other provinces. He apparently hoped that this move would weaken officers' ties to their home provinces and make them more loyal to the imperial regime, but it may well have had the opposite effect. Officers and their families suffered considerable hardship and many complained that they could not properly manage their households while stationed away from Bahia. Since the war was over, they could not see any reason to be kept away from home.

The year 1831 brought sudden changes to Brazilian and Bahian politics. Facing increasing opposition from moderate liberals in the parliament and radical liberals who occasionally took to the streets in Rio de Janeiro, Emperor Pedro I abruptly abdicated on April 7, 1831. A moderately liberal parliamentary government took power in Rio de Janeiro in the name of Emperor Pedro II, then only five years old, and instituted numerous changes in Brazilian society, among them an important devolution of power to the provincial governments and significant reforms to army organization. The liberal Regency government reduced the size of the army, returned its battalions to their home provinces, and created a civilian militia, the National Guard, as a way to empower citizens and to replace the army-controlled militia. Sometime in the middle of 1831, Daniel and the artillery arrived back in Salvador, a city going through a period of unrest. Around the time of the abdication, there had been large-scale anti-Portuguese riots, which had forced the provincial president (governor) and garrison commander to resign. Several radical liberal newspapers had appeared in the city, fanning the anti-Portuguese flames and calling for federalism and equality before the law. Cipriano José Barata de Almeida, one of Brazil's best-known advocates of liberal reform, had just been arrested on trumped-up charges of fomenting African slave revolt.

The return of Bahia's troops and particularly officers like Daniel, still under suspicion because of their role in 1824, worried provincial authorities. They kept the artillery in its traditional quarters in Fort São Pedro and tried to limit the soldiers' contact with civilian society. This treatment greatly upset enlisted men, who naturally wanted to see their friends and family in the city, and on the night of August 31, 1831, they mutinied, declaring that they no longer would sleep in the barracks, eat in the mess, or wear leather uniform collars, adding that they wanted to be discharged. Apparently, Daniel sympathized with his soldiers' demands, for he was arrested the next day for complicity in the mutiny. Daniel's timing could not have been worse. On that very day, the commission investigating disputes about seniority and promotions had ruled that

Daniel should be promoted and regain the seniority that he had lost during his imprisonment in the 1820s. When this good news reached Salvador, Daniel was in jail facing a court-martial and thus could not be promoted. While in prison, Daniel no doubt heard about two other radical liberal rebellions, an abortive rising of an infantry battalion in October 1831 and a short-lived federalist revolt that briefly held the town of Cachoeira in early 1832. Eventually, all of those arrested for complicity in the various liberal and federalist revolts, including Daniel, were transferred to the round fort located in Salvador's harbor, the most secure prison in the province.

In early 1833, Daniel appeared for the first time as one of the leaders of a revolt when the prisoners took over the fort, apparently as part of a larger liberal-federalist plot to gain control of Salvador. For three days the prisoners exchanged artillery fire with land batteries; few men were killed but there was considerable property damage. When they realized that their position was hopeless, they raised a white flag of surrender to replace the blue and white banner of federalism that they had designed. The detailed rebel proclamation found afterward indicates that the insurrectionists had given much thought to the new society that they envisioned. The elderly Cipriano Barata likely had a hand in this document, for he was by far the most intellectual of the radical leaders. (He did not, however, take part in the fighting.) Speaking in the name of the people against the aristocrats, they called for the establishment of a provisional government, the election of the provincial president, the release of political prisoners, and full freedom of the press. Like previous radical liberal manifestoes, this one contained anti-Portuguese clauses seeking to exclude them from retail commerce and civil service jobs. It also pledged to improve food supply to Salvador and to eradicate the counterfeit currency and black marketeering that particularly hurt the poor.

The rebels also envisioned more fundamental economic reform, calling for the end of entails (rare in Brazil) and the redistribution of land to Brazilian patriots who would put it to productive use. Perhaps because they had experienced prison conditions firsthand, penal reform figured prominently in the manifesto, as did judicial reform, in which they stressed the importance of eliminating favoritism, instituting equality before the law, and making courts accessible to the poor by eliminating the fees and emoluments that plaintiffs paid. But Pedro I, should he dare to return to Brazil, would receive no due process from the rebels, who authorized any Brazilian to kill him on the spot. The manifesto, however, had its limits. Nowhere did it mention slavery, and racial discrimination was only addressed implicitly in the calls for equality before the law. In this sense, Daniel and his companions spoke for the free, not for slaves; by stressing the importance of equality and due process, they were seeking to consolidate and extend the opportunities that the 1824 constitution had offered them.

Within two and one-half years, Daniel was out of prison and being considered for assignment to one of the vacant posts in Bahia's artillery battalion. In this case, the garrison commander named a more junior officer to the post, but in 1836, as the most senior unemployed second lieutenant, Daniel was assigned to another vacancy in the Third Artillery. This sudden reversal of fortune was due both to the lax legal system, which almost always acquitted "middle-class" conspirators like Daniel after they had spent a few years in prison, and to army officers' corporate loyalty to one another. No officer wished to set a precedent for cashiering his colleagues, for under different political circumstances, such a precedent might be turned against him. Daniel's difficulty in finding employment after his release from prison also reflected another feature of officers' life in the 1830s. Given the army cutbacks early in the decade, there was a great surplus of officers; while these men were paid, they had little to do, and they did not gain the salary supplements that officers serving in battalions received. Moreover, given the surplus of officers and tight budgets, the government suspended promotions. Not surprisingly, army officers complained a great deal about these cutbacks and came to nurture deep grievances against the regency government. The civilian National Guard added insult to injury, especially since the old militia had been under army control and a place where many army officers spent part of their career. Earlier in the decade (while Daniel was still in prison), they formed the Sociedade Militar (Officers' Club) to lobby for their interests and published a newspaper, *O Militar* (The Officer), that expressed their concerns. By the time that Daniel was released, both the club and the newspaper were moribund, but officers' professional concerns remained.

Army officers' grievances and the long tradition of radical liberal and federalist agitation merged in the Sabinada Rebellion that, for a brief time, catapulted Daniel to prominence. The origins of this rebellion, which broke out on the night of November 6–7, 1837, remain obscure. Moreover, Daniel's memoir of the rebellion is missing its beginning pages, removed in all likelihood to destroy incriminating evidence. As a result, we know nothing of Daniel's role in the preparations, but it must have been significant, for he took the post of war minister in the rebellion's government. The Sabinada officially justified itself as a response to the Regresso, the conservative turn of the imperial government in September 1837, promising to address radical liberals' concerns. Both of Salvador's army battalions supported the movement, while the National Guard mounted only ineffective opposition. Once in control of the city,

the rebels convened a meeting of the city council at which they proclaimed a republic and declared Bahia to be completely independent of
Rio de Janeiro. Like the federalists of 1833, they promised elections and
a constituent assembly. That day, the rebels also addressed military grievances, promoting the principal conspirators (Daniel vaulted four grades
from second lieutenant to lieutenant colonel) and promoting all officers
by two ranks. Generous salary increases were awarded to officers and
men. They also established a civilian government, which was dominated
by Francisco Sabino Álvares da Rocha Vieira, who officially held the
post of government secretary. Like Daniel and Sabino (who lent his name
to the movement), other members of the rebel cabinet had long histories
of involvement in radical politics, including a briefly lucid Manoel Pedro
de Freitas Guimarães, who served as navy minister.

Four days later, the rebels had a change of heart and revised their
declaration of independence to limit it to the remaining period of
Pedro II's minority, expected to end in 1844 when he turned eighteen.
This curious decision, which drew much mockery from the rebellion's
enemies, reflects the durability of the monarchy, its symbolic importance,
and perhaps also a hope that Pedro II would reverse the Regresso when
he came to rule directly. For the rest of November, the rebels gradually
defined their political aims. They talked a great deal, condemning the
domination of Brazil by the imperial government in Rio de Janeiro and
stressing their love of order and their determination to protect private
property. Anti-Portuguese rhetoric once again came to the fore. The
government abolished the National Guard and called up officers and
men of the old army-controlled militias.

Although the Sabinada had triumphed in Salvador, it failed to carry
the Recôncavo. There, much as they had in 1822, sugar planters mobilized their forces and laid siege to the city. The imperial government,
already facing rebellions in two other provinces, sent the troops that
could be spared and imposed a naval blockade on Salvador. As war minister, Daniel had overall responsibility for the defense of Salvador and,
more important, for offensive operations, for he and other rebel leaders
recognized that if they were confined to the city, they would share the
fate of the Portuguese troops in 1823. Unfortunately, the rebel forces
were singularly unsuccessful in extending the rebellion's reach. An attack on Itaparica island, opposite Salvador, failed. Only late in the war
did they manage to launch a significant expeditionary force into the
Recôncavo, but it was soon dispersed. Both the besiegers and the rebels
dug themselves in, and the war quickly turned into a stalemate that the
rebels could not win.

Early in the rebellion, Daniel suffered from erysipelas, an unpleasant skin inflammation, which made it difficult for him to inspect the

front lines. Rather, he busied himself with overseeing the all-important production of ammunition. The city's arsenals were well equipped for the manufacture of cartridges, and large quantities of supplies were on hand. According to Daniel, he managed to increase output so that the rebels' troops never suffered shortages. Daniel's memoir also hints at disagreements among the rebel leadership over military strategy, squabbles over seniority, and disputes over policy toward those who wished to flee the city and toward those who wanted to continue trade with the Recôncavo. Looking at these problems from a tactical and strategic angle, Daniel was willing to permit the emigration of women, children, and the elderly, but not that of able-bodied men and slaves who could be put to use. He complained bitterly about the issuance of licenses to export food from the besieged city.

Two major problems bedeviled Daniel in early 1838. As the city's position became increasingly hopeless, the lower classes became more and more restive, with violent attacks on individual Portuguese taking place and sporadic attempts to burn the properties of Sabinada enemies or those who (worse yet for the plebeians) deserted the cause. Daniel was horrified by these outbursts of popular violence by what an English doctor called the "infuriated black and mulatto mob,"[3] and he repeatedly detached troops to keep order and to protect property.

Slavery posed a more complex problem for Daniel and the rest of the rebel leadership. Initially, they gave it little thought, except to declare that they considered abolition to be "supine stupidity," possibly an attempt to deflect the inevitable accusations that they were fostering slave rebellion.[4] They hired the slave porters who usually worked on the docks to carry supplies to the trenches and likely intended nothing more than using slaves in such support roles. By the end of December, it became clear from masters' complaints that some rebel commanders were admitting slaves into their units. Daniel repeatedly ordered that such slaves be returned to their owners, especially since their enlistment was causing problems in the ranks because some free men refused to serve alongside them. Daniel opposed the solution that the civilian government found in early January—the creation of a battalion of Brazilian-born black freedmen, whose owners would be compensated by the receipt of half of their former slaves' salary. Late in February the rebel government went one step further, proclaiming the freedom of all Brazilian-born slaves who would take up arms in the Sabinada's defense. Daniel vigorously protested this measure as well, declaring that he took no responsibility for the outcome and implementing it with extreme reluctance.

The refusal of free soldiers to associate with slaves and freedmen reflects one of the major fissures in nineteenth-century Brazilian society, as does the Sabinada government's decision to free only creole slaves.

Creoles were only a minority of Salvador's slaves, two-thirds of whom were Africans. While the rebels could conceive of Creoles as part of their defense forces, they did not see Africans as even potentially part of the Brazilian community. The great 1835 slave rebellion, led by African Muslims, reinforced this view, and when the Sabinada's enemies accused the rebels of enlisting Africans, one of its newspapers declared that "the simple fact that we are Bahians, and free Bahians," belied the imputation.[5] Africans were simply not part of the "nation" as the rebels envisaged it, and many had doubts about creole slaves as well.

While Daniel's memoir of the Sabinada is an invaluable historical source, it is strikingly devoid of political content. He did not, for instance, comment on the racial politics of the revolt. As the white upper classes fled Salvador in November and December, outside observers came to see the Sabinada as a race war: "Appearances are materially changed since the commencement of the insurrection and . . . are at present more those of a war of color than anything else," wrote the British vice consul in January 1838.[6] Rebel newspapers expressed the frustrations of upwardly mobile men of color for whom the constitution's provisions of equality were insufficient protection against discrimination. One declared of the Sabinada's enemies: "They are warring against us because they are whites, and in Bahia there must be no blacks and mulattoes, especially in office, unless they are very rich and change their liberal opinions."[7] Supporters of the Sabinada were also divided over racial questions, with some calling for radical solutions. Late in the revolt, a black militia officer, José de Santa Eufrásia, declared "that he was [all too] used to being ruled by whites" and that "blacks should govern the Republic."[8] Where Daniel stood on these issues is impossible to determine from his memoir, but his silence about race is consistent with army policy toward officers— they were assumed to be white men—and with the views of an upwardly mobile elite of "men of color" who sought integration into the upper class on the basis of full equality, which meant that they avoided explicit discussions of race.

Daniel's memoir resembles, as Paulo Cesar Souza has put it, the report of a "zealous functionary" rather than that of an ideologically motivated rebel leader.[9] He once noted that enthusiastic civilians took out a field gun amid shouts of "Long live liberty!" and "Death to the [Portuguese] rogues!" but most of the passage is devoted to criticism of the officer who permitted them to take the weapon that they did not know how to use.[10] In another passage, he expresses his disgust at fellow officers who continued to accept slaves in their units, despite explicit orders to the contrary, wondering what would happen to a government "whose orders were mocked at every turn by those who called themselves leaders of the Revolution fighting for equality and [proper] execution of the law."[11] By contrast, Daniel considered himself to be an exemplary and upright servant of the republic: "I resolved never to tolerate immorality and crime, having delinquents punished with the sanctions that were within my competence, as soon as they were convicted of their evil-doing, as is well-known [and evidenced] by the numerous decrees and orders transcribed in the newspapers."[12] For Daniel, adherence to law, due process, and correct procedure constituted the way to a better society.

On the morning of March 13, 1838, Daniel and another officer set out in a launch to inspect the escarpment along the city's west side with an eye to improving the defenses against seaborne assault. When they returned to the docks, disastrous news greeted them. Enemy forces had breached the city's defenses on the north side and were rapidly advancing toward the downtown, with Sabinada troops retreating even faster. At this point, the focus of Daniel's memoir narrows to that which he experienced personally, as soldiers' recollections of combat typically do. He hastened to Fort São Pedro, on the city's south end and close to the arsenal, where he oversaw the supply of munitions to those rebel troops still under discipline. Perhaps because of his distance from the fighting, he reported nothing about the massacres of defenders. However, the official report by the commander of imperial forces put the number of rebel dead at 1,091 against only 40 government soldiers, and there were later numerous allegations of murders and atrocities committed by the victorious soldiers, especially against black defenders of the Sabinada.

From the fort's parapets, Daniel saw many downtown buildings ablaze, as the arsonists whom he could not contain took revenge on their enemies. Much to his disgust, he witnessed the breakdown of discipline, as retreating soldiers broke into stores and got thoroughly drunk instead of facing the enemy. Worse yet, he saw rebel officers in civilian dress abandoning their posts, and watched another wander around the fort in a stupor, perhaps because he had tried to poison himself (the man eventually recovered). By March 15, the situation around the fort was desperate, with government troops only a few blocks away. Daniel and a few other officers considered organizing a retreat up the coast, hoping to break through thinly held enemy lines, but they found that they had insufficient slaves to carry their supplies. (That they might carry their own supplies apparently did not occur to them!) Finally, at 4:00 P.M., Daniel and a small party, including a few officers and soldiers, abandoned the fort, successfully eluding the government forces closing in from the south and east.

At this point, Daniel's narrative ends abruptly, giving no indication of how he managed to avoid arrest for three years. He only resurfaced in 1840, after the prematurely crowned Pedro II issued an amnesty to all those who had taken part in rebellions against his reign. Rumors occasionally placed him in other provinces, but none was confirmed. During that time, authorities charged him with numerous offenses. No court-martial records from the Sabinada have come to light, but civilian authorities threw the book at him, charging him with everything from destroying the independence and integrity of the Empire, offending the constitution and the royal family, and attacking the regent to fraud, piracy, murder, bribery, and assault. Probably the most serious indictment was that of fomenting slave insurrection, defined as participating in a violent movement of twenty or more slaves to win their freedom. This crime carried the death penalty (as did the murder charge). But the wheels of justice turned slowly in imperial Brazil, and in 1840 the charges against those of Daniel's companions who had been captured were still being appealed. All of them survived to claim the benefits of the amnesty in 1840.

Little is known about the rest of Daniel's life. By the amnesty's terms, he was ordered to reside in São Paulo, where he again tried to resume his army career. He had the nerve to request back pay for the time that he had been in hiding, noting that he had already reimbursed the salary that he had illegally drawn during the Sabinada (since he had been acquitted of all crimes, he judged that he had the right to the salary that he would have otherwise received). This argument had little legal merit and was rejected out of hand. In 1842, Daniel apparently took part in the brief liberal rebellion in São Paulo, after which he disappeared, reportedly joining the remnants of the Farroupilha Rebellion, a republican movement in the extreme south of Brazil.

Second Lieutenant Daniel Gomes de Freitas was only thirty-six when he dropped out of sight. In his short life (or at least the part of it that we know about), he experienced all of the complex and difficult issues that Brazilians struggled with after Independence. The numerous rebellions in which he participated clearly demonstrate that Independence was not a peaceful, consensual process and underscore the fact that Brazilians were deeply divided over fundamental issues. Independence, as far as Daniel was concerned, settled little or nothing; rather, it opened up Brazilian society to a broad debate over the form of the state and the nature of society. His adherence to liberal ideals may seem naive to us today, but it highlights just how powerful and attractive concepts of equality before the law were at that time. Of course, slavery was always a stumbling block for liberals, and it was difficult for them to envisage slaves (and especially Africans) as part of the nation. Effective liberal reform would have opened Brazilian society and satisfied many of the aspirations of men like Daniel, for whom Independence offered the prospect of social mobility and a greater say in the organization of their state and their nation.

NOTES

1. Francisco de Sierra y Mariscal, "Idéas geraes sobre a revolução do Brasil e suas consequências," *Anais da Biblioteca Nacional* 43–44 (1920–21): 65.
2. Daniel Gomes de Freitas, "Narrativa dos sucessos da Sabinada," *Publicações do Archivo do Estado da Bahia* 1 (1937): 275.
3. Robert Dundas, *Sketches of Brazil . . .* (London: John Churchill, 1852), 395.
4. Proclamation, November 14, 1837, *Jornal do Comércio* (Rio de Janeiro), November 27, 1837.
5. *O Sete de Novembro* (Salvador), November 25, 1837.
6. Vice consul to minister to Brazil, Salvador, January 13, 1838, Great Britain, Public Record Office, Foreign Office 13, vol. 143, vol. 187v.
7. *Novo Diário da Bahia*, December 26, 1837.
8. Freitas, "Narrativa," 341.
9. Paulo Cesar Souza, *A Sabinada: A revolta separatista da Bahia (1837)* (São Paulo: Brasiliense, 1987), 49.
10. Freitas, "Narrativa," 269.
11. Ibid., 277.
12. Ibid., 286.

SUGGESTED READINGS

The principal sources on Daniel Gomes de Freitas are his petitions file in Rio de Janeiro's Arquivo Histórico do Exército (D-5-135) and his memoir of the Sabinada Rebellion, "Narrativa dos sucessos da Sabinada," in *Publicações do Archivo do Estado da Bahia* 1 (1937): 261–333. There are numerous additional references to him scattered through archives in Rio de Janeiro and Salvador and the contemporary press. On the Sabinada see Paulo Cesar Souza, *A Sabinada: A revolta separatista da Bahia (1837)* (São Paulo: Brasiliense, 1987); and Hendrik Kraay, " 'As Terrifying as Unexpected': The Bahian Sabinada, 1837–38," *Hispanic American Historical Review* 72:4 (November 1992): 501–27. Three English-language monographs provide the essential context for the society in which Daniel lived: Hendrik Kraay, *Race, State, and Armed Forces in Independence-Era Brazil: Bahia, 1790s–1840s* (Stanford: Stanford University Press, 2001); João José Reis, *Slave Rebellion in Brazil: The Muslim Uprising of 1835 in Bahia*, trans. Arthur Brakel (Baltimore: Johns Hopkins University Press, 1993); and Roderick J. Barman, *Brazil: The Forging of a Nation, 1798–1852* (Stanford: Stanford University Press, 1988). Hebe Maria Mattos's suggestive essay, *Escravidão e cidadania no Brasil monárquico* (Rio de Janeiro: Jorge Zahar Editor, 2000), also influenced this chapter.

CHAPTER 2

Agostinho José Pereira

The Divine Teacher*

Marcus J. M. de Carvalho

The story of the Divine Teacher (Divino Mestre), Agostinho José Pereira, pairs well with the preceding biography of Daniel Gomes de Freitas. Whereas Daniel might have been a light-skinned mulatto and was from a relatively privileged family, authorities described Agostinho as "black" and, even though he was a freeman, from more humble social origins. Whereas Daniel represented the aspirations of many Brazilians from the middle sectors of urban society, Agostinho gives us a rare glimpse of how some Brazilians of African descent understood events and the language of liberty, equality, and brotherhood that Independence, regional rebellions, and late-eighteenth-century revolutions had evoked. It should be emphasized that the views of these individuals and their compatriots should not be construed as typical of all free poor Afro-Brazilians or middle-class "whites," but they probably did reflect the sentiments of many who shared their backgrounds. Although a variety of viewpoints existed in these communities, certain events or issues could galvanize or split them. For instance, fear of the Portuguese, or Lusophobia (an important component of early Brazilian national identity, much like fear of the British in the United States), could unite the Brazilian-born across racial lines. Fear of slave rebellion or a race war, however, tended to bring Portuguese- and Brazilian-born whites together.

Marcus J. M. de Carvalho, associate professor of history at the Universidade Federal de Pernambuco in Recife, Brazil, has published on a broad array of issues related to the history of Pernambuco. He has analyzed the political transition from the colonial period through the first decades of Independence and the role that Pernambucan Indians played in political violence between rival elite factions. His book Liberdade: Rotinas e rupturas do escravismo no Recife, 1822–1850 *(2001) explores slavery in one of Brazil's most important urban centers. In this chapter, he highlights the hybrid and varied nature of religious practices and beliefs and how they were deeply interconnected with post-Independence political struggles for many Afro-Brazilians.*

*Translated by Peter M. Beattie.

*I*n 1846 police jailed the free black man Agostinho José Pereira in the streets of Recife, Pernambuco, along with six other black men and six black women who referred to Agostinho as the Divino Mestre (Divine Teacher). Despite their black skin, none of the prisoners was a slave, and in a nation where most whites were illiterate, they all knew how to read. At least one of the detainees went to jail of his own free will because he did not want to leave Agostinho's side in his moment of misfortune. The provincial chief of police said that Agostinho had preached for five years in Recife, but he suspected that his "sect" was a front for an organization plotting a black uprising, and that the detainees were in contact with secret societies established in other provinces that also planned similar insurrections. This suspicion was a damning one. If proved, it would likely lead to Agostinho's execution as well as to sentences of *galés* (life at hard labor in fetters, a punishment often reserved for slave convicts) for his principal followers. The Divino Mestre's adversaries wrote almost all that we now know about him. Court authorities preserved his only chance to speak for himself in the testimony he gave during his trial. In Brazil, very few blacks were literate and they left behind few written accounts of their own perceptions. This lack of documentation contrasts with the relative abundance of slave and free black narratives and memoirs published by abolitionists in the United States. Thus, the testimonies of the spiritual leader Agostinho and his followers are of particular value because they shed light on how some of the mostly nonwhite free population made sense of Brazil's political independence in Recife, the country's third largest city in the mid-1800s.

After Agostinho's imprisonment, the authorities detained nine more suspects, but the press speculated that there were about 300 members of the Divine Teacher's sect in Recife, the majority of whom were women. Pernambuco's highest court interrogated seven black men and seven black women about their relationship with the Divine Teacher. They learned that Agostinho had taught them all how to read and write, a fact that in itself made the authorities suspicious because it was so uncommon. Agostinho's testimony confirmed that he had taught many black men and women how to read and write to better instruct them in the Holy Scriptures. He also admitted that he believed that images and statues of the saints had no spiritual value, but he denied the rumor that he had symbolically drowned an image of Christ to make this point. For Agostinho, what really mattered was the Word of God, which he claimed to have come to know through "divine inspiration" by way of a holy "vision." The court's judges openly laughed at this assertion. But the black pastor was not shaken, and he argued that it was among the simple folk that God chose His prophets.

For Recife's officials, it was difficult to place the Divine Teacher within more run-of-the-mill popular religious practices that they had come to tolerate, even though they found most of them distasteful. For instance, there were many spiritual leaders of religions imported from Africa in makeshift religious houses, known as *terreiros*, on Recife's outskirts. As in other parts of Brazil, Recife's blacks crowned their kings of Congo, gave parties, organized impromptu drumming sessions, and practiced their cults at the margin of Catholicism. Outsiders tended to view these religious rituals with suspicion, and from time to time the authorities repressed them. There was also "black" Catholicism, sometimes insincere but often real, even fervent. One of Recife's principal churches was the headquarters of the lay black sisterhood of Rosário dos Pretos, one of the oldest in Brazil. This church tended to the Catholic religious needs of blacks, primarily slaves, who donated most of the resources and labor for its construction. The Divine Teacher, however, did not fit these religious categories. Brazilian authorities, most of whom saw themselves as defenders of Catholicism, the nation's official religion, found it distressing that a poor free black man was preaching a different kind of Christianity, namely, Protestantism, in Recife's streets. That the judges of Pernambuco's highest court and not lower-level justices of the peace interrogated Agostinho makes it clear how disquieting his activities were to the province's most powerful leaders.

Agostinho's arrest, however, contradicted Brazilian law that had established limited tolerance for Protestant religious observances since 1810. It is important to recall that when Brazil was still a Portuguese colony, the Napoleonic invasion of Iberia forced Portugal's royal family to flee Lisbon and establish the headquarters of their empire in Rio de Janeiro in 1808. The British provided protection and transportation to the beleaguered Portuguese crown, which in return opened Brazil's ports to free trade. Treaties signed in 1810 between Lisbon and London mandated religious tolerance for British merchants who sought to practice their religion while resident in Brazil. The law allowed for the construction of Protestant churches, as long as their exteriors gave no indication that they were places of religious worship, and forbade public proselytizing of the Protestant faith. If these rules were disobeyed, the criminal code directed that the offending church's membership be dispersed and fined. Their church's religious objects would be destroyed, but no one would be imprisoned for this crime.

The Protestants who came to Brazil after 1810 practiced their faith without incident. The Reverend John Penny signed the first baptismal certificate of Recife's Anglican Church in 1822, the same year that Brazil became an independent nation with Britain's crucial support. In 1823 an

American pastor distributed more than fifty Protestant Bibles in Pernambuco. Ten years later an Englishman left a box full of Scriptures for whoever desired to take them. At the end of 1830 an American pastor named Kidder commented that the religious tolerance for his faith in Recife contrasted greatly with other parts of the world. In 1839 the Anglican Church inaugurated its place of worship in Recife, an imposing building of neoclassical design on the Capibaribe River and upscale Aurora Street adjacent to Recife's city center. Despite the 1810 treaty, the building had all the exterior appearances of a religious temple.

Britain also had the world's largest abolitionist movement, whose leaders had often been influenced by Protestant ideas of the dignity of physical labor. The British government had been pressuring Brazil to end the international slave trade since the 1810s, and it abolished slavery in its Caribbean colonies in 1833. Given this pressure, one can better see why Protestantism might appeal to members of Recife's nonwhite population.

The Padroado Régio (a treaty with the Vatican) conferred on the Brazilian state the right to directly influence the Catholic Church's administration in Brazil in return for the state's financial aid and support of Catholicism as the official national religion. The limits of the state's intervention in the business of the Church, and vice versa, were motives for disputes between the imperial government and the Vatican. During the Regency (1831–1840), when Pedro II was too young to assume his throne, the head regent Father Diogo Antonio Feijó, who was himself a Catholic priest, considered the possibility of forming a Brazilian church like England's Anglican Church—that is, a national church independent from the pope's authority. Brazilian priests openly disobeyed the Catholic Church's celibacy requirement, and some, like Feijó, called for its abolition. Priests in Brazil and much of Latin America often played important roles in public life in the 1800s, and many became influential politicians. The sons and daughters of many clergymen took their fathers' surnames with pride, like the descendants of one of the martyrs of Brazil's struggle for Independence, Padre Roma. His heirs have continued to pass down his name across the generations.

One could accurately say that Brazilian Catholicism was much more Brazilian than Roman. Catholicism in Portuguese America had developed in relative isolation from direct Vatican oversight for three centuries, and it was shaped by a variety of native and transplanted religious traditions and cosmologies. In Brazil, after all, traditional Portuguese Catholics lived alongside and interacted with Indians, forcibly converted Moors and Jews, Africans, gypsies, and a host of Catholic religious orders from different parts of Europe that congregated in novel combinations across Portuguese America's vast territory. The interpenetrating conflicts, inquisitions, compromises, adaptations, and resistance that occurred as these different traditions jostled against one another in the New World gave Brazilian culture a creole flexibility. Thus, the Christianity that Brazilian "Catholics" practiced in Recife had its own unique traditions, which up to the 1840s had been little influenced by attempts to bring greater cohesion and conformity to Catholicism in Europe since at least the sixteenth century.

One of the great strengths of Catholicism historically has been its ability to incorporate aspects of pagan religious practices. An example of this adaptability is the marriage of a black Brazilian-born groom to a brown bride in the respectable "white" Church of Our Lady of Penha on the last day of Carnival to the music of African and indigenous instruments. Another example is the celebration of All Saints Day, when women sway their hips sensually to the sound of *lundum*, a rhythm and dance of African origin whose seeming lewdness shocked many devout European Catholics. But, despite the disapproval of more orthodox Catholics, there was much faith invested in the gods, goddesses, saints, *mestres*, and other entities and divinities whom Brazilians worshipped according to their preferences. The joy of religious processions, the parallel devotions to entities and divinities of diverse religious traditions, their messianic and millenarian beliefs, and the contracts believed to exist between divinities and humans were all manifestations of the intense religiousness that pulsed through the tension-ridden streets of Recife in the post-Independence period. These beliefs could turn at times against the slavocratic regime supported by formal Catholicism just as it could against the followers of Agostinho.

If there was a certain tradition of religious tolerance, even within Catholicism, in Recife and other parts of Brazil in the mid-1800s, why did Agostinho make authorities so nervous? Why did the suspicion that he was furtively organizing a rebellion among Recife's black population exist? A wider view of the historical context makes this inquiry more understandable.

The city of Recife (literally, reef) grew out of the settlement of an isthmus between the Capibaribe River and the ocean that was protected by a line of reefs that formed a natural harbor for commerce. In 1836 the British naturalist Charles Darwin marveled at the extent and straightness of Recife's reefs. After its port opened in 1537, Recife became one of the most important centers of transatlantic trade because of the natural harbor and because of Pernambuco's rich coastal soils that were ideal for sugarcane. After riding the crest of a economic boom in the seventeenth century, the fortunes of one of the oldest commercial ports in the Americas began to waver in the eighteenth century due to increased competition in sugar production from the Caribbean. Even though Pernambuco would never again attain the commercial heights it once enjoyed, sugar production continued to rise through the end of the 1800s. As long as shipping depended on the sail, Recife enjoyed economic advantages that secured its continued, if somewhat sluggish, growth. Recife's port and its position on the easternmost part of the South American continent, favored by trade winds, gave it privileged access to markets in Africa and Europe.

After 1808, Recife grew more rapidly when the Portuguese crown allowed for free trade in Brazil's ports. With Independence in 1822, Pernambucan men of property who wanted to play a role in politics built houses in Recife, the center of regional and provincial politics and soon to be home to one of two national law schools that trained most of Brazil's politicians and bureaucrats. This influx of well-to-do families called for a small army of slave and free servants. The expansion of trade and the creation of a provincial bureaucracy offered new opportunities in Recife for rich and poor citizens, and it led to a growth in urban population. By 1840, a census showed that Recife was home to some 40,000 residents, about one-fifth of whom were slaves. Even though slaves constituted a minority of the urban community, most of the city's population was non-white. Brazilian masters manumitted slaves at much higher rates than did their counterparts in the United States, and Recife's population had practiced more than three centuries of race mixture. In 1842 a census that included parishes outside the urban boundaries of the city indicated that browns and blacks accounted for 58 percent of the population. Of the some 18,443 slaves counted in 1842, 52 percent were African-born. This high percentage of African slaves reflected the ongoing international slave trade to Brazil that only came to an end in 1850, and also the fact that the slave labor force depended on importation rather than natural reproduction to sustain itself. The census likely minimized the non-white population's size. Slaves were the most important measure of wealth in Brazil, where land was abundant and relatively cheap, and many masters sought to hide the actual numbers of slaves they owned from census takers to evade taxes. Also, many wealthy Brazilians with swarthy skin and African features (some of whom owned slaves) were counted as "whites" because, in a race-based slave society, to be characterized as brown or black held a stigma that most social climbers sought to avoid. As a popular Brazilian expression notes, "money whitens."

The large number of free black and brown Brazilians in Recife made it easier for runaway slaves to pose as free men or women and to find work in the growing anonymity of the city's urban labor market. Even though most of these fugitive slaves would eventually be discovered and returned to their owners, Recife's multiracial labor market made it difficult for the authorities to distinguish between slaves and free people of color and frustrated those who wanted to enforce the discipline of the slave regime. The political turbulence that rocked Recife in the first half of the 1800s redoubled these frustrations. Historians refer to this period as the "cycle of liberal insurrections of Brazil's northeast." These uprisings included the Pernambucan Insurrection in 1817, the Equator Confederation in 1824, and the Praieira Revolt in 1848; each centered in Recife. These political insurgencies began as conflicts between factions of powerful, mostly "white" Brazilians, but the instability they generated made it possible for expressions of black rebellion to surface. After all, liberal rhetoric of equality, liberty, and natural rights must have appealed to the slaves and free people of color whose opportunities and freedom were severely limited by law and custom. Men of color and slaves who joined liberal insurrectionary factions often had very different visions of what they were fighting for.

In 1846, at the time of his trial, Pastor Agostinho testified that he was born in 1799 in the Recife borough of Boa Vista, the son of a Brazilian-born slave mother. In Recife, Agostinho would have witnessed many of the bloody struggles fueled by liberal rhetoric. He was fifteen when officials publicly whipped a large number of bondsmen suspected of plotting a revolt rumored to be planned for June 29, 1814—the day of the Holy Spirit, an important religious holiday. To ensure public order, officials transferred the province's principal army battalion from nearby Olinda to Recife. The travel writer Louis François Tollenare wrote that some of these conspirators were executed for their parts in the plot. Among those implicated were the freed slaves Domingos do Carmo, the "king of Congo and of all the nations of Guine," and Joaquim Barbosa, the "captain of the *ganhadores*." *Ganhadores*, or *escravos de ganho*, were most often urban slaves who lived on their own and worked for wages, a large share of which they regularly paid to their owners.

Soon thereafter, the Insurrection of 1817 began with a barracks putsch led by local army officers in Recife who were supported by most of the city's merchants, lawyers, priests, and rural property owners linked to the city's Masonic lodges, the hothouses of liberal thought in the Americas and Europe. These rebel factions took over the local government, and they instituted a provisional republic that governed Pernambuco for seventy-one days until they were defeated by royal troops. The short-lived republic did not advocate the abolition of slavery, but its need for well-trained soldiers led it to entrust the defense of two of the city's principal forts to the Henrique Battalion, a militia composed of free black men who were reinforced by slaves owned by the rebellion's supporters. To further protect the "republic," the rebel government armed several hundred slaves to patrol the city. The Henrique Battalion's barracks were located in the borough of Boa Vista, where Agostinho had been born.

The forces that ultimately defeated the liberal rebels included many local property owners, who armed their paramilitary retinues of black troops in defense of the Portuguese monarchy. During the confusion of battle, many slaves took advantage of the disorder to run away and to hide in the forests outside of Recife. Mopping-up operations by royal forces included hunting down slaves who had fled, some of whom had fought with the rebels. Royal troops publicly whipped any slaves found with arms and then returned the injured bondsmen to their owners.

Brazil's course toward independence was accelerated by an 1820 revolt in Porto, Portugal, whose leaders demanded that their king, João VI, leave Brazil and return to rule in Portugal. Dom João VI preferred living in Brazil, and he had happily ruled his far-flung kingdom from Rio de Janeiro long after Napoleon's ultimate defeat in 1815. The Porto accords gave Brazilian provinces the right to form their own local governments and to select representatives for a constitutional assembly that would meet in Portugal. The competition for public offices that this agreement instigated sometimes led to conflicts. Local elites often mobilized their black and brown clients to support their political ambitions and to intimidate their opponents. Amid these local conflicts, Pedro I, the son of Dom João VI, who had remained in Brazil after his father returned to Portugal, declared Brazil's independence. Pedro assumed the title of emperor and called for the election of a constitutional assembly to draft a charter for the new nation in Rio de Janeiro. In February 1823 disputes over these elections led the black and brown militia forces of Recife to impose martial rule over the city for a week under the command of the brown officer Pedro Pedroso. The racial and ethnic tensions that marked this week were apparent in the lyrics sung by many of Pedro Pedroso's supporters:

Portuguese and Brazilians who paint themselves white	Marinheiros e caiados
All have to go	Todos vão se acabar
Because only blacks and browns	Porque só pardos e pretos
Are bound to inhabit Brazil.	O Brasil hão de habitar.

At the end of 1823, Pedro I summarily closed the constitutional assembly that he had called together months earlier. Many representatives thought that Pedro had acted illegally in disbanding an assembly that drew its authority from the electorate (a liberal ideal of the social contract that gives government legitimacy) rather than the monarch (whose legitimacy is assumed to be divine). Pernambuco's assembly representatives returned to Recife at the same time as the Pernambucan troops who had fought for Brazil's independence against Portuguese loyalists in Bahia. These forces brought to power a faction in Recife sympathetic to federalism (which favored greater powers for local government) and liberal constitutionalism that was critical of Pedro, who desired a strong central government based in Rio de Janeiro. Since the emperor would not recognize the legitimacy of this local government, its leaders declared their secession from the rest of Brazil in July 1824. They called their new state the Equator Confederation, but it was destined to be short-lived. When Pedro's imperial navy blockaded Recife, throngs of mostly black and brown Recifenses took to the streets and threatened to sack the stores and warehouses of Portuguese merchants. The city's police and militia forces contained the riotous mob. Ironically, those on the front lines of the forces of public order were the brown and black militia. Oral tradition has preserved protest songs sung in the streets during those heady days of disorder:

I will imitate [Henri] Christophe	Qual eu imito a Cristovao
That immortal Haitian leader	Esse imortal haitiano
Hurrah! We will imitate his people	Eia! Imitai a seu povo
Oh, my sovereign people!	Oh, meu povo soberano!

Henri Christophe, the famous emperor of Haiti, was already dead in 1824, but the news of the Haitian Revolution had spread throughout the Americas. Haiti had become an internationally recognized independent government in 1804 after a long struggle fought mostly by Haitian slaves had liberated the former French colony. Haiti was the first nation in the Americas to abolish slavery and the first black republic. Slaveowners throughout the Americas feared the example set by Haitian slaves, but many black and brown Brazilians, slave and free, obviously drew inspiration from it.

In his 1846 testimony, Agostinho admitted that he had defended the Equator Confederation as a militia officer, but he qualified his support by stating that he had done so because of his commander's orders. This experience must have influenced Agostinho's views. The Equator Confederation included radical liberals, and in its final days it declared an end to the international slave trade. The victorious imperial forces executed the movement's leaders and flogged lesser supporters. As further punishment, some were pressed into the imperial army as common soldiers; many of them were soon transferred to Brazil's southernmost reaches to fight in the Cisplatine War of 1825–1828 against Argentina. What happened to Agostinho as a result of his involvement in this rebellion is uncertain. But his testimony revealed that he was on duty outside of Pernambuco in Rio de Janeiro and Bahia in the years after the conspiracy. The judges suspected that the Divine Teacher was an army deserter.

Whether Agostinho was an army deserter or only a militia officer, as he alleged, he had served outside of Pernambuco. His military training and his experience with other men from different regions who shared similar social origins, hopes, and ambitions must have been a transformative experience for him. During his travels, Agostinho must have acquired a larger vision of the world than that permitted by the limited everyday lives of most poor Brazilian-born men and women. Many impoverished Brazilians lived and died in the same province, the same town, and some even on the same street or plantation.

The Divine Teacher claimed to have learned how to read and write from his slave mother's mistress. Literacy likely made it possible for him to advance to an officer's rank in the colored militia at a young age. Who knows if he had already begun to teach literacy to his counterparts at that time? Captain Pedro Pedroso, who led the barracks revolt of the nonwhite militias in 1823, taught algebra to his cellmates when he was imprisoned for his role in the uprising of 1817. A black man who knew how to read and write had additional arms to deploy: the capacity to transmit information and the authority that knowledge of the Holy Scriptures gave to religious Christians.

One can only speculate about what happened to Agostinho after the Equator Confederation revolt was crushed in 1824. Perhaps he fought in the Cisplatine War against Argentina. If he had, Agostinho would have witnessed the mobilization of the Brazilian army to fight a war against republican adversaries who advocated the abolition of slavery. If he had stayed in Pernambuco in the 1820s, he would have witnessed other creative combinations of political struggle and religiosity. The golden days of the runaway slave community called Catucá began in the wooded suburbs of Recife and then snaked its way north in between sugar plantations. In 1827 the Pernambucan government suspected that Catucá's leader, Malunguinho, planned to attack the city. Officials thought that this bold plan had been inspired by a rebellion in Salvador, Bahia, that had seen cooperation between slaves and members of runaway or maroon communities. It was yet one more indication that Brazilian slaves had developed complex channels of communication that kept them abreast of the news of slaves in other parts of the Americas. Undoubtedly, black sailors, slave and free, spread news of the revolt in Recife's port because officials did their best to censor public accounts of these events.

The controversy and struggle with the maroon community of Catucá had an impact on the spiritual life of blacks in Pernambuco. The Pernambucan Cult of the Sacred Jurema (a small sweet fruit, sometimes used to make wine) combined Catholic, indigenous, and African religious practices and beliefs. As in most Afro-spiritist religions, different divine spirits were invoked during religious rituals. Some of these divinities were African in origin, such as Ogun and Exu, but in Brazil new divinities based on local archetypes became part of popular religion, such as the *mestre* and the *caboclo* (backwoodsman). But in Pernambuco, Catucá's maroon leader, Malunguinho, became a sacred entity still invoked to this day before the altars of the Sacred Jurema. Perhaps this cult of Malunguinho already existed in the 1840s when Agostinho was arrested. While other historical leaders of maroon communities became part of Afro-spiritist cults in other parts of the Americas, as Makandal did in Haitian Vodun, this was not common. Thus, Malunguinho had achieved a distinct place in popular memory and religion. Apparently, the Divino Mestre was not the only one to combine religious fervor and political struggle.

The limited information we have about Agostinho forces us to speculate about possible influences in his life because we know little for certain about his activities between 1824 and his arrest in 1846. We do know that if he served in the army or the militia in the latter half of the 1820s, he would have witnessed intense agitation in the barracks in almost any part of Brazil. The lengthy delays in the payment of soldiers' wages, the poor quality of mess food, coercive recruitment practices, and the floggings to which privates were subject heightened tensions in the ranks across Brazil. In 1827 and 1828, German and Irish mercenaries hired by Pedro I in the wake of the Cisplatine War rioted in a number of provinces to complain about the lack of pay and Spartan conditions. Among Brazilian-born soldiers and officers, there was the impression that their emperor favored the Portuguese-born for promotions and plum postings. The hostility between Portuguese- and Brazilian-born officers and soldiers also had a latent racial underpinning that fueled suspicions. More courts-martial sentenced officers and soldiers for insubordination, disseminating political pamphlets, and inciting riots. In 1830, Pernambuco's army commander reported to the war minister in Rio that among his troops and officers, there were men with very different and strongly held political views: conservative monarchists who supported Pedro I's right to rule as an absolutist, liberal constitutionalists, and even republicans. He concluded that these political divisions made it impossible to maintain order among the men.

These growing tensions became more aggravated in the following year when a parliamentary crisis led Pedro I to renounce his throne in favor of his five-year-old son. Riotous protests in the streets of Rio surrounding the imperial palace precipitated Pedro's 1831 abdication. Enlisted soldiers and the city's mostly nonwhite poor played the most prominent roles in these disturbances. The radical liberal politician, journalist, lawyer, and native of Pernambuco, Borges da Fonseca, had been a key player in inspiring and orchestrating these effective acts of popular protest in Rio. Fonseca himself reported that troops from Pernambuco stationed in Rio had been among the most active participants in the protests that forced Pedro's abdication. Coincidentally, Fonseca, who later returned to his native Pernambuco, would serve as Agostinho's defense attorney in 1846.

In Pernambuco, agitation in the barracks reached its height in September 1831 when soldiers once again took over Recife's streets and promoted looting and loud protest marches. Many of Recife's poor black, brown, and white citizens joined the soldiers. Not one army officer, however, supported this uprising. Enlisted men had abandoned their appointed posts and duties en masse but repression came swiftly. Army officers along with militia and the irregular forces of prominent plantation owners surrounded and then massacred several hundred protestors in the streets. Those who survived and were apprehended were sent as prisoners to other provinces.

It is possible that Agostinho had not witnessed any of these events and had somehow managed to distance himself from these tumultuous episodes that shook the public institutions and ruptured the political stability of imperial Brazil. Interestingly, the judges of Pernambuco's highest court in 1846 seemed to worry most about the uncertainty that surrounded Agostinho's activities since 1824. During his interrogation, they asked Agostinho repeatedly if he had participated in the Sabinada Rebellion in Salvador, Bahia, in 1837–38—yet another liberal rebellion in the northeast that probably posed a more serious threat to Brazil's unity than any other. Agostinho denied that he had taken part. When asked if he knew the leader of the Sabinada, a brown radical liberal by the name of Sabino, Agostinho replied that he did. But, he added, he had met Sabino when the brown rebel was imprisoned in a Rio de Janeiro cell that Agostinho guarded.

The suspicion that Agostinho was a *sabino* had grave implications. The Sabinada began with a barracks revolt led by military officers and other local leaders dissatisfied with Bahia's provincial leaders and the Conservative policies put in place by the new Regency government in Rio de Janeiro in 1837. Under siege by imperial troops, the rebels who dominated Salvador recruited, armed, and mobilized Brazilian-born slaves to defend the "nation." The exclusion of slaves of African birth demonstrated the fragility of the alliances that rebel leaders hoped to sustain to defend their uprising. Soon enough the rebellion's initial leaders lost control of those whom they hoped to mobilize. Salvador's mostly nonwhite poor took to the streets and sacked properties owned by Portuguese merchants. The repression of this revolt was particularly violent, complete with executions and whippings, but three years later the government, seeking to quell regional rebellions, offered amnesty to all

Sabinada participants. Even if the judges could prove that Agostinho had taken part in the Sabinada, they could not legally prosecute him for it. However, if they knew that the Divine Teacher had been involved in the Sabinada, there would be little doubt about the dangers he potentially posed because of his contacts with black and brown radicals in other provinces.

The attention of the Pernambucan authorities, though informed by the broader historical context, was riveted by events in 1846. Recife had been peaceful for some time, but tensions underlay this placid surface. In 1845 a liberal opposition political party called Praieiro won provincial elections over Pernambuco's Conservative government. The electoral disputes between Liberals and Conservatives had been far from peaceful. Between 1841 and 1848, elections for justices of the peace, provincial deputies, and senators produced brawls at polling places across the province. In 1845 the most popular plank in the Praieiro Party's electoral platform was a proposal to "nationalize," or to prohibit the Portuguese and other foreigners from participating in retail trade. A similar nativist policy had been espoused during the Sabinada Revolt years earlier and in other regional rebellions. The nativist discourse of Liberals emphasized that Brazil's independence from Portugal remained partial because its commerce was still dominated by Portuguese businessmen who preferred to hire, train, and promote their fellow countrymen over the Brazilian-born. Relatively poor Portuguese immigrants to Brazil stood a much better chance of upward social mobility in the world of commerce in which the ladder of ascent stood blocked to most Brazilians. In truth, few of these Portuguese immigrants rose notably, and their fellow countrymen in the Brazilian retail trade often exploited them ruthlessly, but the perception was that Brazilians remained locked out of commerce.

Resentment toward retailers was especially harsh because of the inflation that had its roots in the national government's monetary policies. For Brazil's mostly nonwhite poor, however, it was the local retailer who seemed to be arbitrarily raising prices and profiting from the misery of the workers. Ambitious Brazilians of modest means often saw humble Portuguese immigrants as direct competitors. These ethnic and racial resentments encouraged violence during elections, as noted. Between 1844 and 1848, there were at least seven instances where Recife's popular classes, stirred up by anti-Portuguese rhetoric, went on looting sprees against Portuguese stores and warehouses, shouting, "Mata marinheiro!" (Death to the Portuguese).

The most violent of the *mata marinheiro* disturbances would occur in 1847 and 1848, but there had already been similar nativist attacks of lesser intensity in Recife during the elections of 1845. Nonwhites and their poor white compatriots took advantage of the agitation that elections produced to defy public authority. One episode in 1845 is symptomatic of this climate. As two professional runaway bounty hunters returned a fugitive slave to his owner in Recife, a crowd of blacks attacked them. The assailants almost succeeded in liberating the fugitive before a number of army soldiers who happened to be nearby intervened.

In October 1846, when a petition of habeus corpus was entered for Agostinho, the Conservative and Liberal parties disputed a senatorial election. As noted earlier, Agostinho's lawyer, the radical liberal Borges da Fonseca, had made a political career as a street agitator who had promoted *mata marinheiro* riots that had precipitated Pedro I's abdication in 1831. In the 1840s, Fonseca became a member of Brazil's as-yet small movement to abolish slavery. He did not refrain from producing political tracts that informed "men of color" about their constitutional rights. In defense of Agostinho, Fonseca, a member of the white elite, criticized the racism of the authorities who arrested his client. He probably sought to use Agostinho's persecution to remind nonwhite voters in Recife to vote for the Liberal Party candidate he supported. The trial was thus something of a showcase for political posturing and vote mongering. With this background, it is possible to address the central question of this essay: Why did Recife's authorities find Agostinho's ideas and preaching so threatening? The answer seems to be distilled in a verse found on the person of Agostinho's wife and entitled *The Source of the* ABCs." Unfortunately, the police did not transcribe the exact words of the verse for us to analyze, but its contents are mentioned. It was a poem that spoke about liberty; and, worse still, its verses alluded to Haiti.

The police also confiscated the Divine Teacher's personal Bible in which passages that referred to "liberty" and the end of slavery had been highlighted. In defense of his client, Borges da Fonseca asked, "What crime is it to be a *cismático* [Protestant]?" But the judges believed that Agostinho was not a run-of-the-mill Protestant. His reading of the Bible was not the same as that of white priests and pastors. After all, religious texts can serve just as well to justify domination as they can rebellion. Agostinho had made his choice, and therein lay his interpretation of the Scriptures. In his analysis of slavery in the United States, the historian Eugene Genovese demonstrated how black pastors contributed to the creation of a unique religious and social culture among slaves. In Brazil the rigidity of the Catholic hierarchy and the cooperation between Church and state made it difficult for a black man to become a priest. Besides, it would have been difficult for any Catholic priest to preach a message of rebellion to slaves without breaking with the Church hierarchy and thereby with Catholicism itself. Agostinho broke with the Church by attributing his ministry to a divine revelation unmediated by priestly authority.

One cannot know how aware Agostinho was of the political implications of his ministry. He may have calculated that his confident responses would mask his seditious intentions, but perhaps it is wrong to impute such a political consciousness to Agostinho. It is possible that he did not see himself as a rebel who transgressed the order of the slave regime. He himself claimed to follow "the law of Jesus Christ" and could have seen himself as a simple preacher, but the authorities did not share this view. They feared the implications of Agostinho's interpretation of Christianity that seemed to contain elements of millenarianism (the belief that the Second Coming of Christ was at hand in which God would smite the wicked and exalt the poor and oppressed). According to his followers, Agostinho's wife had been pregnant for five years, and she would give birth only when the Messiah returned to Earth. Millenarianism had manifested itself periodically in Brazil in conjunction with violent political rebellion. The Cabanos Revolt (1832–1835), centered in Pernambuco, had been the post-Independence rebellion that proved the most difficult local insurgency to repress in part because of its millenarian impulses. Like the Romans before them, Portuguese authorities knew that religious fervor could add a wild-card element to rebellion that could prove difficult to contain, especially in a slave society.

The notion of God that Agostinho espoused also had novel elements. Under interrogation, the literate Magdalene of the sect claimed that she had also come to know God through a vision. She was seated when the clouds descended and then opened to reveal Him in a purple robe as the Master of the Martyrs. When asked whether God was black or white she responded that He was *acaboclado* (a brown mix of Indian and European)—a mestizo God much more in keeping with Brazilian racial realities than the lily-white portraits and statues of Christ found in churches throughout Brazil. Upon hearing this testimony, the judges of the tribunal once again laughed. But the Divino Mestre's followers remained confident in their convictions despite the derision of these powerful and learned men. Nothing seemed to shake their faith. When asked if he knew why he and his fellow believers had been jailed, one follower of the Divino Mestre answered simply, "because they imprisoned us!"

Clearly, even in slave societies where Protestantism predominated, both masters and the authorities limited the autonomy of black Christianity by subordinating black religious community to white pastors. The tension between a master's assumed responsibility to civilize Africans by Christianizing them and maintaining the discipline of slave labor was great. In an attempt to limit the free interpretation of the Holy Scriptures, laws and practices in slave societies across the Americas generally discouraged literacy among slaves and free blacks. By addressing Agostinho as the Divino Mestre, his followers highlighted his mission of religious liberation and salvation through teaching literacy. That the verse found on Agostinho's wife mentioned Haiti and the "ABCs" was an especially damning association in the eyes of the authorities who were investigating the rumors surrounding this black pastor. Agostinho was not the only social reformer interested in education as a means of liberation. When Agostinho's lawyer and republican agitator, Borges da Fonseca, had been imprisoned by Pedro I in 1829, the white radical's lawyer certified that his client worked in Paraíba do Norte as a teacher of mutual education as outlined by the Lancastrian method (whereby students are taught and supervised by other students).

Among Agostinho's followers there was no one whose race was recorded by court authorities as brown or mixed, only "black" men and women. We know little else about the hundreds of followers of Agostinho who the authorities claimed existed in Recife other than that most of them were women. When asked about his flock, the Divino Mestre declared that there were more women than men in his sect because men were more morally lax. Men had a harder time accepting the asceticism he demanded from his followers. As noted earlier, the seven women arrested with Agostinho knew how to read. Courageously, his wife affirmed that she carried the verses to the poem about the origins of the ABCs because she thought that they were beautiful. Even though the followers of Agostinho all claimed to be free, at least one master placed an ad in a Recife newspaper in 1847 that described his fugitive slave, the "black Joaquina," as one who had attended the "Divino Mestre's clubs." Obviously, Agostinho's ministry provided a space for slave and free blacks to congregate, which disturbed authorities.

One year later, Agostinho had returned to preaching. Why would officials allow such a potentially dangerous religious leader to go free? Perhaps because they had no legal foundation on which to prosecute him or perhaps they hoped his arrest and interrogation would intimidate him and his followers. In any case, Recife's priests must have taken precautions and possibly turned to the leaders of the black and white Catholic lay brotherhoods to warn against the Protestant preaching of Agostinho and his followers. A newspaper article of October 1847 reported that each time one of the Divino Mestre's followers was arrested in Recife, a pack of unruly adolescent black boys appeared and physically attacked the victims of police persecution. The journalist feared that these gangs could turn against "any honest man" and disrupt public order. In truth, this had already started happening, because in June and then in September 1847 there were *mata marinheiro* riots in Recife during which various Portuguese citizens were injured by the furious multitude of young, mostly nonwhite, adolescents.

The participation of mostly nonwhite adolescents in attacks against the followers of the Divino Mestre confirms that the black population of Recife was not united by a single worldview or cosmology. Many black Recifenses maintained the religious practices of their African forebears and only adopted the outward forms of Christianity. But other poor Brazilians of all races were devout "Catholics."

The last time Agostinho and his followers appear in the sources is in late 1847, when the authorities coercively recruited a number of his adherents into the army as enlisted men. Even though their occupations and their positions as household heads should have legally exempted these men from military impressment, sometimes the authorities ignored the legal rights of poor men. After their induction, those who could not prove their legal exemption from military service in a timely fashion were likely to be transferred to other provinces.

Agostinho disappeared from sources just when the last of the post-Independence liberal insurrections, the Praieira Revolt of 1848–49, broke out in Pernambuco. It seems that no space was left in newspaper columns to worry about the Divino Mestre's doings. In the only case of its kind, two different senatorial elections that favored candidates of the Pernambucan Liberal Party, more popularly known as the Praieiro Party, were annulled in the late 1840s; then elections brought the Conservative Party back to power in 1848. When a new party came to power, it removed officials nominated by the previous administration and appointed its own cronies. When the Conservatives began this process, a number of prominent Praieiro Party members refused to surrender their political posts as justices of the peace, National Guard officers, and police commanders. As a result, an armed struggle began in November 1848. Praieiro forces attempted to take control of Recife, and rumors flew of new conspiracies led by Brazilians of African descent. For example, two freed slaves born in Africa were imprisoned for plotting just such a revolt. One of them was popularly know as Benedito, "the governor of the blacks from the African Gold Coast." Another man imprisoned under the same accusation was a militant Liberal, Francisco Borges Mendes, who was probably white because court records almost always stated the race of suspects when they were men of color. Mendes had been born and raised in Bahia, but he had lived for six years in Recife. He is not the only example of links between insurrectionary forces in Bahia and Pernambuco. The scrivener Francisco José do Rego, a supposed "seducer of the people," was arrested in Recife and accused of belonging to radical clubs in Bahia that plotted rebellion.

Most of the individuals arrested in the wake of the Praieira Revolt did not undergo a separate inquiry and trial. They were caught up in the typical steamroller of repression aimed at the political opposition in general. Imperial army troops allied with local forces loyal to the provincial government crushed rebel forces. The authorities pressed some of the defeated rebel troops that they captured and transferred them to other provinces as punishment. Unlike previous revolts, however, there were no executions. The very last Praieiro to be granted amnesty was Agostinho's former lawyer, the radical liberal leader Borges da Fonseca, who was freed in 1852.

The attempted invasion of Recife by Praieiro forces in February 1849 produced hundreds of casualties on both sides. In this battle, tailors formed the group of artisans who were the most prominent in the rebel army. In a city where tradesmen often interacted in social and professional organizations, it is perhaps not surprising to note that Agostinho was a tailor. Perhaps his contacts within this group and his brush with the law the previous year led Agostinho to steer well clear of involvement in this rebellion. His name does not appear on the list of tailors, five of whom were captured, named in the inquiry that investigated the revolt. Three witnesses accused the tailor Manoel Joaquim da Costa of holding seditious rebel meetings in his shop. When the Praieiro army invaded Recife, witnesses testified that gunfire at government troops came from his residence. The same accusations were leveled against the tailors Manoel do Amparo Caju, whose nickname was Pardo Caju or Brown Cashew, and José Romão de Freitas. Both these men were also accused of "seducing men" to join the rebel fight, but it was clearly Borges da Fonseca who was known to be the main recruiter of supporters for the Praieiro army in Recife and the surrounding countryside.

Even though little is known about the Divino Mestre, the stories generated about him by the press and the courts permit rare glimpses of how black and brown Recifenses responded to Independence and the struggle to build a national state. The liberal rhetoric that accompanied Independence preached lessons of equality, liberty, and natural rights that were contradictory in a slave society whose order was predicated on ideals of racial and ethnic hierarchy. The cases examined in this essay suggest the numerous connections that likely existed between black and brown men from different parts of Brazil who participated in radical politics. Sometimes in alliance with more radical white men, these non-white Brazilians dreamed of creating a new political and social order in Brazil for which some were willing to fight and die. The connections between men of color in Bahia and Pernambuco seem particularly striking even though the ethnic origins of their bondsmen were distinct for the most part (the Gulf of Benin in the case of the former, and Angola and the Congo in the latter).

The hybrid nature of Brazil's cultural and genetic makeup made possible solidarities and divisions among its populace. Fragile webs of information were woven by a variety of actors who sought to form secret organizations and conspiracies. The numerous black sailors who regularly traveled up and down Brazil's coast transporting goods, slaves, prisoners, soldiers, and government officials were undoubtedly key sources of information for these underground networks. The domestic servants of politicians could provide intelligence about the plans of the rich and powerful whose private conversations they overheard from time to time. Even prisons became schools where radicals sought to educate and to indoctrinate converts to their cause.

As this essay has shown, rebel troops were most commonly punished with service as enlisted men in the regular army in distant provinces. In theory, the authorities sought to avoid inducting black (particularly African-born men) into the regular military forces up to the 1860s, but in practice, these rules were disregarded. In truth, perceptions of race could change from observer to observer according to circumstances. The suspicions about networks of secret societies that linked black men and radical liberal abolitionists, such as Borges da Fonseca, from different provinces was not so farfetched as to be dismissed as the collective paranoia of a master class who feared the example of Haiti. Even though documentation does not give us explicit information about these alternative political and religious visions, officials seemed ready to believe in their existence and their danger.

SUGGESTED READINGS

For an overview of Brazilian politics and the challenges to national unity in the early Independence period, see Roderick Barman, *Brazil: The Forging of a Nation, 1798–1852* (Stanford, 1988). For an excellent collection of documents, see Robert Edgar Conrad, *Children of God's Fire: A Documentary History of Black Slavery in Brazil* (Princeton, 1983). On Pernambuco's economy in the 1800s and its place within Brazil, see Peter Eisenberg, *The Sugar Industry in Pernambuco: Modernization without Change, 1840–1910* (Berkeley, 1974). For the classic interpretation and apology for Brazil's heritage of African and Indian slavery, see Gilberto Freyre, *The Mansions and the Shanties: The Making of Modern Brazil* (New York, 1963). On Lusophobia and Pernambuco's place in early national struggles, see Jeffrey C. Mosher, "Pernambuco and the Construction of the Brazilian Nation-State, 1831–1850" (Ph.D. dissertation, University of Florida at Gainesville, 1996); and idem, "Political Mobilization, Party Ideology, and Lusophobia in Nineteenth-Century Brazil: Pernambuco, 1822–1850," *Hispanic American Historical*

Review 80:4 (2000): 881–912. Also see the author of this chapter, Marcus J. M. De Carvalho, *Liberdade: Rotinas e rupturas do escravismo no Recife, 1822–1850* (Recife, 1995); and idem, "Hegemony and Rebellion in Pernambuco, Brazil, 1821–1835" (Ph.D. dissertation, University of Illinois, Champaign-Urbana, 1989).

PART II

THE GENERATIONS OF THE LATE EMPIRE (1870–1889) AND THE OLD REPUBLIC (1889–1930)

*D*uring the last third of the nineteenth and the first third of the twentieth centuries, Brazilians experienced momentous changes, but stubborn continuities persisted in many sectors of society. In 1870 the Brazilian imperial government celebrated victory over Paraguay after a five-year war on a distant inhospitable front. The Paraguayan War (1864–1870) was South America's largest international military conflict, and most Brazilians were stunned that it took five years to defeat the tenacious forces of Paraguay, a nation with a much smaller economy and population. Military officers believed that their role in the war had earned them the right to a greater voice in national affairs, and they resented civilian politicians for their miserly support of the war effort and their reluctance to fund military reforms after the war. Many younger officers became alienated from the imperial government because of this neglect, and some began to espouse republicanism—that is, government with an elected head-of-state rather than the emperor. The military, an important pillar of support for Brazil's imperial order, began to fissure.

The Catholic Church also distanced itself from the emperor. A dispute known as the Religious Question led Pedro II to arrest and to prosecute two Catholic bishops in 1873 who defied his authority. The clerics were jailed despite protests from the Vatican. Yet another persuasive pillar of support for the imperial order had been weakened. New and increasingly important constituencies in Brazilian history began to raise their voices against imperial neglect. Members of the petty bourgeoisie and incipient labor organizations in burgeoning urban centers complained that too little imperial attention and treasure were expended on urban improvements to better the security, health, housing, sanitation, transportation, and quality of city life.

Wrangling over electoral and recruitment fraud between Liberal and Conservative politicians during the Paraguayan War pushed a faction of more radical Liberals to found an official Republican Party in 1870. It would remain a small third party during the Empire (1822–1889), but it opened a front of direct public criticism of the monarchy. Republicans viewed the aging Pedro II, who was afflicted with diabetes, as a symbol of a bygone degenerate era, and some derisively referred to him as "Pedro Banana." Republicanism was strongest in the states of São Paulo and Rio Grande do Sul. The leaders of these growing provinces, like military officers, saw themselves as vanguards of much-needed modernization within Brazil.

The city and province of São Paulo were the main beneficiaries of the spectacular boom in coffee, the commodity that came to constitute most of the value of Brazil's exports in the second half of the 1800s. This economic boom attracted investment and population to the province, and the wealth generated by coffee exports supplied much of the imperial government's tax revenue. The province's now-heavy labor demands led coffee planters to buy slaves from masters in the economically torpid northeastern sugar provinces after the international slave trade ended in 1850. Economic malaise and cycles of drought in the northeast in the 1870s began a pattern of outmigration from that region to others in Brazil (particularly São Paulo) that continues to this day. Despite its rapidly growing wealth and population, São Paulo did not enjoy commensurate representation in Brazil's parliament because the imperial constitution made no provisions for reapportionment. Frustration with the imperial political order led many planters and politicians in São Paulo to embrace the Republican Party. Because São Paulo had become a principal slaveowning province after 1850 as well as the stronghold of republicanism, the party's leadership was slow to support abolitionism. This legacy estranged most of the African-descended population from the Republican Party.

By 1872, slaves only constituted about 15 percent of the national population, down from nearly one-third in 1850. Brazil's bonded population had been sustained by importation, and natural reproduction among slaves was much too low to replace an aging black work force. By the 1880s, abolitionism became fashionable, particularly among educated urbanites and in the north and northeastern provinces where the slave and master populations had dwindled. Slaves themselves sensed that change was in the air, and many ran away from their masters or resisted in other ways to undermine the discipline of the slave labor regime. They became important protagonists in their own struggle for freedom. In May 1888, Pedro II's daughter, Princess Isabel, signed into law legislation pushed through by a Conservative parliament that completely abolished slavery. This law generated much sympathy among Afro-Brazilians for the monarchy and the Conservative Party (a party that ironically had long defended the rights of slave owners). The law, however, included no provisions to help former slaves make the transition to life as free citizens, nor did it offer compensation to slaveholders. Many slavocratic landholders and merchants who had been staunch supporters of the monarchy now believed that the imperial government had abandoned them.

The decline of the slave population made it more and more impera-
tive to find a new source of laborers. The booming coffee economy of
São Paulo pushed leaders in this state to grapple with this issue with
greater urgency. Many came to advocate replacing the slave labor force
with European immigrants. Unable to convince the imperial parliament
to subsidize European immigration, politicians in São Paulo used provincial funds to bring European workers into the coffee fields. Italians,
Spaniards, Portuguese, Germans, eastern Europeans, and peoples of the
eastern Mediterranean began to arrive in increasing numbers through
the early 1900s. Besides supplying needed labor, many white leaders believed that one of the dividends of supporting European immigration
was that it would help to "whiten" Brazil's population and dilute the
influence of African and indigenous peoples, whom they assumed to be
congenitally inferior. Some Brazilians justified this policy by appealing
to ideas of social Darwinism that became popular in the late 1800s. Social Darwinism was a "scientific" apology for European domination of
colonial subjects across the world because it argued that Europeans were
racially superior. In brief, social Darwinists suggested that it was only
"natural" for Europeans to dominate inferior peoples who were fated by
evolution to die out or to be absorbed by the superior white race. This
empirical bigotry reinforced traditional ideas of racial hierarchy and prejudice among Brazil's mostly white elite toward their mostly racially mixed
fellow citizens.

In November 1889 a group of military officers and cadets orchestrated a bloodless coup that led to the promulgation of the Republic,
which sent the ailing Pedro II into exile. None of the imperial
government's traditional allies stood up to defend the monarchy, and the
Afro-Brazilian population was not in a position to fight for their beloved
emperor.

Brazil's 1891 Constitution took much of its inspiration from the U.S.
Constitution. It gave more power to state and local governments to regulate their affairs, policies that particularly pleased the leaders of São Paulo
who had chafed under central imperial rule. Many republican leaders,
civil and military, believed that modernization was the answer to all of
Brazil's woes. Some embraced North Atlantic fashions, architecture, technology, science, sports, cultural output, and economic and political models
with the fervor of true believers. They rarely stopped to consider fully
the consequences of these choices for Brazil's poor. For instance, republican leaders remodeled the capital's downtown district along the lines of
Haussmann's Paris and callously demolished many colonial buildings and
tenements that had provided affordable lodgings for the city's working
class. In 1904 a citywide riot exploded in which elements of the popular

classes attacked and destroyed many of the symbols of the city's modernity, such as gas street lamps and streetcars. This eruption of violence and vandalism exemplified the growing sense of social distance that existed between ordinary Brazilians and republican leaders and their supporters. Indeed, in their tastes and policies, the privileged distanced themselves from their nation's creole Iberian heritage. For instance, the republican elite prided themselves on wearing the latest northern European fashions whether or not they were suited to Brazil's tropical climate. Many republican youths turned their backs on Catholicism, and instead joined or were influenced by the Positivist Church, which preached a message of order and progress that is still emblazoned on Brazil's flag.

Despite their confidence in modernization, republican leaders found the task of implementing their heterogeneous ideals of national reform and renewal tough going. After surviving a number of regional rebellions that threatened to topple the Republic, the military leaders who had dominated the state in the early 1890s agreed to turn power over to civilian Republican politicians. In the early 1900s a new Republican political order emerged known as the Politics of the Governors. During Brazil's Old Republic (1889–1930), political parties were state-based rather than national in scope. This new system strengthened the hands of local political bosses, the *coronéis*. State governors agreed to respect the autonomy of *coronéis* to administer their bailiwicks as long as they delivered the majority of votes from their district to the dominant state party. The republican Constitution failed to guarantee citizens the right to a secret vote, so powerful local leaders could easily intimidate voters; and if that did not work, officials stuffed ballot boxes to favor their candidates. On their part, governors made a similar pact with leaders at the federal level. They would deliver their states' vote to presidential candidates with the understanding that the federal leadership would respect the governors' right to administer their states without undue federal intervention. In practice, however, weaker states were less able to resist federal intervention.

The Old Republic's Politics of the Governors placed local, state, and national governments once again largely at the service of the traditional agro-export sector. The economic policymakers of the Old Republic preached the mantras of early twentieth-century globalization: free trade, free markets, and comparative advantage. In theory, they believed that government intervention in the marketplace would create distortions that would hamper rather than enhance economic growth. Following the dictates of classical liberalism, the government's role should be limited largely to providing for national defense and internal security, delivering the mail, and enforcing the laws that protect private property. Therefore, they rejected plans hatched by the Republic's early military leadership to create a system of tariffs to stimulate industrialization. However, when overproduction threatened the price of coffee on the world market, the federal government demonstrated a keen willingness to intervene in the marketplace on several occasions. In truth, free markets and free trade are ideals that have never been fully implemented by any nation.

World War I shook the faith of many Brazilians in the principles that girded the Old Republic. It was one thing for Europeans to use their military might to run roughshod over the rights and lives of colonial peoples in Asia and Africa, but the industrial-scale barbarism of European against European made many educated Brazilians question whether northern Europe was a model of civilization worth emulating. The debut of total warfare made it clear to military and civilian leaders in Brazil how vulnerable they were in the face of industrial war machines. During the war, the Brazilian military was unable to purchase crucial armaments and consumers had to go without many industrial goods. By following the economic philosophy of comparative advantage, Brazilians had come to depend on industrial imports from North Atlantic nations, a danger that many military officers never tired of reiterating.

Brazilians soon found that they had little capability of their own to produce weaponry and goods of similar price and quality. In 1916 the government scrambled to implement a modern recruitment system based on a draft lottery, but routine health inspections revealed a disturbing fact. Most draftees were in poor physical condition, suffered from many preventable ailments and diseases. They also lacked the basic education that facilitated the use of modern military hardware, training, and tactics. One public health authority coined the phrase, "Brazil is an immense hospital." World War I even brought into question the wisdom of Rio's policies of subsidizing European immigration to "whiten" the national race. The authorities worried whether German and Italian immigrants living in isolated colonies in Brazil's south, where few bothered to learn Portuguese, might become beachheads for foreign imperial domination.

For their part, many Afro-Brazilians after abolition became marginalized from formal institutions and the formal economy. In areas where European immigration was heavy, Afro-Brazilian laborers were squeezed out of higher-paying skilled labor jobs and other potential avenues for social mobility in commerce. Congress never passed laws that segregated Afro-Brazilians or outlawed interracial marriage, but racial prejudice was real, even if it was less formal than its manifestations in the United States, Cuba, and South Africa. Racial prejudice limited the opportunities and rights of African-descended people and dealt them humiliations, especially if they did not "know their place." Despite these tremendous disadvantages, some African-descended Brazilians managed to better their lives. A few became prominent and respected members of their community.

Many indigenous Brazilians struggled to maintain their culture and communities by both fighting off "white" settlement and retreating to isolated regions to escape the danger represented by settlers. Settlers brought with them communicable diseases that could devastate Indian communities, and many whites often did not hesitate to kill Indians in order to secure their claims to frontier lands.

Even though European immigrants enjoyed many advantages in Brazil, many of them became exploited laborers in agriculture and incipient industries. The leaders of Brazil's early trade union movement were often foreign-born men who brought the ideas of anarchism and socialism with them. They sought to form unions to improve their wages and working conditions, but Brazilian industrialists and authorities had little patience with strikes and protests. After World War I the government cracked down on labor unions, exiled many foreign-born labor leaders, and intimidated workers (both Brazilian and foreign-born). In the wake of the 1917 Bolshevik Revolution in Russia there were rising fears of labor radicalism internationally. In rural areas where most Brazilians continued to live, powerful oligarchs continued to use patronage and, if necessary, violence to maintain a pliant work force and deferential sharecroppers.

Brazilian women made some grudging gains in these years of transition. The 1916 legal code gave women the right to manage marital property if their husbands were sentenced to two or more years in jail. While male jurists and legislators lauded this enlightened reform, many wives and daughters likely found it risible because they lived in the shadow of patriarchal power. Violence perpetrated against wives by husbands largely went unpunished, and juries rarely convicted husbands who claimed to have murdered their wives because they had committed adultery. Women workers earned lower wages, which limited their ability to support themselves and a family on their own, but despite these difficulties many women managed to head their own households. Young women who did not enjoy the protection of a stable family or influential patron might be forced into prostitution. Conversely, some women preferred this often higher-paying profession to the alternatives of work as domestic servants and factory workers where they still faced the danger of sexual harassment and abuse by male employers, employees, and managers. In the 1920s more and more middle- and upper-class women began to leave the home to take up work as teachers, secretaries, and civil employees and to enjoy public entertainment in dance halls, movie theaters, and parks.

The practice of cloistering wives and nubile daughters in the home to protect their reputations began to slowly relax as the age of the automobile offered prosperous young sweethearts new mobility and opportunities for private intimacy. A new romantic ideal of a companionate marriage between husband and wife began to emerge that emphasized a relationship between more equal partners rather than between a dominant (male) and passive (female) one. The feminist movement had laid tenuous roots in Brazil in the 1800s, but it began to pick up steam in the 1920s, the decade when women in the United States gained the right to vote. Still, feminist ranks remained small, and most women who participated were educated members of the middle and upper classes. Social conservatives condemned feminists and "modern women" as *mulheres homens*, or "he-women," and predicted that social chaos would result from the breakdown of gender roles and the traditional patriarchal family.

After World War I the government faced increasing demands for state intervention to improve public health, education, and sanitation. Some important initiatives began, but they were far too small in scale to satisfy the growing number of Brazilians who insisted on more meaningful government action and reform. In the 1920s young educated Brazilians became increasingly critical of the Old Republic's political and economic order. One symptom of youthful protest was the 1922 Modern Art Week in São Paulo. There, young artists and writers celebrated the nation's centennial by brazenly stating that Brazilians had declared their political independence from Europe in 1822, and in 1922 they were finally declaring their intellectual independence. Modern artists, writers, and scholars sought out "Brazilian" cultural themes as raw materials from which to create high art that was uniquely Brazilian in character. They began a vogue for Afro-Brazilian and indigenous manifestations that they saw as untouched by the desire to imitate European culture and therefore were more genuinely "Brazilian" in character. The self-conscious effort to create truly national art, literature, architecture, and music ironically drew much of its inspiration from the modern art scene in North Atlantic nations.

On another nationalistic front, junior officers in Brazil's military launched a series of rebellions known as the Tenente (Lieutenant) Revolts (1922, 1924–1927). These officers sought to topple the Old Republic's regime that they viewed as dominated by rural oligarchs who had little interest in modernizing the nation and improving the health and welfare of Brazil's majority. The young rebels' platform of reforms was rather vague and moderate, but they called for, among other things, secret ballots for elections and state efforts to encourage industrialization and social welfare. Although their daring efforts of military defiance failed to topple the government, these idealistic young officers won the admiration of many Brazilians who agreed with their critiques of the status quo. The Tenente Revolts helped to sharpen disillusionment with the main philosophies and practices that guided the Old Republic, but the effectiveness of these critiques only became apparent in 1930 when a military coup led by the civilian politician Getúlio Vargas brought an end to the Old Republic's political order.

∽

The life story of Juca Rosa demonstrates how people of African and European descent interacted and how their practices interpenetrated one another in the late imperial capital to create a rich creole mix. However, the elements of Afro-Brazilian spiritist religion and formal legal and religious institutions based on European models coexisted uneasily. Famous healers such as Juca could develop an impressive following among privileged white Brazilians and enjoy powerful protectors in high places, but if their activities drew too much attention, they could fall victim to police and judicial crackdowns. Religion also played an important role in the European immigrant communities of temperate southern Brazil. While Juca's black skin and African heritage lent authority and legitimacy to his potions and spells, Jacobina Maurer demonstrated that women could also become influential mystic leaders. Her following consisted of first- and second-generation Protestant German immigrants who felt alienated and threatened by the larger Brazilian society and even by the Catholic German immigrant population that lived in close proximity. Her religious community's decision to cut themselves off from the contaminating influences outside their faith led to a clash that was ultimately much more violent than the repression of Juca Rosa's cult. The authorities worried about the abilities of Afro-Brazilians and European immigrants to assimilate to mainstream Brazilian culture in the late empire when the institution of slavery had entered a phase of decline and European immigration began to increase. They were also disturbed that a second-generation Afro-Brazilian man and a German woman could wield such influence over their followers.

While Juca and Jacobina represent examples of how "outsiders" responded to official ideas of national community in the late empire, the life stories of Adolfo Caminha and Cândido Rondon demonstrate how ambitious young men privileged with education embraced ideals of nationalism, modernization, positivism, and republicanism. Both became military officers, although the navy's high command forced Caminha to resign his commission at an early age. Caminha then turned to literature as a means of expressing his sense of nationalism and critiquing injustices that continued to plague Brazilian society without losing his faith in republicanism. Rondon struggled to reform Brazilian governance from within the system by changing the way the state dealt with uncontacted Indian communities that were mostly located on the nation's vast western frontiers. Both Caminha and Rondon struggled with the relationship between ideas of race and national community, and they exemplify the heterogeneity and contradictions that characterized nationalist thought in regard to race in Brazil.

CHAPTER 3

Juca Rosa

Spiritual Leader and Healer

GABRIELA DOS REIS SAMPAIO

Juca Rosa drew his authority not from science but from the creole tradi-
tions of Brazil's African, indigenous, and European heritages of popular
religion, medicine, and magic. In this realm, Juca's black skin enhanced
his authority because most Brazilians assumed that people of African de-
scent were by nature closer to the spirit world of magic, which white au-
thorities associated with pagan savagery. A growing number of public
officials resented and feared the renown of Juca's practice; they also prob-
ably relished, consciously or unconsciously, the fact that he seemed to con-
firm many of the racist stereotypes that Afro-Brazilians were dishonest,
libertine, and superstitious. On his part, Juca sought to use some of these
very prejudices as tools to improve his own circumstances while defying
other stereotypes that whites held about blacks.

Juca provided services for a wide variety of problems. He not only
treated his clients' health but his practice also embraced their emotional,
carnal, and worldly desires. Juca's following consisted largely of poor, mostly
nonwhite women with dubious claims to respectability, but as his reputa-
tion as a faith healer (especially known for his love incantations) grew,
ladies from the more privileged classes came to consult him. His very suc-
cess as a faith healer and reputedly as a lady's man eventually led to his
downfall. Accusations that he had seduced white women of high rank
brought about a criminal investigation of Juca Rosa. Keep in mind that in
the post-Reconstruction U.S. South, such an accusation against a black
man would likely lead to a public lynching. In Rio, authorities sought to
enforce lines of racial and social status and separation by less violent means.
They likely hoped that the public investigation would discredit Juca as a
charlatan and shame his wealthy clients for being hoodwinked and seduced
by a black man. It would be a lesson for those members of the elite who
sought out the services of faith healers.

While this turn of events was a misfortune for Juca, it is a rare bounty
for social historians. The testimony of Juca and his followers and the sen-
sationalist newspaper coverage of the scandal provide unique information
about the lives, beliefs, and practices of poor Brazilians and how they in-
teracted with members of the elite. They also reveal the sexual, gender,
racial, social, and cultural tensions that riveted Brazil as the institution of

slavery began to decline after the end of the international slave trade in 1850. The story reveals both the fascination and revulsion that members of the white elite felt toward Afro-Brazilians and popular cultural practices in an age when scientific reason and method became international touchstones of civilized Western worldviews.

Gabriela dos Reis Sampaio is an assistant professor of history at the Universidade Federal da Bahia. Her essay is based on a much broader study of this faith healer's life and times, "A história do feiticeiro Juca Rosa: Cultura e relações sociais no Rio de Janeiro imperial" (2000). She is also the author of Nas trincheiras da cura: As differentes medicinas no Rio de Janeiro imperial *(2002).*

José Sebastião da Rosa, or Juca Rosa, as he was popularly known, was one of the most important folk healers (*feiticeiros*) in nineteenth-century Brazil. His African-born mother gave birth to Juca in Rio de Janeiro in 1834. He probably learned from her many of the religious rituals he conducted at his house. He lived in downtown Rio, the capital of Brazil's monarchical empire, and grew up amid the city's large population of slave and free people of African descent. Rosa's house became a place where mostly nonwhite members of Rio's working poor went to look for help with problems related to money, love, and illness. But Juca was no stranger to many rich white men and women who showed up at the faith healer's home for advice, spells, and medicines.

In 1870 officials accused Rosa of sexual involvement with a number of rich white women and charged him with charlatanism. He was the favorite subject of the press for months and, due to these newspaper reports as well as courtroom testimony, we can learn much about this intriguing character, the people who sought out his services, and the officials who prosecuted him. This essay will tell his story in relation to the important political, social, and economic transformations of his times.

A PUBLIC SCANDAL

In the last months of 1870 the newspapers of Rio de Janeiro published articles denouncing the mysterious and immoral activities of a famous black *feiticeiro* who had a large number of followers. Under headlines such as "Witchcraft" or "Dark Mysteries," they described the ceremonies held at his house, where, according to reporters, women danced naked to the sound of drums, the leader entered into a trance and spoke in African dialects, and animals were sacrificed during strange rituals. Even worse for journalists was the allegation that Rosa seduced white women, some of whom were members of important families. Reporters accused the black necromancer of menacing women with his poisons, charlatanism, and bad influence. In their words, lust, immorality, and vices learned from the "barbarian" people of Africa had violated the "sacred" houses of "decent white people."

At the time of his arrest, the healer Juca Rosa was thirty-six years old. His imprisonment had been prompted by an embittered, 20-page, anonymous denunciation that detailed information about him and his followers, including their names and addresses. The chief of police read the unknown author's report and then went to Rosa's house and arrested him without hesitation. However, Juca was a well-known figure. He had been practicing as a healer for many years, at least since the beginning of the 1860s, without being bothered by any authority. It was said that he was protected by important people, powerful politicians, and even some police officials. But in 1870 something happened, or probably many different things happened, and his peaceful existence as a respected healer ended.

The first and most obvious cause of his fall from grace was his reputed sexual liaisons with the wife of an important person, probably a member of the parliament. This unknown political figure became upset enough to denounce Rosa in writing, and he was powerful enough to make sure that the chief of police would put the healer in jail. He also chose the right police officer for the job: Miguel Tavares had become famous for hardline law enforcement, especially in cases related to slaves. A scrappy public official whose post gave him police powers as well as those of a public prosecuter, Tavares had even threatened to prosecute masters and mistresses who profited by leading their young female slaves into work as prostitutes. Based on the chief's record, we can believe that any important patron whom Juca Rosa may have had would not easily suborn the ambitious Tavares, a practice that was not uncommon in Brazil at the time. Tavares himself conducted the investigation and instigated criminal proceedings. He kept Juca Rosa in jail during the eight long months of the investigation and trial.

The criminal case resulted in a more than 400-page document, with testimonies from several of Juca's followers. This extraordinary court document makes it possible to learn a lot about the healer's ceremonies, rituals, and mysterious cult. It also provides other clues as to why he was jailed and put on trial. It is important to remember the fundamental importance of the political moment during which the case became a public scandal. Broader changes in Brazilian society shaped the development of Juca Rosa's arrest and trial. By placing his story in this context the historian can put together the different pieces of this complicated puzzle. But let us start by going to Rosa's house to attend a ceremony and by trying to understand why this Afro-Brazilian healer attracted so many followers from different races and classes.

JUCA ROSA'S CEREMONIES AND HIS FOLLOWERS

On the night of August 14, 1870, a big initiation celebration took place at the house of one of Juca Rosa's most loyal followers, Henriqueta. Like most of Juca Rosa's devotees, Henriqueta was a woman of color. The authorities recorded the race of the women whom Juca Rosa referred to as his "daughters" as "black" or "brown." Henriqueta, however, was also the mother of two children sired by the healer. Records reveal only one white disciple in Juca's coterie, a Portuguese woman named Mariquinhas da Europa. While few white women became part of Juca's inner circle of devotees, various witnesses noted that many white women often went to Rosa's house for consultations and believed in his power. There were also some men who regularly helped Rosa in the ceremonies, played musical instruments, or just attended the rituals. To become a "daughter," each woman had to swear an oath promising to give to the "Father" (Juca Rosa) the guardianship of her spirit as well as her body. These female initiates had to perform certain rituals that included taking herbal baths and making animal sacrifices. They also had to pay a monthly fee to Juca, bring candles and offerings (usually animals and food) to the saints, and give occasional presents to Rosa. This last requirement was not asked for directly by Juca Rosa but was implicit, and the "daughters" would tell every new member that it was necessary, in order to please the "Father."

The August 14 celebration was held for the initiation of Leopoldina into Juca Rosa's ritual family. Leopoldina had visited Rosa a week before at his home to ask him to bring back a sailor whom she was in love with but who had left her. Leopoldina had been directed to consult with Juca Rosa by a fellow seamstress, Mariquinhas da Europa, who happened to be Rosa's favorite "daughter." According to her, Rosa had "as much power as God" and the "ability to get anything that people asked from him." One of Rosa's specialities was love spells, and he told Leopoldina that he could solve her problem, but she would have to become an initiate of his cult first. She agreed and testified that the healer's presence and manners had impressed her. According to Leopoldina and other witnesses, Juca Rosa was a strong, tall black man with lively, penetrating eyes. She and others admitted that they found Juca very attractive. He dressed well, wore jewelry, and had a fancy watch and chain. The mystery that surrounded him aroused in Leopoldina a mix of fear and respect. She had met several healers before, who were common in Brazil at that time, but none had made her feel the way that Juca did. She started to believe the rumors about him.

When she arrived at Henriqueta's, around thirty people, mostly black and brown women, filled the house. At the end of the living room was an altar covered with a lace tablecloth. On the altar there were images of the Virgin Mary, the Senhor do Bonfim (literally, the lord of the good death, a popular Catholic designation for God), and a crucifix, all lit by candles. In the center of the altar a vase held a root: on getting closer, she saw five or six small daggers stabbed in the big root, in all directions. Later she asked another "daughter" what the root was for, and she was told that it was a spell to make a man sexually impotent. On the same altar, there were also containers and pots filled with different liquids and powders, a large decorated pipe, leaves, talismans, stones, and all kinds of strange objects. In another room, Leopoldina saw some women sitting around a big table where there were glasses of sugarcane brandy and wine; in that room she spied some hens, roosters, pigeons, and a sheep.

After a while, the ceremony really started. Some black men began to play and sing: Joaquim shook a tambourine; Lúcio, Juca Rosa's main assistant, played drums; João Maria scratched a long wooden instrument called a *macumba*. Juca Rosa's followers called him "the chief of the *macumbas*." Another black man led the dancing. When Rosa showed up, everyone made a circle, singing, dancing, and clapping. The "daughters" were barefoot, and some reports claimed they were naked. Leopoldina did not know the words to the songs—to her they sounded like African dialects—but she felt comfortable enough to join in and feel part of the group. Rosa, dressed ceremonially, wore blue velvet pants, a short-sleeved shirt, a velvet hat, but no shoes. Suddenly, he fell down and everybody stopped dancing. He entered into a trance, shaking his body and speaking words that Leopoldina did not understand. The others explained that Juca Rosa had been possessed by spirits who would speak through him. He had "the saint in his head."

In that state, after all of those present had kissed his hands and bowed to him, Rosa turned to Leopoldina. That was a moment of astonishment for her. Impressed by all she had seen and full of respect, she told Rosa her problems and desires. The healer told her to take good care of her body because that would help her "keep all men around" and "make her lover give her everything she wanted." He also gave her a root to always carry with her, worn on her chest, and told her to bring offerings to the spirits: two chickens, a sheep, candles, and oil. She then swore an oath and became an initiate of the cult. She promised to keep secret everything that happened there, to trust the "Father" in all circumstances, and to give him guardianship over her spirit and her body. In return, Juca

Rosa would give her protection against all evil. Later, after being part of the cult for some time, Leopoldina felt stronger and safe; she had a deep faith in the "Father" and tried to do exactly what he told her. She also realized that all the other "daughters" were, like her, Rosa's lovers.

Juca Rosa's incarceration led many of his "daughters" to tell the police much more than their oath to him would have allowed. Very few had the courage to deny their activities to the police chief, and even when they did, they could not sustain the denials for very long. During the interrogations, all of the "daughters" admitted that they were Rosa's lovers—except for one, Mariquinhas, the woman who had introduced Leopoldina to the cult and the only "white" initiate who gave testimony to the court. Her race may have helped Mariquinhas, who probably had the money and influence to resist the pressures of the police inquiry. Later in the case, officials accused all of the "daughters" of being prostitutes, including Mariquinhas, and Juca Rosa of being their pimp. When Leopoldina testified that Rosa had told her to take care of her body in order to "keep all men around," the prosecution concluded that this phrase alluded to prostitution. All of the "daughters" declared that they were seamstresses, the profession most prostitutes claimed when the police arrested them.

For most doctors and lawyers, women such as Leopoldina, Mariquinhas, Henriqueta, Leocádia, Júlia, Emília, and others who gave testimony in the case were certainly "prostitutes," because they were either single or married but not living with their husbands. (Divorce was not legally recognized at the time.) All of these women had lovers. It was clear, moreover, that the "daughters" expected presents and money from their lovers, and that the money was, in most cases, their principal income. But that admission does not necessarily mean that they were not dressmakers too or that they considered themselves prostitutes. These women may have accepted money for sexual favors from time to time, but even some of the men who were their lovers testified that they were not prostitutes. No doubt, standards and practices of morality and status were different among the free poor than among the white elites.

Were the "daughters" prostitutes or dressmakers? This is not the most important question even if we could answer it. Although the interrogation reveals how the poor—both white and especially nonwhite—in the 1870s lived, survived, and loved, few sources reveal what the Brazilian free poor believed, how they resolved problems, and what their values were like. In a racist society based on slave labor dominated politically and economically by a few rich white men, poor free people had to fight hard to survive and to assert their freedom. They searched for ways of avoiding the authorities, who persecuted them and who considered the poor inherently "dangerous." But they also had lighthearted moments, when they would share with partners their beliefs and construct identities and solidarity.

Juca Rosa's cult demonstrates the importance of religion and faith in the life of African descendants in Brazil. Faith in the spiritual leader made the "daughters" and many others continue to go to Juca's house even when his spells or prayers did not heal them or when their lovers did not return—although many times his magic did work, according to their testimonies. Under police pressure, many of the "daughters" admitted that they were attached to Rosa only because of their fear of their "Father." But their testimony belies their tenacious faith in Rosa. They told the police that despite any fights or disagreements with Rosa, they would always go back to him if they had any problems, physical or emotional. They would follow his prescriptions, pay the fees, and bring the offerings—in short, they would trust him.

Religion, for many African descendants in Brazil, was an essential part of their social life, and it is important to understand that fact in order to better understand the society and the relations between different social groups. For black and poor people in Brazil as well as in many societies in Africa—especially from West Central Africa, the homeland of most Brazilian slaves—religion was a foundation of sociability. It was also how people understood their daily life; it was where they looked for relief from their pains, for cures for their diseases, and for solutions to their problems. In that context, the healer or spiritual leader had a vital role, not only to solve individual problems but also to answer social questions. Such was the case in many societies in Africa and then in Brazil where different religious traditions came together. Belief in magic and witchcraft helped people to shape their understanding of the world and their relationship to others. This strong faith helps us to understand the power of Juca Rosa's influence. His power and fame became so strong that even white people sought his advice. The cultural life of blacks, browns, and whites influenced each other.

Some elements of the experience described by Leopoldina and other "daughters" illuminate the confluence of African and European cultures. In the rituals led by Juca Rosa we find crucifixes and references to Catholic saints, the Virgin Mary, and Senhor do Bonfim as well as roots, stones, powders, liquids, daggers, and alcohol. Europeans had colonized parts of Africa long before they came to America, and Catholic priests had been trying to convert Africans long before they became slaves in Brazil. Thus, when black Africans arrived in Brazilian cities, many already had had some familiarity with the saints and other Catholic traditions. They created new creole habits and rituals that can only be understood within the social and political contexts in which they lived. Understanding something of African and Portuguese religions is a start, but only the context of cultural transformations that took place in Brazil gives us a clearer picture of what all these things meant to different individuals. For example, court testimony reveals the importance of drums and dance for Juca's trance. In some parts of Africa, drums were fundamental to sorcery, and healers wore hats similar to the one Juca used during his religious rites. Clearly, the "Africanness" of Juca's magic lent it greater legitimacy, but it also borrowed from Iberian Catholic traditions to enhance its potency.

The role of love spells and other necromancy to make men impotent, so central in Rosa's cult according to his "daughters," is related to the environment in which all those women lived. Men dominated Rio's society, and poor women had very few employment opportunities that enabled them to maintain a household on their own. Respectable Brazilians considered most women wanton who did not live under the protection of a husband, father, or other male relative. They viewed women who married but who later separated from their husbands and lived on their own the moral equivalents of prostitutes.

The limited opportunities for respectable female independence reveal the importance of a leader such as Juca Rosa, and they help to explain why so many of his followers struggled to keep on paying their fees to Juca Rosa. Some "daughters" committed petty crimes to be able to do so. Leocádia, for instance, sold some furniture in her charge that belonged to a rich family. Mariquinhas was sued by a shop for goods bought on credit that she never paid for, and Miguel had almost all of his few belongings taken by the police for not paying rent for several months. In this last case, Miguel was saved at the last minute: his landlord, after seeing how poor he was—and perhaps under one of Rosa's spells—dropped the complaint. These followers of Rosa lived under difficult conditions in which they had little power or room for negotiation, but they still did what they could to pay their obligations to the leader in order to have the "Father's" protection and approval.

FROM THE CASE TO THE CONTEXT

In the mid-1860s, when Juca Rosa was at the height of his fame and had many clients and followers, most of Rio de Janeiro's population was of African descent. Slavery still existed, even though the international slave trade had been abolished in 1850, but most of Rio's black population was composed of free men of color (*pretos livres*) and freedmen (*libertos*). Since 1860 there had been an increase in the number of manumissions in Rio, and the number grew after 1867 as a result of the Paraguayan War. The government had bought slaves at market prices and freed them on the condition that they serve in the armed forces and fight at the Paraguayan front. Some patriotic masters donated bondsmen to the war effort. After completing their service contracts, these former slaves would become free Brazilian citizens.

In 1849 slaves constituted almost 42 percent of Rio de Janeiro's population: 110,602 slaves out of 266,466 residents. At the time, Rio had the largest urban slave population in the Americas. There were still around 10,800 freedmen, plus around 30,000 *pardos* (brown Brazilians of mixed African and European descent) as well as *pretos livres*. In 1872 the population had only a modest increase from 266,466 to 274,972. However, the number of slaves had diminished dramatically: they formed only 17 percent of the city's population.

This high number of free and freed black people lived mostly in the city's center, the "black city." There, free black and brown Brazilians could afford cheap rented rooms in crowded tenements, called *cortiços* or beehives, where many slaves also lived. Many urban slaves in Brazil lived on their own and paid their masters a regular part of their earnings. It was often very difficult to tell whether most people of color were free or slave in the city's black borough by the way they dressed and looked or by their lifestyle. It was an ideal hiding place for runaway slaves, and members of the mostly white elite considered the "black city" vice-ridden, dirty, and dangerous. Urban reformers at the end of the 1800s and the beginning of the 1900s, yielding to "white fear," targeted major urban reform projects in and around the "black city" to displace these mostly poor black and brown residents from the city's downtown.

The majority of Juca Rosa's followers was composed of blacks who, like him, lived in the "black city." This gritty but lively borough of Rio encompassed the largest concentration of cheap and unsanitary tenements, gambling houses, bordellos, and places of Afro-Brazilian worship (*candomblés*). Many *capoeiras*, or men who practiced the uniquely Afro-Brazilian martial arts and who often belonged to urban gangs, also called the "black city" their home. Alongside these street toughs, strumpets, grifters, and shamans dwelt most of the city's poorly paid day laborers who lived in this sector because it was the only housing that they could afford. Among these people were the followers of the city's most renowned faith healer, Juca Rosa.

It is interesting to note that close to that depressed part of town were the cafés, theaters, elegant shops, and even residences of wealthy families and important politicians. Besides the extreme social and economic inequalities that separate groups and social classes, the proximity of the space they occupied at times led to conflicts but at other times to cultural mixing. In Juca Rosa's case, as noted earlier, many rich and elegant ladies frequented his house. There were also some important men who visited Rosa, a fact that should not surprise us. Similarly, the strong ties between some *capoeiras* and politicians (particularly members of the Conservative Party) were public knowledge. *Capoeiras* served as body-guards and paramilitary thugs during elections where voting sometimes became a contact sport.

The fears of prosperous and mostly white Rio residents of the danger represented by the strong concentration of blacks in the cities, especially in Rio itself, was ever present during the nineteenth century. Although rich whites interacted with blacks in their everyday lives—especially with black servants living in their homes—at the same time the threat of slave rebellions was constant. This fear prompted the authorities to regulate bondspeople whenever they were not under the watchful eyes of their masters or overseers. It was against the law, for example, for blacks to hold meetings lest they might plan sedition. For this reason, the police often repressed parties, dances, or religious rituals that concentrated large numbers of blacks. The ghost of "Haitianism" had terrified mostly white elites for years and had been an inspiration for many blacks. Slaveholders in Brazil observed with concern many of the efforts made by slaves to obtain their freedom from running away to riots, criminal activity, and everyday strategies of resistance. It was in these years when slavery in Rio had entered a phase of rapid decline that Juca Rosa became rich and powerful.

Politicians discussed the growing pressure of the slaves for their freedom after the Paraguayan War when many ex-slave-veterans came to reside in Rio at war's end. Moreover, the 1871 Free Womb Law would free the children born of slave mothers. For the first time the end of slavery seemed real, and all the dangers and stereotypes that white people had associated with blacks and their presence in society became magnified. The debates about the end of slavery that took on new vigor after the Paraguayan War also were related to Brazil's economic future. What would happen to agriculture without slave labor? Who would work in the fields? How could immigrants be brought in to work on the farms and plantations? And what should be done with the immense number of newly freed blacks, considered immoral and inferior by most white intellectuals and physicians? How could officials manage them when they were released from slavery and able to act without the control of their masters?

Brazilian society was undergoing a crucial moment of change when the police jailed Juca Rosa. To justify the idea of black racial inferiority, new scientific theories were gaining more acceptance. Among the theories of "scientific racism," North Atlantic social Darwinists apologized for European imperialism by arguing that there was a natural hierarchy of races, which, in most instances, placed northern Europeans on top and black Africans on the bottom. Social Darwinists tried to explain the inferiority of the black race and in turn justify the repression, discrimination, and subjugation of nonwhites in Brazil and other parts of the world. If slavery was no longer a stable marker of inferior status in Brazil, then scientific racism provided a new way to justify bigotry against blacks. Most advocates of scientific racism believed that miscegenation or race mixture weakened both races by tainting an imagined racial purity. Brazil's long history of race mixture was criticized by a number of North Atlantic travelers who believed that it had condemned this colossal nation to backwardness. These views clouded the hopes of even fervent Brazilian nationalists that their country would one day be united and modern.

This climate of self-doubt about Brazil's racial composition may have heightened interest in the scandal surrounding Juca Rosa. The faith healer's sexual dalliances with rich white women, and especially the wife of an important but unnamed politician, are certainly what initiated the case. But this reason alone does not explain why he was kept in jail for eight months during the investigations, or why the case aroused so much discussion in the newspapers. The Juca Rosa scandal even became the subject for a play. In 1870 the very presence and influence of blacks in the cultural life of whites were being questioned and criticized in new ways. Even for those who defended the end of slavery in the parliament, the press, and the street, the case of an important black man who had influence over not only blacks but also prominent whites (especially women) became much bigger than it would have otherwise.

WHAT HAPPENED TO JUCA ROSA AND WHY?

The parliament approved the 1871 Free Womb Law in the same year that Juca Rosa was condemned for charlatanism. Apparently, he had been operating for many years with police tolerance, as one newspaper reported. He had earned the respect of powerful white men who had protected him from prosecution. His condemnation at that particular moment is certainly related to the intellectual and political debates of his day. Juca Rosa embodied what many whites feared that a society without slavery could bring about. As a socially mobile black man who dressed well and wore expensive jewelry, Juca Rosa defied the stereotypes of black men as poor, unrefined, humble, and pliable. But he had acquired his money and influence by defying conventions important to an emerging generation of police officials, intellectuals, and physicians who were eager to prove scientific theories of racism correct. Juca Rosa's power derived from his reputation as a faith healer who relied on African-influenced religious practices. All this was bad enough in the eyes of many privileged Brazilians, but his sexual involvement with white ladies was the last straw. His scandal became an explicit example of the bad influence of the "lustful and evil black nature" that many white intellectuals preached against. These authorities fought to preserve white supremacy by trying to eliminate African cultural, social, and genetic influences in Brazil at a time when slavery's decline seemed poised to erode cherished standards of status.

During the second half of the 1800s, most of Brazil's intellectual elites stepped up attacks against what they considered to be the immoral and corrosive influence of black and uneducated people in the realm of customs and habits. Physicians, jurists, writers, politicians, police officials, and others fought to eradicate popular practices that they considered barbaric. One example was the *entrudo*, the rowdy horseplay and mockery associated with pre-Lenten Carnival celebrations that often involved dousing passersby with liquids, including urine. Despite police attempts to end this practice, some members of the elite continued to participate in the *entrudo*—the equivalent of "slumming" to enjoy the thrill of the forbidden and exotic. The police also attempted to suppress Afro-Brazilian *capoeiras*, but many wealthy and influential politicians employed these street-fighting toughs. Many African-influenced religious practices—especially those connected to African traditions such as *festas* (popular street festivals), *batuques* (Afro-Brazilian drums and dance), or Afro-spiritist cults like Juca Rosa's—were suppressed. Measures to stop those practices ranged from the police's direct repression to denunciations in journals, church sermons, and parliamentary speeches.

In the same way, practices of healing that were different from the official "scientific" medicine of Brazil's medical schools came under attack from physicians and public health officials who justified their sometimes more deadly treatments on the basis of "science." Most Brazilians had long relied on faith healers, midwives, and barbers to treat their ailments and attend in dangerous procedures such as childbirth, but in 1850 the government created a special unit—the Junta Central de Higiene Pública—to deal with problems of public health. The entire country, and especially the capital, suffered many serious epidemics, among them yellow fever and cholera. Rio's international insalubrious reputation was bad for business because the city was Brazil's major port. It also deterred foreign immigrants from moving to Brazil and to Rio in particular. During the 1870s, politicians, merchants, and plantation owners began to lobby for government subsidies to attract European immigrants to work in the fields, factories, and shops. This policy dovetailed well with the elites' desire to "whiten" their "national race" in order to ensure that

Brazil's modernization and future would not be blemished by its heritage of race mixture.

After 1850, fighting problems of public health increasingly became synonymous with solving social problems, and physicians played a very important role. Areas where poor and black people lived, like Rio's "black city," tended to attract the habits and diseases that the authorities wanted to eradicate. This was a classic case of blaming the victim for the poverty and misery that racism thrust upon most brown and black Brazilians and those whites too poor to live or make a living elsewhere, but to public health officials it was more a crusade for national salvation. With the support of "science," these officials felt empowered to act in the name of vague ideals of "civilization" and "progress" in order to free the Brazilian nation from the sins of the colonial past. In the 1890s they destroyed tenement housing without providing any alternative for thousands of people and built in their stead parks and broad Paris-style avenues. They attacked the traditions and habits of the population's majority and attempted to force them to adapt to imposed standards of public health. One of the pivotal conflicts was the 1904 Vaccine Revolt, when the parliament passed a law making smallpox vaccination obligatory for all citizens. The law's passage resulted in a citywide riot in Rio, but ultimately the conflict furthered the government's efforts to condemn the practices of popular healers and medicines.

After 1850 the power of physicians started to grow inside the government, and they started a crusade against all kinds of practices, especially those used by poor people, calling everything charlatanism. All over the country, the law subjected different kinds of healers—*curandeiros* and *benzedeiros* (faith healers), *espíritas* (spiritualists), *barbeiros* (barbers), *boticários* (apothecaries), and even foreign doctors without valid diplomas—to legal prosecution and forbade them to practice. Still, the state did not possess the power to enforce these laws. Many Brazilians successfully pressured the authorities to release faith healers who had been arrested, and many local officials refused to carry out these laws because they respected the power of traditional healers. In this context, the presence of a leader such as Juca Rosa in Brazil's capital seemed particularly threatening to the authority of physicians who were trying to persuade their patients of their superiority over their rivals, the "charlatans." The fact that Juca Rosa was prosecuted for charlatanism rather than for pimping is telling in this regard.

As stated in newspapers of the time, Juca Rosa was well known throughout Brazil and even in Europe. For some of his adherents, he had the power to do whatever people asked him, including to cure disease. Many people of that time—blacks and whites, poor and rich—had faith in Juca's powers and believed that he was capable of performing miracles. Some publicly testified that Juca had cured them of strange illnesses or helped them to ensnare rich lovers or get old lovers back. Others, like Leopoldina, did not have their desires fulfilled. Her lover in the navy never came back to her, but she never lost her faith in the "Father." The "daughters" found ways to pay the fees and attend the ceremonies. Ironically, we know less about how wealthy white ladies viewed Juca Rosa because they had enough influence to avoid testifying about their relationship with the black healer in a public venue. Still, many had risked their names and positions to go to Juca Rosa's house and ask for his advice, and many probably sought out other faith healers after Juca Rosa's arrest. In newspapers, memoirs, chronicles, and other documents, witnesses reported the presence of many rich white ladies in the black healer's house. While their reasons for seeking a black healer's advice were certainly different from those of the poor blacks who were culturally more connected to the practices of Juca Rosa, it is undeniable that the influence of black practices and beliefs reached all classes of Brazilian society. There was no pure "black" culture or "white" culture in Brazil, although some historical actors may have believed that they existed. In Brazil, a mix of African, indigenous, and European beliefs and customs had come together over the centuries.

Even with all his power—Rosa's magic spells, the expensive lawyer he hired for his dramatic courtroom defense, the appeals to the emperor—the "Father" was found guilty. He spent six years in jail and, after his conviction, disappeared from the available documentation. What became of him is a mystery. But his imprisonment was not enough to undermine the importance of black healers or Afro-Brazilian spiritual leaders (*país de santo*), who today still have followers from all social classes.

SUGGESTED READINGS

For more about Juca Rosa and his world, see Gabriela Sampaio, "A história do feiticeiro Juca Rosa: Cultura e relações sociais no Rio de Janeiro imperial" (Ph.D. diss., Departamento de História do IFCH/UNICAMP, São Paulo, 2000). On disease and Afro-Brazilian culture, see Sidney Chalhoub, *Cidade febril: Cortiços e epidemias na Corte imperial* (São Paulo: Cia das Letras, 1996). On working-class sexuality and the state, see Martha Abreu Esteves, *Meninas perdidas: Os populares e o cotidiano do amor no Rio de Janeiro da Belle Époque* (Rio: Paz e Terra, 1989); Luis Carlos Soares, *Rameiras, Ilhoas, Polacas . . . A prostituição no Rio de Janeiro do século XIX* (São Paulo: Ática, 1992); and Sueann Caulfield, *In Defense of Honor: Sexual Morality, Modernity, and Nation* in *Early-Twentieth-Century Brazil* (Durham, NC: Duke University Press, 2000).

On the culture of Brazilian slaves and their lives, see Sidney Chalhoub, *Visões da liberdade: Uma história das últimas décadas da escravidão na Corte* (São Paulo: Cia das Letras, 1990); Sandra Graham, "Slavery's Impasse: Small-Time Mistresses and the Brazilian Law of 1871," in *Comparative Studies in Society and History* 33:4 (October 1991); and Mary Karash, *Slave Life in Rio de Janeiro* (Princeton, NJ: Princeton University Press, 1987). On popular protest in Rio, see Teresa Meade, *Civilizing Rio: Reform and Resistance in a Brazilian City, 1889–1930* (University Park: Pennsylvania State University Press, 1997). On ideas of race and nation in Brazil, see Lilia Schwarcz, *O espetáculo das raças: Cientistas, instituições e questão racial no Brasil, 1870–1930* (São Paulo: Cia das Letras, 1993). On Afro-Brazilian culture in Brazil, see Roberto Moura, *Tia Ciata e a Pequena África no Rio de Janeiro* (Rio: Secretaria Municipal de Cultura, 1995); Eduardo Silva, *Prince of the People: The Life and Times of a Brazilian Free Man of Color* (London: Verso, 1993); and Robert Sienes, " 'Malungu, Ngoma Vem!': Africa coberta e descoberta no Brasil," *Revista USP* 12 (December/January/February 1991–92): 48–67. On West African religion and culture, see John Thornton, *The Kongolese Saint Anthony: Dona Beatriz Kimpa Vita and the Antonian Movement, 1684–1706* (New York: Cambridge University Press, 1998); Willy de Craemer, Jan Vansina, and Renée C. Fox, "Religious Movements in Central Africa: A Theoretical Study," in *Comparative Studies in Society and History* 18:4 (October 1986): 458–75; and Sidney Mintz and Richard Price, "The Birth of African-American Culture," in Timothy E. Fulop and Albert J. Raboteau, eds., *African-American Culture: Interpretative Essays in History and Culture* (New York: Routledge, 1997), 37–53.

CHAPTER 4

Jacobina Maurer

German-Brazilian Mystic

Roger A. Kittleson

The life stories of Agostinho José Pereira and Juca Rosa have demonstrated the anxieties that officials expressed about the Afro-Brazilian population. These apprehensions led many influential policymakers to advocate European immigration as an alternative and superior answer to Brazil's labor needs over African slaves. In addition, most of these officials believed that European laborers were naturally harder working and more civilized than Brazil's native and racially mixed free working population. The introduction of European immigrants had the added benefit of "whitening" Brazil's population in an age when social Darwinists argued that northern Europeans were racially superior to other peoples in the world.

The Brazilian government attracted the first waves of European immigrants with promises of land grants mostly in Brazil's sparsely inhabited southern provinces, where the temperate climate was thought to be more suitable for Europeans than the tropics. Similar homesteads were not made available to native Brazilian workers, and even the land grants that the parliament promised to veterans of the Paraguayan War never materialized for the vast majority of the surviving troops. Large-scale European immigration to Brazil, however, only began after the complete abolition of slavery in 1888 and the promulgation in 1889 of the Republic, which subsidized the passage of European and later Japanese immigrants to Brazil. Most of these newcomers would settle in the state of São Paulo and the three states to its south: Paraná, Santa Catarina, and Rio Grande do Sul. In this southern region, immigrant communities of Germans, Italians, Poles, and Japanese were established.

Life was tough for the first waves of these immigrants. The lands designated for immigrant colonization were often located in isolated frontier regions that lacked roads, reliable river transportation, or railroads to facilitate travel and trade. The tragic life story of Jacobina Maurer and her followers reveals many of the difficulties faced by German Protestant immigrants in their new Catholic homeland. It also reveals the ambivalence of Brazilian political and economic leaders toward these immigrant populations, especially when they began to become more integrated into

state and national political and economic networks. While Europhile Bra-
zilian politicians believed that European immigrants would promote the
nation's economic development and civilization, they also were concerned
about the presence of isolated immigrant communities where many mem-
bers worshipped in the Protestant faith and most never bothered to learn
Portuguese. How would these foreign elements be integrated into a homo-
geneous national community? As Roger Kittleson notes, these immigrant
colonists tended to refer to those outside their settlements, often derisively,
as "Brazilians." Thus, they did not necessarily identify themselves as being
Brazilian or part of a broader imagined national community. As we see in
the government repression of the Muckers, a Protestant splinter group led
by Jacobina Maurer, these anxieties perplexed local and national leaders
and could erupt into violent conflict. The Muckers' vision of a religious
community largely separated by language, ethnicity, and belief from the
national and even the local urban immigrant community threatened the
visions of those who sought to unite Brazilians of all races, religions, and
ethnicities behind a common nationalist cause.

Roger Kittleson is assistant professor of history at Williams College.
He is currently completing work on a book manuscript provisionally en-
titled "A New Regime of Ideas: Plebeians and the Transformation of Po-
litical Culture in Porto Alegre, Brazil, 1845–1900." He has published
articles on a variety of topics that include the themes of gender, abolition-
ism, and state building in Brazil, but his abiding research interest lies
with analyzing the culture, beliefs, and politics of urban plebeians in Porto
Alegre, Rio Grande do Sul.

*I*n February 1873, Jacobina Maurer sent an open letter to her oldest
brother, Francisco (Franz) Mentz, publicly chastising him for having
abandoned the religious community that had formed around her in a
German immigrant settlement (*colônia*) near São Leopoldo, Rio Grande
do Sul. Convinced that the end of the world was near, she worried that
he had placed his soul in peril by leaving the Muckers, as the group was
known: "And what do you intend to do," she asked him, "on the day of
tribulation and adversity, which is coming soon?" She also appealed to
his "fraternal love" for her and the many other relatives and friends in
the tightly knit group he had deserted. "Return," she pleaded, "and leave
behind the tumult of the world, for you have injured me in my heart,
which is bleeding drop by drop. What will our good mother say when
she finds out?"[1] Because Francisco refused to rejoin his sister and her
followers, he did not witness their bloody destruction; over the course of

five weeks in 1874, the Brazilian army, assisted by local residents who bitterly opposed what they considered a heretical and immoral sect, crushed the Muckers. Among the dead after the final battle lay Jacobina, shot in the chest, although no one could say who had killed her.

Hostility toward the Muckers did not, however, end with the brutal repression of the "female Christ" and those who believed in her preaching. Just over twenty years later, suspicions arose once more in the *colônia* when a group that included Jacobina's daughter Aurélia cut off relations with their neighbors. Anxieties quickly escalated into violence when rumors blamed the "new Muckers" for the 1898 murder of a child in the *colônia*. Fueled by gossip and mistrust, some 200 enraged residents of the region took up arms, killing several leaders of the latter-day Muckers. A century later, descendants of German immigrants in Rio Grande do Sul still vehemently condemn Jacobina and her followers as savage libertines who burned alive whole families and tried to dismantle the institution of marriage. Echoing nineteenth-century critics, they single out Jacobina for special attacks, asserting that the Muckers' female spiritual leader murdered her own child to avoid capture by government soldiers and urged others to follow her example of switching husbands freely. "Mucker," or false saint, is one of the milder epithets applied to Jacobina.

What explains the extraordinary hatred toward Jacobina and the Muckers that erupted in the early 1870s and lingers on even today? How did a community of mostly poor, mostly Protestant, first- and second-generation immigrants come to face a military expedition organized specifically to stamp out their beliefs and practices? Scholars have long argued the guilt or innocence of Jacobina and her followers in the events leading up to their demise. While some portray the Muckers as humble folk who became victims of others' prejudices or political machinations, others depict them as a true threat to the social and spiritual order. To understand the reaction that the Muckers and their "new Messiah" provoked, however, it is not enough to focus exclusively on the nature of the group and its doctrine; we must look at the evolving relationship between the Muckers and nineteenth-century Brazilian society as a whole. When we do so, we see that the emergence of Jacobina Maurer and her followers highlighted fault lines within European immigrant populations in southern Brazil and between those immigrants and the broader society they had entered. Everyone involved wondered how Europeans would integrate themselves into the country's seigneurial, patriarchal, and (until 1888) slave society. Most significant, the trajectory of Jacobina's group pointed out how partial and tension-laden the consolidation of Brazil's national state was one half-century after Independence.

⌒⌐

The woman who caused such widespread consternation actually spent her entire life in a small corner of Brazil. Born Jacobina Mentz in Hamburger-Berg (later Hamburgo Velho), Rio Grande do Sul, in 1842, she died less than thirty kilometers away, in the woods that covered Ferrabrás hill; only two stays in the provincial capital of Porto Alegre had taken her beyond the "colonial" zone centered on São Leopoldo. She never learned the national language of Portuguese, communicating in German throughout her life. Within her circumscribed world, she was an odd child who did not display any exceptional talents. Her formal education was brief and hardly productive; in the year or two that she attended a private school, her sister Carolina later wrote, Jacobina was a poor student, "scarcely learning to read and write, at great sacrifice."[2] In fact, it was only when trying to interpret the Bible as an adult that she became literate, although even then her reading was slow and hesitant. Many witnesses have contended that Jacobina was a sickly child, beset with "crises" that included melancholy, trances, or epileptic attacks. She denied these rumors, as did Carolina and other relatives and adepts, asserting that she had merely had a single, traumatic illness at age twelve. That episode was alarming enough, however, for Jacobina's mother to seek out Dr. João Daniel Hillebrand, a tremendously influential figure in the area; Dr. Hillebrand prescribed marriage as the best treatment for the nervous young woman. In fact, it was after her marriage that Jacobina's "crises" started in earnest.

She most likely met her husband, João Jorge Maurer, when he was working in her uncle's carpentry shop. Maurer, too, was a child of the colônia, having been born in the picada of São José do Hortênsio in 1840 and living most of his life near the settlement of Padre Eterno, on the south side of Ferrabrás hill. In contrast to Jacobina, however, Maurer was a robust figure with little unusual about him. He not only worked as a cabinetmaker but, like many other artisans in the region, farmed his own small property as well. Garrulous and generally well liked, he also impressed others with his entrepreneurial drive. Sometime around 1868, Maurer began to apply that energy in a new field after meeting a healer (curandeiro) named Bucchorn and accompanying him for a short while on his wanderings. When he returned home, Maurer set up on his own, administering herbal remedies and forcing his patients to take the kind of rest that their usual routines made impossible. In a society rich in popular forms of medicine and very poor in formally trained physicians, word of his skills spread and people with all manner of ailments, from back pain to blindness to tuberculosis, sought him out. They all received the same oily herbal medicine, although the methods of its application varied. Whether it was the treatments themselves or the rest that seemed efficacious, João Jorge's patients believed that he helped them. As a result, his business expanded, so that soon he was treating the sick not only from nearby settlements but even from Porto Alegre, Pelotas, and other major cities in the province, all of whom came to consult the *wunderdoktor* (miracle doctor).

Jacobina was at first her husband's assistant, helping to prepare his infusions, plasters, and salves, and tending the growing number of patients who stayed at their house. She underwent her own transformation, however, after Maurer made himself into a renowned healer. Jacobina had begun to suffer "crises" about the time she and her new husband moved out of her mother's house in 1867, and they became more frequent and more dramatic over time. According to Dr. Hillebrand, who examined her again in 1873, she maintained her normal pulse rate and coloring during a spell but entered into a trance-like state where she was oblivious to pain or other stimuli. (The good doctor tested his unconscious patient's sensitivity by pricking her with a needle and by holding ammonia under her nose.) For many in the *colônia*, Jacobina's "syndrome" was somnambulism, a phenomenon that was the topic of much conversation in the São Leopoldo region after a book on the subject made its way into the settlements. Jacobina herself may have shared this belief about her condition, for in later descriptions she asserted that she experienced mystical revelations while in the throes of a crisis. As she emerged from unconsciousness, Jacobina made proclamations about the remedies that her husband should prescribe and prophecies about the futures of individuals around her. For Jacobina and the handful of people who heard and believed in her visions, her special understanding came from a "Natural Divinity" that called to her soul and filled her with knowledge. On the strength of her new gift, Jacobina's reputation rapidly outshone her husband's; although João Jorge continued to treat his loyal patients, more and more people were interested in what the "Prophetess" had to say. It was those folk gathering at the Maurers' house who became known as the Muckers.

Far from a rigidly insular or exclusionary sect, their group was at first loosely organized around the Muckers' "natural faith." Everyone, even the merely curious, was welcome to hear Jacobina's "clarifications" at their meetings. Furthermore, to join their ranks one merely had to embrace their beliefs; no strenuous rite of entrance was required. The articles of Mucker faith reflected this openness as well. They held that the "Natural Spirit" alone would lead each person to happiness and health; things beyond faith in the "Natural Divinity"—worldly wealth, in particular—were unimportant for achieving "clarity" but not so evil that the Muckers had to abandon them. More important, the Muckers did not withdraw from the world at this stage. Their children continued to attend school, and their families still participated actively in their churches, both Catholic and Protestant. Indeed, the Muckers remained part of the communities of the *colônia* through 1872, when local and provincial authorities began to investigate the meetings of believers at the Maurers' house.

Sweeping changes in the first few years of the 1870s turned the Muckers into a secessionist insular religious community centered increasingly on the figure and preaching of Jacobina. Mucker beliefs had always had an obvious spiritual element, but from 1871 on, they became much more the tenets of a distinct religion that derived from, but ultimately renounced, the Christianity in which the immigrants had been reared. In this latter stage, the reunions at Ferrabrás for the first time included readings from the Bible and the singing of Protestant hymns. The focus of the meetings, and the great draw for many adepts, were the interpretations that Jacobina now made of Biblical passages. Once again, as with the discussions of somnambulism, ideas from the outside seem to have played a part in shaping Jacobina's evolution here. A mysterious, itinerant Protestant preacher (known to many witnesses as Hardes Fleck but identified by historian Moacyr Domingues as either Gerhard or Gotthard Fleck[3]) found his way to the Maurer household in this period. There, he encouraged Jacobina to read the Bible for herself, perhaps telling her that she showed some special aptitude for its exegesis. Fleck soon disappeared, but Jacobina's engagement with the Bible deepened and became linked to her crises. She now emerged from her trances, witnesses asserted, with messages about their religion and the fate of the world. "God is present!" she exclaimed upon regaining consciousness. "My heart exalts with pleasure! The angels of Heaven are descending! Oh, what a beautiful sight!" Whereas earlier her visions had dealt with cures or individuals' lives, she now issued grand and increasingly millenarian prophecies. The Muckers had to remain pure in their faith, she told them, for the end of the world was coming soon.

For some of those present on such occasions, Jacobina was no longer just a neutral vehicle for divine revelations; indeed, some assigned divinity to their Prophetess herself. Augusto Wilborn was most adamant on this point, declaring to the police that for him, Jacobina was Christ, if only because of her manner of revealing the truth held in the Bible. It is unclear how many of the Muckers accepted this idea, but at least part of her flock came to see her as more than simply inspired by God. Jacobina's own assessment of her role is still more difficult to ascertain. If she claimed to be a new incarnation of Christ, as her critics accused her of doing, she did so only off the public record; all that she told the authorities who interrogated her was that "between herself and the divinity there [was] no person serving as intermediary." At the very least, Jacobina cultivated an air of the supernatural in her performances at meetings. In early 1873, for instance, she spoke of her upcoming ascension to Heaven and, several witnesses alleged, appeared before her followers dressed in a flowing white robe, with a wreath of flowers on her head, looking like someone who had already left this world. Whether or not Jacobina wanted to convince people that she had risen toward Heaven but then opted to return to her earthly flock—as gossips of the time charged—she was certainly fashioning herself into the oracle and leader of a new, true faith.

At the same time, the nature of the Mucker community was evolving. Up to that point the core of the group had consisted of Jacobina's five brothers and two sisters, together with a few families whose patriarchs had brought them en masse into the Mucker band. By 1871, however, waves of newcomers interested in Jacobina's preaching threatened the dominance of the original elements, most of whom had come to Ferrabrás in search of medical cures, and the "natural faith" that they had helped fashion in the Maurers' home. The influence of the more religiously oriented, later entrants derived principally from their loyalty to João Jorge and, especially, to Jacobina. One key figure, known as Jacó Mula ("Jacob the Mule") because he had worked as a muleteer, became the butt of affectionate jokes for his undying devotion to Jacobina. Indeed, he followed her around so eagerly that other believers called him "the sacristan of the Prophetess." His efforts won him the reward of intimacy with power; he was the only one who enjoyed unlimited access to the Maurers' room. Others such as Carlos Eisenfeldt and Jorge Robinson ("Robinson the Redhead") also rose to prominence in the Mucker community by demonstrating strict obedience to the couple. Some of these men, contemporary observers averred, even gained the status of "apostles" of the "new Messiah" of Ferrabrás. The rumor that Jacobina had designated her own apostles was, of course, part of the charge that she was pretending to be Christ. In fact, it is improbable that the Muckers used the word "apostles" as anything like a formal title; most likely, the word was merely a synonym for "disciples" or "believers."

Some of the most energetic adepts, like Jacobina's brother Jacó Mentz, emulated João Jorge in recruiting acolytes in nearby towns. Spreading news of Jacobina's preaching at stores and taverns and throughout the settlements, they invited everyone they met, even Protestant pastors, to sample their meetings. This campaign was not, however, a continuation of the group's earlier openness. On the contrary, it was based on a growing sense of society's division into two camps, the believers and the unbelievers; the Muckers were just attempting to bolster their side with new converts. In a letter that Jacobina sent to her cousin Matthias Schroeder she went so far as to label her enemies "anti-Christ"—not the

Anti-Christ, but against Christ nonetheless. With that kind of bifurcated vision of the world, it only made sense for Jacobina and her followers to close ranks. By 1873 the Muckers had removed their children from schools and themselves from churches, for neither institution was teaching the "true doctrine" available through Jacobina. From a modest band of peasants seeking cures for physical ailments, the Muckers had become a separate community united in their religious beliefs around their prophetess.

 ∾

That the rise of this sect centered on a woman was an extraordinary occurrence. Nineteenth-century Brazil, after all, was a patriarchal society that severely restricted "decent" women's participation in public life. Along with the enslaved and the poorest free men, women formed the majority of the population excluded from formal political citizenship. Moreover, although dominant notions about "natural" female traits portrayed women as having a special capacity for spirituality, women were prohibited from holding formal institutional power in Brazilian churches. The influence that Jacobina attained, then, was part of the "perversity" that nonbelievers attributed to the Muckers.

Certain facts do, however, make her rise to a position of leadership less surprising. For one thing, her parents' families were not only fervently but also somewhat unconventionally religious Protestants. Her mother was said to be highly devout but did not legally marry Jacobina's father until 1850, a year before he died and left her a widow; common-law marriages, while prevalent in the population at large, were much less typical of immigrant settlements. More notorious still was the background of the family of Jacobina's father. According to most accounts, her paternal grandfather, João Libório Mentz, brought his wife and children to Brazil in order to escape religious persecution in his home city of Tambach. The Mentzes had been part of a small faction that had split off from the Lutheran church in the region; much as the Muckers did decades later in the New World, these German schismatics, labeled "Anabaptists" by anti-Mucker journalists in Rio Grande do Sul, undertook the schooling of their children and the celebration of baptisms and other religious sacraments in their own homes and meeting places. We cannot, however, be too quick to assume that Jacobina was merely a direct product of her grandfather's faith. For one thing, the family patriarch died before she was born and thus exercised no direct influence on her; neither Carolina nor any other witness mentioned the impact of Jacobina's grandmother. Furthermore, her father, who might have transmitted his parents' ideas, nonetheless consented to her brief time in school and then died when Jacobina was only nine years old. At best, the religious formation of Jacobina's family served as the context for her later transformation into a religious leader.

Other features of life in the *colônia* more immediately laid the groundwork for the development of the Muckers. Prominent among these was the semi-frontier nature of immigrant society in Brazil. For the first decades after their founding, the settlements of European groups existed on the fringes of national society and government. This tendency was true even of São Leopoldo, which enjoyed such impressive growth and economic development that politicians and scholars hailed it as the birthplace of European immigration to Brazil, although four other projects for immigrant colonies had preceded it. Those Germans who made their way across the Atlantic, through cities such as Rio de Janeiro and Porto Alegre, and up to the *colônia* of São Leopoldo found themselves very much in the hinterlands. Like the others who came in this first wave of immigrants, Jacobina's grandparents, the Müllers and Mentzes, must have tried to take possession of the lands that the Brazilian government had promised them.

Imperial officials provided little, however, in the way of support and infrastructure; often the immigrants had to push and prod local and provincial authorities first to survey and then to distribute the plots of land promised to settlers. In their petitions and other written protests they often shocked officials who, unused to such formal demands of legal rights, labeled them "litigious." Later, when the lines were laid out, the immigrants had to turn their new properties into farmland. A first step was to hack out a rough road (*picada*) through the forest; lots fronted this basic route of communication and transportation and ran back into the woods. Clearing the land was only the first of the arduous tasks necessary to bring the property into production. Plowing and harvesting were particularly difficult for those who had been merchants or artisans in Europe, but even the majority who were knowledgeable farmers were starting from scratch in unfamiliar surroundings.

Above all, these new residents of the Empire struggled with an isolation they had not known in their native countries. This is not to say that their new lands were uninhabited; although disease, warfare, and enslavement had reduced their numbers, the remaining indigenous peoples in the area resented, and resisted, the inroads that new settlements made. Local authorities reported raids on *colonos* (settlers) by Indians into the 1860s and 1870s. To a great degree, however, the immigrants lived outside the mainstream of their new country's official life. In the first few decades of organized immigration, when they lacked reliable means of transportation to cities like Porto Alegre, the *picadas* seemed distant from potential markets where they might sell their produce and buy goods they could not make for themselves. Few of the *colônia*'s men, moreover, were able to become citizens until the mass naturalization implemented by the Republic in 1891.

The remoteness of the settlements, however, was not only a commercial or political but also a social and cultural fact in the lives of the *colonos*. The relative absence of contacts with urban centers or with non-immigrant populations (whom the Germans called, sometimes derisively, "Brazilians") meant that the immigrants could develop their society relatively free of outside influences. They did not, it is crucial to understand, simply create a copy of Germany within Brazil. Indeed, for most of the nineteenth century, there was no single, unified Germany; the immigrants who showed up in São Leopoldo came from disparate regions and states and spoke dialects that could be mutually unintelligible. In Brazil they drew on their diverse European backgrounds but also incorporated some features of the Brazilian language, dress, foods, and so on to forge a novel, German-Brazilian culture. The resulting dynamic mixture led European visitors to conflicting impressions of São Leopoldo; some, such as the Englishman Michael G. Mulhall, thought that they had unexpectedly encountered a German town in South America, while others, such as the Austrian Joseph Hörmeyer, were moved to complain about the immigrants' excessive assimilation.[4]

One of the most troubling aspects of this new culture for Brazilian authorities was its religious diversity. The mere fact that most of São Leopoldo's population was Protestant (between 60 and 65 percent at midcentury) was already unsettling in the officially Catholic empire. The widespread observance of Protestant rituals in Protestant churches in São Leopoldo challenged the imperial constitution's restrictions on the public practice of non-Catholic religions. Worse still, the "colonial" zone threatened to produce a range of heterodox versions of both Catholic and Protestant faiths. No institutional church maintained a stable presence in the *colônia* in the early decades of immigration; German-speaking Catholic priests arrived only in 1849. The few clergy serving the area tended, moreover, to stay in the center of São Leopoldo. In the absence of the guidance of priests and pastors, residents of outlying settlements took initiatives to take charge of their own spiritual needs. Community associations sprang up to coordinate efforts to erect church buildings and maintain congregations. They also elected laymen to oversee regular meetings and minister to the local populace. To the horror of both Catholic and Protestant officials, these stand-ins at times celebrated the sacraments. The more informal nature of religious practice in the rural *picadas* may also have given women a stronger voice in spiritual matters and in that way facilitated the rise of a female leader such as Jacobina.

From the 1850s on, however, changes would sweep across the "colonial" zone and begin to close the frontier. The official churches attempted to correct any errors that might have appeared by imposing their control over their immigrant flocks. Jesuit priests and Lutheran ministers began to arrive in greater numbers to "conquer" the rural *colonos* who had strayed from orthodoxy. Those clergy proved to be some of the most iron-willed enemies of the Muckers, who, after all, ultimately attempted to synthesize their own religion.

In the economic and political spheres as well, the isolation of the *colônia* was breaking down. From the civil war that blazed across Rio Grande do Sul between 1835 and 1845, São Leopoldo was drawn into Porto Alegre's economic orbit. Settlers in the *picadas* had produced mostly for subsistence, both in their farming and in the small artisanry that most families also practiced. By disrupting normal commercial patterns, however, the war opened the urban market for *colonos'* goods. The process really took off after midcentury, when merchants oversaw the transformation of the Porto Alegre-*serra* (mountain) region into a complex, interconnected economic zone. The links between settlements and capital so energized Porto Alegre that some visitors described the "colonial" region as the motor of the regional economy. In fact, ties to the city led to the diversification of São Leopoldo's economy, spurring a wide range of artisanry and simple manufactures. The introduction of steamship routes (1852) and a railroad (1874) between Porto Alegre and São Leopoldo symbolized and further invigorated this development.

The growth of the "colonial" economy brought wealth but also inequality into the São Leopoldo area. The great beneficiaries in the *serra* were the thriving center of the old colony (elevated in 1846 to the status of *vila*, or town) and the merchants based there. More direct exchange with Porto Alegre meant competing with that city's large commercial houses, but São Leopoldo merchants managed to secure their hold on much of the *colonos'* production. They also expanded their activities, helping to create larger-scale commercial agriculture and manufacturing. These men formed the rising elite of São Leopoldo and strove to establish not only social status but also political power commensurate with their wealth. To enter Brazil's clientelistic political system on the best terms possible, they tried to harness the votes of the increasing numbers of settlement residents (particularly the Brazilian-born children of immigrants) who were attaining political citizenship. The people whom those would-be political bosses tried to manipulate came from the other end of the social scale, which saw many rural settlers sliding into a poverty that they had not known before. Flourishing production in the town of São Leopoldo and the influx of imported goods spelled doom for small artisans working independently in the countryside. At the same time, smallholding farmers fell under the increasing power of the merchants, who not only bought agricultural products but also controlled the supply of credit. As land prices crept upward, some settlers were forced off their plots; many more found themselves unable to leave sufficient lands for all of their children. In the end, the economic turn after midcentury engendered socioeconomic and political stratification in the *serra*.

The Muckers were the result of both the *colônia*'s early cultural isolation and the later integration of São Leopoldo into broader economic and political systems. The relative lack of official controls on settlers opened the way for diverse popular religious practices; Jacobina's group was the most dramatic result of that potential. The appearance of a large, newly impoverished rural populace, furthermore, supplied most of the believers who gathered at Ferrabrás. Indeed, the body of Jacobina's followers was in many ways representative of that segment. Her acolytes were overwhelmingly but not entirely Protestant (the Protestant majority tended to be poorer than the Catholic minority in the region); worked as farmers, with some artisans; lived in the *picadas* rather than in the town of São Leopoldo; were poorly educated; and, with few exceptions, spoke only German. Like much of the general population of the "colonial" zone, they were also bound to each other through kinship; the most active Muckers generally came from a few extended families (the Maurer, Mentz, Fuchs, and Sehn clans).

∾

From the earliest meetings at the Maurers' house, the small community of these humble *colonos* set off sparks in the region. At first, they were primarily the target of jokes and malicious gossip up and down the *picadas*. Neighbors portrayed the Muckers as simple-minded rubes who had fallen under the spell of a charlatan. The tone of popular rumors grew more sharply critical by 1872–73, however, as opposition to the Muckers flared up among religious and civil officials and the wealthier elements of São Leopoldo society. Soon, nonbelievers in the region were condemning the Muckers as diabolical and dangerous. Jacobina, as one of her followers related afterward, was attacked as a witch and a seductress; allegedly, she had thrown over João Jorge in favor of Rodolfo Sehn, the young married adept who became the "interpreter" of Jacobina's utterances during her "crises" and who had encouraged other couples to break their marital vows. At Jacobina's prodding, the Muckers were supposedly also building a fortress and amassing weapons and ammunition with which to resist all authorities.

In May 1873 a petition from forty-six residents of the fourth district of São Leopoldo crystallized this early opposition. Reflecting the resentment of the institutions the Muckers had abandoned, a Lutheran pastor and a schoolteacher headed the petition drive. They found support mostly among the wealthy in São Leopoldo, but they also convinced several small farmers and even some direct relatives of the Muckers to endorse their complaints against the group. Accusing Jacobina of declaring herself Christ and of threatening social peace, these citizens sent their petition to their police *delegado*.

By addressing the matter to that official, they also brought the question of the Muckers into the web of local and provincial politics, a development that pushed all involved toward confrontation. Key politicians in the area had their own grievances against the Muckers and their own partisan interests to defend. One of the most tireless persecutors of the group (although also a cousin of Jacobina's), the police official Lúcio Schreiner, blamed João Jorge Maurer for a recent electoral defeat; he had counted on Maurer to deliver the votes of his followers, but João Jorge and other Muckers had stayed away from the polls. Allied with others who resented the Muckers' independence, he pressured higher authorities to intervene. As soon as the Liberal Party newspaper *A Reforma* latched on to the story of the Muckers, provincial-level politicians also gave the reclusive sect their full attention. In the aggressively competitive climate of nineteenth-century politics, the Liberals, who were then out of power, used the rise of the Muckers relentlessly to condemn the ruling Conservatives as weak and ineffective; if the Conservative president (or governor) of the province could allow such an immoral sect to flourish, the Liberals argued, then it must be time for a different party to take over. With the entrance of politicians into the fray, the anti-Mucker forces had come into alignment.

From that point, the pace of events accelerated. Just eleven days after the first petition appeared, the provincial president sent the chief of police of Rio Grande do Sul, backed up with fifty soldiers, to investigate. They took João Jorge and several other Muckers in for interrogations immediately but came back two days later for Jacobina, who was apparently in a trance. After questioning the men and ordering Dr. Hillebrand to examine Jacobina, the chief of police sent the Maurers under escort to Porto Alegre. There they remained in custody for forty-five days, with Jacobina confined in the hospital of Santa Casa da Misericórdia. In their absence the group at Ferrabrás demonstrated impressive cohesion, for the members who remained organized a great meeting for Pentecost; even the police, who broke up the gathering and forced those present to sign formal pledges of good behavior, did not dissuade the Muckers from continuing their activities.

The return of Jacobina and João Jorge caused not only celebration but also a strengthening of reserve in the Mucker community. The disciples took up an old project and began the construction of a new meetinghouse next to the Maurers' home. Large enough for the increased number of *colonos* who were showing up to hear Jacobina, the building was also to be a solid, stonework structure; in the nightmares of nonbelievers, it became a military fort. Beginning with the funeral of one of the oldest Muckers, the eighty-one-year-old Jorge Jacó Fuchs, the group also began to bury their dead not in church cemeteries but on the property at Ferrabrás.

The distrust and contempt that the Muckers and non-Muckers held for each other color the accounts of what followed. It is, however, clear that the contending sides matched each others' ever-greater determination and violence. Passions ran especially high among Jacobina's opponents after a policeman, João Lehn, accused Rodolfo Sehn and another Mucker of shooting him. Although it apparently has not survived, a second, more vehement petition presented further allegations against the Muckers; the signatories now called for the deportation of Jacobina and her followers. Meanwhile, although Lehn's injuries halted his actions, other policemen continued their vigilance over the goings-on at Ferrabrás, arresting João Jorge and thirty-two others briefly after the attack on their colleague. In a punishment usual in the period, five of the younger Mucker men were pressed into the army as common soldiers, although the provincial president quickly rescinded that order. The Muckers countered with their own petition. Having lost faith in Rio Grande do Sul's authorities, they sent their grievances directly to the emperor, who had visited São Leopoldo ten years earlier. João Jorge and two or three companions took the document, with its thirty-one signatures and detailed complaints about the outrageous and arbitrary behavior of neighbors and the local police, to the court in Rio de Janeiro. When a copy made it to the desk of the provincial president, he ordered investigations by his subordinates; those men, some of whom were mentioned in the petition, found the Muckers' assertions to be groundless.

The failure of the Muckers' petition to win them protection from the emperor would not have surprised any politically savvy observer at the time. It did, however, contribute to the further radicalization of the group's ideas and practices. The months that João Jorge spent away from Ferrabrás seem to have shifted power even more fully to Jacobina and her closest disciples. It was, not coincidentally, in this period that rumors appeared about Jacobina's betrayal of her husband; although denied by Rodolfo Sehn's wife, the story was that Jacobina had not only taken up with her "interpreter" but also became pregnant with his child. Certainly, the Prophetess was leading a core of her followers to much more hard-line positions. Jacobina's message focused increasingly on the imminent and violent end of the world; she thought that catastrophe would come about in a war among men. For a time she preached that the Muckers were the elect, those who had received God's truth and who would be welcome in the Kingdom of Heaven; an especially unpleasant end lay in store, she explained further, for the nonbelievers of São Leopoldo, who had heard but rejected that truth. By 1874, however, Jacobina was characterizing her followers not only as the "illuminated" but also as agents of God who had to use the force of arms to defeat the evil and unholy in the final battles of this world.

The actions of the Muckers paralleled the extremism of Jacobina's visions. Pooling their labor and money, they completed the construction of their imposing meetinghouse and bought up all the arms and ammunition they could find. During nights of true terror, Jacobina's followers also seemed to confirm the most horrifying rumors about themselves. From the attempt on Lehn's life forward, the Muckers' enemies had blamed them for a series of atrocities. The incidents that began in May 1874—much more assuredly the work of the Muckers than previous acts—stunned and infuriated the population of São Leopoldo. The night of May 30 brought the murder of Jorge Haubert, not only a former Mucker but also the godson of Jorge Robinson, one of the most militant of Jacobina's acolytes. Removed by the police from Robinson's custody, Haubert had become an opponent of the sect in the town of São Leopoldo. When two figures in disguise shot him there, even the more urban space no longer seemed safe from Jacobina's "ruffians." Assassins did not manage to find another of their targets, former Mucker Martinho Cassel, on June 15, but they killed his wife, along with three of their children and a stepdaughter, and set fire to their house. On June 25, after ten days of preparations, the Muckers truly began to wage war on their most vocal enemies in the *picadas*. Although their activities probably fell short of the rumored destruction of fourteen households, squads of five or so Muckers murdered at least twelve people and burned down homes and businesses.

The panic that this wave of violence caused in São Leopoldo, along with the outcry it occasioned in the partisan press, forced provincial politicians to abandon their earlier reluctance and mobilize a repressive force. From a demented woman suffering from "religious monomania," Jacobina had, in officials' eyes, become the chief of a rebellion that endangered her neighbors and the reputation and control of those in power. With outrages by both Muckers and non-Muckers becoming commonplace in the region, the provincial government stepped in to turn the situation into a regular war. Officials, army troops, and equipment were flooding into São Leopoldo within twenty-four hours of the fiery incidents of June 25; the state was amassing a substantial force, under the command of Colonel Genuino Olympio de Sampaio, a decorated veteran of the Paraguayan War (1864–1870). Including National Guard squads and local residents who eagerly offered their help, Colonel Genuino counted on over 500 fighting men at one point.

Jacobina's followers made up a much smaller host, although we cannot be sure of their number. Assured by their leader that they were the Divine Right fighting against the representatives of a morally sick and sinful world, the Muckers fought with a passion and a unity of purpose that the official military could not match (although the anti-Mucker irregulars impressed government officers with their ferocity). The government's campaign struggled, in fact, to achieve a definitive victory over Jacobina's holy warriors.

The first great battle ended in ignominious defeat for the forces of legality, when a guide led Colonel Genuino's men to a field that turned out to be too close to the Muckers' stronghold. Surrounded by rebels who knew the terrain and unable to count on their artillery, which either floundered in the mud or fell apart, the government side retreated; five soldiers were killed and dozens more wounded in that initial contact with the "fanatics." The shock of this loss led both military and civilian authorities to redouble their preparations for the next battle. Not all of the arms and men were of great use—National Guardsmen proved especially prone to desertion—but Colonel Genuino grew more confident in his ability to bring down Jacobina and her disciples. Proceeding toward the Maurer house on July 19 (after bad weather had caused a one-day delay), the assembled soldiers, guardsmen, and irregulars attacked the Muckers. From their positions in the two buildings and behind felled trees, the believers mounted a tenacious defense of their spiritual home, at one point greeting a demand for their surrender with a burst of rifle fire. Despite the Muckers' zealous resistance, the cannons and sheer size of Colonel Genuino's army wore down the rebels, and the battle began to shift in the government's favor. When the commander ordered that the Maurers' house be set aflame, everything dissolved into brutal chaos. It is probable that more than fifteen rebels died in the battle, eight or ten more in the fire. Soldiers took prisoner as many as fifty-two more Muckers (reports vary on the exact figure), some of them women who had tried to throw themselves into the flames to avoid capture. Those who lived became the victims of rape and other violence at the hands of government fighters.

The victory that Colonel Genuino announced did not, however, come until August 2. João Jorge, Jacobina, and other Muckers had fled the army's advance on July 19. Maurer did not, however, stay with his wife and the infant that she had recently borne. According to one witness, Jacobina gave her husband some food and sent him off, saying, "[Here] I will have my death, and I will take my child with me. I can't let her wander the world accompanied by provocations and ridicule." It was allegedly to protect their hiding spot that Jacobina had her child killed that night; we cannot know, however, exactly when the infant died or by whose hand.

Jacobina and the others, meanwhile, regrouped in the forest. Around three o'clock in the morning of July 20, rebel shots tore into the army's camp. The commander, who was speaking with four or five of his men, received a bullet in his leg. By chance it nicked an artery, and within two hours, Colonel Genuino was dead. After some wrangling among military and political authorities, Captain Francisco Clementino de San Tiago Dantas took over for the hero, who was buried with great pomp in Porto Alegre. Left with much-reduced resources but benefiting from information that a Mucker deserter had provided, Dantas cornered Jacobina and her remaining followers in the woods. Although they still needed two hours of battle to complete their mission, the soldiers and their allies overcame the defiant rebels. Jacobina and Rodolfo Sehn were the last to die that day. When only the two of them were alive, Sehn tried to shield Jacobina with his body, but to no avail. In a volley of rifle fire, they fell dead together.

∽

The emergence and repression of Jacobina and her followers played out against a backdrop of ambivalence about European immigration. Throughout the Mucker drama, Germans in Rio Grande do Sul took pains to assert their loyalty to Brazil, ostentatiously cheering on official actions and offering their assistance in preserving order in São Leopoldo and Porto Alegre. They had reason to be anxious, for anti-German feelings had spilled onto the streets of the provincial capital in a riot in 1863, after the immigrant journalist Carlos von Koseritz dared to question Brazil's position in a diplomatic dispute with Britain. Across Brazil, moreover, elites had long expressed reservations about the utility of German immigration. For plantation owners in the center-south, who wanted hands to replace a declining slave force, programs to install European workers initially seemed a poor investment; experiments with Swiss *colonos* in São Paulo taught planters that they could not merely plug European workers into a slave system. Even for those who, like most elites in Porto Alegre, backed the creation of an immigrant smallholder population, German settlements were at times troubling. Fearful about a German state within the Brazilian nation, they tended to blame immigrants for the isolation into which they had been placed. Moreover, some of the qualities that Germans were expected to inject into their new country—

from their discipline and "love of work" to their European civilization—might actually make them appear threats to existing Europhile powerholders in Brazil.

Ultimately, however, the course of events leading up to the violent climax of Jacobina's life demonstrated the limits of elite anxieties about European immigration. Reactions to the Muckers and their female leader did not portray them as representing the unhealthy potential of German "colonization" programs. Indeed, appearance of such "bad" immigrants effectively underlined the "goodness" of the others, and policymakers focused on the purported benefits that white Europeans were to furnish.

Much less sanguine, of course, was the campaign that civilian and military men staged against the Prophetess and her acolytes in 1874. This most unfortunate aspect of the story turned out to be a precursor to subsequent actions by the Brazilian state in the late 1890s at the northeastern town of Canudos and during the 1910s in the Contestado region of southern Brazil. In both of those regions, millenarian movements faced repressive expeditions that in central ways repeated the experience at Ferrabrás—indeed, Colonel Genuino's old battalion and other soldiers who fought the Muckers also took the field at Canudos. The Republic that waged war on those later communities of believers exhibited the same exaggerated desire to assert its control over the national territory and populace that the imperial state had displayed in crushing Jacobina Maurer, the immigrants' daughter turned oracle, and the *colonos* who believed in her preaching.

NOTES

1. Ambrósio Schupp, *Os "Mucker": A tragédia histórica do Ferrabrás*, 4th ed. (Porto Alegre, 1993), 69–70.
2. Moacyr Domingues, *A nova face dos Muckers* (São Leopoldo, 1977), 40.
3. Ibid., 73–74.
4. Michael G. Mulhall, *Rio Grande do Sul and Its German Colonies* (London, 1873); Joseph Hörmeyer, *O Rio Grande do Sul de 1850: Descrição da Província do Rio Grande do Sul no Brasil meridional*, trans. Heinrich A. W. Bunse (Porto Alegre, 1986).

SUGGESTED READINGS

Much of the official correspondence and local journalism about the Muckers is collected in the three volumes of Códice 605 at the Arquivo Nacional in Rio de Janeiro. Other crucial documentation, including the testimony that Jacobina and other Muckers gave before the police, exists in the Arquivo Público do Rio Grande do Sul and the Arquivo Histórico do Rio

Grande do Sul, both located in Porto Alegre. On German immigrant communities in Brazil in the 1800s, see João Guilherme Biehl, "Jammerthal, the Valley of Lamentation: *Kultur*, War, Trauma, and Subjectivity in Nineteenth-Century Brazil," *Journal of Latin American Cultural Studies* 8:2 (November 1999): 171–98. On the German population in Brazil in comparative perspective, see Frederick C. Luebke, *Germans in Brazil: A Comparative Study of Cultural Conflict during World War I* (Baton Rouge: Louisiana State University Press, 1987). For more on politics and ideology in the provincial capital of Rio Grande do Sul, see Roger Kittleson, " 'Ideas Triumph Only after Great Contests of Sorrow': Popular Classes and Political Ideas in Porto Alegre, Brazil, 1889–1893," in *Liberals, Politics, and Power: State Formation in Nineteenth-Century Latin America*, ed. Vincent C. Peloso and Barbara A. Tenenbaum (Athens: University of Georgia Press, 1996); and idem, " 'Campaign All of Peace and Charity': Gender and the Politics of Abolitionism in Porto Alegre, Brazil, 1879–1888," *Slavery and Abolition* (December 2001).

For scholarly treatment of the Muckers, see especially Janaina Amado, *Conflito Social no Brasil: A revolta dos "Mucker," Rio Grande do Sul, 1868–1898* (São Paulo, 1978). Other studies with rich documentation are Moacyr Domingues, *A nova face dos Muckers* (São Leopoldo, 1977); Elma Sant'Anna, *Jacobina Maurer* (Porto Alegre, 1985); Leopoldo Petry, *O Episódio do Ferrabréz (Os Mucker)* (São Leopoldo, 1957); Ambrósio Schupp, *Os "Mucker": A tragédia histórica do Ferrabrás*, 4th ed. (Porto Alegre, 1993); and Eduardo Marques Peixoto, "Questão Maurer, os Muckers," *Revista do Instituto Histórico e Geográfico Brasileiro* 68:2 (1907). One of the best contemporary Gaúcho novelists, Luiz Antonio de Assis Brazil, has written a fictional version of the story of the Muckers, *Videiras de Cristal* (Porto Alegre, 1990); see also the film, *Paixão de Jacobina*, that director Fabio Barreto based on that novel. On German immigration to Rio Grande do Sul, see Emílio Willems, *A aculturação dos alemães no Brasil* (São Paulo, 1946); Jean Roche, *A Colonização Alemã e o Rio Grande do Sul*, 2 vols. (Porto Alegre, 1969); José Hildebrando Dacanal, org., *RS: Imigração e colonização* (Porto Alegre, 1980); and Cláudia Mauch and Naira Vasconcellos, eds., *Os alemães no sul do Brasil: Cultura, etnicidade, história* (Canoas, 1994).

CHAPTER 5

Adolfo Ferreira Caminha

Navy Officer, Ardent Republican, and Naturalist Novelist

PETER M. BEATTIE*

While religious fervor inspired the impassioned loyalties of Jacobina Maurer and the Muckers to their community of faith, secular nationalist fervor stirred the hearts of others who strove to reform and unify Brazilian society. Abolitionism and republican nationalism among other intellectual and political movements became fashionable in the 1880s, and they shaped the coming of age of educated youths such as Adolfo Ferreira Caminha and his peers. Many republican sympathizers believed that monarchy, aristocracy, cruel punishments, the Catholic Church, and a lack of more widespread education had retarded Brazil's progress. Caminha was an outspoken abolitionist, but like many of his generation, he also expressed ambivalence about the role that former slaves and their descendants would play in postabolition Brazil. Both his life and his literary work exhibit a series of contradictions that show us how reform-minded Brazilians lived through and made sense of the transition from a constitutional monarchy to a republic, and from an economy dependent on slave labor to one that relied on free labor.

Caminha's biography indicates how some young men from middle-class origins made sense of the dramatic changes occurring all around them. His views of institutions, values, and practices were not typical, but his firmly held beliefs reveal much about the dramatic changes and stubborn continuities that characterized his times. Caminha and many of his peers shared a strong faith in science, technology, rational analysis, and North Atlantic civilization that would be shaken by economic depression, political instability, corruption, and war in Brazil in the 1890s. His life and work reveal a young man who was very critical of his society, but who also expressed pride and faith in Brazil's promise.

Peter M. Beattie's research focuses on the intersection between the growing influence of public institutions and the lives of Brazil's free poor. One theme of his book, The Tribute of Blood: Army, Honor, Race, and Nation in Brazil, 1864–1945 *(2001), is how coercive recruitment for the military played a central role in the fledgling penal justice system.*

*The author thanks James N. Green for his helpful comments on an earlier version of this chapter.

Here, he points out that a major theme of Adolfo Caminha's oeuvre is a critique of military impressment (coerced induction) and the flogging of sailors as injustices that survived slavery's abolition. He argues that Caminha associated these and other Brazilian social problems with the legacies of monarchy and slavery that the new republican government needed to address forthrightly.

Adolfo Ferreira Caminha's life and work made him one of the most controversial, uncompromising, and tragic figures of a youthful generation that embraced republicanism, abolitionism, and modernization. He thrived on controversy and rivalry; his friends commented on his talent for making enemies. His novels explored taboo social subjects in a frank, realistic style, and in this way he unflinchingly challenged Brazilian mores, institutions, and practices that he regarded as misguided or hypocritical. His penchant for tweaking bourgeois moral pretensions earned him admiration from a handful of freethinking literary lights as well as repudiation from more conservative readers and critics. As a result, triumphs and calamities marked his short and sometimes bitter career. Tuberculosis, the poet's disease, brought an untimely end to Caminha's life in Rio at the tender age of twenty-nine.

Caminha was born in 1867 in the small town of Acarati not far from the dazzling coastal dunes of Ceará, a state that rests east of the Amazon Delta and just south of the equator. Ceará's humid coastal zone produced profitable sugarcane for export, and African slaves and their descendants provided most of the plantation labor. But in Ceará's hinterland, the landscape becomes more arid and forbidding. This region is not appropriate for thirsty sugarcane, but it is suitable for less labor-intensive crops and cattle. These backlands are very fertile when rains are plentiful, but when periodic droughts strike, the landscape becomes desolate and its scrub forests desiccated. The sun bakes shallow rivers into mud-caked snaking trails that many migrants trudged along to escape certain death in their search for potable water, food, and shelter on the muggy seaboard.

At a young age, Caminha's life was marked by the most horrific natural disaster in Brazil's history: the Great Drought (1877–1880), which forced tens of thousands of parched Ceará residents to abandon their homes. Most migrants lost their livestock and crops to the harsh elements, so they arrived on the coast destitute with only the few belongings they could carry in bundles on their heads. Government efforts to aid drought victims floundered. Relatives and many charitable individuals helped the refugees, but others took advantage of their vulnerability. Most refugees found little in the way of help, and some resorted to crime. For this reason, those living near the coast, like Caminha's family, often feared the wretched and desperate backlanders when they arrived in large numbers. It is estimated that some 250,000 perished, but many of those who survived returned when the rains greened the hinterlands again. Others migrated to less arid regions of Brazil in search of a better life. Indeed, the Great Drought helped to establish a pattern of migration by poor northeasterners referred to as *retirantes* (derived from the verb "to retreat") that continues to this day. Caminha witnessed the devastation that nature could wreak on the innocent and immoral alike, and how this misfortune could be compounded by government ineptness, corruption, and indifference.

It is interesting to speculate about how Caminha's youthful memories of this cataclysmic event influenced his life course and the worldview he adopted as a young man. Perhaps this tragedy contributed to the acerbity of his personality and his impatient desire to reform and modernize Brazil. Passages in Caminha's novel *A normalista* (The school girl) relate the Great Drought's devastation, complete with the description of a dried-up corpse at the side of the road whose eyes and intestines had been eaten by buzzards and flies. Caminha's childhood memories of the drought were punctuated by personal tragedy: his mother's death in 1878. As a result, he later went to live with an uncle in the nation's capital, Rio de Janeiro.

In 1882, Caminha won, on the basis of a competitive entrance exam, a government-sponsored education at the Navy Academy in Rio. Despite its vast coastline, Brazil's navy remained a small entity of some 3,000 men. While the larger army had some nonwhite junior officers, the navy's officer corps remained a more exclusive bastion of "whiteness." Unlike army personnel, naval officers often traveled to foreign ports where they met local dignitaries, procured supplies, and explored the sites. In contrast, most common sailors were black or of mixed African and European heritage and were restricted to their ships or dock areas when abroad. Brazil's leaders wanted foreigners, especially Europeans, to see their nation as "white," even though the majority of its population was nonwhite.

This bigotry was given "scientific" impetus in the late 1800s by social Darwinism, a theory that posited the existence of a natural hierarchy of races that placed northern Europeans at the top and Africans and American Indians at the bottom of an imagined scale of evolutionary development. This theory served to explain, justify, and apologize for European imperialism and the dominance of Brazil's mostly white elite.

Caminha drank in the intellectual and political currents that swirled through Rio in the 1880s. Like many cadets of his day, Caminha took a great interest in the humanities. These young men followed the lead of the sons of elite families who attended one of two Brazilian law faculties where rhetoric and a knowledge of literature were touchstones of

educational prestige. As a nationalist, Caminha argued that "the literature and arts of a country are much more serious matters than is commonly thought." He criticized Brazilian writers for their lack of discipline
and their fondness for bohemia and shallow praise. Caminha's taste in
literature favored the works of naturalist authors such as Emile Zola of
France and Eça Queirois of Portugal. Caminha, like the U.S. novelist
Stephen Crane (author of *The Red Badge of Courage*), found inspiration in
European naturalism.

Naturalism is characterized by a number of conventions. Naturalists
believed that nature was indifferent to human affairs, and instead impersonal scientific laws governed the universe and could even determine the
actions of human beings. In short, neither nature nor God intervened to
reward the deserving or smite wrongdoers. Many readers and critics found
naturalist novels to be shockingly amoral because villainous characters
often went unpunished while the innocent suffered unjustly. Naturalists,
however, did not see themselves as amoral but instead considered themselves social critics who sought to realistically depict social problems and
inequities in the light of contemporary science. Perhaps Caminha's
traumatic experience with the drought in Ceará made this approach to
nature and human affairs even more attractive. Naturalists placed taboo
social subjects, including prostitution and marital infidelity, under the
microscope of their unblinking prose. Caminha would take these controversial conventions to extremes that made Crane appear tame by
comparison.

Beyond naturalism and social Darwinism, other influential schools
of thought and political movements influenced Adolfo Caminha and his
generation. In the 1880s positivism was the most prevalent school of
philosophical thought, particularly among military cadets. Inspired by
the French thinker Auguste Comte, positivists had an almost mystical
faith in science and human progress. Comte believed that civilization
passed through three progressive stages of development: theological,
metaphysical, and, finally, scientific or positivistic. These stages roughly
correlated to evolving political systems from theocracies to monarchies
to representative governments. Positivists believed in the ability of mathematics, science, and technology to unify and modernize a nation and to
create rational institutions that would operate in harmony with natural
laws to form more just societies. While positivism had broad influence
within Brazil, it was far from monolithic. Brazilian positivism appealed
to civilians and military officers, and it exhibited a variety of schools of
thought that ranged from orthodox Positivist churches to eclectic het-
erodoxy. Todd Diacon's biography of General Cândido Rondon that fol-
lows later in this volume examines Brazilian positivism more fully.

Alongside positivism, abolitionism became trendy in Brazil during the 1880s. As a committed abolitionist, Adolfo likely took pride in his home state's leading role in the nation's abolitionist struggle. Ceará's legislature ended slavery within its borders in 1884, four years before most of Brazil, as the result of a strike in the provincial capital, Fortaleza. Its port was too shallow to accommodate oceangoing ships, and instead, smaller boats, or lighters, transported goods between the docks and vessels anchored offshore. Commerce depended on stevedores and seamen who manned the lighters and who were mostly free men of color. Since 1850, Brazil's government had abolished the international slave trade, but thereafter, an internal trade in bondage developed that followed the same routes of many migrant *retirantes* who had left the northeast for the southeast where coffee production fueled a booming economy. In 1883 one black seaman, Chico da Matilde, was so ashamed of his role in this slave trade that he organized a strike among Fortaleza's sailors, who refused to handle goods on any ship that trafficked in slaves. This humble seaman became a celebrity known as the "Sea Dragon." His actions show how common free Brazilians in the provinces, not just well-educated abolitionist politicians in Rio, worked to undermine slavery. Abolitionists in Rio invited and received the Sea Dragon as a national hero, and his fame emboldened abolitionists across Brazil. It seems probable that Caminha witnessed or was at least aware of the Sea Dragon's triumphant welcome to Rio.

Caminha and many who espoused abolitionism also held republican sympathies, but Brazil's Republican Party had been slow to advocate the end of bondage. Republicanism was strongest in São Paulo, where the internal slave trade had concentrated the dwindling bonded population after 1850. Careful not to offend powerful São Paulo masters, the Republican Party leadership did not speak out vociferously for abolition at first. Indeed, much of the nonwhite population associated abolition with the monarchy and the Conservative Party, which finally passed a national abolition law in 1888. Mostly nonwhite *capoeira* toughs (practitioners of Afro-Brazilian martial arts and often members of urban gangs), sympathetic to Emperor Pedro II and sometimes in the pay of Conservative patrons, disrupted Republican political rallies by instigating street brawls. One colorful Afro-Brazilian leader in Rio, Cândido Fonseca da Galvão, who called himself Dom Obá II, warned about the threat of Republican plots posed to Brazil's imperial monarchy in the 1880s. Most members of the establishment, however, viewed Dom Obá as an eccentric sot and dismissed his editorials as deluded maundering. Many Republicans who came to power in 1889 were fearful and suspicious of Rio's black and brown community and their royalist sympathies. Once in power, Republican police vigorously repressed Rio's vibrant *capoeira* organizations.

Most Republicans believed that Pedro II and the monarchy were anachronistic. An official Republican Party had formed in 1870, but it remained a weak third party in a parliamentary system dominated by the Conservative and Liberal parties. Radical Republicans doubted the likelihood of toppling the monarchy by the ballot, and they began to hatch seditious plots. Some Republican leaders made allies within the military officer corps, especially the army. A new generation of military officers became impatient with the monarchy and the civilian political elite. They believed that civilian leaders did not give a high priority to Brazil's military modernization. Naval officers were on the whole more royalist than army officers, but some young ones like Caminha became enamored with republicanism. Caminha gave voice to his republican sympathies at a literary ceremony that marked the death of French author Victor Hugo, a ceremony that the emperor himself attended. Caminha's speech insulted Pedro II by praising Hugo's republican beliefs and lamenting that the author of *Les Misérables* would not witness the triumph of republicanism in Brazil. This disrespect for the monarchy in the presence of the emperor infuriated the Navy Academy's commandant, who wanted to punish Caminha, but the temperate Pedro II insisted that no action be taken. This act of imperial clemency, however, did not win over Caminha; he went on to pen many literary barbs against monarchism.

Caminha did not limit his criticism of Brazil's navy, monarchy, and imperial society to public speeches. While still a cadet, he published a short story, "Chibata," that was serialized in a Rio newspaper. The title referred to the practice of flogging common sailors, barbarous treatment that resembled punishment meted out to slaves. Henceforward, Caminha borrowed from his own experiences to compose a number of naturalist novels that criticized social injustices.

The navy commissioned Caminha in 1886 to voyage on a vessel especially built as Brazil's exhibit at an international exposition in New Orleans. Brazilian engineers designed the steamship equipped with sails, a symbol of national pride because all of its components were made and assembled in Brazil. With this exhibit, Rio's leaders hoped to impress upon North Americans and other foreign delegates that Brazil was a modern nation attuned to industrial progress. In 1895, Caminha published an account of these travels, *No país dos Ianques* (In the country of the Yankees), which recorded the reactions of astonished North Americans who arrogantly declared that it was impossible for a backward nation like Brazil to build steamships.

Soon after Caminha returned from his duties abroad, Brazil abolished slavery, and in 1889 an army coup unseated Pedro II and promulgated the Republic. These events encouraged Caminha, who had expressed outspoken faith in republican ideals and institutions. With slavery and monarchy gone, many now thought that Brazil's march toward its destiny as a wealthy, modern, influential, and ultimately "white" nation was assured. The republican government, influenced by the scientific bigotry of social Darwinism, subsidized European immigration and banned African immigration in order to "whiten" Brazil's population. These mostly European immigrants began to fill many of the more desirable positions that Afro-Brazilian free workers and slaves had once held. Neither the imperial nor the republican Brazilian government made any attempt to smooth the transition from slavery to freedom in a manner similar to the Freedmen's Bureau in the United States. The fate of black and brown Brazilians in the labor market and in the imagination of "white" republican nationalists was one of displacement. Intellectuals rejected the fears that many Europeans expressed about miscegenation and instead claimed that Brazil's heritage of race mixture accelerated the whitening process. They based this argument on the supposition that women would tend to choose lighter-skinned sexual partners as well as the erroneous belief that "white" genes were more powerful than "nonwhite" ones. While many citizens applauded slavery's abolition, uncertainty about the role of black and brown Brazilians in the new republican order abounded. Most intellectuals believed firmly that people of Indian and African descent were inferior to Europeans. Some even posited that nonwhites were "natural monarchists" stuck at a stage of positivist development that white European civilization had already surpassed. Many questioned whether nonwhites were able to understand and to carry out the duties required of republican citizens. Social Darwinism popularized by writers such as the Englishman Herbert Spencer helped to justify the economic and political exclusion of former slaves in the new Republic.

An illustration of Caminha's doubts about the role of former slaves in "civilized" nations is perhaps nowhere more clearly demonstrated than in his depiction of Annapolis, Maryland, in *No país dos Ianques*: "Annapolis is like a dissonant note in American civilization. Imagine an African maroon (runaway slave) community, a large village dissected by narrow, uneven, and unaligned streets, with the somber aspect of an old colonial burg, where a population, for the most part black and backward, circulates—and you have the antithesis of the modern city. . . . Insipid, monotonous, and sad like a pagan cemetery, Annapolis is a protest, an anathema against the natural evolution of things, a repugnant blemish on the U.S. map." Caminha's text clearly associates blackness and Africanness with all that is the opposite of modern and progressive in the United States—and by extension in Brazil. He also expresses pessimism about Brazil's "race" and "manhood" when compared to the United States:

"It was not without some sadness that we Brazilians—a degenerated and sluggish race—observed the formation of a strong and happy [U.S.] race with all the characteristics of virility and independence." At other points, however, Caminha had doubts about the influence of genetics on nations and individuals. In an 1894 editorial he noted that a French scholar had demonstrated that environment and education influenced human potential by showing that crimes were more common among the poor and less educated. Like others of his generation, Caminha expressed ambivalence about his nation's racial composition and the role of education and environment in shaping its destiny.

As a naval officer, Caminha had to wrestle with his contradictory views on race and national destiny because the military's enlisted ranks remained dominated by black and brown men. To fill the lower ranks, both the army and the navy continued to rely heavily on impressment, which targeted young men who were in trouble with the law or unemployed. From time to time, police made recruiting sweeps in city taverns, on the streets, and in the countryside. Impressment resembled the methods of African and Indian slavers. Once in the ranks, sailors were legally subject to being flogged in front of the entire crew, a practice that resembled the punishment of slaves at the public whipping post. This practice was even more shocking to many reform-minded men like Caminha because whipping posts in the 1830s had been taken down in favor of more "civilized" floggings of law-breaking slaves behind prison walls. The imperial government even outlawed the flogging of slaves in 1888. After "Chibata," Caminha would be pushed by events to revisit this subject in 1895 in his best novel, *Bom Crioulo*.

In 1889 the new republican government outlawed flogging in the navy, a reform that had been legally granted to army troops in 1873. Soon thereafter, it also banned military impressment. By outlawing these abuses, the army-dominated republican government sought to distinguish its rule from that of Pedro II. Events, however, soon led the government to renege. Insubordination in the navy led authorities to reinstate flogging soon after its abrogation. In 1891 the Republic's first president, Marshal Deodoro da Fonseca, was forced to step down after he illegally ordered army troops to close Congress. In 1892, Vice President Marshal Floriano Peixoto's regime was rocked by a failed barracks putsch, and then from 1893 to 1895 a major rebellion broke out in Brazil's southernmost state, Rio Grande do Sul. As the government cast about to put down this rebellion, disgruntled naval officers turned their guns on Rio in yet another insurrection and carried on the fight around the capital for months in 1893.

To make matters even worse for the new government, the economy bottomed out in 1893 as part of an international depression. Then, in

1896–97 the state mobilized the greater part of the federal army to defeat the irregular troops of a millenarian religious community, which allegedly pined for a return to monarchy, in the dusty backlands town of Canudos in the northeastern state of Bahia. To fill the military's ranks to quell these revolts, the central government violated the Constitution and resorted to military impressment. These dramatic events probably led Caminha to begin thinking of a story that would highlight the injustices of flogging and military impressment. Personal experiences and disillusionment with the military likely gave impetus to his plans.

In 1888 the navy transferred Caminha to Fortaleza for health reasons. He sought an assignment in his home state, but after years of study in Rio and duty abroad, Fortaleza may have seemed somewhat stultifying and provincial. However Caminha felt about life in Ceará, we know that he began a scandalous affair with the wife of an army officer there. Adulterous affairs with married women could end in socially sanctioned murders. Cuckolded husbands, subject to humiliating comments that questioned their manhood, were goaded into seeking revenge to still wagging tongues.

A contemporary of Caminha, Euclydes da Cunha, became the victim of his own act of revenge. A military officer, journalist, and later a much more famous author than Caminha, da Cunha died in the early 1900s when he tried to kill an army officer who was having an affair with his wife. Da Cunha surprised his rival and shot him several times at close range. The injured officer had only enough strength to grab his own revolver and slay da Cunha in self-defense before passing out. After the bullet-ridden officer recovered from his wounds and the courts dismissed the charges against him, he married da Cunha's former wife. Later, da Cunha's son, who was studying at the Navy Academy, was apparently spurred to action by cadets who demanded to know how "a man" could allow his mother to marry his father's assassin. Like his father, da Cunha's son surprised the army officer and shot him several times. His wounded stepfather then reluctantly raised his own pistol and killed the young man.

While such spectacular cases fueled the sensationalist press, most affairs did not end in such dramatic violence, despite stereotypes that insisted that a betrayed husband could only cleanse his dishonored reputation in his wife's blood. By contrast, Caminha's affair with a married woman shows that not all cases of adultery resulted in murder, but even so, there was often a high price to pay. Caminha's lover left her husband after an argument, and she began to live publicly with Caminha. The army officer reported the situation to his superiors, who ordered Caminha to terminate the affair, but he refused. When the high command ordered Caminha to embark for Europe to separate him from his lover,

Caminha resigned and took a low-paying position as a bureaucrat in Fortaleza. We must remember that there was no legal divorce in Brazil until the 1970s, and though there were ways for a married couple to separate, they could not contract a legal marriage to another unless their spouse died. This affair made Caminha and his "wife" the objects of gossip in Fortaleza, but Caminha had thick skin. He now had more time to dedicate to his writing, and he would swipe back at those in Fortaleza society who snubbed or rebuked him by depicting aspects of their hypocrisy in his novel, *A normalista*.

In 1893, Caminha decided to move to Rio with his partner to pursue a career as a journalist and novelist. To support them and their two children, however, he continued to work as a federal bureaucrat. Even in Brazil's largest city, few writers managed to make a living by their pen alone, an injustice that Caminha complained about in his editorials. After publishing several books, he died a man of modest means despite his education, talent, and literary notoriety.

In his short life, Caminha managed to collect a number of axes to grind as well as principles to advocate. *A normalista* attacked the vicious rumor mill that had made his life difficult in Fortaleza. The novel's plot drew from his own life and, like many naturalists, he often based his characters on individuals whom Caminha knew or observed firsthand. This approach gave naturalist writing its realistic edge, but it could upset those who recognized themselves in supposedly fictional characters. Caminha's novel tells the story of a young woman, Maria do Carmo, raised in Ceará's interior until the Great Drought forces her family to flee to Fortaleza. The harrowing journey ends with the death of Maria's mother. Distraught by his wife's death and disenchanted with his prospects in Ceará, Maria's father decides to seek his fortune in the Amazon and leaves his daughter behind in the care of her godfather, a scrivener employed in a Fortaleza government bureau.

As the schoolgirl Maria matures into an adolescent beauty, she becomes the object of desire for young suitors and, most disturbingly, for her godfather. She begins to flirt with the governor's son, a vain but sentimental ladies' man and law student. When the governor learns that his son has been courting Maria, a woman well below his social station, and that his gallantries have become the subject of gossip, he orders his son to stop seeing her. Maria's godfather, jealous of this relationship, abuses his power as the girl's patriarchal protector to seduce the innocent country lass, and Maria becomes pregnant. When the rumor spreads that Maria is with child, the townspeople assume that the father is the law student, and he hastily flees the state to return to his studies in distant Recife. As the governor's enemies conspire to use the scandal to undermine his administration, he unexpectedly dies.

Meanwhile, Maria's godfather sneaks her off to the country to quietly give birth. After a long and painful labor, the infant is stillborn. Upon recovering, Maria returns to her school in Fortaleza whose curriculum had been modernized to conform to models espoused by, among others, social Darwinist Herbert Spencer. By then, the attention of Fortaleza's citizens has turned to new subjects of real importance in the wake of the army coup that had unseated Pedro II and established the Republic. No one speaks of the scandal that involved Maria and the governor's son. In fact, the novel's last sentence relates that she is engaged to a republican police lieutenant and foresees a "luminous" future for herself.

Caminha could not resist taking a final poke at the monarchy in the novel. The only character who complains about the Republic and its treatment of Pedro II is Maria's godfather. Here, Caminha associates the transition to the Republic with Maria's return to a healthy life free of malicious rumors. Her liberation from her depraved godfather and engagement to a republican police lieutenant coincide with the overthrow of the monarch, the ultimate patriarch. The monarchist stepfather's progeny is stillborn, and Maria is poised to found a healthy, legitimate family with her fiancé under the new Republic. Caminha's bitingly realistic depiction based in part on recognizable figures in Fortaleza society may have been a way of avenging himself on those who had shunned him. This approach along with the delicate sexual subject matter of Caminha's novel led some critics to declare it immoral, but the ever-combative Caminha defended *A normalista*'s morality in a vitriolic newspaper column. One might expect the author to seek safer ground, but instead Caminha ventured farther onto thin ice.

Caminha's next major novel, *Bom Crioulo*, depicts a tragic romance between a handsome black sailor and a winsome blond, blue-eyed cabin boy, Aleixo. In *Bom Crioulo* the metaphor of slavery and freedom plays a constant refrain in the relations between characters, and it reveals Caminha's preoccupation with this issue in postabolition Brazil. He sets the novel in the late Empire before slavery and monarchy had been abrogated. The black sailor's name is Amaro, but his shipmates dub him Bom Crioulo, which may be translated as "good nigger," but it could also be used as an endearing term of intimacy for a good-natured black man. The protagonist's irresolute nickname presages his portrayal.

The title *Bom Crioulo* was likely intended as an ironic evocation of Bom Selvagem (the noble savage) and the supposed natural goodness of men uncorrupted by civilization. This romantic ideal made popular by philosophers such as Jean-Jacques Rousseau inspired Brazilian elites in the mid-1800s to physically incarnate the nation in the form of a Tupi Indian warrior in newspaper cartoons, novels, and official government artwork. Unlike the Indians of the Americas, Africans did not awaken the same fantasies of natural man and noble savagery in Brazilian minds and literature. Clearly, Caminha was pushing a lot of racial and nationalist buttons in this novel.

Bom Crioulo is a runaway slave apprehended by the authorities, who force him to serve in Brazil's navy probably because they assumed he was a vagrant free man of color. *Bom Crioulo* is one of a small number of nineteenth-century novels whose plot depicts a same-sex romantic relationship. Caminha used this controversial protagonist and subject matter to condemn military impressment and corporal punishment in the navy as well as Brazil's heritage of monarchy, slavery, aristocracy, and "perversion."

Caminha's portrait of the "unnatural" relationship between Aleixo and Bom Crioulo is freighted with racial and gender stereotypes. "Only one thing vexed the cabin-boy—the black man's sexual whims. Because Bom Crioulo was not satisfied merely with possessing him sexually at any hour day or night . . . He obliged the boy to go to extremes, he made a slave of him, a whore of him. . . . The first night he wanted Aleixo to strip, to strip right down to the buff. . . . Aleixo replied sulkily that that was not something you ask a man to do! Anything but that." Here stereotypes of slavery and freedom are reversed in an effort to shock the sensibilities of bourgeois readers. Most Brazilians of the time would expect the white man to be the dominant partner in sexual intercourse. The active partner would take on a manly identity as the sexual aggressor, and the passive partner, an emasculated femininity or at best that of a "boy." Thus, to stand exposed for another man's sexual pleasure was not "something you ask a *man* to do."

When men were segregated from women in prisons, barracks, ships, or even elite boarding schools, the unstoppable male sex drive—or so physicians believed—impelled men to dominate other males sexually. Brazilian military tribunals sometimes pursued men accused of homosexual acts, and some told of their liaisons with other soldiers. Tradition-bound officers and common soldiers thought sodomy to be an abominable sin, while reformers such as Adolfo Caminha understood it to be the result of degenerative medical pathology. Others at least partially rejected these conventions and engaged in forbidden sex themselves.

Caminha's story suggests that Bom Crioulo's "inverted" sex drive resulted from the inhumanity of slavery compounded by impressment and flogging. On the contrary, Bom Crioulo believed his desire for young men to be "natural." Here, Caminha appears to suggest that Bom Crioulo's lack of education and the gender segregation common to both slave quarters and military barracks encouraged same-sex liaisons. As a parallel, he presents an esteemed navy captain, a scion of the imperial nobility, who was "known" to be an active sodomite, "an aristocratic military gentleman . . . completely indifferent to the fair sex, who sought out his innate, ideal model of beauty in male adolescents. . . . The captain . . . preferred to live in his own way, with his own people, with his sailors. And there is always a touch of respectful hypocrisy, of malicious hesitation when the captain was mentioned. [But] no one spoke disrespectfully of him. Everyone wanted him to remain as he was . . . gentle at times, an implacable disciplinarian, a model officer."

In Caminha's ambivalent view of sodomy in the navy, he makes it clear that the captain and Bom Crioulo desired young males to the exclusion of women. Even though sailors furtively smirked about the captain and Bom Crioulo, they respected and feared their masculine authority, implying virility and a rugged individuality. Here, Caminha vents his republican animus toward the monarchical Empire by insinuating that slavery, impressment, and aristocratic privilege warped its social and sexual order. The extremes of the old regime's social scale reversed the "natural" desires of the most privileged and most exploited. Abolitionists had similarly argued that slavery debased not only the slave but also the master.

Navy historian Gastão Penalva suggests that the steamship's captain in *Bom Crioulo* was a thinly veiled reference to Admiral Saldanha da Gama, an officer under whom Caminha had served during his voyage to New Orleans. If his contemporaries recognized some of Caminha's scandalous characters as men whom he had met in the navy, then many of them must have been enraged by the novel. Caminha took satisfaction in airing some of the navy's dirty laundry after he was unceremoniously forced out of the ranks for heterosexual impropriety—that is, his affair with a married woman. But *Bom Crioulo* was much more than a political tract; it was a naturalist novel that critiqued social problems.

Caminha was not the only one to suggest a connection between corporal punishment, mental instability, and "sodomy." An 1877 appeals court in Recife settled a dispute over the sale of a slave who, the buyer claimed, had unbeknownst to him suffered from "mental illness" and the "nefarious vice of sodomy." The defense argued that the slave had neither suffered from mental illness nor practiced sodomy before his sale. Rather, they blamed the new owner, whose excessive punishment had so tormented the slave that he was driven to mental illness and sodomy. Though the argument did not sway the court, slaveowners, or at least their lawyers, had appropriated medical assertions that associated excessive flogging with sexual perversion to serve their interests.[1]

Most physicians in the 1800s viewed nonreproductive sex, even masturbation, as deleterious to male health and psychological stability. Caminha suggests that "unnatural" sex is pathological when he relates that as Bom Crioulo carried on his year-long affair with Aleixo, he inexplicably began to grow thinner, to tire more easily, and to feel "pains of weakness in his chest." Bom Crioulo becomes even more sick and forlorn when he is transferred away from Aleixo to a steamship whose captain refuses him shore leave and flogs him. During their separation, Aleixo, who has grown ashamed of his sexual domination by the black man, does not seek out Bom Crioulo and proudly begins his own "manly" affair with a Portuguese prostitute, Carolina. When Bom Crioulo's health gives way, he is sent to the hospital. Giving up hope that Aleixo will visit, he is gripped by "a deafening despair, an incredible despair, augmented by pathological accidents, fomented by a type of contagious leprosy." Here the "pathological accidents" appear to refer to Bom Crioulo's "unnatural" sexual relations with Aleixo. Bom Crioulo learns of Aleixo's betrayal from a comrade. In the final scenes, the black sailor leaves the hospital in a demented state and brutally takes Aleixo's life to avenge his honor. The cautionary tale implies that deadly physiological and psychological consequences resulted from this "waste" of a man's "generative juices" in infertile same-sex copulation.

While Caminha treated the affair between Aleixo and Bom Crioulo in a sympathetic light, his novel does not condone their relationship. Bom Crioulo's death is tragic because he does not recognize his sexual behavior as an "illness" that violates "natural" laws. Rather, Bom Crioulo's lack of education and the inhumane abuses visited upon him by his former master and then the navy captain had twisted his "natural" desires.

While some critics sympathetic to naturalism's goals did not find Caminha's depiction of same-sex relationships offensive, most found it to be pornographic. One sharp-tongued critic suggested that Caminha himself had been a passive sodomite, but the author pointedly rebuked this reviewer. He asked, "What is more pernicious: *Bom Crioulo*, which studies and condemns homosexualism, or these publications out there that preach, in a philosophical tone, the dissolution of the family, concubinage, free love, and every type of social immorality?" Despite the hyperbole and controversy, the book sold well, but after its initial edition it was not reprinted and most critics ignored it for almost a half-century.

Perhaps understandably, most scholars who have analyzed Caminha's body of work gloss over his interest in criticizing military impressment and flogging in favor of his depictions of transgressive sexuality. But as suggested above, these issues were intertwined. Impressment even arises in Caminha's novels that focus on other issues. In *A normalista*, one of Maria's uncles was punished as a youth with impressed service in the army because he was a *peralta incorrigível*, which can be translated as an "incorrigible fop" or an "incorrigible idler or vagrant." Both meanings were clear to Caminha's well-educated readers in the 1890s. Many Brazilians associated the military enlisted ranks with sexual depravity and as an emasculating punishment for wayward poor men. The practice of disciplining vagrants and troublemakers with military service was not unique to Brazil. It had been a venerable European practice up to at least the mid-1800s. England impressed American seamen into the Royal Navy in the 1700s and early 1800s (one of the abuses that helped to spark the War of Independence and the War of 1812). The struggle to abolish impressment and slavery in the Atlantic world shared deep historic parallels. Members of Oliver Cromwell's New Model Army in seventeenth-century England compared military impressment to slavery. They then extended this critique to call for an end to slavery in the English colonies. Of course, these protests did not stop England from becoming the greatest European imperial power whose colonies depended on slavery. As in Brazil, the coercive methods used to fill the navy's ranks created an off-color image of intemperance, impropriety, and sadism; no less than Winston Churchill allegedly once said that the Royal Navy's history was one of "rum, sodomy, and the lash."

Caminha's depiction of Bom Crioulo's induction tells us, with allusions that would have been obvious to his contemporaries but not to later critics, that the former slave had been forced into service. The opening chapter relates that before his health inspection by the navy, Bom Crioulo had spent the night in a jail cell. Thus, like most enlisted soldiers and sailors of his day, the police had apprehended Bom Crioulo and sent him to serve in the military. Caminha later clarifies: "Bom Crioulo only experienced an equal pleasure when they obligated him to become acquainted with liberty by impressing (*recrutando*) him into the navy's ranks." In the late 1800s, "recruiting" was a synonym for impressment. Initially, Bom Crioulo was happy with a sailor's life; he worked hard because he had better food and better treatment than he had had as a slave. Later, however, he changes his attitude when he is brutally flogged and navy officers restrict his liberty. Then Bom Crioulo muses, "A sailor and a black slave, in the long run, they come down to the same thing." Caminha wanted to see not only slavery abolished but also the slave-like conditions under which many Brazilian sailors and soldiers lived in the postabolition era.

Bom Crioulo was in many ways a model eugenic citizen in Caminha's text. A handsome "colossal, savage figure," he defied with "formidable muscles the diseased softness and weakness of a whole decadent, enervated generation." Here we hear echoes of Spencer's social Darwinist maxim: "To be a good animal is the first condition for success in life; to be a nation of good animals is the first condition for national prosperity." Bom Crioulo exhibited a nobility of physical strength, dexterity, and charisma—"a man to be watched" who exercised a "decisive influence over the crew" despite his low rank. When sober and well treated, Bom Crioulo was generous, hardworking, tolerant, and philanthropic; in most respects, he was a Brazilian Billy Budd—the virtuous and virile "handsome sailor" whom Herman Melville made famous. Like Bom Crioulo, Melville's Billy Budd had been impressed, flogged, and victimized by the corrupt justice of the British navy of the early 1800s. I have found no direct evidence that Caminha read Melville, but it is likely that he had heard of this revered American author and his seagoing novels during his New Orleans tour.[2]

Unlike the uncorruptible "white" Billy Budd, Bom Crioulo was more human because his positive traits could be subverted. When poorly treated, Bom Crioulo became "rebellious," given to drinking too much *cachaça* (sugarcane brandy) and provoking fights. His jealousy for the object of his affections, the cabin boy, consumed him. Caminha evinces doubts about Bom Crioulo's race and political loyalties when he notes that the boardinghouse room he shared with the cabin boy when on leave had a newspaper portrait of the emperor on the wall. This symbol hints at the monarchist sympathies of most Afro-Brazilians, and the way republicans stereotyped nonwhites as "natural" monarchists whose lack of education left them unprepared for the duties of republican citizenship. His description of Bom Crioulo's vices recalls that of Cesare Lombroso, the Italian criminologist who, according to one of Caminha's own editorials, "considered the criminal a type of unconscious and uncouth savage, who reappears in civilization because of atavism."

Caminha's deeply ambivalent depiction of Bom Crioulo and his choice of a controversial tragic hero to condemn impressment and flogging distracted readers from his critique. *Bom Crioulo* presaged the 1910 Anti-Flogging Revolt, a rebellion led by Brazilian sailors to protest corporal punishment, impressment, and poor conditions in the navy's enlisted ranks that nearly led to the bombardment of the nation's capital. Few readers paid close attention to Caminha's condemnation of impressment and flogging, but he recognized them as part and parcel of a struggle against slavery and its legacy. Impressment and flogging would come to an end in Brazil's navy only in the World War I era.

Based on his own passionate beliefs and experiences, Caminha's most important novels criticized aspects of the subordination of women and nonwhites and advocated greater equality, but he also expressed fears and doubts about what these new freedoms and rights might entail. For instance, if nonwhite men and women could indulge their own sexual freedoms, they might subvert the republican "whitening" project which assumed that women would "naturally" seek out lighter-skinned mates. Also, Caminha depicted same-sex relations as crimes against nature and nonproductive. In the sparsely populated, continent-sized country of Brazil, leaders saw population growth as essential to national development and defense. Caminha treats Bom Crioulo sympathetically because in part he sees him as the victim of forces beyond his comprehension and control rather than as a conscious degenerate. Like other nationalists of his day, Caminha expressed the hope that education and humane treatment would make nonwhites and women into responsible and productive citizens, but he also betrayed his fears about the dangers they could pose to a healthy republican moral, social, and political order.

Adolfo Caminha reveled in the role of literary rebel. He used his fiction to critique Brazilian society, advocate causes, and discredit his rivals, all the while creating memorable literature, much more than political tracts or slanderous diatribes. It would be overly simplistic to say that after taking a swipe at members of Fortaleza society in *A normalista*, Caminha turned his attention to the navy in *Bom Crioulo*, but it seems to account for part of his motivation and selection of subject matter. Caminha's *Bom Crioulo* leaves his careful reader with unresolved questions that still trouble us in the twenty-first century. Were Bom Crioulo's "crimes" his own fault? Or did his social pathology result from an unjust social order that failed to educate him or to treat him humanely and as an equal because of his race? Did Caminha see Bom Crioulo as worthy of citizenship in Brazil's national community? Or did he believe that Bom Crioulo's race, lack of education, and sexual leanings disqualified him from full membership? The ambiguities in Caminha's *Bom Crioulo*, one of the first Brazilian novels to feature a black man and former slave as the protagonist, reveal much about the anxieties that haunted the consciences of reform-minded republican nationalists of this generation in relation to manhood, sexuality, freedom, race, citizenship, and nationalism.

NOTES

1. Apelado Manuel Alves Vianna, Tribunal de Relação, Arquivo do Instituto Arqueológico, Histórico e Geográfico de Pernambuco, Recife, 1877, caixa II, Pasta 2.

2. In *Billy Budd*, Herman Melville describes the "handsome sailor," a type that closely resembled Caminha's depiction of Bom Crioulo.

> In certain instances they (mariners) would flank, or, like a body guard, quite surround some superior figure of their own class. . . . I [once] saw . . . a common sailor so intensely black that he must have been a native African of the unadulterated blood of Ham. A symmetric figure much above the average height. . . . At each spontaneous tribute rendered by the wayfarers to this black pagoda of a fellow—the tribute of a pause and stare, and less frequent an exclamation—the motley retinue showed that they took that sort of pride in the evoker of it which the Assyrian priests doubtless showed for their grand sculptured Bull when the faithful prostrated themselves.

Both Billy Budd and Bom Crioulo were foretopmen, a job high in the rigging that required courage and skill. Melville's *Billy Budd* was published posthumously, so it is doubtful that Caminha read it, but he might have been familiar with Melville's novels with similar themes such as *White Jacket* or *Moby-Dick*.

SUGGESTED READINGS

The only Adolfo Caminha novel available in translation is *Bom Crioulo: The Black Man and the Cabin Boy*, trans. E. A. Lacey (San Francisco: Gay Sunshine Press, 1982). A recent assessment of *Bom Crioulo* that focuses on literary criticism is Robert Howes, "Race and Transgressive Sexuality in Adolfo Caminha's *Bom Crioulo*," *Luso-Brazilian Review* 38:1 (Summer 2001): 41–62. See also Sânzio de Azevedo, *Adolfo Caminha (vida e obra)* (Fortaleza: Universidade Federal de Ceará Edições, 1997). For a more focused analysis of *Bom Crioulo* in the context of military impressment, see Peter M. Beattie, "Conflicting Penile Codes: Modern Masculinity and Sodomy in the Brazilian Military, 1860–1916," 65–85, in *Sex and Sexuality in Latin America*, ed. Donna Guy and Daniel Bouldersten (New York: New York University Press, 1997). On the life of enlisted military men, see Peter M. Beattie, *The Tribute of Blood: Army, Honor, Race, and Nation in Brazil, 1864–1945* (Durham: Duke University Press, 2001). On slaves and military service, see Hendrik Kraay, "The Shelter of the Uniform: The Brazilian Army and Runaway Slaves, 1800–1888," *Journal of Social History* 29:3 (1997): 637–57. On "whitening" theory, see Thomas E. Skidmore, *Black into White: Race and Nationality in Brazilian Thought* (Durham: Duke University Press, 1993). On same-sex romance and community, see James N. Green, *Beyond Carnaval: Male Homosexuality in Twentieth-Century Brazil* (Chicago: University of Chicago Press, 1999). On black and brown political sympathies, see Eduardo Silva, *Prince of the People: The Life and Times of a Brazilian Free Man of Colour*, trans. Moyra Ashford (London: Verso, 1993). On police and *capoeiras*, see Thomas H. Holloway, " 'A Healthy Terror': Police Repression of *Capoeiras* in Nineteenth-Century Rio de Janeiro," *Hispanic American Historical Review* 69:4 (1987): 733–56; and Carlos Eugênio Líbano Soares, *A negregada instituição: os capoeiras do Rio de Janeiro* (Rio de Janeiro: Biblioteca Carioca, 1994). On military impressment and its links to abolitionism in the British and U.S. context, see Peter Linebaugh and Marcus Rediker, *The Many-Headed Hydra: Sailors, Slaves, Commoners, and the Hidden History of the Revolutionary Atlantic* (Boston: Beacon Press, 2000). Caminha's literary criticism and editorials cited in the text can be found in *Cartas literárias* (Fortaleza: Universidade Federal de Ceará Edições, 1999).

CHAPTER 6

Cândido Mariano da Silva Rondon

One Man's Search for the Brazilian Nation

Todd A. Diacon

Up to this point the biographies in this volume have revealed much about the lives and perceptions of Brazilians of African and European descent, but what about the indigenous population? These numerous ethnic and linguistic groups have held perhaps the most ambivalent of positions in the imaginations and policies of Brazil's political and economic leaders. In the mid-1800s an Indian craze swept members of the elite, some of whom went so far as to adopt indigenous names and proudly declare descent from indigenous forebears. A consequent Indianist literary boom brought forth some of Brazil's most treasured early national novels. Conservative senator José de Alencar's O Guarany *inspired an operatic adaptation by the Brazilian composer Carlos Gomes—one of the best-known Latin American operas performed across Europe at the time and more recently in New York by Placido Domingo. The Tupi-Guarani warrior symbolized for cartoonists the Brazilian nation in the 1800s much as Uncle Sam personified the United States.*

The most radical Indianists proposed that the indigenous lingua franca, Tupi-Guarani, replace Portuguese as the official national language because it was "truly Brazilian." This linguistic appeal would remain an element of ultranationalist rhetoric for decades. In the twentieth century, modernist poet Oswald de Andrade borrowed from Shakespeare's Hamlet *to parody this nationalist fetish: "Tupi, or not Tupi." In part, this Indianist craze was a way for Brazilians in the mid-1800s to assert their nationalism by distancing themselves from their former colonial overlords, the Portuguese. Who could be more "Brazilian" than the original inhabitants? Or so elites in coastal urban centers reasoned. But independent indigenous peoples did not call themselves Brazilians.*

Even while nationalist intellectuals celebrated their romantic visions of Indians to create myths of Brazil's origin and identity, the decimation of indigenous peoples continued. An estimated pre-Contact population of some five million indigenes had been reduced to 100,000 by 1900. Most of the violence against Indians in Brazil was not carried out by the armed forces, but by frontier settlers who sought to despoil Indians of lands they claimed were rightfully theirs as citizens. The romantic Indianist craze died down during the Paraguayan War (1864–1870) when Brazilian soldiers fought

Paraguayan troops who were mostly of mixed indigenous and European descent (even though some Indians fought alongside the Brazilian army as allies). Brazilian propaganda often demonized the enemy as a band of Indian savages, whereas the Paraguayans counterattacked by portraying the Brazilians as barbaric Africans. After the war, some Brazilians with republican sympathies criticized the use of an Indian warrior to represent the nation and civilization. When republican leaders came to power in the 1890s, some predicted the inevitable elimination of the indigenous population, but there was no complete consensus on government policy toward the Indian peoples. Even so, Brazilian nationalist rhetoric continually returns to Indianist rhetoric and imagery even though its popularity waxed and waned over time. Despite this special position in nationalist mythology, Brazil's Indians are subject to humiliating abuses and violence to this day.

In this chapter, Associate Professor Todd Diacon relates the life story of Cândido Mariano da Silva Rondon, who grew up in late-1800s Mato Grosso, a vast western frontier province where many Indian peoples still lived in close proximity to "white" settlements, towns, and ranches. Rondon had both European and Terena Indian blood, as did many hinterland inhabitants. He gained entrance to the Military Academy in Rio, one of the few opportunities available to young men of relatively modest means for higher education, where he became influenced by the creeds of positivism and republicanism. As an army engineer, he was in charge of integrating communications on the isolated western frontier by stringing telegraph lines across Brazil's inhospitable interior. Due to his background, experience, and education, he sought to use the power of the federal government to protect Indians from the abuses of settlers and missionaries. Rondon is most famous for his efforts to protect the interests of Indians, but, as Professor Diacon shows, there is much disagreement about the legacy of these efforts.

Todd Diacon earned his Ph.D. in Latin American history at the University of Wisconsin, Madison. He recently finished a book-length manuscript entitled "Stringing Together a Nation: Cândido Mariano da Silva Rondon and the Construction of a Modern Brazil, 1889–1930," forthcoming from Duke University Press. Professor Diacon is currently head of the History Department at the University of Tennessee, Knoxville.

Cândido Mariano da Silva Rondon found himself in a familiar spot in late 1913. At that moment he was hundreds of miles from the nearest town of any size—indeed, hundreds of miles from the nearest road. Such isolation was nothing new for him; for more than twenty years he had been directing the construction of telegraph lines through the most isolated regions of his native Brazil. For more than twenty years, to be more exact, he had been directing telegraph construction in his native state of Mato Grosso.

Mato Grosso in 1913 was an enormous state (it has since been divided into two). It comprised 15 percent of Brazil's total land mass and was larger than any South American country except for Argentina. Rondon knew the state well, from its gentle, rolling pastures in the south to its vast swamp, the Pantanal, in the west. Now, however, he was surrounded not by grass, nor by swamps, but by a thick, seemingly impenetrable jungle. Working in northwest Mato Grosso, he was in the sixth year of his tireless effort to string a telegraph line across the Amazon Basin.

Rondon was not alone. An army officer with a degree in engineering, he commanded some 400 soldiers as they fought diseases (especially malaria), construction injuries, and insects and wild animals of every description. In a land crossed by rivers of crystal clear waters, men refused to bathe for fear of piranhas. In a land full of wild game, men preferred to go hungry for fear of getting lost in the dense forest and for fear of surprise attacks by the always threatening, but seldom seen, Nambikwara indigenous people.

Late in October 1913, Rondon stood in the middle of the forest directing survey and line placement efforts when a winded soldier arrived with an urgent telegram. It had taken some twenty-four hours to deliver it from the nearest telegraph station on the line Rondon was constructing. The foreign minister ordered Rondon's immediate return to Rio de Janeiro, Brazil's capital. The reason? Former U.S. president Theodore Roosevelt wished to explore the Brazilian Amazon, and Rondon, who knew the place better than anyone, would be his guide. He was needed in Rio to plan the expedition and to brief the foreign minister on what Roosevelt could expect in the Amazon. Ultimately, Rondon, Roosevelt, and a handful of men would descend the so-called River of Doubt, which Rondon renamed the Roosevelt River. For fifty-nine days they would shoot rapids and map the course of the river, while Roosevelt would battle a leg infection and high fevers that nearly killed him.

Rondon was honored and excited to be given such a mission. At the same time, however, the proposed expedition would delay telegraph construction. And, as he noted that night in his diary, to travel from northwest Mato Grosso to Rio de Janeiro would be no easy task, and it certainly would not be a quick trip. For over a week, Rondon rode his horse northwest along the 30-foot-wide path his men had cleared through the jungle to the Jiparaná River. He boarded a heavy, dugout canoe for the difficult passage on the Jiparaná, which included shooting numerous rapids and many laborious portages. Once on the Madeira River he took a steamer to the growing city of Manaus, on the mighty Amazon River, another steamer to Belém, on the Atlantic coast, and then sailed to Rio de Janeiro. Five weeks after receiving the telegram in the jungle, Cândido Mariano da Silva Rondon finally stepped foot in the capital.

In the early 1900s there was no easy route between Rio de Janeiro and Mato Grosso. Rondon chose to travel on the Amazon to return to the capital. Many times he chose the other route, which meant boarding an ocean liner in Rio de Janeiro and sailing south to Buenos Aires, Argentina. There he boarded a smaller vessel for the long ride up the Paraguai River and into Mato Grosso. In other words, to go from one Brazilian state to another required passing through three foreign countries: Uruguay, Argentina, and Paraguay.

It is no coincidence that Brazil's government sent Rondon to construct telegraph lines in one of the most isolated regions in the country. The area was a national security nightmare. In 1865, Paraguayan troops had invaded southern Mato Grosso and occupied a wide stretch of territory. Incredibly, the lack of roads and modern communications meant that leaders back in Rio de Janeiro heard of this invasion nearly six weeks after the fact! Twenty-four years later, in November 1889, soldiers in Rio de Janeiro overthrew their emperor, Dom Pedro II, and instituted a republican government. Residents of Cuiabá, the capital of Mato Grosso, however, celebrated Christmas that year by toasting the emperor and the monarchy. Why? Because news of the overthrow still had not reached Mato Grosso's state capital more than a month after the demise of the Empire and the creation of the Republic.

The telegraph, a relatively new technology, promised to end Mato Grosso's isolation. A metal wire would sew together a vast country. A metal wire, with its "electric hum of progress," promised to connect Brazilians in growing cities such as Rio de Janeiro and São Paulo with the nation's enormous hinterland. Technology promised to bring the Brazilian state—that is, the national government—to the far-off countryside. Urban beliefs and practices, which city dwellers considered to be "Brazilian" life ways, now would be introduced to a people who lived in Brazil but were considered foreigners by the citizens living along the Atlantic coast.

Because he commanded the telegraph construction campaigns in Mato Grosso, Cândido Mariano da Silva Rondon serves as a perfect example of the attempts to create a unified Brazilian country and nation. Rondon, it should be noted, did not spring from the powerful landowning families or commercial leaders. Instead, he hailed from a small town in Mato Grosso and was orphaned at an early age. Raised by a humble but not impoverished uncle, Rondon embarked on a career in the army.

Service in the military was one of the only paths to a higher education available to most Brazilians in the nineteenth century. As one of only two truly national institutions in Brazil at the time (the other was the Catholic Church), the military shaped Rondon's life. It led him to consider Brazil's future not only as a country of urban dandies or country bumpkins but also as a unified nation with a promising future.

Rondon formed part of a generation of Brazilian reformers in the late nineteenth and early twentieth centuries. Members of his generation abolished slavery (1888) and established the Republic. The reformist impulse in part drew from changes unleashed by Brazil's growing trade in agricultural products with Europe and the United States, which was encouraged by advances in technology (such as steel-hulled ships that could transport more cargo) and in finance (limited-liability corporations and investment banks). With Brazilian commodities such as coffee now affordable for even the working poor in Europe, agricultural production and export skyrocketed. This expansion of production then drew once-isolated lands into the nation's, and the world's, economic orbit.

The impetus for reform also came from within. The war with Paraguay (1865–1870) demonstrated Brazil's problems. The country suffered from the near absence of a transportation infrastructure. At times it was difficult, or even impossible, to move troops to the theater of war in remote Mato Grosso. In light of these difficulties, Brazilian intellectuals and political leaders questioned the foundations of their nation. Did the country's ills spring from a lack of civic pride and national spirit? What did leaders need to do to produce a strong, unified nation of citizens who thought of themselves as belonging together?

Conditioned by historic ties of colonial rule and by new market ties, leading Brazilian intellectuals looked to northern Europe for ideas on how to build a supposedly modern nation. Rondon gained his first exposure to European notions of nation and nationhood as a cadet in the Military Academy in Rio. In particular, his mathematics professor, Benjamin Constant Botelho de Magalhães, introduced him to a curious ideology from France. That philosophy, which later became a religion, was Positivism.

On a quiet side street near the center of Rio de Janeiro stands the Positivist Temple of Humanity. In front of the building the flags of Brazil and France float in the breeze, the latter in honor of the nationality of Positivism's founder, Auguste Comte. Inside, the visitor quickly notices the garish statues ringing the sanctuary. Bright red lips and tongues, coal black eyes, and gray heads and beards of historical figures such as Descartes, Shakespeare, and Julius Caesar stand silently. These are the heroes of Humanity, the beings believed most responsible for the progress of civilization and mankind. There is not a Brazilian face among them.

Auguste Comte developed Positivism in the decades following the fervor and unrest of the French Revolution. He believed in the need to improve the lives of the poor in order to prevent future unrest, rebellion, and revolutions, but he also believed that such reform should be implemented in a tightly controlled, top-down fashion. To explain such an elite-led project of controlled reform, Comte identified what he considered to be the "natural laws of the universe." Only a very small, educated elite, he argued, could understand these laws and then implement them for the good of all.

Having identified these natural laws, Comte divided the history of humanity into three stages of social evolution. In the "Theological Stage," humans could explain their world only through the mediation of spirits. In the "Metaphysical Stage," humans began to seek answers through observation and rational thought. Such scientific searching prepared Humanity (Positivists always capitalized the word) for the third and final stage of social evolution, the "Positivist Stage." A few, enlightened Positivist "priests" would guide society as determined by the natural laws that they alone truly understood. The result would be happiness, solidarity, proper behavior, and the end of world conflicts. The result, in Positivist parlance, would be the triumph of Humanity.

Positivism developed a dedicated following in Brazil. It appealed to reformers such as Rondon, who believed in the need for change but who also feared class conflict and social unrest. It appealed especially to military men such as Rondon, who sought to modernize Brazil in the wake of the Paraguayan War but hoped to do so in an orderly and controlled fashion that would ensure the power of rulers over the poor. Because of Positivism's emphasis on rational thought and scientific investigation (so as to explore and demonstrate natural laws), it appealed also to those members of the middle class schooled in the sciences and engineering. Indeed, nearly 80 percent of the early Brazilian Positivists were army officers, physicians, engineers, and professors.

Positivists supported the overthrow of the monarchy in 1889 as a necessary step toward the social evolution of the country. They shaped legislation separating Church and state during the early years of the Republic. They also designed the national flag, which includes the Positivist motto "Order and Progress." Indeed, that motto tell us much of what we need to know about the philosophy and its supporters in Brazil: reform (progress) was the goal, but it had to take place in a controlled fashion (order).

Support for Positivism entered into a long decline shortly after the declaration of the Republic. In part this decline was due to the fact that for many intellectuals, it was merely one of several fads from Europe. The strict moral code that Brazilian Positivist leaders implemented further alienated potential followers. Sunday morning services at the Positivist Temple of Humanity lasted, for example, for three or four hours. In addition, Positivist leaders prohibited followers from exercising a wide range of professions. Nevertheless, Rondon remained a passionate adherent for his entire life. Indeed, as we shall see, it shaped his vision of the Brazilian nation, and it gave him the strength to survive the difficulties of telegraph construction in the jungle.

Given the popularity of Positivism among Brazilian army officers, it is ironic to note that Positivists opposed militaries and militarism. Science and technology, followers argued, would bring peace and prosperity to mankind and eliminate the need for armies and wars. Armed conflicts, Positivists claimed, were relics of previous stages of social evolution and would disappear when Humanity reached the Positivist stage of progress. Positivists, including Rondon (who eventually attained the highest rank of marshal in the army) and Benjamin Constant (the long-time professor in the Military Academy and later the minister of education), believed that the armed forces should be reorganized into a simple police force. In the future, they predicted, armies would become national development brigades led by military engineers.

Rondon's career of building telegraph lines in the interior is an especially appropriate example of the Positivist plan for the nation. It promised to integrate the Brazilian west through infrastructure development. It would connect peoples in the interior with enlightened Positivists on the coast, and this link would then speed the social evolution of all Brazilians. With its botanical and geological explorations and surveys, Rondon's commission would study nature to serve Humanity.

Rondon's Positivism, and his belief in the need to create a single, homogeneous Brazilian population in order to create a strong nation, help to explain some of the more curious aspects of life on the telegraph line. No matter how hard his troops had labored that day, or no matter how many miles they had marched, Rondon always ordered a tree felled and a flagpole fashioned so that the Brazilian national flag could be raised. It did not matter if he was leading a small squadron that had spent the day hacking its way through the jungle. It did not matter if they established camp in the dark of night, which made felling a tree that much more difficult. It did not matter if he was with 300 or 400 men in a more permanent camp. The Brazilian flag always fluttered above the tents of the Rondon Commission.

This rite was Rondon's method of asserting the presence of the Brazilian nation as well as the unity of the country. This is why he wrapped Indians in the Brazilian flag when taking their pictures, in what became a kind of routine after the establishment of peaceful relations with indigenous peoples. Literally, he wrapped these people in the flag of the nation as a symbol of their incorporation into that nation. Moreover, we should not forget that this same Brazilian flag was also the Positivists' flag, and their motto always dominated staged photographs.

Positivism and the Brazilian nation were one and the same for Rondon. As a way of asserting a new federal presence in the interior, Rondon exchanged local, indigenous place names for those of Brazilian statesmen and heroes. Many of these were associated with Positivism. For example, Rondon renamed one river the "Festival of the Flag" (Festa da Bandeira) in honor of the Brazilian/Positivist flag. He renamed another river in honor of one of the heroes of the declaration of the Republic, Benjamin Constant. Slowly, as Rondon and his men surveyed and mapped the lands of the northwest, indigenous places that no one in Rio de Janeiro would recognize now gained familiar names on government maps. A new, unified concept of the nation was emerging, led by leaders from Rio de Janeiro. No one paid much attention to what peoples indigenous to that region thought of this assertion of nationhood.

This need to impose a particular image of the nation on the interior led to what today we might consider to be rather comical activities and rituals. Rondon carried a gramophone with him, on which he played the national anthem as well as other Brazilian songs in camp at night. He did so in part for his soldiers. But he did so as well for any indigenous peoples who might be within earshot. Likewise, Rondon traveled with an early version of a slide projector, known as a "magic lantern" (with bulky glass plates as slides). At night he would use the forest canopy as a screen to show pictures of the president of Brazil and other national leaders. Camp thus became, for soldiers and anyone else who might be watching, an ongoing civics lesson.

If you were to ask a Brazilian today about Cândido Mariano da Silva Rondon, he or she would likely respond with the phrase: "to die if necessary, but to kill . . . never!" This oft-repeated phrase of Rondon's referred to his activities in regard to Indians. In fact, Rondon is much more famous for his policies toward Indians than for his telegraph construction campaigns. He is remembered chiefly as the founder and first director of the Indian Protection Service (SPI). Established in 1910, this federal agency has directed Indian-white relations in Brazil until this day.

Rondon used the SPI and his telegraph campaigns to implement the Positivist blueprint for Indian-white relations. In a nutshell, Positivists argued that Indians lived in the first, or Theocratic Stage, of social evolution. The proper course, therefore, was to establish peaceful relations and then to encourage the evolution of Indians into the Positivist Stage of development. First and foremost, this Positivist analysis meant that Indians should be protected—from invasions and attacks on them by whites. Indeed, a Positivist leader argued in the early 1900s that indigenous groups should be recognized as sovereign nations. Doing so would allow for their slow, inexorable acculturation into "Brazilians."

Positivists believed that revolutionary change was impossible. The highest form of social evolution (Positivism) had to be reached without force or coercion. It had to be reached, in other words, via an evolutionary process, for if force was used, how could one tell if change had really occurred? The forced incorporation of Indians into the Brazilian nation would, Rondon and other Positivists argued, merely create an illusion of change.

Positivists, in conclusion, believed that Indians were not racially inferior but were living in an earlier stage than whites of social evolution. As such, they were to be protected and taught by example. Eventually, with the proper training, they would become "Westerners" or, more specifically, "Brazilians." Positivists maintained that Indians should be allowed to continue speaking in their own languages (this policy differed starkly from that of the United States toward Indians of the day). They believed that Indians should be allowed to follow their existing customs. And Positivists especially opposed Christian missionary efforts vis-à-vis Indians, for forced conversions violated, they felt, the laws of nature and society.

Cândido Mariano da Silva Rondon actively implemented his Positivist plan for Indian-white relations as the director of the SPI. He lectured to dignitaries about the need to protect Indian landholdings. He ordered his SPI personnel to fan out across the country to survey and protect Indian lands. While directing telegraph construction in Mato Grosso he denounced cases of violence, invasion, and destruction of Indians and their properties. All the while, he and the SPI employees built posts to "attract" indigenous peoples, in what became known as Rondon's "pacification" strategy. This strategy involved placing gifts of machetes, cloth, beads, and other items along the trails used by the Indians. By demonstrating their peaceful intentions (hence his motto, "to die if necessary, but to kill . . . never!") and by leaving the gifts, SPI workers then made peaceful contacts with indigenous peoples. The goal was to convince these people to adopt Western dress, habits, and tools—that is, to acculturate them and turn them into Brazilians.

It is interesting to note that virtually every attempt by Rondon and his men to protect Indian holdings and peoples failed. In Mato Grosso, Rondon protested attacks against Indians and the theft of their lands. He visited the governor of the state and other officials to demand an end to white violence against Indians. He called for armed expeditions not to punish Indians, but to punish their white attackers. But in case after case the attacks continued, and Rondon and his officers were reduced to publishing appeals in newspapers, for public opinion was their only source of support. Landowners and leaders in Mato Grosso held far more power than did Rondon, his telegraph commission, and the SPI.

These failed attempts at protection demonstrate a useful lesson about the nature of Brazil in the early twentieth century. The national government seated in Rio de Janeiro exercised little authority over most of the country's lands and people. In other words, the central state wielded little influence over powerful landowners and their political supporters. In Rondon's case, his inability to intervene successfully is not surprising. Operating in a state (Mato Grosso) the size of Alaska, he never commanded more than 350 to 600 men in the region at any one time. Furthermore, his soldiers were split into units and subunits and distributed across thousands of square miles of territory. At a time when reformers such as Rondon and the Positivists sought to create a unified Brazil peopled by a homogeneous population, central government representatives seemingly could not arrest even a single individual as long as that person enjoyed the protection of local potentates.

Many of Rondon's contemporaries believed that his policies were far too respectful of indigenous practices. For many Brazilian scholars today, his policies accomplished far too little. Such differences of opinion remind us of another valuable lesson when studying Rondon and, indeed, Brazilian history in general: the need for historical context. Was Rondon a saint, a tireless and selfless individual who struggled to save Indians, as his supporters argued at the time? Or, as many scholars argue today, was he little different from the slave drivers of the colonial era and thus bent on the eventual elimination of indigenous peoples in Brazil?

In the early 1900s prominent landowners in Mato Grosso resented what they saw as Rondon's meddling in their internal affairs. They denounced his Indian policy as being far too tolerant. They complained that his policy of respecting indigenous practices prevented the transformation of Indians into "good citizens." Furthermore, they attacked Rondon in racist terms, for he was himself the descendant of a Terena Indian, and he was proud of his ancestry. Rondon's problem, his landowner opponents asserted, was that he was an uncivilized half-breed and was thus incapable of "improving" other Indians.

These racist attacks help us to situate Rondon and his policies as they developed in the early twentieth century. Rondon and the Positivists rejected race as a variable crucial to explaining the differences between populations. Instead, as good followers of Comte they emphasized sociological, and not racial, differences between groups and argued that all of the world's population was composed of the same biological (racial) material. In contrast, other powerful Brazilians adopted another European intellectual trend to explain the nation's ills: "scientific racism." For them, Brazilian Indians were a subrace. Their inferiority was racial, and they were destined to disappear. Indeed, that disappearance was the goal of these intellectuals. For Brazil to become a modern nation (and modern meant more European and white), they argued, Indians would have to give way to whites. Civilization, they maintained, did not include Indians, and thus they were doomed to extinction.

An extended confrontation in 1909 highlighted these different understandings of, and approaches to, Indian-white relations in Brazil. Herman von Ihering, the director of the Museu Paulista (a museum in the state of São Paulo), wrote a series of guest editorials in Brazilian newspapers on the subject. Indians were incapable of learning in the Western sense, he argued, and thus could not be assimilated into the larger population. Because of their inferiority they would disappear, no matter what Rondon and his associates did to help them. Von Ihering argued that the future of Brazil rested with the waves of European immigrants then entering the country. These immigrants, and not the Indians, merited support and protection.

In light of the above, we see that Rondon's policies were far more respectful of indigenous rights and life ways than the policies proposed by others at the time. While key intellectuals engaged in a racist discourse on the future of Brazil, Rondon argued for basic indigenous rights. While prominent Brazilians called for the extermination of Indians, Rondon cried out for the protection of indigenous landholdings and opposed attempts at forced conversions to Christianity. In comparison with the governments of the United States, Canada, and Australia, which all made the separation of *indigene* children from their families a centerpiece of official Indian policy, Rondon ordered his men to respect native languages, practices, and familial integrity.

Yet the current critics of Rondon's legacy make many legitimate points, and herein rests the final lesson to be drawn from the study of his life: people can act in contradictory ways, and their policies may contain many intended and unintended consequences. As such, it becomes difficult, if not impossible, to answer with a simple "yes" or "no" the question of whether Rondon's policies were "good" or "bad" for indigenous peoples in Brazil. They were both, it seems fair to say. By contrast, most current critics would say that they were uniformly harmful.

Two principal arguments emerge from recent Brazilian examinations of the life and times of Cândido Mariano da Silva Rondon. The first is that the SPI and Rondon engaged primarily in expanding the power and reach of the central government. That is, their expressed interest in aiding *indigenes* primarily was the rationale for expanding the authority of a particular bureaucracy. Studying Indians, and asserting their rights in regard to landowners, was really more about establishing federal power over local landowners than it was about helping indigenous peoples. In other words, the goal of state actions was not really the support and protection of Indians but the expansion of federal authority in the hinterlands. In addition, current scholars argue that the Brazilian government exercised a kind of ultimate power: it reduced what were once myriad nations of peoples with different languages, beliefs, and practices into a single, generic "Indian" category. In the name of "protection," critics argue, people such as Rondon created "Indians" out of groups that always identified themselves as Nambikwara, Terena, or Bororo.

Indeed, critics call this a conquest of sorts. By redefining separate nations of indigenous peoples as generic "Indians" and then by trying to turn them into "Brazilians," Rondon and others were little different from the settlers who attacked and raided indigenous communities. And, they say, even if we grant that Rondon was truly trying to help and protect Indians, he did so in a paternalistic manner that robbed them of their right to define their own futures. This condescension can be seen best, critics note, in the 1916 Civil Code. In the name of protecting Indians from wily speculators out to rob them of their lands, the Civil Code declared Indians to be "relatively incapable" for legal purposes. Indians could not (and still cannot) purchase, sell, or transfer their lands without the federal government's approval. They became minors, in effect, with the government as their tutor.

This system, known as *tutela* in Brazil, meant that individuals such as Rondon decided the future of indigenous peoples without necessarily taking into account the wishes of those peoples. And Rondon and government officials concluded that what was best for Indians was for them to become, over time, more like whites. Or, to use a phrase Rondon would be familiar with, to become "Brazilians." There was seemingly no attempt to judge what Indians wanted. There was, instead, a solution, a specific end point, and it was decided by non-Indians.

A brief biography is not the place to debate these varied opinions on the legacy of Cândido Mariano da Silva Rondon. It is appropriate, however, to remember the historical context within which he operated. If today we find his programs problematic, it is certainly fair to explain why. However, this should not lead us to forget what others said and proposed about Indians in Brazil at the turn of the twentieth century. In contrast to those who sought extermination, Rondon sought protection. Such protection was, admittedly, paternalistic, but was it not preferable to death and destruction? Or, to adopt the tone of current critics, was it only a different form of death and destruction?

Late in his life, Cândido Mariano da Silva Rondon granted an interview to a Brazilian journalist in which he reviewed his ninety years of life and his seventy years of policy making. He defended his work but wondered aloud if it might not have been better simply to have left indigenous peoples alone. As much as he had tried to protect and to serve these peoples, ongoing clashes between Indians and whites had caused the aged Rondon to question his pacification policy. His attempts to turn Indians into Brazilians had not, it seemed, contributed to their happiness and prosperity, although these had been his goals throughout his life. Had he done the right thing by seeking out Indians who had not yet been contacted by whites? Or did his own attraction and assimilation policies simply begin the march toward suffering and death?

The offices of FUNAI, the government Indian agency that replaced the SPI, are located in Brasília, which is now the national capital. In the neighborhood that surrounds its offices, many houses have been converted into extended-stay hostels for visiting Indians who are either working for FUNAI or who have traveled to Brasília in search of a solution to a particular problem. On a typical day indigenous children play in the streets and alleys of the neighborhood, while their mothers wash clothes and their fathers conduct business with the government's Indian agency.

Galdino Jesus dos Santos, a 44-year-old Pataxó Indian, was in Brasília in 1997 to demand federal guarantees for tribal lands. Late at night on April 19, the "Day of the Indian" holiday in Brazil, dos Santos made his way back to his hostel after his business at the FUNAI offices ended. At such a late hour the doors were locked, and his attempts to wake residents failed. At a nearby square, dos Santos approached a concrete bus stop, of the kind ubiquitous in Brasília, with its cement pillars and flat roof. A bench there seemed like the best place to await the sunrise, and he settled down for some welcomed sleep.

At some point an automobile full of five teenagers noticed the sleeping figure at the bus stop. These kids all belonged to wealthy families, and one of them was the son of a judge. Seeking a few thrills, they circled their car back around the square and stopped. One of the boys—it is not clear which one—grabbed a can of gasoline from the trunk. Just for fun, as they put it later, they doused the sleeping figure with the gasoline and struck a match. At that moment, a simple concrete bus stop became a funeral pyre. At that moment, in a small square in a residential neighborhood in Brasília, the nation's capital, Galdino Jesus dos Santos perished. Later, the boys explained that they would not have harmed dos Santos if they had known he was an Indian. Instead, they thought he was "merely" a homeless person.

After weeks of intense media coverage and indignant protests by Indians and non-Indians alike, the case reached a predictable conclusion. The defendants, benefiting from their family connections, managed to avoid murder charges when a judge reduced the case to simple assault and battery. A slap on the wrist was the only punishment for their heinous crime. In 1997 the power and influence of well-connected individuals continued to trample on the basic rights of other citizens.

In Brazil the genie is out of the bottle, and there is no going back. Would those indigenous people whom Rondon contacted have been better off if they had been left alone? Probably so. But would they have been contacted eventually? Absolutely. So, what are the best policies for Indian-white relations today? In light of the 1997 incident in Brasília, perhaps the answer rests not only with defending the rights of indigenous Brazilians but also with carving out rights for all citizens, regardless of their class, ethnicity, race, or gender. When all Brazilians can obtain justice, then all indigenous Brazilians will too.

SUGGESTED READINGS

There is surprisingly little written about Rondon in English. Basic starting points include Theodore Roosevelt, *Through the Brazilian Wilderness* (New York: Charles Scribner's Sons, 1916); Joseph R. Ornig, *My Last Chance to Be a Boy: Theodore Roosevelt's South American Expedition of 1913–1914* (Mechanicsburg, PA: Stackpole Books, 1994); Donald F. O'Reilly, "Rondon: Biography of a Brazilian Army Commander" (Ph.D. diss., New York University, 1969); and David Hall Stauffer, "The Origins and Establishment of Brazil's Indian Service, 1889–1910" (Ph.D. diss., University of Texas, 1955). The leading Brazilian critic of Rondon is Antonio Carlos de Souza Lima. In English see his article "On Indigenism and Nationality in Brazil," in Greg Urban and Joel Sherzer, eds., *Nation States and Indians in Latin America* (Austin: University of Texas Press, 1991), 237–57. In Portuguese see his important book *Um grande cerco de paz: Poder tutelar, indianidade e formação do Estado no Brasil* (Petropolis: Vozes, 1995). Another starting point in Portuguese is Esther de Viveiros, *Rondon: conta a sua vida* (Rio de Janeiro: Livraria São José, 1958).

PART III

THE POPULIST-ERA GENERATIONS (1930–1959)

Elections during the Old Republic had largely been engineered in smoky back rooms where political bosses from state-based Republican parties came together to select a presidential candidate who usually won 80 or 90 percent of the vote. In 1929, however, a dispute between state delegations led to a rare contested presidential electoral campaign. The powerful leaders of São Paulo and their cronies backed the candidacy of one of its native sons, but a number of other states supported the election of a politician named Getúlio Vargas from Brazil's southernmost state, Rio Grande do Sul. Vargas lost the election to the connivings of the Old Republic's dominant political machine, but he was not prepared to give up his bid for the presidency so easily. He plotted with his civilian political allies as well as with army officers and even participants in the Tenente Revolts of the 1920s who lived in exile. In 1930 he led a military coup that quickly fought its way into power. The façade of the Old Republic was more rickety than many had suspected.

The year 1930 was an ominous one for a head of state to come to power anywhere in the world. The Great Depression was ravaging world economies, and it hit Brazil's agro-export economy especially hard. The price of coffee on the international market plummeted, and this fall generated widespread financial panic and unemployment. Politically, Brazilians remained divided. Some continued to have faith in the model of liberal democracy and free enterprise as practiced in the United States or Great Britain, while others looked to the state-directed economy of the Soviet Union as an alternative route to development with social justice. Others found the corporatist fascism of Benito Mussolini's Italy a more appealing model in part because it seemed a conservative compromise between capitalism and communism. Throughout much of the decade, Brazilians who backed these very different visions for the nation's future vied for power and influence, and groups within each faction attempted to overthrow Vargas's government through force of arms. Vargas maintained a delicate balancing act between contending political factions by playing them off against each other and by reaching out via state programs and radio to the formerly politically untouchable class of Brazil's urban workers. He was indirectly elected president in 1934, but in 1937 he ousted all political parties and began to rule as a dictator again under what he dubbed the Estado Novo, or New State (1937–1945). Vargas claimed that authoritarian rule was necessary to prevent the political extremism that threatened to undermine Brazil's stability, unity, and sovereignty.

Unfettered by legislative debate, Vargas decreed a corporativist state that structured many aspects of society—from trade unions to sports leagues, tourism, museums, historic preservation, education, Indian policy, and even Rio's Afro-Brazilian Carnival parades. His reforms focused on Brazil's growing urban centers, but they also had an impact on rural areas. Vargas tried to co-opt those who opposed him, but if that failed, he was not above jailing or exiling political opponents. He used censorship and state patronage to shape public perceptions in the media and popular culture, but his government was never as powerful or repressive as the totalitarian states of Europe. Vargas portrayed himself as a benevolent dictator, and he adopted the epithet "Father of the Poor." While many Brazilians despised Vargas and his regime, he was a popular dictator during most of the Estado Novo.

As a leader, Vargas had two overarching goals: to strengthen the power of the central government, and to use state intervention to create market conditions that would allow Brazil's economy to diversify through industrialization. Vargas railed against the faith that leaders of the Old Republic had held in the economic philosophy of comparative advantage and free trade, and he derisively referred to the agro-export economy as one of "desserts": coffee, sugar, cocoa, and fruits. He advocated tariffs, tax breaks, and state ownership of key resources and industries to lay a foundation that would allow both Brazilian and foreign capitalists to participate in industrial development. Foreign policy would advance this strategy, which later came to be known as import-substitution industrialization. When the United States declared war on Japan, Germany, and Italy in 1941, its diplomats began to court Vargas's support for the Allied cause. Vargas knew that the Roosevelt administration needed Brazilian territory for air bases in order to conduct its campaign against Axis forces in North Africa. In return for joining the Allies, Vargas secured guarantees that the United States would help to build a modern state-owned steel factory, Volta Redonda, in Rio de Janeiro. Brazil, the only Latin American nation to mobilize land forces to support the Allies, sent an expeditionary force of 25,000 men that fought alongside the U.S. army in Italy. While his policies helped Brazil to industrialize and to assert itself on the global stage, Vargas had joined an alliance that claimed to be fighting to defend democracy. Toward the war's end he anticipated what seemed to be an inevitable return to democracy, and he began to organize not one but two political parties. Before he could marshal his new political organizations, however, Vargas was forced out of office in 1945.

During the new era of populist democracy from 1945 to 1964, Vargas had given women the right to vote (in 1932, only twelve years after women in the United States gained this right). While there was still a literacy requirement, Vargas had overseen a vast expansion of public education that qualified more Brazilians to vote, especially in urban areas. The U.S. government applauded Brazil's return to democracy, but by the late 1940s it largely ignored its giant ally to the South as it focused attention on the Cold War in Europe and Asia. In Brazil, in an era of pork barrel politics, conservative, moderate, and leftist politicians vied for the votes of the newly enfranchised urban poor by promising state patronage in return for political support. It was an age rife with political corruption, but for a change, humble Brazilians had a better shot at enjoying some of the benefits of venality. In this new political environment, a famous Conservative politician in the industrial city of São Paulo, Adhemar de Barros, won over working-class voters by promising public sector jobs, public works, and other favors. His unofficial campaign slogan was "He steals, but he gets things done." Barros kept his name in the newspaper headlines, and he gleefully acknowledged that "they speak badly of me, but they are speaking about me." Knavish as some populist politicians were, they now had to pay attention to the needs and desires of the working class at least occasionally to remain in power.

Proving his talent as a vote-getter, Vargas re-entered the political fray and eventually won election as Brazil's president in 1950. He succeeded in fulfilling his campaign promise to nationalize the petroleum industry, but inflation and government debt began to eat away at his popularity. Offended by the unrelenting and stinging criticism of Carlos Lacerda, a Conservative journalist and politician, the president's brother, Benjamin, organized a botched assassination attempt against the newspaper and radio pundit that was soon traced to the presidential palace. Vargas's opponents savored the implications of the crisis for their political fortunes, but Vargas, rather than face political humiliation, committed suicide. He left behind a note accusing vague international and national forces of conspiring against his government and his commitment to the autonomy and prosperity of the common people. Most Brazilians reacted to the news with an outpouring of grief for the fallen leader who, more than any other figure, had shaped the contours of contemporary Brazilian society.

In 1955 a moderate Vargas protégé, Juscelino Kubitschek, was elected president by promising voters fifty years of economic development in one five-year presidential term. At this time, Brazilians exuded great optimism and confidence in their future as an industrialized nation and world power. Kubitschek continued the protectionist, state-led development policies that Vargas had championed, and he oversaw the construction of a bold new national capital, Brasília, in the country's central west region. The capital itself symbolized the heady exhilaration of the times. Laid out in the shape of a giant jet airplane, the most modern mode of transportation of the day, the city would pilot Brazil to a glorious futuristic destiny. Its design, landscaping, architecture, and monuments gave the visitor a glimpse of a tropical space-age city. To pay for Brasília's construction as well as industrial development projects, however, the government began to run up a steep debt with foreign banks. While Kubitschek asserted that import-substitution industrialization policies would make the national economy more autonomous, in reality Brazilian industry continued to depend on foreign technology, credit, investment, and markets. While Kubitschek's economic nationalism fed the expansion of the economy for most of his term, problems of inflation and slowing growth indicated difficult financial times ahead.

Brazil's populist era was characterized by a burst of artistic, literary, and scholarly creativity that reflected a certain self-conscious nationalism. During the World War II period, U.S. and European consumers became enamored with Brazilian samba music as popularized by Hollywood's highest-paid female actress, Carmen Miranda. In the late 1950s the hip, sophisticated bossa nova created another international musical sensation. In the realm of high culture, the original orchestral compositions of Heitor Villa-Lobos earned him renown, and the modernistic architectural designs of Oscar Niemeyer won international prizes.

The vogue for Afro-Brazilian and indigenous culture that began in the 1920s took off in the stormy years of the 1930s. Gilberto Freyre's *The Masters and the Slaves* (1933) praised the contributions that Africans had made to Brazil's culture and apologized for its history of slavery. Freyre gave intellectual credence to the myth of racial democracy that held that Brazil was unique among nations in that racism was not a significant part of its tradition. By expressing pride in Brazil's African heritage, Freyre challenged aspects of social Darwinism that had made Brazilians uncertain about their national destiny because of their history of race mixture. Vargas's administration welcomed the unifying myth of racial democracy as a national credo, but official pronouncements and practice did not always coincide. For instance, while Vargas promoted Afro-Brazilian Carnival parades as tourist attractions to showcase the nation's African heritage, he also chose the blond, blue-eyed sons of German immigrants for the presidential honor guard to prove to foreign dignitaries that Brazil was a "white" nation. And when Vargas's Estado Novo in 1937 closed down all political parties, he included the fledgling movements of Afro-Brazilians. It would be another generation before dynamic black political organizations reappeared on the national scene.

Somewhat like the myth of Horatio Alger in the United States, the concept of racial democracy helped Brazilians to imagine that they belonged to a leveled and homogenized national community that provided opportunities to all. Such imaginings, however illusory, allowed strong feelings of nationalism to flourish among Brazil's populace. These sentiments went hand-in-hand with populist political mobilization and the policies of economic nationalism of the period. The myth of racial democracy did not change the fact that most Brazilians of dark skin encountered real racial prejudice. A disproportionate number of black and brown Brazilians remained unemployed or in low-paying jobs that kept them in poverty, and few of African descent could be counted among the growing middle class. Only a miniscule number reached influential positions in politics, commerce, and the liberal professions. Still, any acceptance and recognition that racial democracy sanctioned, though often patronizing, must have been appreciated by many Brazilians of African descent, especially given the influence of social Darwinism on the thinking of intellectuals and leaders during the Old Republic.

❧

Samba composer Geraldo Pereira's life provides a glimpse of the opportunities and perils confronted by a young Afro-Brazilian migrant to the capital. Rather than choose a stable, if modest, career as a public employee, Pereira set his sights on fame and fortune in Rio's emerging music industry. His story illustrates the difficulty that many Brazilians of African descent faced in translating recognized talent into a profitable career. In a similar vein, mixed-race soccer player Domingos da Guia took advantage of his athletic talent to become a star and defended Brazil's national honor on soccer fields around the world. After his career ended, however, Domingos's life of celebrity faded quickly. He ended up as an obscure public functionary with a modest salary. While sports and music offered new opportunities to many Brazilians of African descent, the fruits of their labors were often ephemeral.

Norma Fraga's story reveals how a black woman became part of a small but prestigious educated elite. Her life as a student illustrates the varied struggles experienced by an emerging, if disproportionately small, black middle class in the 1930s. She recalls how she responded to the elaborate rallies orchestrated by the Vargas regime to inculcate patriotism, national unity, and pride in the "Brazilian race." Vicente Racioppi's biography reveals how the son of Italian immigrants became a successful lawyer and a fervent nationalist who dedicated much of his free time to the preservation of historic buildings and artifacts. His sentiments dovetailed well with those of the Vargas regime, and at least initially he won recognition and support for his efforts to preserve the historic treasures of the colonial boomtown, Ouro Prêto. Soon, however, federal officials, annoyed by Vicente's criticisms, forced out this local preservationist and asserted the authority of the national government over historic sites. Norma and Vicente's vignettes demonstrate how individuals participated in and shaped the cult of Brazilian nationalism.

CHAPTER 7

Geraldo Pereira

Samba Composer and Grifter

Bryan McCann

Manifestations of Afro-Brazilian culture evoked starkly ambivalent responses from the mostly white and light-skinned Brazilian authorities and business leaders who dominated the dissemination of cultural products to the broader public. Tolerance and even a nativist appreciation for aspects of Afro-Brazilian religion, dance, martial arts, music, and folkways (mostly practiced on the margins of formal institutions and commerce) gave way from time to time to violent repression. Many Europhile republican officials and intellectuals associated these manifestations of African culture with savagery and backwardness, which needed to be eradicated for Brazil to progress. For them, the complexion of the population not only needed to be "whitened" by subsidizing European immigration, but the tone of the national culture needed to be bleached as well.

During the 1920s and 1930s, a new appreciation of Africa's contributions to the development of a uniquely Brazilian national culture became fashionable among white intellectuals, artists, and consumers. Samba, based on African rhythms, descended from the slums in the hills surrounding Rio to its wealthy downtown. Instead of trying to suppress African cultural influences, political leaders such as President Getúlio Vargas used government funds to promote Carnival parades and the samba music that accompanied them as tourist attractions. The city of Rio was Brazil's cultural and political axis, and its influence increased under Vargas. It is no accident that samba, a musical genre that took its definitive form in Rio, became identified as Brazil's "national" music. Samba was not only good music, but its success was buttressed by federal support and the new technologies of radio and the recording industry, which were centered in the capital. Brazil had a wealth of other musical genres that could have been selected over samba for promotion as the national sound, but these genres mostly came to be identified as "regional" musical traditions.

Geraldo Pereira came from a provincial city to Rio as a young man, in search of a better life. He became celebrated as an archetypical Carioca (resident of Rio), the malandro *(streetwise hustler), and an innovative samba composer. As Bryan McCann's biography of Pereira shows, he never managed to make a fortune from his hard-won fame. As a dark-skinned man from the slums, Pereira's recording career was stunted. Instead, the mostly white performers who crooned Pereira's catchy tunes and the re-cording moguls who produced their records enjoyed the financial rewards of his labors. Pereira led the life of a malandro to the hilt: hard drinking, womanizing, fast talking, and street fighting. He often lived from hand to mouth but never failed to dress elegantly. Pereira's life and songs helped to define the iconic image of the malandro and the uniquely Carioca flavor of Brazil's "national" music.*

Bryan McCann is assistant professor of history at Georgetown University. His biography of Geraldo Pereira comes out of his much broader project on Brazilian radio and music that are the subjects of his book Hello, Hello, Brazil: Popular Music and the Making of Modern Brazil *(Durham: Duke University Press, forthcoming, 2004). His next project will examine the social history of Rio's swank southend neighborhoods (the Zona Sul) in the 1950s, when they began to develop rapidly.*

*M*alandros are like sharks of the asphalt: if they stop moving, they die. During the peak years of their circulation, from the 1920s through the early 1950s, they moved in the interstices of Rio de Janeiro, sliding back and forth between the underworld and the world of law-abiding citizens, between poverty and the middle class, between night and day. They gathered in the dancehalls, cafés, and corner bars of the city and scattered in the back alleys of its red light zones. Dressed in the most dashing attire—a pressed linen suit, a natty straw hat, patent leather shoes with spats—they moved with rhythm, grace, and flair. They strove to remain one step ahead of the police who hounded them, the women who suffered for their broken promises, and the creditors who held their worthless debts. Geraldo Pereira was the model of a *malandro*, and this was his world. As he cruised the streets of the city he wrote, sang, and peddled sambas that translated this world into rhythm and melody, revealing its intricacies and its dilemmas with perfect economy and arresting insight. At the age of thirty-seven, a single punch from a rival *malandro* knocked him cold on the sidewalk outside a downtown bar. He died days later.

To backtrack a little: the *malandro*, or rogue, is an iconic figure of modern Brazilian life. The term apparently comes from an Italian word for petty thief or brigand. In the early decades of the twentieth century in Rio, it came to signify a man who lived on the margins of the law, surviving by his wits in the brothels and gambling dens of the city. The stereotypical *malandro* was black or of mixed race and a sharp-dressed, heart-breaking hustler. He was associated with samba from the early stages of the genre's growth. As samba evolved in the 1920s from a ludic, impromptu form played by amateurs for a group of onlookers into a commercial, composed form played by professionals for a paying audience, sambas about *malandros*, or in the voice of *malandros*, became a staple of the genre. Indeed, it was samba that turned the *malandro* from mere stereotype into cultural icon. It was also samba that gave the *malandro* his ambiguity—he was disdained by elites and bureaucrats and alternately feared and admired by the members of the lower orders. To residents of the city's growing *favelas*—the hillside shantytowns that were spreading rapidly over Rio's sheer granite peaks—the *malandro* could be a powerful symbol of the evasion of authority, a feat much to be admired among the illegal squatters who were generally treated as natural criminals by the authorities.

To a young man who had traded rural poverty for urban poverty, who could not suppress his vaulting ambition to move in higher circles, and who discovered in himself a marvelous inclination for samba, the *malandro* was an enormously seductive figure. This pull goes a long way toward explaining Geraldo Pereira's studied *malandragem*, or *malandro* practices. Pereira was not a natural-born *malandro*—that creature does not exist. Instead, he sought to give flesh to the icon of the period's sambas, including his own. In the process, he drank, danced, and hustled himself into an early grave, but not without leaving behind some seventy sambas, including a dozen that figure among the genre's all-time greats and that marked an important stage in its evolution.

TO THE METROPOLIS

Geraldo Pereira was born in Juíz de Fora, Minas Gerais, in 1918. Today, Juíz de Fora is one of Brazil's leading provincial industrial cities, but at that time it was a dusty rural outpost largely controlled by local land barons. Pereira's family was of the kind who depended on such patrons for sustenance and security and who pledged their labor and their votes in return. Pereira later recounted that in his childhood he worked as a *candeeiro de boi*, or cattle drover, leading the herd from corral to pasture on the dirt paths of Minas. If he attended school in Juíz de Fora, he had little to show for it. By all accounts, he was illiterate when he arrived in Rio de Janeiro.[1]

He came sometime between 1929 and 1931, following his older brother Mané, his mother's child from a previous union, who had migrated to the city years earlier. Mané had established himself in Mangueira, a *favela* just north of downtown and one of the early strongholds of samba (a distinction it still maintains). He arrived at a moment when Mangueira, the city surrounding it, the genre of samba, and Brazil itself were undergoing transformations that would mark them profoundly. In the realm of high politics, Getúlio Vargas in 1930 led a coup that brought to a close a long-running political confabulation between the landowners of São Paulo and Minas Gerais and that initiated Vargas's own long chokehold on the presidency. He would remain in office until 1945, presiding over the dictatorial Estado Novo between 1937 and 1945, and would later return as elected president from 1950 until his suicide in office in 1954. Vargas brought a centralizing, industrializing energy to his long tenure, attempting to transform Brazil from agricultural exporter into modern industrial giant. His efforts in this regard did not entirely succeed, but they did help to modernize Rio—the capital until 1959—and make it more than ever the bureaucratic and cultural center of the country.

Rio failed utterly to reckon with the unforeseen consequences of its modernization—the unplanned, unregulated *favelas*, populated primarily by rural migrants such as Pereira who were drawn to the city by its promise of opportunity. Upon arrival, they found that employment was hard to come by, and the pay insufficient to fulfill any aspirations of an apartment in the city when they could find it. Mangueira, for example, was surrounded by a glass factory, a hat factory, and a ceramic factory, all of which depended on the labor of the *favelados* and none of which paid common workers enough to live anywhere else. The *favela* became almost a captive labor pool for such industries as well as for the unskilled occupations of the growing city's service sector—delivery boy, seamstress, shoeshine boy, *pau para qualquer obra* (jack of all trades).

Samba, in the meantime, was going through its own transformation, and it drew on the same pool of talent. In the late 1920s a group of young, untrained *sambistas* from the neighborhood of Estácio, just across the valley from Mangueira, tinkered with the samba rhythm, emerging with an infectious 2/4 swing that lent itself to syncopated percussion and brief, catchy melodies. Their sambas were simple enough to be learned, played, and sung by almost anyone, making them perfect for Rio's many *blocos*, or informal Carnival parade bands. At the same time, the Estácio composers decided to turn their own *bloco* into something more formal and permanent and founded the samba school of Deixa Falar, or Let Them Talk. Other neighborhoods began their own samba schools, and these became the principal attractions of the city's increasingly spectacular Carnival parade. Mangueira's foremost samba school, Estação Primeira da Mangueira (First Station of Mangueira), quickly became one of the largest and best organized.

The growth of the broadcasting and recording industries signalled even more profound transformations for samba. Around the same time that Geraldo Pereira arrived in Rio, the multinational recording companies RCA Victor and Odeon established affiliates in Rio. The city already had a handful of radio stations, which were quickly growing more commercial, more professional, and more dedicated to promoting popular music. Above all, they sought talent among the young performers of the city's hottest music, samba—with one important reservation. In the 1930s and through most of the 1940s, radio and the recording studios were limited to white and nearly white Brazilians. This restriction was neither a policy nor an acknowledged practice, but the expression of a deep-seated and covert racism that limited the opportunities of black Brazilians at every turn. Dark-skinned musicians such as Geraldo Pereira and his closest peers might play on records or in radio backup bands, but they would not be stars, at least for the time being. As a result, the composers of Estácio and Mangueira were far more likely to sell their sambas to white singers than to taste fame and fortune themselves.

SANTO ANTONIO

Much was made at the time of the distinction between *cidade*, the city, and *morro*, the hill, or *favela*. The *cidade* stood for order, wealth, and work, while in the vision of most elites the *morro* stood for chaos, poverty and idleness. The racial overtones of these stereotypical characterizations were inescapable: in the discourse of *cidade* and *morro*, the *cidade* was figured as white and the *morro* as black, or more generally Afro-Brazilian. In truth, Rio's *favelas* were home to a diverse population but were certainly predominantly black and brown. If the discourse of *cidade* and *morro* tinged *favelados* with the label of idlers, it also gave them cultural capital. But the *morro*, with its all-night samba jams, its communal intimacy, its old women from Bahia—the keepers of African traditions—also stood for play, spirit, and deep cultural roots. These qualities became highly prized among *morro* residents themselves, who looked upon Carnival, and samba in general, as an opportunity to display these attributes before the stodgy lower city.

The *morro*'s separation from the *cidade* also permitted the rise of local strongmen who filled the gaps of commerce, justice, and rule. Geraldo's brother Mané was one such figure, directing local affairs in Santo Antonio, a section of Mangueira. (The *favela* itself was already the size of a bustling town, with its own discrete neighborhoods.) Mané owned a bar that served beer and *cachaça* to the residents of Santo Antonio. He built and rented out several shacks in the neighborhood. (*Favela* life, unregulated though it was, did not necessarily free residents from the burden of rent.) He loaned money, charged interest, and sent enforcers when the payments were delayed. And he mediated neighborhood disputes, encouraging reluctant grooms to keep the implicit promises they had made to their "dishonored" conquests. In the absence of formal justice, Mané's decrees were more or less binding. Residents of his patch of turf either conformed or left.

Geraldo Pereira thus arrived in Mangueira impoverished but with a powerful patron on the hill. Mané quickly put his brother to work in the bar and to selling vegetables door to door in the neighborhood. Pereira, for his part, took every opportunity to flee from his brother's watchful eye, preferring to spend his time instead taking in the sambas performed by a local *conjunto*, or regular group. He attended elementary school, desultorily. Outside of school, however, he showed a tremendous ambition to learn, convincing neighborhood residents to teach him to read. A few years after his arrival, he also studied guitar with a local composer, quickly absorbing enough to start composing his own sambas and then leaving off his training. Guitar would remain for him primarily a composition tool rather than a means of expression.

By 1937, Pereira was spending a great deal of his time hanging out in the *quadra*—a kind of open dance floor and training space—of the samba school Unidos da Mangueira, which briefly shared the hill with the better known Estação Primeira. Unidos da Mangueira was based right in Santo Antonio, and its *quadra*, like those of most samba schools, served as a community center. Here, Pereira learned the methods of the school's composers, testing out his own first attempts at rhyming quatrains in improvised sambas.

He also undertook the far more unusual task of producing his own play in the school's *quadra*. If inventing a few samba verses was almost an expected rite of passage for the young *favelado*, writing plays was only slightly more common than playing polo. Theater in Brazil was strictly a middle-class phenomenon. Geraldo Pereira, however, produced a play set in the *favela* that spoke intimately of its conflicts. No script survives, and it seems likely that Pereira never wrote any formal dialogue, preferring to create a rough plot and to let his actors—friends from the neighborhood—improvise their parts. The sketch concerned a young *malandro* whose girlfriend, returning to the *favela* from her daily work as a maid in the city, is beaten by another man. Outraged by this affront to his honor, the *malandro* confronts his rival and shames him. Not surprisingly, Pereira took the leading role for himself.

The plot established several of the themes that Pereira would continue to explore in his samba compositions. The young woman's work takes her out of the *favela* and thus exposes her to danger. The *malandro* reacts possessively but entirely without compassion—what angers him is not that his girlfriend has been beaten, but that another man has encroached on his territory. Relying on a combination of physical force and verbal agility, the *malandro* then asserts his power and makes his rival look like a fool.

The production in the *quadra* closed with the cast singing a Pereira samba recounting the plot, largely from the perspective of the *malandro*. Several years later, Pereira sold the samba, "Na Subida do Morro" (Going Up the Hill), to the singer Moreira da Silva, who recorded a successful version that added his own impromptu verses to Pereira's original lyrics. These lyrics are extraordinarily violent in their description of the *malandro's* confrontation with his rival, but this description is ambiguous: it is impossible to tell whether the lyrics recount a bloody beating or are merely threats and boasting. This ambiguity is itself a key to Pereira's work, which frequently alludes both to the power of language as a weapon and to its slippery nature. The *malandro's* hustle, in this work, is a confidence game that depends on his stylish and powerful image and above all on his silver tongue.[2]

Pereira never again tried his hand at playwrighting or production (although he did appear several times as an actor). His early venture in the theater, however, reveals his ambition to make his mark in some way. His potential avenues for success were few. It must have been clear to him that a job in one of the factories surrounding Mangueira would lead nowhere. He could become a boss on the *morro* like his brother, but the endless responsibilities of that course did not suit him. He could aim for a job in the lower ranks of the expanding civil service, an opportunity for occupational respectability. This he tried, working in the stockroom of the city administration's Schools Department, until he concluded that the job's demands of attendance and punctuality outweighed its security and benefits. Or he could attempt to parlay his musical ability and his imagination into success as a *sambista*, beyond Santo Antonio and Mangueira, in the city below.

FROM THE PRAÇA TIRADENTES TO THE CAFÉ NICE

The greater population of Rio de Janeiro never heard of Pereira's play, but in Santo Antonio it was a hit. Alerted to Pereira's growing reputation, the directors of Estação Primeira soon seduced him away from Unidos. Pereira became one of a stable of extraordinarily talented *sambistas* at the larger school, and his name would forever be linked to its tradition. Unidos dissolved several years later, essentially swallowed up by its neighbor.

Pereira's association with Estação Primeira brought him into contact for the first time with the music market. Composers such as Cartola, one of the founders of Estação Primeira, were regularly approached by white singers with access to radio shows and to record companies who were looking for material. At times, these singers bought compositions outright, registering the copyrights in their own names. More frequently, they gave at least some credit to the real composer, registering themselves as "collaborators." This was business as usual, and no one at the time looked upon it as exploitation.

Indeed, middle-class composers occasionally engaged in the same sorts of practices, despite their greater access to the music market. For most composers, the goal was to get one's material before the public in any way possible, letting copyrights take care of themselves. This practice was a rational response to the nature of the market. Although Getúlio Vargas had done a great deal to strengthen copyright protections in Brazil, helping to make music a viable industry, the payment of royalties was still extremely unreliable. Everyone knew that only the big-name singers got rich in music, by selling tens of thousands of records and demanding high performance fees.

The relaxed attitude of many composers toward copyrights also reflected the transition of popular music from pastime to profession. Not so long ago, samba had been a collective activity and its refrains had derived from multiple, anonymous sources. As with every popular genre, many of the early recorded samba hits were slightly more polished versions of these urban folk creations. By the late 1930s samba was already well on its way to becoming an art of individual stars and established authorship, but it still retained enough of the collective spirit of its origins to make rigid adherence to the idea of individual intellectual property unlikely. For a composer on the *morro*, as a result, trading copyrights of dubious value for an immediate payment equivalent to perhaps a month's minimum salary seemed like not a bad deal at all.

Geraldo Pereira got his first break in the music market late in 1939, at the age of twenty-one, when the singer Roberto Paiva recorded "Se Você Sair Chorando" (If You Leave Crying), a samba that Pereira had co-written with Nelson Teixeira. Pereira collaborated with nearly twenty different composers over the course of his career, and that collaboration ranged from the nominal participation of famous singers to true mutual authorship. This helps to explain the lack of coherence in his work, which varies widely in subject matter, perspective, melodic approach, and quality. The best of his compositions bear the unmistakable mark of his genius for incisive portraits of daily life in the marginal neighborhoods of Rio de Janeiro, rich in the slang of the *favelas* and with a singular melodic buoyancy. "Se Você Sair Chorando" does not fall into this category—it is undistinguished and formulaic. Paiva was a second-rank singer, not the type who could make a hit out of ordinary material, and the samba was not a great success.

Pereira was thrilled that the tune was recorded but disillusioned when it brought him neither fortune nor fame. What it gave him was an entrance into the world of samba in the *cidade* and its peculiar routines, quite different from those on the *morro*. He began hanging out around the Praça Tiradentes, a downtown plaza surrounded by nightclubs and theaters that staged musical revues. The sidewalk on one side of the plaza was known as the *calçada de fome*, or walk of hunger, a parody of Hollywood's *calçada de fama*, or walk of fame, because of the penniless composers who gathered there to peddle their sambas to singers, revue producers, and nightclub managers. Pereira became a regular on the *calçada de fome*, buttonholing the star singers with whom he became increasingly familiar. Eager to come across as something other than an impoverished *favelado*, he dressed always in a pressed suit and shirt, sprinkled himself with cologne, and manicured his nails. He also continued to study the elements of writing, taking great pains to avoid the embarrassment—common among *favela* composers—of presenting a samba with spelling and grammar errors.

The popular singers, for their part, were in a much better bargaining position, but they too were always on the lookout for talent, and Pereira clearly had it in abundance. By late 1940, Ciro Monteiro and Moreira da Silva, the two men who would become Pereira's greatest interpreters, had already recorded his work. Monteiro was white, and Moreira da Silva was of mixed racial descent, with fair skin. Both had greater access to the music market than the dark-skinned Pereira, who dreamed of his own singing career. To be fair, both were also superior singers: Ciro Monteiro had a gift for hitting the perfect emphasis on Pereira's unusual melodies, playing with the beat with relaxed verve. And Moreira da Silva acted the part of the *malandro* with consummate flair, embodying the rough-and-tumble characters of Pereira's work.

As Pereira became better known in the early 1940s, he spent less time on the *calçada de fome* and more at the tables of the Café Nice, located a few blocks away on stately Rio Branco avenue, the city's main thoroughfare. The Nice was known as the samba stock exchange: it was where composers, performers, and radio producers gathered to talk shop, trade information, and collaborate. At the Nice, white middle-class composers and ambitious *favelados* such as Geraldo Pereira came together on roughly equal terms, a rarity in the context of Rio's implicit racial hierarchy.[3] With his good looks, his smooth talk, and his enormous talent, Pereira did well for himself in this environment. He was soon finding singers to record his work at the rate of about four sambas per year, mostly just before Carnival, when Rio's music industry kicked into high gear.

He soon discovered that the recording was only half the battle. Once the recording was made, composers were expected to join forces with the singers in promoting it in any way possible—making the rounds of the radio stations, asking producers to play the record, or, better yet, inviting the singer for a live performance. It meant visiting the local nightclubs and requesting the tune from the house band. And at Carnival, it meant hiring a group of musicians to parade through the streets, playing the composition over and over and hoping a crowd would follow along. When undertaken by a street-smart operator such as Geraldo Pereira, all these activities could come under the heading of *malandragem*, depending as they did on charm and *jogo da cintura*—literally, play of the waist, and figuratively, subtle maneuvering. But taken together they proved harder and more time-consuming than real work. Pereira quit his job at the Schools Department in order to dedicate all his time to this exhausting routine. He did so uneasily, however: his samba was not making him wealthy by any stretch, and its precipitous changes in fortune were the very opposite of the civil servant's secure monotony.

EARLY WORKS

Pereira's first hit was a 1940 collaboration with Wilson Batista on a samba entitled "Acertei no Milhar" (I Hit the Lottery), recorded by Moreira da Silva. Batista was several years older than Pereira and had been a significant composer since the early 1930s. His portraits of crafty *malandros* and hard-luck characters from the lower rungs of Rio society had a deep influence on Pereira's own work. "Acertei no Milhar" portrayed one such character—a working-class stiff named Vargulino who dreams that he has won the lottery and can indulge all his yearnings for wealth and leisure, only to awaken with a start to the dull routine of his daily job. Moreira da Silva later stated that this samba was Batista's alone and that the older composer had merely added Pereira's name at the behest of the singer himself, who knew that Pereira would dedicate considerable energy to promoting the samba if his name were attached.

This explanation is plausible—the samba is more typical of Batista's work than Pereira's. While the composers shared similar subject matter (with Batista leaning more toward working-class characters and Pereira more toward the *favela*), Batista more commonly used clever twists such as the "surprise" ending of "Acertei no Milhar." More indicative was their use of language: Batista relied on narrative and rarely used slang, while Pereira used images and dialogue and reveled in slang. "Acertei no Milhar" is a first-person narrative and contains almost no slang. What Pereira probably gave the composition is the unusual name of Vargulino's wife, Etelvina, which happened to be the name of one of Pereira's nieces. And the way in which that name is invoked as the samba's first word—an abrupt, rising four-note melody—is typical of Pereira's striking opening statements.

Over the next four years, Pereira wrote a number of semi-successful sambas, but nothing that would establish him as one of the most talented composers of the city. That recognition came in 1944 with his enormous hit, "Falsa Baiana" (False *Baiana*). Like the *malandro*, the *baiana*, or woman from the northeastern state of Bahia, was a cultural icon in Brazil. *Baianas* represented African tradition in cuisine, music, and attire—the latter a flowing white lace dress with numerous beads and amulets. The iconic *baiana* was seen as the carrier of African rhythm who, by migrating to Rio, had enabled the creation of samba. There was some truth to this image; samba had originated in the 1910s in house parties hosted by old *baianas*. But the link between *baianas* and samba had outgrown any historical foundation and had become part of national lore. (Indeed, by regulations approved by Getúlio Vargas, every samba school in the official Carnival parade had to feature a wing of *baianas*.)

Pereira's samba compares the false *baiana*, who merely puts on the costume for Carnival, to the real one, who has samba in her every movement. When the false *baiana* enters the samba circle she just stands there. No one claps, no one sings, and the samba dies. In contrast, when the real *baiana* enters, she swivels her hips and leaves her onlookers with their mouths watering, saying, "Hail, Bahia!" The melody skips along the rhythm like a stone skipping over rolling waves. Ciro Monteiro's recording brought the *baiana* to life perfectly, making the samba one of the biggest hits of the year and, eventually, a standard of the genre.

If Pereira had never written another samba of note, "Falsa Baiana" would have been enough to establish him as a significant composer. As it happened, he wrote several more of similar grade, rounding out a body of work that, while small in comparison with that of Batista, for example, is nonetheless captivating. Months after Monteiro recorded "Falsa Baiana," the Anjos do Inferno, or Hell's Angels, recorded Pereira's "Sem Compromisso" (Without Commitment). (The Anjos do Inferno were a mild-mannered, clean-cut vocal quartet and had nothing to do with motorcycles.) In "Sem Compromisso," the scene is one of Rio's *gafieiras*, or dancehalls. Ranging from working-class dives to posh salons, they constituted one of the city's principal forms of leisure. They featured live bands (decked out in tuxedos, brass instruments gleaming, in the fancy joints) playing the popular music of the moment and were often graced by star singers who stopped in to plug their tunes. The *gafieiras* were one of the few venues where a respectable young couple could grab hold of each other without condemnation. The speaker in "Sem Compromisso" is a young man hoping to take advantage of this situation. His girlfriend, however, keeps dancing with another man (although she swears it is "without commitment"). The speaker threatens and cajoles, but his girlfriend dances away.

As in "Falsa Baiana," the melodic line bobs and weaves in the basic samba beat, creating a rhythmic tension that seems to pull the lyrics along irresistibly. In the words of Roberto Paiva, "only the mute cannot sing 'Sem Compromisso.' "[4] These two 1944 compositions helped to inaugurate a strain known as "samba teleco-teco," an onomatopoeic term referring to the syncopation of the vocal line and the underlying rhythm. The emphases in Pereira's melodies sometimes fall on the strong beat, sometimes on a weak one, and not infrequently on a weak beat and then held through the strong one. The effect of these rhythmic tensions is similar to that of a polarized electromagnetic track that pulls along a train, with the distinction that before the listener can get accustomed to the polarities in Pereira's melodies, he sprinkles his lyrics with clusters of plosive and sibilant consonants that echo the sounds of samba percussion. Indeed, the percussive nature of Pereira's lyrics makes the vocal line itself an adequate substitute for varied instrumentation, a quality that João Gilberto emphasized in his stripped-down bossa nova recordings of Pereira's work twenty years later. In Gilberto's voice and guitar rendition of "Sem Compromisso," the lyrics take the place of tambourine and hand drums.

This syncopated style was one of Pereira's hallmarks. The other was his incisive vision of *favela* life. His most compelling early expression in this vein was the samba "Golpe Errado" (Unfair Blow), which Ciro Monteiro recorded in 1945. The lyrics to "Golpe Errado" begin with a brief, quasi-cinematic description of a *malandro* strolling with his girlfriend ("Here he comes in his starched, white suit . . ."), and then note that his real woman is off working as a maid in a white man's house. The narrator notes that this woman—not necessarily his wife, but at least his domestic partner—will even bring him his supper later, and observes that his callous exploitation of her is an "unfair blow." All this is expressed in seven brief lines. The first three are sprinkled with references to color, referring to the *malandro's* white suit, his brown girlfriend, his black woman, and, finally, her white employer. This quick survey of the spectrum shows us the *malandro's* style but also suggests that in this case, at least, this style merely perpetuates Brazil's phenotypical hierarchy. The following four lines then pass judgment on the *malandro*—this is an unfair blow. A second verse adds further incriminating evidence, describing the *malandro* leaving for the samba jam just as his woman returns from work.

The moral judgment of the refrain is unusual in Pereira's work; he ordinarily limited himself to dispassionate reporting on the lives of his characters. The explicit condemnation of "Golpe Errado" seems to stem not so much from the *malandro*'s mistreatment of his woman—not at all unusual in Pereira's work—but from the fact that this particular mistreatment forces the woman to go work as a maid to support his lifestyle and his adulterous affairs. The true *malandro*, the samba implies, should be self-sufficient. The perfect economy of the lyrics opens up these interpretational possibilities rather than prescribing them strictly—another characteristic of Pereira's work.

A *MALANDRO* IN SEARCH OF HIMSELF

"Golpe Errado" might have been a self-portrait but for the fact that Pereira's wife did not bring him supper. While still in his teens, Pereira had become a ladykiller in Mangueira. In 1938, just as he began to break into the world of samba, one of his seductions reaped the inevitable consequences. The young woman's father learned of the affair and came after Pereira demanding that he "repair her honor" by marrying her. Pereira's brother Mané had built his reputation on settling such disputes in Santo Antonio, and he forced his younger brother to go through with the marriage. By all acounts, Pereira did not even bother to return with his wife from City Hall. He never lived with her, limiting himself to occasional visits—one of which apparently produced a son—and providing no financial assistance. The marriage had no noticeable effect on his habits of seduction.

Pereira was only too eager to leave behind his wife and Santo Antonio. He began renting a series of rooms in working-class, often squalid neighborhoods in the city, hoping to remain close to the dancehalls, the recording studios, and the radio stations. When money ran out, he retreated up the hill to friends and family. Only with the success of "Falsa Baiana" did he make the residential transition from *morro* to *cidade*. Even then, his financial problems were far from over. In 1946, despite the fact that he had several hits to his name, he returned to civil service, finding a job as a truck driver hauling trash for the city. At least, that was the job description, and Pereira registered for a license to make the job legal. He never slowed down his constant circulation in samba circles, however, making it impossible for him to show up for any regular work. According to his girlfriend at the time, he struck a deal with a local politician, swinging votes for the politician in Mangueira in return for a no-show job in the Sanitation Department. According to Moreira da Silva, ever so often Pereira gave a free show to bureaucrats in the department to maintain his cushy deal. Such arrangements were far from unusual in the government ranks. The job paid poorly, but it guaranteed Pereira a pension he would not survive to collect and health benefits that could not save his life.[5]

In the *gafieiras* that he attended both to plug his music and to cruise for conquests, he cultivated the image of a *malandro valentão*—a tough guy, *que topa qualquer parada*, ready for any scuffle. Out of the spotlight he was less courageous, or more sensible, backing out of fights when he could, limiting the blows when he could not. According to one fellow composer who had had a stormy relationship with Pereira, "he always wanted to fight embracing," grabbing his opponent in a boxer's clinch. He found it easier, apparently, to fight with Isabel Mendes da Silva, his on-and-off girlfriend throughout much of the 1940s. The two cultivated a pattern of abuse and reconciliation, each spending the night in jail at least once for domestic violence.[6]

Mendes da Silva interpreted Pereira's violence as the consequence of racial anxiety stemming from Pereira's fear that the color of his skin was holding him back. In her words, "he really wanted to get rich, but he had a complex . . . he had some kind of shame because of his color." Other observers came to similar conclusions, reporting that "he had a persecution anxiety, and he thought color was the problem."[7] Such psychological interpretations would be debatable even with far richer knowledge of Pereira's personality. Coming as they do secondhand and at a great chronological remove, they cannot be considered reliable as a character assessment. But they do point to the fact that Pereira, unlike virtually any composer of his generation, was willing to address racial inequality explicitly. The black women in his sambas go work for white families, and that is an unfair blow. While this observation hardly seems radical by any current standard, it was unusually frank in a context in which references to racial inequality were deeply discouraged.

If Pereira did believe that the color of his skin limited his material success, he was certainly correct. By the late 1940s, there were a few, isolated black singers beginning to hit the big time, but they were an anomaly. (Indeed, the nickname of one of them—Blackout, or Blecaute, as it was usually spelled—suggests just how uncommon it was to see a black face in the glossy magazines that chronicled the world of radio stars.) As a composer who hoped to cross over to success as a singer, Pereira faced imposing odds.

LATE WORKS

Whether or not Pereira himself had a persecution complex, many of his sambas portray characters experiencing disillusionment, betrayal, or persecution. In most cases, these misfortunes are purely romantic—the woman goes off with another man—and thus differ little from the themes explored by any number of contemporary *sambistas*. In a few cases, however—and most of these are among Pereira's best works—the calamities described speak more directly to the dilemmas of *favela* dwellers and *sambistas*. While this portrayal is often satiric, it helps to reveal a side of Rio that the daily newspapers completely ignored. Pereira's 1947 samba "Pisei num Despacho" (I Stepped on an Offering), for example, is told in the voice of a *sambista* who has, as the title suggests, trod on an Afro-Brazilian spiritual offering. These offerings—perhaps a candle, some flowers, and one or two objects of significance to the supplicant or to the spirit being invoked—are frequently placed at the corners of crossroads, which are sacred spaces in all Afro-Brazilian sects. As a result of his pedestrian insensitivity, the speaker in "Pisei num Despacho" loses his ability to dance and to compose sambas. He goes to the *gafieira* but has no luck with the ladies. His only cure will be to journey to the distant suburbs to visit a *pai de santo*—an enlightened elder capable of reading the spirits' will and appeasing them.

The depiction of Afro-Brazilian spirituality in the samba is neither exotic and mysterious nor mocking and simplistic. The speaker's dilemma is comical, but his resort to a *pai de santo* is entirely reasonable. As listeners in the *favelas* and the working-class neighborhoods would know, the suburb mentioned in the samba—Caxias—was indeed home to several esteemed *terreiros*, or spiritual centers. Pereira gave his work the specificity of local detail that would make it resonate with listeners—primarily poor and working-class Afro-Brazilians—who had themselves journeyed to such *terreiros*. (Ironically, a few years later, Pereira's former girlfriend Isabel Mendes da Silva would give up her hard-drinking life in the city to become the leader of a spiritual sect in the suburbs.)

The following year, Pereira had what was perhaps his most lucrative hit, "Que Samba Bom" (What Great Samba). The composition is unusual in Pereira's work in that it is unabashedly enthusiastic and positive, relating neither deception nor disillusionment. It describes a hot samba jam, with plenty of booze and women to spare, where even fools are "*se arrumando*," or taking care of themselves. The melody is also simpler and more direct than Pereira's syncopated marvels. In the recording by Blecaute, "Que Samba Bom" became one of the year's top-selling records.

Despite its success, Pereira soon returned to a more complex approach. His "Ministério da Economia" of 1951 satirizes the proposed creation by Getúlio Vargas—newly returned to office as the elected president—of a Ministry of the Economy to guard against inflation. The lyrics take the form of an open letter to the president, praising him for a step that will doubtless lift *favelados* out of poverty. In contrast to the nationalistic sambas that characterized the late Estado Novo, however, the praise of government here is clearly tongue-in-cheek: "Sir President . . . Now everything will be cheap/ Now the poor will be able to eat . . . I won't have to eat cat anymore." The closing line repeats this sentiment; the cats on the hill will laugh with pleasure, knowing they will now be safe from the *favela's* stew pots.

Eating cats was by no means common in Mangueira. Pereira, rather, makes use of an exaggerated image of extreme poverty to give his samba a more sarcastic bite. The real power of the lyrics, however, comes from the speaker's exultation that now he will be able to call home his *"nega bacana,"* or righteous black woman, from her job as a maid in a rich woman's apartment in Copacabana. It is unclear whether the speaker is intended as another *malandro*, who takes advantage of his woman's hard work to fund his own idleness, or a more typical *favelado* worker himself. The sly tone of the lyrics shows that he is no stranger to *malandragem* and thus may give some weight to the first interpretation. Regardless, what is perfectly clear is that the overarching economic structure has forced the black woman into menial service in the home of a wealthy white woman. In its sarcasm, the samba suggests that Vargas's economic overtures toward the poor would do nothing to change this basic, demeaning truth—an allegation that turned out to be completely correct.

Pereira followed "Ministério" with two sambas that show *favelados* attempting unsuccessfully to mitigate this inequality through *malandragem*. In both "Polícia no Morro" (Police on the Hill, 1951) and "Cabritada Malsucedida" (Unfortunate Goat Stew, 1953), a *malandro* named Bento steals a goat from a *doutor*, an elite gentleman. In "Polícia no Morro," Bento uses the goatskin to make a drum, and in "Cabritada Malsucedida," as the title suggests, he intends to make goat stew. In both cases, the police climb the hill in search of the goat. In "Polícia no Morro," they shut down the samba and prevent the school from parading. In "Cabritada," they break up the party and arrest everyone in sight. The hapless narrator of that samba only gets out of jail when his wife's employer goes to the police station and pulls some strings. The pessimistic implication is that the *favelados* are ultimately at the mercy of the authorities and the elites. Only the ruling classes can manipulate the workings of justice, and the best that the *favelados* can hope for out of interaction with the *cidade* is a good patron.

In "Escurinha," a 1952 samba, Pereira suggests that complete separation might be a better course. *Escurinha* literally means "little dark girl."

To a reader from the United States, this term comes across as inevitably racist. In the Brazil of 1952, this was not so. The myth of racial democracy—the idea that Brazilians lived in prejudice-free racial harmony—had prevented diminutive race-based terms from taking on any apparent deprecatory meaning. Thus, when the *"negro"* or black man of "Escurinha" pleads with the title figure, he does so in a tone of affectionate intimacy. He urges her to leave her work as a maid and return to the *favela*. Instead of promising her a palace, he promises to share his *barraco*, rigorously and honestly listing its appointments: four earthen walls, a zinc roof, a floor of wooden slats. More important, he claims that as director of the samba school, he will make her its queen. He offers, in other words, no material luxuries, but rather a cultural glory within a small, closed community. This life is a long way from racial democracy.

"Escurinha" also marked the height of Pereira's use of percussive sounds in his lyrics. Its opening lines, written (and sung) in rough Portuguese typical of the *favelas*, sound like a rhythm section working at full strength: "Escurinha/ tu tem que ser minha/ de qualquer maneira/ te dou meu boteco/te dou meu barraco. . . ." (Escurinha, you must be mine, in any way, I'll give you my bar, I'll give you my shack. . . .) The director of the samba school, fittingly, speaks in pure samba.

DECLINE

Pereira's success as a composer brought him no peace. On the contrary, the experience of frequently hearing his sambas on the radio without getting rich made him bitter and suspicious. On many occasions, he accused the composers' association charged with distributing royalties of fraud and corruption, to little avail. He found no great fortune as a singer. He had rhythm and style, but in comparison with masters of the genre such as Moreira da Silva, his voice was thin. He recorded many of his own compositions, but they tended to sound much better in versions by other singers. Although he sang frequently as a guest on various radio programs, no station ever hired him as a regular performer.

Pereira allegedly had his tonsils removed at least partly because he believed they were interfering with his singing. He responded poorly to the operation and bled profusely for days. In the early 1950s his health began to decline rapidly. He ate little and drank constantly; and the more he drank, the more he looked to fight. In the words of one colleague, "Geraldo, when he drank, asked for consent to be irritating, and then he abused that consent . . . when drunk, he was obsessively truculent."[8] As the mid-1950s approached, he was drinking almost all the time, from the start of his day at around 11 AM to its finish, when the *gafieiras* closed at around 4 AM. Toward the end of his life he supposedly drank cheap cognac by the liter, hoping that it would cure impotence.

At the same time, he never gave up his ambition to keep learning, to keep improving his skills. He made several attempts in this period to learn to write music, believing that it would bring him greater respect among his colleagues. Distracted by drink and his constant round of Rio's nightspots, he never followed through. He gained a reputation as unreliable when he broke contracts with singers and with other composers. In 1954 he signed on for a prestigious long-running gig in São Paulo, but he could not bear to be away from the *gafieiras* and the girls of Rio on the weekends. He missed so many shows that his co-stars eventually gave up on him.

In 1954, Pereira wrote "Escurinho," his final composition of note, a samba that reads like autobiography. The *escurinho* of the title "used to be a good little black man," but since he got out of jail he cannot stop brawling. He threw over the *baiana*'s tray of delicacies and went up to the *favelas* looking for a fight. Worst of all, he found it. He disrupted the samba on the hill, bringing it to an end. For a *malandro*, there could be no worse sin.

In early May 1955, shortly after his thirty-seventh birthday, Pereira had a barroom disagreement with Satã, or Satan, a famed *malandro* of Lapa. Satã, as everyone knew, was homosexual and liked to cross-dress. Later, he became known as Madame Satã (whose biography is featured in Chapter 14). Satã had lived, drunk, and fought in the streets of Lapa since Pereira was just a boy, in the early 1930s. Then, that downtown neighborhood was a buzzing hive of cafés, cabarets, and brothels frequented by locals and travelers of all classes. By the early 1950s it was decidedly down at the heel. The cabarets had shut down, the cafés had lost most of their customers, and most of the brothels had been pushed farther away from middle-class neighborhoods. A few of the old bars remained, and it was in one of these that Pereira and Satã had their notorious encounter. Both its causes and course are mysterious. Pereira may have mocked Satã for his sexual proclivities, or he may have merely told Satã to be quiet. He may have thrown the first punch, or taken it. What everyone agrees on is that Pereira provoked the fight and that Satã knocked him out (although witnesses differ as to whether this happened in the bar or on the sidewalk out front).[9]

Satã later claimed that medical negligence—a delayed ambulance, careless doctors—caused Pereira's death. More likely, Pereira's health was so ruined that he could not recover from even minor trauma. He died of internal bleeding several days later in the Public Servants' Hospital. He was admitted there not because of his public service as *sambista*, much less *malandro*, but rather because of the job he rarely showed up for, that of truck driver for the Department of Sanitation.

NOTES

1. For basic biographical details see Alice Duarte Silva de Campos et al., *Um Certo Geraldo Pereira* (Rio de Janeiro: FUNARTE, 1983).

2. On ambiguity in "Na Subida do Morro," see Claudia Matos, *Acertei no Milhar: Malandragem e samba no tempo de Getúlio* (Rio de Janeiro: Paz e Terra, 1982), 195–97; on the general importance of verbal skills to the *malandro*, see pp. 85–86.

3. Nestor de Holanda, *Memórias do Café Nice* (Rio de Janeiro: Conquista, 1969).

4. Roberto Paiva, as cited in Campos et al., *Um Certo Geraldo Pereira*, 143.

5. Campos et al., *Um Certo Geraldo Pereira*, 103. Moreira da Silva also held a civil service sinecure as an ambulance driver. By his own reckoning, at least he went to work more often than Pereira. Author's interview with Moreira da Silva, 1997.

6. Campos et al., *Um Certo Geraldo Pereira*, 77, 88, 91–92, 103, 106.

7. Isabel Mendes da Silva and Luiz da França, as quoted in Campos et al., *Um Certo Geraldo Pereira*, 27, 103.

8. Fernando Pimenta, as quoted in Campos et al., *Um Certo Geraldo Pereira*, 24.

9. For various versions of the fight between Pereira and Satã see Luis Fernando Vieira et al., *Um Escurinho Direitinho*, 58; and Campos et al., *Um Certo Geraldo Pereira*, 132–36.

SUGGESTED READINGS

There are two full-length biographies of Geraldo Pereira: *Um Certo Geraldo Pereira*, by Alice Duarte Silva de Campos, Dulcinéa Nunes Gomes, Francisco Duarte Silva, and Nelson (Sargento) Matos (Rio de Janeiro: FUNARTE, 1983); and *Um Escurinho Direitinho*, by Luis Fernando Vieira, Luís Pimentel, and Suetônio Valença (Rio de Janeiro: Relumo Dumará, 1998). Claudia Matos offers a fascinating analysis of the representations of *malandragem* in Pereira's work in *Acertei no Milhar: Malandragem e samba no tempo de Getúlio* (Rio de Janeiro: Paz e Terra, 1982).

There are several excellent works in English on the general history of samba. For the roots of the genre, see Peter Fryer, *Rhythms of Resistance: African Musical Heritage in Brazil* (Middletown, CT: Wesleyan University Press, 2001). For the rise of samba as the dominant national genre, see John Chasteen's translation of Hermano Vianna, *The Mystery of Samba* (Chapel Hill: University of North Carolina Press, 1999). For samba's importance in everyday Brazilian life, see Alma Guillermoprieto, *Samba* (New York: Vintage, 1990). For a more general survey of Brazilian music, see Christopher McGowan and Ricardo Pessanha, *The Brazilian Sound* (Philadelphia: Temple

University Press, 1998). My own forthcoming book analyzes popular music and the formation of a national popular culture in Brazil between 1930 and 1954. *Hello, Brazil: Popular Music and the Making of Modern Brazil* is tentatively scheduled for publication by Duke University Press in 2004.

CHAPTER 8

Domingos da Guia

A Mestizo Hero on and off the Soccer Field*

LEONARDO AFFONSO DE MIRANDA PEREIRA

Historian Leonardo Affonso de Miranda Pereira tells us a story of triumph and tragedy as lived by one of Brazil's first international soccer stars of African descent. Domingos da Guia was one of the most prominent members of the first generation of professional nonwhite athletes who broke through the color barriers that limited the acceptance of brown and black players on Brazil's most prominent club teams as well as on its international teams. For the first time in 1938, Brazil sent a national team to Europe that included black and brown players. These men were to defend their country's honor on the soccer fields of France, a nation that most Brazilians considered the epitome of culture, taste, and civilization. At the time, sports competitions had become a venue for demonstrations of national superiority. Adolf Hitler attempted to capitalize on this concept when Berlin hosted the Olympic Games in 1936. Germany and the United States were awash at this time in racist and nationalist ferment ranging from the black-shirted ideologues of the Nazi Party to the white-sheeted members of the Ku Klux Klan. Nations contested ideas of racial and national superiority through sports in a period of tense international relations that ultimately erupted into the violence of World War II. Brazilian sports journalists and intellectuals depicted Domingos da Guia as the perfect representative of the nationalist myth of racial democracy in the 1930s because of his mixed racial heritage. However, like composer Geraldo Pereira (see Chapter 7), Domingo's life and his words belie the very idea of Brazil's racial democracy that he was said to represent.

Soccer has long been one of Brazil's greatest sources of pride. The national team has the best record of any in the world, and it is the only team to have won the coveted World Cup soccer championship five times. This recognition, however, did little to remove important barriers to the ability of Afro-Brazilians to fully participate and compete in the areas of commerce, education, and government. Entertainment and sports provided one of the few avenues to fame and fortune that opened up for nonwhite Brazilians in the 1920s and 1930s. But, as Professor Pereira's biography of Domingos shows, these advances were often fleeting.

*Translated by Peter M. Beattie.

Leonardo Affonso de Miranda Pereira has a Ph.D. in history but teaches Brazilian literature in the Department of Literary Theory at the Universidade de Campinas, in the state of São Paulo. His research interests focus on cultural history. He authored a study of Carnival, O carnaval das letras *(1994), and more recently a study of urban protest,* As barricadas da saúde: Vacina e protesto popular no Rio de Janeiro da Primeira República *(2002). Professor Pereira's biography of Domingos da Guia springs from the research for his book on the Brazilian obsession with soccer,* Footballmania: Uma história social do futebol no Rio de Janeiro (1902–1938) *(2000).*

𝒯he 1938 World Cup soccer tournament held in France marked a significant moment in the history of Brazilian soccer. Even though the sport had been played in Brazil since the late 1800s, many believed that for the first time Brazil's very best players represented the nation in an international tournament. In previous competitions numerous social, racial, and regional restrictions made it difficult to form a national soccer team of Brazil's best athletes, but the team sent to Paris in 1938 mixed players from different regions, social classes, and ethnic origins. The complexions, accents, physiognomies, and backgrounds of this team came much closer to representing the diverse composition of Brazil's population, and these attributes augmented the enthusiasm of its fans who came to see the players as legitimate representatives of their nation. The 1938 team incorporated athletes who, despite their well-known skill, would not have been invited to be part of Brazil's national delegation in years past. Such was the case of Domingos da Guia, a starting fullback, who was known by his contemporaries as the "Divino Mestre" (divine master).

At twenty-seven, Domingos was at the top of his career in 1938. According to journalists and spectators, he had first distinguished himself as an "excellent fullback" during Rio's Metropolitan League championships, when he defended his team Bangu in 1931. Bangu derived its name from a working-class suburb of western Rio de Janeiro where new industries had attracted manual laborers of various races and ethnicities. Sports columnists praised Domingos's spectacular, "often magisterial" moves as a precursor of a new style of play for defensemen. More than a mere "defender," he was, according to the coach who recruited him for a position on an all-star team representing the city of Rio in 1931, "a player who worked with his brain," who did not depend solely on his superior physical strength and speed. With a confidence never before seen on the soccer fields of Rio, the national select team eventually invited him to join them and he quickly won a starting position. The Brazilian and the international press acclaimed Domingos for his prowess on the field, and he soon became a true legend of Brazilian sports.

Beyond his undeniable soccer skills, another factor appeared to guarantee Domingos special attention: his capacity to combine traits understood as innate in individuals of African origin with others attributed to whites and Europeans. His dark skin and African features clearly distinguished him from the players who had been selected to represent Brazil internationally in the past. Those teams had been formed exclusively by white players, who came from the better educated, so-called good families of Brazil's wealthiest cities: Rio de Janeiro and São Paulo. Domingos was not the only black player who broke through this racial barrier in the 1930s, a decade of strident militarist nationalism, domestic instability, and diplomatic tensions. Soccer's professionalization and the competition it inspired made it more acceptable to include Brazilians of African descent who possessed obviously superior talent on the national team. In short, the desire to seek recognition from other nations by winning international soccer matches began to overcome the urge of Brazilian coaches and authorities to represent their nation internationally as essentially white. Domingos, however, seemed to surprise mostly white journalists who heaped praise on the intelligence and elegance of his play.

For journalists and fans, Domingos brought together the deceptive agility and rhythmic strength naturally attributed to African-descended soccer players with a European risk-averse, no-nonsense, team-oriented playing style and refined technique. Some observers of the era suggested that Domingos was the perfect embodiment of an "authentically" Brazilian soccer style. This was what the already renowned Brazilian sociologist Gilberto Freyre saw in Domingos. Freyre, who had earned a master's degree in anthropology from Columbia University, returned to his native Brazil and became an intellectual sensation when he published *The Masters and the Slaves* in 1933. In this influential book, Freyre attacked the racial theories of social Darwinism that since the end of the nineteenth century had dominated debates over Brazil's national identity and destiny. Social Darwinists generally praised what we now know are fictitious ideas of "racial purity" and argued that race mixture had a detrimental effect that combined the worst attributes of both races. Since Brazil had been characterized by a long history of race mixture, these theories troubled Brazilian intellectuals who feared that their racial heterogeneity would prevent them from ultimately becoming a modern and unified nation that they generally associated with "whiteness." Ashamed of Brazil's mostly nonwhite population that social Darwinists associated with barbarism and backwardness, most Brazilian intellectuals advocated whitening the population by encouraging European immigration. In the unabashedly imperialist world of the late nineteenth and early twentieth centuries where races were often depicted as if they were single organisms in a struggle for survival with other races, Europeans saw their success in subjugating other peoples as proof of their innate racial superiority. It was little wonder that the Brazilian government became careful to send abroad only white diplomats, navy officers, and other delegations (such as soccer players) to represent Brazil to Europeans as a "white" national race.

In contradistinction to social Darwinism, Freyre tried to demonstrate the advantages of Brazil's heritage of racial diversity and race mixture over the centuries. He praised the contributions of Africans and their descendants in the development of a uniquely Brazilian culture that mixed European (mostly Portuguese), African, and, to a somewhat lesser extent, indigenous, Moorish, and Jewish traditions and genes. He used his scholarly authority to attribute positive connotations to racial and ethnic heritages that had long been seen as traits that foredoomed Brazil's national destiny. Freyre, like many other Latin American intellectuals of his day, embraced Brazil's tradition of race mixture as a positive national trait that made its culture creative and unique.

It is thus understandable why Freyre became one of the first to applaud the presence of soccer players of African descent on the Brazilian national team. In a newspaper interview, Freyre affirmed that the national team's triumphs were the fruits of the "courage that we have finally had to send to Europe a team that is strongly Afro-Brazilian," where the white players mixed with the "big black men who are really Brazilian, and the mulattos, even more Brazilian." For Freyre this racial mixture and interplay shaped the essence of a uniquely "Brazilian soccer style" that would be characterized by "something between dance and *capoeira*." Brazil's national team players would distinguish themselves from the European athletes "by an agglomeration of traits of surprise, of skill, of astuteness, of agility, and at the same time of individual brilliance and spontaneity." For Freyre, the Brazilian players thus had a special quality guaranteed by the harmonious integration of different ethnic groups that had shaped Brazil's unique national history and character.

This Brazilian team also received the unreserved support of President Getúlio Vargas during the World Cup tournament of 1938. Vargas had borrowed many of Freyre's interpretations of Brazil's unique racial heritage to support his political platform. Vargas had maintained his grip on power, surviving several attempted coups and revolts against his government, in part by mastering the art of popular appeal. In 1937, with the support of his military, the indirectly elected President Vargas closed

Congress and all political parties to implement a new regime that he called the Estado Novo (New State). He claimed that the reform was needed to maintain Brazil's national unity at a time of international turmoil and domestic conflict between factions that supported fascism, socialism, or liberal democracy as alternative paths for the nation's future. Vargas appropriated some of Freyre's nationalist theories of Brazil's unique traditions of racial and class harmony to give legitimacy to his dictatorship that closed down meaningful political debates and disputes. Soccer players such as Domingos da Guia served President Vargas well as an ally in his propaganda and political project because they embodied the ideal espoused by Freyre of Brazil's unique heritage of "racial democracy," or the idea that racism was not a prominent characteristic of Brazilian society.

These factors help to explain why Freyre depicted Domingos da Guia as a prime example of his thesis of racial democracy that in the 1930s became a stock part of sports journalism in Rio de Janeiro. Freyre made this association explicit in a 1947 preface he wrote for the sports journalist Mário Filho's book, *O negro no futebol brasileiro* (The black man in Brazilian soccer). The sociologist Freyre associated Apollonian (referring to Apollo, the Greek god of the sun and public probity, justice, physical strength, and decorum) traits with Europeans while he attributed Dionysian (the Greek god of wine, mirth, and humor) traits to the African tradition. For Freyre, the national team's style was "a little bit of samba, a pinch of boyish Bahian pranksterism, and even a little *capoeira*. . . . With these components Brazilian soccer moved away from the original well-ordered British style to become a dance full of irrational surprises and Dionysian variations" that gave substance to a new style whose forms the legend of Domingos da Guia would forever shape.

Before he reached this summit of nationalist adulation, however, the young Domingos Antonio da Guia had to travel a long and difficult road that he described in an interview for posterity at Rio's Museum of Image and Sound in 1967. This author also interviewed Domingos twice thirty-one years later, when his advanced age led to some lapses in his memory. Domingo's childhood was similar to that of many other poor children. Born on November 19, 1911, in the industrial borough of Bangu, about an hour's train ride from Rio's downtown, he had eight siblings and was the youngest of four brothers. Like almost all of Bangu's residents, his father worked in a textile factory owned by the Campanhia Progresso Industrial do Brasil, which had transformed a predominately rural area into an industrial zone by the early 1900s. For most boys raised in Bangu at that time, their highest realistic ambition for the future was a factory job.

The textile factory provided primary schooling for the children of its employees. Domingos finished eight years of school, but, like most Brazilians of his class, he never went on to secondary education. Many boys in Bangu lacked educational, career, and leisure options, and they found inexpensive release and diversion in spirited games of soccer, the preferred sport of all classes in Rio de Janeiro by 1900. This passion for soccer deepened when Rio hosted a South American championship tournament in 1919 that the Brazilian team won. In Bangu, the interest in soccer was evident early. The factory sponsored a team to represent the borough in 1904. Bangu's team proudly took the name of its neighborhood, and for a time it was the only team in Rio's top league whose players came almost entirely from the working class. In the 1920s, Rio's most prominent teams hailed from wealthy neighborhoods near the city's center. Aristocratic sports clubs catered to prosperous and mostly white Brazilians, and they barred Rio's mostly darker-skinned working-class men from joining their teams. Bangu's success inspired the formation of other working-class teams in the borough and other parts of the city. By the time Domingos began to take his first kicks, soccer had already become a working-class obsession capable of causing young students such as Domingos to cut classes for a game.

More than a simple diversion, the game already seemed to Domingos a concrete alternative path to a better life for himself and his family. Until the 1930s, soccer remained an amateur sport and league officials prohibited direct payments to players. Domingos's three older brothers played for Bangu teams, and he witnessed firsthand the advantages offered to worker-athletes: sometimes players won cash bonuses, and companies rewarded prized worker-athletes with cushy, higher-paying jobs. Contemporaries labeled these practices that ran counter to the spirit of amateur sporting ethics "brown professionalism" (a reference to the race of many of the working-class players). "Brown professionalism" began to transform the city's sporting scene by promoting the increasing incorporation of the working-class suburban teams into the most competitive first-division league dominated by the more venerable white soccer clubs. Young soccer players and their promoters transformed a leisure activity into a new, if narrow and unstable, avenue of social mobility that tended to reinforce the devotion of poor fans to their neighborhood teams, players, and soccer itself.

As Domingos himself recalled in 1967, "my interest in soccer at first came from necessity." Domingos had already worked as an adolescent drudge at a number of low-paying manual labor jobs. Like other young men, he knew that "soccer players had greater chances for financial success." Confident in his sporting abilities, he endeavored to use soccer as a vehicle for raising his income.

As a teenager, Domingos knew that until he played on the more prominent teams, his athletic success would be limited. To practice and gain experience, he banded together with a group of young boys from his neighborhood to form a new team called Julius Caesar, which played in a field near the local church. Because the boys lacked the means to buy shoes and jerseys, they borrowed equipment from more established neighborhood teams. One neighborhood team, Esperança, was especially helpful to Julius Caesar. Some of Domingos's older brothers played for Esperança, a team in Rio's second-division league (roughly equivalent to American baseball's minor leagues). Esperança's players, in turn, depended on used equipment provided by the borough's sole first-division team, Bangu, the only club that promised a higher standard of living for its players.

Only in 1929 at age eighteen did Domingos's years of practice finally pay off; he became a second-string player for Bangu. Even though he rode the bench and played in only four games in his first season, by making the team Domingos won a job at the textile factory. In 1930, Domingos got a break: a starting fullback for Bangu suffered a serious injury. His brother, Luiz Antonio, who had been a starting fullback for Bangu years earlier, was now a club coach who had the responsibility for naming substitutes. Those who followed the club closely suggested Domingos, who had been playing well on the club's second team. Luiz Antonio, however, was reluctant at first because he thought his younger brother was "too thin, too weak" for a defense position usually reserved for more burly players. In the end, Luiz Antonio gave in, and Domingos started in his first game in a key match against one of Rio's perennial powerhouse teams, Flamengo. According to Domingos, "That was my start, and I was happy. We won by a margin of 3 to 1, and I never left Bangu's starting team thereafter."

More than prestige, Domingos's promotion to the first team earned him a substantial pay raise. By starting for Bangu in Rio's citywide championship, Guilherme da Silveira, the owner of the textile factory that sponsored Bangu, began to pay Domingos bonuses for his play in amounts that varied between 500 and 1,000 reis per game. Beyond these bonuses, he received a monthly salary from the factory. Until this point, Domingos had played for teams where the players "paid to play," but Bangu "gave him a small salary." "I worked in the factory office or I worked at this or that and I played for Bangu," Domingos recalled. His narrative reveals how club owners indirectly paid amateur players in the system of "brown professionalism." At a time when a factory worker had to work hard to gain just enough to sustain his household, Domingos now earned an income that was much higher than most common laborers. Despite the barriers that he had to overcome because of his race and class, Domingos beat the odds and became one of the few players who succeeded in making his living by playing soccer.

As a professional player, Domingos's ascent was meteoric. His great play for Bangu won him renown that led to his nomination to a citywide all-star team in 1931. This annual tournament pitted players from Brazil's second largest city at the time, São Paulo, against those from the nation's largest city and capital, Rio de Janeiro. That same year he formed part of Brazil's national team that took on neighboring Uruguay for the Rio Branco Cup. His superior play earned him a starting position, making him the only black player on Brazil's national team. Against Uruguay, Domingos's skill and pluck won over Brazil's fans. One cheering fan yelled out, "I am going to have that *crioulo* [roughly equivalent to 'nigger'] plated in gold." The comment reveals the deep-seated contradictions that underlay the popular celebration of Domingos's athletic brilliance and racial attitudes. Brazil defeated Uruguay by a score of 2 to 1. Domingos emerged as one of the best players on the field and was "praised by all."

Soon after this triumph, other wealthier white soccer clubs became interested in acquiring Domingos. The need to attract fans to pay for tickets to attend the games required victories. Some of Rio's more traditional teams began to slowly integrate players from the working classes to improve their records. Domingos and other players with dark skin from humble backgrounds profited from a wider process of professionalization that transformed soccer into an industry capable of generating vast financial resources and inspiring passionate loyalties from fans in increasingly impersonal urban environments. These players' athletic gifts allowed them to surmount the racial prejudice that had limited the careers of those who came before them.

In January 1932 rumors began to spread that Domingos would be transferred to América (one of the most popular and successful of Rio's teams in the 1930s). Like Leônidas da Silva, another black athlete invited to play for América, Domingos signed a request to be registered as a club member of América. Nevertheless, Domingos desisted from joining the club. To justify his position, he alleged to the press that he had not joined América because he did not want to offend his brothers, part of the Bangu team's faithful. Years later, in 1998, he admitted that "Bangu was not a first caliber club. . . . It was not a Fluminense, a Vasco, a Botafogo, nor an América. It did not have that kind of money." As it seemed clear to most of the sports journalists of the period, Domingos's desire to move to another club was fueled primarily by a desire to increase his income and fame. In confirmation of these suspicions, Domingos signed with another club, Vasco da Gama (a team named for the famed Portuguese navigator), and Bangu cancelled his membership with the accusation that he sought to join other clubs.

Even though Vasco da Gama did not have the prestige and tradition of Rio's most aristocratic and venerable teams such as Fluminense, Flamengo, and Botafogo, it managed to become one of Brazil's elite soccer teams at the beginning of the 1920s. Rio's large Portuguese immigrant community, which dominated retail commerce in the city, founded and financed Vasco, a team that began defeating the city's premier teams because it began to contract black working-class players whom other, more exclusive clubs barred. The success of this strategy was such that this up-and-coming club won its first citywide championship in 1923. Thus, it is fitting and perhaps natural that Vasco was one of the first major teams interested in signing Domingos.

His new contract gave Domingos wealth he had not known as a player for Bangu. "It meant brand-new socks, shoes, knee pads, and shin guards," recalled Domingos. While these acquisitions seem rather modest, for Domingos, "it was paradise." More than brand-new equipment and uniforms, Domingos began to earn substantially more than he had for Bangu without having to put in hours at the factory. For transferring to Vasco he was paid 5:000$000 with a monthly salary of 500$000 reis, a veritable fortune for a working-class man during the Great Depression. In a vain attempt to contain the progressive professionalization of soccer in Brazil, the league put in place new rules that worked to contain the social ascension of renowned athletes such as Domingos. One new rule prohibited players who had switched clubs from taking part in the annual citywide tournament; it obliged Domingos to play on Vasco's second team, which vied for a championship in a much less prestigious tournament. Even though professionalism was still technically illegal in Brazilian soccer, Domingos already had in soccer a well-paid profession with a salary and prestige beyond the reach of a factory worker.

Domingos's social and professional climb was only at its beginning in 1932 when he was once again called on to be a starting player for Brazil's national team in a battle for the Rio Branco Cup, this time in Montevideo. With the help of Domingos, Brazil triumphed by a margin of 2 to 1 over Uruguay. Brazil's press acclaimed the victory as "a notable achievement" and a worthy motive of "just pride" for the Brazilian people. For his formidable performance, Domingos garnered his highest accolades. The Uruguayans themselves declared Domingos the "best fullback on the entire continent." The Montevidean newsmen described him as a "fortress" that secured Brazil's defense. When he returned to Rio with his teammates, Brazilian fans carried Domingos on their shoulders in triumph and thousands thronged Rio's principal streets to honor the national team. The press described the spontaneous welcome accorded the players as the "most moving and impressive reception ever given to a national sports team." From being players only reluctantly accepted on the national team, players of African descent such as Domingos had become national heroes with international athletic reputations.

It did not take long, however, for this international prestige to change Domingos's life. In 1933, Nacional (a principal Uruguayan team) offered Domingos an even more financially lucrative contract. Uruguay, unlike Brazil, had already instituted a professional soccer league. The deal included a monthly salary of 1:500$000 with a bonus of 43:000$000 reis just for signing. The contract's value was more than eight times what Domingos earned with Vasco. He hesitated for about a month before signing the contract because he was not happy about the idea of leaving Brazil. He later observed, perhaps revealing the growing nationalism of the period, that "no one leaves his birthplace happily" and that he did not look with approval "on those who left to make their living in foreign lands." In the end, Domingos thought that he could not pass up this golden opportunity to improve the lives of his family and himself. Before leaving for Uruguay, he left with his brother-in-law money to buy a new house for his parents as well as a piece of land for himself in Bangu. It was, in truth, the beginning of a new life.

For the next three years, Domingos accepted new contracts, each involving ever larger sums of money, and transferred from team to team. His success in Uruguay was crowned by leading his team to a national championship, but his confessed desire was to return to play in Brazil, which he did after Brazil instituted its own professional soccer league in 1933. Bangu, the pioneer of "brown professionalism," won Rio's citywide tournament in 1933, and this victory may have inspired the directors of Vasco to hire more players of African descent. In 1934 they offered Domingos a large sum to return to Rio to play for them. His return did not disappoint fans because Vasco would win the city's tournament the following year. In 1935 a new offer from abroad, this time from Boca Juniors (later the team of Diego Maradonna) of Buenos Aires, Argentina, won Domingos a contract worth more than four times the amount paid to him by Nacional two years earlier. Domingos proved he was worth the investment by leading Boca Juniors to a national championship in 1935. He was the only player of his era who could lay claim to be part of a national championship team in three different countries, a feat that confirmed his prowess on the field and made him Brazil's first truly international soccer star.

Soon enough, yet another Brazilian team resolved to invest the capital necessary to bring Domingos back to Brazil. Rio's traditional teams began to turn their backs on their aristocratic snobbery in order to increase revenues. Flamengo would be the first to build a strong team around a number of nonwhite players. Its goal was to popularize the team to increase the number of club members and fans who would pay to watch Flamengo play. In 1935 the club's leadership began to hire black players such as Domingos's brothers, Otto and Ladislau. In 1936 they also contracted another brother of Domingos, Médio, and other more prominent black players such as Fausto and Leônidas. Soon thereafter, Flamengo, "with great sacrifice," according to Domingos himself, managed to lure him away from Boca Juniors and back to his native Rio. This recruitment strategy made Flamengo's team look different from most other principal teams in Rio, who had remained reluctant to hire so many dark-skinned professionals.

Leaving behind the series of contract negotiations and transfers that had gained him renown, Domingos would stay with Flamengo until 1943. Now he played for one of Brazil's most traditional powerhouse teams whose popularity grew during the 1930s. As Domingos put it, his years with Flamengo were the apogee of his career. With his fame consolidated and his comparatively high salary, Domingos became a major stadium draw for Flamengo. His spectacular play was even applauded by the opposing team's fans. Domingos had achieved a degree of respect and appreciation from club members and fans who a few years ago had turned up their noses at the prospect of hiring a black working-class player.

It was in this context that the national soccer federation began to make preparations to recruit a select team for Brazil's participation in the World Cup tournament of 1938. Domingos and his Flamengo teammate, Leônidas da Silva, were already national stars who had proven their mettle in international competitions. Their reputations fueled the confident expectations of Brazilian fans for the nation's first world soccer championship. For the first time, the press gave the national team's selection process extensive coverage, and many journalists played up the idea that this team would be selected without regard to the social and racial prejudices that had colored nominations in the past. Popular sports journalist Mário Filho, who had purchased the newspaper *Jornal dos Sports* in 1936, had been a leading promoter of innovations in the coverage of soccer and other sporting events in Brazil since 1930. His journalistic commentary clearly supported the transformations in Brazilian soccer that permitted black players such as Leônidas and Domingos to represent Brazil. Mário Filho sponsored unprecedented coverage of the 1938 World Cup and was an influential propagandist of this international sporting event that inspired nationalist passions. The results of the work of Mário Filho and other radio and print journalists were seen in the streets of Brazil where the intensity of support for the national team bristled. Mário Filho would remember years later, "Every Brazilian was overwhelmed by the most intense passion." With the help of the press, not to mention President Vargas and intellectuals such as Gilberto Freyre, the Brazilian public felt pride and an intense connection to their national soccer team. These were the glory days of Domingos and his teammates.

July 5, 1938, was the date of Brazil's opening game against Poland. Just before the game, Mário Filho telephoned the Brazilian delegation in Paris to conduct an exclusive pre-game interview with the players that he ran in his paper the next day to mark the opening of the World Cup competition. When asked about the game against Poland, Domingos promised to give "his all for the victory," and he hoped to play the "best game" of his life. Brazil went on to defeat Poland in a high-scoring nail-biter by 6 to 5. Domingos had indeed played his best despite running a fever of 102 degrees. Mário Filho confirmed that Domingos was "one of the great players in the match and that he had lived up to his fame."

In its other games, the Brazilian team, captained by Domingos and Leônidas, made a lasting impression on Europe. Foreign players, journalists, and fans noted the mixture of races in the composition of Brazil's team but even so, they described Domingos as "one of the most phenomenal players of the tournament." In the semifinal match, Italy defeated Brazil 2 to 1. The winning goal came off of a play in which Domingos had a decisive role when he aggressively tackled an Italian forward in the goal area. This foul led the referee to make a disputed call that gave Italy a penalty kick that they converted into a goal. As Domingos said in 1967, he had made this mistake "because he did not know the rules of soccer."

The adverse result, however, did not dampen the enthusiasm of Brazilians for their national team idols. They attributed the loss to a mistake by the referee, who had marked a penalty kick when the ball was already out of play. Brazilian fans continued to demonstrate an unshaken faith in the superiority of Brazil's soccer prowess. Even though they did not win the World Cup, the Brazilian press insisted on calling the team "the kings of soccer" because they "were better than all the other teams in the championship." Mário Filho joined the chorus, calling the team members "kings without a crown . . . the crack players of Brazil" had given "the European players a soccer lesson." Brazilians were no longer apprentices of the European sport; they were now masters of the game. The so-called true world champions were praised not only by the press as national heroes but also by government ministers. President Vargas's minister of education, Gustavo Campanema, sent the national team a telegram after their defeat, in which he declared them to be "an affirmation of the admirable strength of Brazil, whose many future glorious sports victories were assured."

By personifying a new nationalist image for Brazil and the political project led by President Getúlio Vargas, Domingos, Leônidas, and the other players on the national team, despite their defeat, consolidated their prestige. Taking the field "with the Brazilian soul," in Mário Filho's expression, they proved themselves worthy of the verses of Gilka Machado, then considered "the greatest poetess of Brazil":

Leônidas and Domingos
Fix on the foreigner's retina
The miraculous reality
Of what the Brazilian man is.

Making these two Brazilian soccer players of African descent into glorious symbols of a "new people," the poetess distilled the sentiments of a movement that made them into true representations of the nation's soul. It is not surprising that Domingos once again received a hero's welcome when he and the Brazilian team returned home. With his fame renewed by his World Cup play, Domingos's likeness was used in advertisements for the Vencedora (victorious) brand of clothes, and he endorsed a number of goods ranging from common household products to department stores. From Flamengo, he received a substantial raise with a new contract that paid 50:000$000 for the signing bonus alone. He became an example for the next generation of young working-class black players who gravitated to Flamengo, such as the future star Zizinho, who had idealized Domingos as a youth. Awash in praise and adoration, it seems only natural that Domingos would assert that he was "very happy with his soccer career."

The intense press coverage he received, however, was a double-edged sword. On the one hand, it reinforced the national prestige of black players such as Domingos, but on the other, it camouflaged the contradictory processes that had made his successful professional career possible. Even though his success had been facilitated by a nationalist movement led by artists, intellectuals, and even sports journalists who portrayed the contribution of Brazilians of African descent in a new positive light, Domingos himself seemed to detect that much of this rhetoric rang hollow. He did not exactly see himself as a symbol of Brazil's "racial democracy" or accept the idea that one's race did not prevent the social ascent of talented individuals of color. He was aware of the role of sports journalists such as Mário Filho in creating his legend as a soccer star of African descent, and he frequently thanked the press for its generous praise. Still, he did not forget the many difficulties and insults that he had confronted during his career because of his race.

He well remembered the case of his oldest brother, Luiz Antonio, who in the 1920s became known as an exceptional fullback. According to Domingos, "In Bangu, they say that Luiz Antonio was better than me." Despite his brother's talent, however, his race prevented him from winning the renown and the remuneration that Domingos would achieve only a few years later. Even though Luiz Antonio was widely recognized as one of the best players in Brazil, not one of the wealthy traditional teams even attempted to sign him, and league authorities and politicians vetoed his nomination to the national select team in the 1920s because he was Afro-Brazilian. Even at the height of his career, Domingos witnessed many examples of the difficulties that talented players of color continued to confront. Few managed to parlay their soccer talents into the public acclaim and financial security that Domingos and Leônidas had secured. Fausto, one of Domingos's teammates on Vasco da Gama and later on Flamengo, had undeniable talent that earned him a contract with a Spanish team early in his career. After his career came to an abrupt end, Fausto soon thereafter died penniless and alone at a very young age in 1939. For Domingos, Fausto's life story and those of other celebrated Afro-Brazilians demonstrated that "blacks have never been accepted in this country."

Racial prejudice in Brazil led Domingos to play down in public his own African ancestry. He realized that Brazilian racism struck hardest against the "really black, black player." To deflect this harsh racism, Domingos declared that he was a "mulatto," and he distinguished himself and his experience from darker skinned players such as his own teammate, Leônidas da Silva. As Domingos put it in a 1995 interview, "he [Leônidas] had a real disadvantage . . . [because] he was black, black, black as tar, . . . [even] with his money he remained that *crioulinho* (little nigger). Not me, I am mulatto, so I was treated differently when I arrived at a social gathering . . . [Folks would say] Domingos is black? What do you mean, black? At parties I would socialize freely with [lighter skinned people] and feel at ease conversing because I was not white but black." Domingos hurriedly answered his own rhetorical question: "Well, no, I am not white, but I am not black either!" He then clarified his own confusing circumlocution: "I am the darkest member of my family because of the sun" that beat down on him during his years of playing soccer in Brazil. But he emphasized again that he was "not black or a nigger."

During his career, Domingos remained conscious of the need to shield himself from the worst forms of social and racial discrimination to which he sometimes fell victim even in his moments of glory. As he admitted soon after affirming the advantages of being mulatto in Brazil, "I did not attempt to mix with the wealthy set because I had the disadvantage of being a person of color: I am not black but I am not white either . . . I recognized that [in some social spaces] especially in the wealthy parts of the city only a white person could enter. I said to myself, I cannot go in there. My hair is bad [a racist expression used by Brazilians to belittle the curly hair characteristic of people of African descent]." To distance himself from "blacks," Domingos took care to shape his public image. In his first appearances with Bangu, he wore a cap to hide the curls that he recognized as a trait strongly associated with "blackness." As he remembered, "I began to wash my hair often and then to comb it down straight." Until he returned to play with Flamengo in 1936, Domingos's cap had been his inseparable companion and a trademark of his public image. He carefully monitored his behavior and image even at the height of his career to avoid a direct association with "blackness." Domingos's actions demonstrate the very limited nature of Brazil's "racial democracy" that he himself had come to symbolize. Individuals of color who wanted to be accepted had to know their place in the social hierarchy, even if they were soccer stars, or else face humiliating social censure. Even though he criticized racial prejudice, Domingos also exhibited his own disdain for "blacks" and a fear of being treated like one.

Once his international reputation had been secured after the 1938 World Cup, Domingos felt comfortable enough to leave his cap at home and to display his woolly hair publicly. From that time on, Domingos lost his interest in playing for Brazil's national team, according to Mário Filho, who observed that he stopped playing with the same enthusiasm to deliberately avoid being tapped for the national team. Still, he continued to help Flamengo win championships and maintained his prestige. Domingos's long stint with Flamengo provided a period of stability in his life during which he played some of his best games. He led Flamengo to back-to-back state championships in 1942 and 1943.

In 1944, Domingos left Flamengo to accept a profitable new contract from the city of São Paulo's most popular team, Corinthians. He played there for four years, and his inspired play for Corinthians earned him one last invitation to play for Brazil's national select team against Uruguay for the Rio Branco Cup in 1947. At age thirty-six, Domingos began the final phase of his soccer career. His skill and experience could no longer fully compensate for his declining physical vigor. In 1948 he decided to return to play for Bangu, the team that had helped him to launch his professional career. Domingos stated that Bangu "is where my spirit is more tranquil." Brazil's greatest fullback played his last season of soccer with Bangu in 1949, when he decided it was time to leave professional sports for good.

Despite his years of lucrative contracts and endorsements, Domingos left soccer without a stable retirement nest egg. "I earned a lot of money," Domingos lamented, "but I did not know how to invest my earnings. One time, someone advised me to invest in some houses in Copacabana. It was at that time still a relatively thinly populated Rio borough. Instead, I invested in a subdivision in Bangu." In the mid-1900s, Copacabana would become one of the most densely populated and wealthy boroughs of Rio where real estate values soared, whereas Bangu remained a working-class suburb where property values did not rise so rapidly. Besides his misguided investments, Domingos claimed that he had wasted a lot of money on "women and drink." As he saw it, "I did not know how to save money, but I did know how to live it up."

From the start, his fame seemed sufficient to secure a financially stable future. Even though he had not invested his earnings from soccer wisely, he had his name, which was still capable of earning him a good income. In 1950 he won a contract to endorse soft drinks, and he then turned his hand to a career as a coach for Olaria, a second-division team that represented yet another of Rio's working-class suburbs.

In a game where heroes succeed one another rapidly, Domingos's name soon became less well known. This process was accelerated by the success of Brazil's national team in the 1950 World Cup held in Rio, where Brazil's team only stumbled in the final game in a heart-breaking loss to Uruguay. In 1955, Mário Filho notes in his memoir that "no one spoke anymore of [Domingos] da Guia." He noted that Domingos then lived in São Paulo where he was the owner of a humble luncheonette. A few months later the journalist reported that Domingos was living "in misery" with financial difficulties unimaginable for someone of such renown. He observed, "With the end of his soccer career, came the end of everything for Domingos." The journalist's statement implied a recognition of the contradictions in the myth of racial harmony that he himself had helped to create around the image of the great black fullback. Away from soccer, Domingos was merely a middle-aged black man who had only a primary education and little work experience in the world of business. His soccer career had not prevented him from facing the severe limitations that his race and class imposed on his future.

Fortunately for Domingos, his miserable situation did not last long. Guilherme da Silveira, the owner of the textile factory where Domingos and his brothers and father worked, soon arranged a job for him. As Domingos's son later recalled, "My father was very lucky that Silveira liked him so much." By virtue of his old boss's patronage, Domingos found work as a modest public employee, a job that he maintained for the rest of his life, even after he no longer could work. Two of his sons followed in their father's footsteps to earn a living from professional soccer. Ademir da Guia had a soccer career nearly as brilliant as his father's.

In the last years of his life, Domingos lived with his sons in the middle-class borough of Meier in Rio. At this late point in his long life of eighty-six years, he mused in a somewhat confused stream of consciousness, "The only reason I did not become arrogant and vain was because I came from such a sad state of poverty. We were born in Bangu, my family did not own a house, we did not have anything. We had a house made of wood, you slept in fear, there was no fence, there was nothing. . . . My good fortune was that God gave me the talent to play soccer." A great soccer player, whom politicians, intellectuals, and journalists had once praised as the embodiment of the Brazilian nation's unique genius, had discovered that outside the sports stadium, limits imposed by his race and his class origins belied the myth of racial harmony and tolerance. His self-made celebrity and fortune had been short-lived, but with the help of his family and an old patron, Domingos had managed to escape the more difficult life of a Bangu factory worker.

The story of Domingos and of the nation he reputedly represented failed to live up to the ideal of racial democracy or the idea that Brazil was uniquely free of racial tensions and discrimination. Nevertheless, the former fullback still expressed great pride in his achievements and his sport. In front of a television set that broadcast a game between two women's national teams, he ended his last interview by declaring his gratitude to soccer. Even if they did not provide him and others with a means of completely overcoming racial and class inequalities and prejudices, he took pride in the role he had played in shaping the history of soccer and Brazil, a nation he had proudly defended on the soccer field. Both had given him the means to change his own destiny. Nodding at the television set, he stated, "As a child I was already watching this game. I knew how to play, I mean to say, my entire life was bound up with sports. . . . I began watching and I ended up playing. Then I was happy."

SUGGESTED READINGS

There are important studies of Brazilian soccer and society published in Portuguese: Mário Filho Rodrigues, *O negro no futbol brasileiro* (Rio de Janeiro: Firmo, 1994); Waldemyr Caldas, *O pontepé inicial: Memória de futebol brasileiro* (São Paulo: IBRASA, 1990); Leonardo Affonso de Miranda Pereira, *Footballmania: Uma história social do futebol no Rio de Janeiro (1902–1938)* (Rio de Janeiro: Nova Fronteira, 2000); J. C. Meihy and J. S. Witter, eds., *Futebol e cultura: Uma coletânea de estudos* (São Paulo: Arquivo do Estado de São Paulo, 1982); Anatol Rosenfeld, *Negro, macumba e futebol* (São Paulo: Edusp, 1993); and Mário de Moraes, ed., *Futebol e arte: Depoimentos e Domingos da Guia, Zizinho, e Pelé* (Rio de Janeiro: Museu da Imagem e do Som Rio de Janeiro, 2002).

On Brazilian soccer in English, see Tony Mason, *Passion of the People: Football in South America* (New York: Verso Books, 1995); Robert M. Levine, "Sport and Society: The Case of Brazilian Futebol," *Luso-Brazilian Review* 17:2 (1980): 233–51; Janet Lever, *Soccer Madness: Brazil's Obsession for the World's Most Popular Sport* (Prospect Heights, IL: Waveland Press, 1995);

José Sérgio Leite Lopes, "Class, Ethnicity, and Color in the Making of Brazilian Football," *Daedalus* 129:2 (2000): 239–70; idem, "Football and the Working Class in Brazil: Colour and Class in the Making of National Identity," Working Paper, Manchester International Centre for Labour Studies, University of Manchester, no. 15 (May 1996); and Alex Bellos, *Futebol: The Brazilian Way of Life* (North Pomfret, VT: Bloomsbury, 2002).

CHAPTER 9

Norma Fraga

Race, Class, Education, and the Estado Novo

JERRY DÁVILA

The music and sports industries began to offer a small number of talented but mostly poorly educated nonwhites such as Geraldo Pereira and Domingos da Guia new possibilities for social mobility and celebrity in the 1930s. Studies by social scientists, however, have shown that level of education is the variable that best predicts future income. Of course, income is only one way of measuring relative success (a subjective concept, especially for poorly paid academics) within a given social system. In any case, unlike a career, a reputation, physical vigor, or belongings, education is a possession that cannot be easily lost or taken away. A good education tends to lend more stability to an individual's position as well as the patina of polish and respectability often associated with superior social and class status. On average, a better-educated person is more able to deal with the adversities and injustices that nature, society, or fate presents them over the course of a lifetime. In the ideal, public educational systems should serve as gateways to achievement and social mobility for all citizens. But in practice, educational institutions often act as barriers to maintain the status quo.

Jerry Dávila's recounting of Norma Fraga's life as a student of African descent during Brazil's Estado Novo (1937–1945) reveals how the public education system worked to the disadvantage of most nonwhites. New standards for teacher certification and higher pay led to both a "whitening" and a feminization of the teacher corps in Rio's growing network of elementary schools during the Vargas years. The system also tended to reflect stubborn ideas of racial hierarchy among an overwhelmingly white teacher population. Thus, white students were more likely to be tracked for achievement and promotion, while black and brown students were more likely to be held to low standards or held back altogether. Most of the architects of the system and the curriculum itself preserved stereotypes of primitive, inferior African culture and assumed that the need to "whiten" those of African descent through education was a matter of national salvation. These practices flew in the face of the nationalist rhetoric of racial democracy that most leaders of the Estado Novo embraced. As Professor Dávila shows, Dona Norma was one of the few persons of color who managed to overcome barriers that kept most nonwhites out of the higher educational

165

institutions and the profession of teaching. Her relatively privileged background and intelligence overcame the social disadvantages of her race. Her biography gives renewed life to the tired cliché of the exception that proved the rule, and it shows how a disproportionately small, but significant, non-white urban middle class emerged despite the many prejudices common to Brazil's institutions.

Jerry Dávila is assistant professor of history at the University of North Carolina, Charlotte. His biography of Dona Norma Fraga comes out of the extensive oral history research that he conducted with Brazilians who were students in the 1920s, 1930s, and 1940s for his book Diploma of Whiteness: Race and Social Policy in Brazil, 1917–1945 *(2003). He continues his studies of the role of racial thought in shaping public policy by exploring Brazil's foreign relations with newly independent African nations.*

On September 4, 1942, some 40,000 public school students assembled in Rio de Janeiro's largest soccer stadium to pay homage to the "Brazilian Race." Under the direction of the country's most famous classical composer, Heitor Villa-Lobos, the students performed "folkloric" African and indigenous songs and sang nationalist hymns to celebrate the Estado Novo dictatorship. They were honoring the dictator, President Getúlio Vargas, and the spirit of Pan-Americanism. Brazil had just entered World War II on the side of the Allies and would soon send soldiers to Europe to fight under the command of U.S. generals. Ironically, this gathering of tens of thousands of students—described as a special "Race" that was "Brazilian"—sang nationalist anthems and celebrated the Allied cause by imitating the public assemblies of fascist Europe. The Estado Novo regime that mobilized these students had been imposed five years earlier as a dictatorship colored by fascistic influences, but this government was never as heavy-handed or supported by well-organized grassroots fascist parties commanded by a national leader such as Adolf Hitler or Benito Mussolini.

One of the 40,000 voices at the stadium on that day belonged to Norma Fraga, a fourteen-year-old student at the nation's most prestigious high school, the federally run Colégio Pedro II. She stood at a historic crossroads for Brazil. Her singing bridged the Allied military cause with the fascist political culture that it fought. What was it like for her? Did she respond to the fascism of the event, the nationalism of the moment, or the world at war? None of the above: "for us at that time, we did not have the slightest notion of what it all was, it was something for the youth to enjoy. There must have been some who detested it, because it was more or less mandatory, and there were always those who would not go, but I went to all of them, because I love big public events . . . it was fascist, it was a fascist regime, but we all loved it."

Norma Fraga's experience was typical in many ways. When she was nine years old, her family moved from the countryside to the federal capital, Rio de Janeiro, at a time when urban populations in Brazil swelled. She attended the public schools that had been transformed and expanded by Anísio Teixeira, a progressive reformer and Rio's director of public education before he was purged from Vargas's government in a 1935 anti-Communist crackdown. Like many young urban women increasingly contemplating professional careers, Fraga dreamed of being a teacher, and indeed would teach history for most of her life. Yet there are also ways in which her story is unique. Standing in the stadium in 1942, she wore the khaki uniform of the Colégio Pedro II, one of the most exclusive schools in Brazil at the time and indeed one of the country's few public secondary schools. She would join the 4 percent of her generation that completed their secondary education. Indeed, according to census data, only 17 percent completed the third grade. What was most exceptional about her experience, however, is that Norma Fraga was a woman of color.

While the 1940 census declared nearly half of Brazil's population to be black, indigenous, or racially mixed, and while Brazilian elites professed that their country was a racial democracy free of tensions and intolerance, it was unusual for a student of color to reach the rarified halls of the Colégio Pedro II, let alone any other secondary school. Of her class of over 500, there was only one other student of color, Fraga recalls, and that pupil was the daughter of one of the school's administrative staff. It was highly uncommon for a young woman like her to be in high school and much more probable that she would work as a domestic servant, the source of employment for one third of black women in Rio over age twelve at the time. Two-thirds of Brazilians of color in her generation were illiterate. Norma was born in the countryside, the youngest of twelve children. The odds that she would escape the almost invisible barriers that systematically marginalized Brazilians of color were high. The odds that she would reach the Colégio, and indeed complete a university education, were astronomically high.

Norma Fraga was an unusual woman in an unusual time. Her experience is evocative of the barriers faced by Brazilians of color like herself, and of the very rare opportunities that made it possible to overcome them. It is a story of belonging and of being able to belong. Interviews conducted between 1999 and 2001 with Norma Fraga, and with other students who studied at the Colégio Pedro II alongside her, make it possible to see her experience not only as an exception but also as a means of understanding the growing complexity of urban life in a country that struggled with its identity, especially in terms of its racial heterogeneity and mixture. The awkward transition from semi-fascist dictatorship to signatory of the United Nations charter, the slow process of industrialization, the quick process of urbanization, the image of racial democracy—lying like a veneer over centuries of slavery and racial injustice—all framed the world in which Norma Fraga grew up.

As Norma's experience shows, there is more than one way to read the patterns of politics and political participation during the Estado Novo. Some white students of the Colégio Pedro II became political activists who first pressed for Brazil's entry into World War II, then for an end to the Estado Novo dictatorship. A few even became members of Brazil's Communist Party. Norma did not take part in these movements. To the contrary, she relished the choreographed moments of nationalist celebration of the Estado Novo regime. Still, her presence at these events, especially as a student of the prestigious Colégio Pedro II, defied the expectations of white educators who, like others of Brazil's mostly white social elite, did not believe that Afro-Brazilians were well adapted or suited to succeed in a modern industrializing society. Norma's presence was in itself a political act: she lived through momentous years in Brazil's history; and, throughout them, she carved out a role as an equal participant.

Norma Fraga was more than a witness to those "Day of the Race" festivities of September 1942. An avid participant who loved to sing, she also enjoyed the great crowds. She attended the rally with her entire eighth-grade class, and indeed with the rest of the students in her school. Along with tens of thousands of other public school children from around the city, she sang songs that had been practiced in class year in and year out. The "Day of the Race" assembly, like many other such gatherings over the course of the year, was a moment in which the regular students in nationalist choral song would be put on display. On this day, or any other, she might sing a short hymn composed by Villa-Lobos that illustrated the musical and cultural march toward whiteness which the composer, like other educators, envisioned as the destiny of the "Brazilian Race." In the hymn, "Rejoicing of a Race," Villa-Lobos composed two choruses, one identified as African, the other as *mestiço*. The African chorus, simple and unsophisticated, was three syllables, continuously repeated: "A - - iu - - ê/ A - - - - - iu - ê." The *mestiço* chorus was more complex, but still repetitive: "Chumba Tuma á - ê - ma, Chumba Tuma á - ê - ma/ Chumba Tuma á - ê - ma, Chumba Tuma á - ê - ma/ Can-ja can-jê - rê tu-ba! Can-ja can-jê - rê tu-ba!" Reflecting Villa-Lobos's views on whitening, lyrics became increasingly complex as the cultural voice transitioned from an African toward a European one, but the African chorus remained primitive in its simplistic repetition.

More complex songs such as "Little Soldiers" reflected the nationalism promoted by the Vargas regime: "We are little soldiers/ Strong in the struggle to find/ The conquests and destiny/ That we offer to our fatherland/ March, little soldier/ Content and happy/ Be guided on your journey/ By your love of the Nation." Another common theme was the cult of personality around Getúlio Vargas. Students sang "Viva Brazil! Save Getúlio Vargas!/ Brazil places its faith/ Its hope and its certainty/ In the future upon the Chief of the Nation."

Norma sang these words, her voice swelled by tens of thousands of others, as generals, ministers, foreign dignitaries—and at times Vargas himself—looked on proudly at the disciplined, nationalist, and Europeanized "Race" that was being forged. While some educators actually believed this race would be physically whitened, most agreed that it could at least become culturally and behaviorally European, and therefore functionally if not physically white. Although educators poured great efforts into the building of such a consciousness, for a student of color such as Norma, none of this really made any sense: "it was a 'Brazilian Race' in quotation marks, you know, because what Brazilian race is there? What does that mean? But that is what they called it . . . but we prepared all those patriotic hymns, and it was that whole pretty thing of the public schools all there and parading, the 'Chief of the Nation,' Getúlio Vargas [would attend], and they called it Day of the Race, which is a totally erroneous expression because there was no race in that, but they called it Day of the Race." The idea of the "Race" had no resonance, she recalled. "It all came out of the heads of the ideologues of the Estado Novo, with their fascist model, which we can criticize today, but at the time I thought it was great to go to the events, to dress in the [school] uniform and parade." Although she identified herself as black, Norma saw no contradiction in her participation in these movements.

These student gatherings took place several times each year, celebrating the Race, Brazilian independence, the proclamation of the Estado Novo, or even the visit of dignitaries from the United States. They were a major logistical operation: for months the school system planned and choreographed special transportation on buses and trolleys for children to gather from around the city. Meeting places, bag lunches, and medical supervision were all carefully arranged. Students rehearsed yearround in their schools. The authorities intended these assemblies to dramatize a united, nationalist support of the regime, confidence in the nation, and adulation for the "Chief of the Nation," Getúlio Vargas. Their complex logistics and fluid, choreographed performances evoked the image of a vigorous government capable of coordinating the nation's energies.

The assemblies conveyed an image of order and progress, but at a price—the regime curtailed democracy, restricted civil liberties, and disbanded political parties in favor of an authoritarian administration that envisioned Brazil as an organism whose constituent parts could be coordinated by an all-powerful central government. Writing from exile, Anísio Teixeira, the reformer who had introduced the choral song program when he directed the school system in the early 1930s, condemned the Estado Novo as "a corrupted and most degrading fascism which is giving life to our most objectionable potential." He continued: "Ours is a phase of putrefaction. And our Government is the result of this putrefaction." Teixeira, who admired the United States, used these strong words to condemn the Estado Novo system of government, which applied a "corporatist" model of social organization developed by Benito Mussolini in Italy and adopted by fascist Spain and Portugal (and to an extent this model was even visible in some aspects of U.S. New Deal policies). Under this system, groups such as workers and industrialists, farmers, intellectuals, and students were seen as distinct corporate entities whose interests would be managed and balanced by the regime. By coordinating the nation's energies, the Estado Novo would project Brazil into the modern age. The assembly of the students acting as a single group and—despite their different ethnic and racial backgrounds—as a single "Race" symbolized the orderly and united society that the Estado Novo architects envisioned. Students would yield their individualism and gain membership in a corporate group that defined them as the future of the nation.

While the idea of a "Brazilian Race" held no special significance for her, Fraga still participated in its elements. Beyond the choral displays, the process of building the "Race"—of carrying out the social engineering that would make Brazil culturally, if not physically, white—was pursued extensively in school programs. Just as there was an irony to fascist assemblies that celebrated the Allied war effort, there was an irony to students of color singing about a "Brazilian Race" that did not quite exist but that, if it did, would be white. It is this irony that Norma negotiated through her education and that highlights the tension between color and status in Brazil. While Brazil is a country that instituted few explicit barriers to the integration and ascension of people of color, subtle obstacles and discrete reminders of the superiority of whiteness dotted the social and institutional landscape. Indirect barriers, ostensibly meritocratic policies, and values that belittled people of color together resulted in the systematic marginalization of those of African descent. Significantly, this system did not totally foreclose social mobility. It permitted the integration of some privileged individuals. In these cases, status became more important than color in determining social place. Norma's relationship with those symbols of status placed her among that privileged group.

The Fraga family moved to Rio de Janeiro in 1937 after Norma's father died. He had been a landowner and political boss in the interior of Espírito Santo. It was uncharacteristic but not inconceivable for a rural landowner in Brazil to be nonwhite. A landowner typically needed extensive networks of patronage and credit, resources available to few former slaves. It is not surprising, then, that her father would have been both a landowner and a bulwark of the ruling Republican Party in the years before Vargas came to power. Economic and political power were close cousins in the countryside, and Norma's father's situation allowed him to send his children to study in the federal capital, where they even attended medical and law schools. Although this experience was uncommon for most Brazilians of African ancestry, we should remember that some families of color had a lineage of freedom that by the twentieth century might stretch over many generations. These families, like that of engineer and abolitionist André Rebouças or President Nilo Peçanha— exceptions whose families experienced prodigious social mobility—would be heralded as examples of racial equality in Brazil, despite the overwhelming evidence to the contrary.

In the decades before Vargas came to power, being a political boss meant delivering the votes to guarantee an election, regardless of the methods. Norma's older brothers would return home at election time with their wrists sore from fraudulently signing names to ballots. Since Norma's mother was staunchly opposed to these practices, she became an ardent *getulista* (supporter of Vargas) in 1937 when the Estado Novo closed the political system, suspended elections, and dissolved the political parties, temporarily ending the corrupt electoral politics that her late husband had encouraged. Since two of her children studied in Rio, Norma's mother resolved to move the family there, and she supported them by running a downtown boardinghouse.

When the family arrived in the capital, nine-year-old Norma enrolled in a public school near her home in the city center, the most economically, racially, and ethnically diverse part of Rio. Although one of her teachers was black, and although she also aspired to be a teacher, she recognized the fact that this profession was increasingly limited to white women. Many Brazilian men and women of color had taught in public schools at the beginning of the century. Most lacked formal training, and their numbers declined as the school system expanded and the government imposed more exclusive selection, testing, and training criteria for teachers. Most new ones were graduates of the Institute of Education, the city's teachers college, which admitted a small number of aspiring candidates and did so only at the beginning of their high-school years.

Admissions committees selected candidates on the basis of their health, appearance, psychological exams, and intelligence tests. The tough selection criteria, based on such vague factors as temperament and appearance, made it easy to exclude nonwhite candidates without explicitly using "race" as a reason. These criteria especially handicapped candidates who came from poorer backgrounds and who in the past had been educated and prepared for teaching by religious charities and orphanages. Although the Institute offered one of the only public secondary educations in the city (along with the Colégio where Norma studied), its admissions criteria were so strict that candidates commonly took a year-long preparatory course for the exams. Since the preparatory courses were private and expensive, they were one more way in which admissions were restricted to well-heeled, generally white candidates. The increased professionalization of the teacher corps, in the guise of tighter admissions standards to the Institute, the restriction that only women could become teachers, and other measures had the cumulative effect of limiting the number of nonwhites who could apply.

These criteria of professionalization were part of a broader reform under way in elementary education. By the time she enrolled in school, public education had been massively reorganized. Education reformers expanded institutions that had once been the province of the privileged in order to reach the masses. The reasons for this transformation had to do with the educational policymakers' preoccupation with race and the creation of an industrial work force. Many feared that the mostly poor and nonwhite population were degenerate, but they believed that the school system could redeem them and thereby save the nation. Consequently, the curriculum, extracurricular activities such as choral assemblies, teacher training, and the process of placing and advancing students were all redrawn with a racialized agenda. Formal barriers were not erected, but the nature of education reform and expansion meant that the newly included groups experienced few opportunities for meaningful advancement.

It was in this context that the "Day of the Race" celebrating the doctrine of a "Brazilian Race" became a centerpiece of the public education offered by the Estado Novo regime. Everyone could belong, regardless of color. Schools would build the "Brazilian Race" by addressing degeneracy. Indeed, for the reformers of the nation's public school system—men such as Minister of Education Gustavo Capanema—the "Brazilian Race" was a work in progress: the country's different ethnicities and races would dilute over time into a healthier and more fit, culturally European, and potentially white Brazilian people. Special attention to maternity, infancy, and youth would gradually transform the nation's diverse phenotypes. Public education would Europeanize the culture. The choral performances of the "Day of the Race" were an allegory of this work in progress. Students would sing "folkloric" African and indigenous music that symbolized a primitive ethnic past. They would hail the accomplishments of the regime, praise Brazil's bright destiny, and laud the qualities of its leader, Getúlio Vargas, who, like the overwhelming majority of public figures, was a white man.

In the rarified atmosphere of the halls of government ministers, Brazil's racial mixture was the topic of serious discussion and planning. Could Brazil become a white country? What did it mean to be a white country? How could Brazil get there? By the 1930s, the consensus was that Brazil could become "functionally" white by training its citizens in the appropriate cultural, moral, hygienic, health, and civic values. Minister Capanema chose to celebrate this historic accomplishment by commissioning a statue of the "Brazilian Man" to be placed outside the Ministry of Education. In 1938, as the statue neared completion, Capanema visited the studio where it was being made and was appalled by a racially mixed, physically unfit figure. This image was not the robust and racially fit "Brazilian Man" that would be the model for his ministry's labors. Capanema fired the sculptor and started over again with a list of precise measurements provided by doctors and anthropologists that defined an Aryan and athletic figure.

While policymakers squabbled over the appearance of the "Brazilian Man" statue, Norma went on with the business of being an elementary school student. Big blocs of her school day were given over to the curriculum of whitening and fighting degeneracy. Her physical education classes were specifically tailored from imported French eugenic standards to increase the health and vitality of the "Race." Her choral songs and the whole civic calendar she followed were tied to a Europeanized and nationalist identity. As a girl, she took regular courses in a discipline called puericulture, which attended to issues of pre- and postnatal child care. For the government agents of the "Brazilian Race," childbirth was a crucial intersection on the road away from degeneracy, and proper maternity care was a commensurately important feature of social policy.

Despite her inclusion in the Colégio Pedro II's student body, Norma's educational experiences reveal frequently hostile attitudes toward Afro-Brazilians such as herself. There was no explicit racism in the school that Norma attended, but there were numerous implicit barriers that very few Brazilians of color were able to negotiate. School system programs that Norma took part in were created by educators who had a deep-seated belief in the "degeneracy" of Afro-Brazilians. Most did not believe Afro-Brazilians to be biologically inferior, but they equated blackness with poor health, poor hygiene, a pre-logical culture, psychological maladjustment, and an inability to work productively. The programs they created—such as Villa-Lobos's nationalist musical program, the textbook vision of Afro-Brazilians, and slavery as folkloric vestiges of a bygone Brazil, and the Health Brigade—all reflected the belief that Afro-Brazilians were at the margins of the national experience, becoming members of the mainstream only as they embraced new "scientific" norms of comportment. While the school system sought to remedy perceived deficiencies, its policies reflected and reproduced a belief in the accumulated inferiority of Brazilians of color.

Returning to Villa-Lobos's choral performances, we can see the ways in which the vision of a disciplined, nationalist and modern Brazil was rife with racial implications. Villa-Lobos saw his musical program as an instrument for the European acculturation of nonwhite students, and for the preservation of social discipline in schools where children from different races increasingly studied together. The presumably white students imagined by Villa-Lobos learned not only "the good teachings of their professors, but sometimes, certain habits and customs from rebellious children, generally influenced by environment or heredity, even though the school should be a temple for developing the soul, cultivating a love of beauty . . . focusing on the qualities and virtues that human progress depends upon."

Villa-Lobos counterposed whiteness—defined in his words by progress, beauty, and virtue—to blackness, which embodied rebelliousness, bad habits, and problems of heredity. His musical program was an educational, disciplinary, and nationalistic allegory of the journey away from blackness, through mixture, into whiteness. One of the traits that Villa-Lobos believed had to be left aside was the "obstinate" and "unconscious" rhythms performed during Carnival, whose sambas were composed by Afro-Brazilians such as Geraldo Pereira (see Chapter 8). Villa-Lobos bemoaned the fact that this enthusiasm was not projected into the singing of the national anthem. But he believed that the transition from street rhythms to forcefully sung civic hymns could be achieved through the "constant exercise of marches and martial songs," which not only sharpened the musical capacity of the population but also awakened "a greater civic interest for things patriotic." Writing of the "race now being created," Villa-Lobos explained: "This is a task of preparing the child mentality to, little by little, reform the collective mentality of future generations." He endeavored to create a new national aesthetic that, among other things, was hostile to Afro-Brazilian culture. He did not try to erase Brazil's African and indigenous cultural expressions. To the contrary, Villa-Lobos gained fame specifically by celebrating Brazilian folklore and weaving African and indigenous elements into his classical compositions. But the structure he brought to musical education assumed the vantage point of a white man looking upon African and indigenous cultures as folk artifacts, vestiges of Brazil's past that needed to be recognized and included but subordinated to its modernistic future.

The condescending vision of Afro-Brazilians typically held by educators was visible in the texts they wrote and the commemorations they planned. Their vision was present as well, though less visible, in school practices which, though based on principles of science and merit, were nonetheless steeped by educators with the sense that Afro-Brazilians were ill adapted to modern, urban, and industrial society. Consequently, schools tracked students based on their perceived state of health, level of intelligence, and degree of psychological adjustment. A review of school records reveals that these were racially coded and subjective criteria that, school reports show, routinely tracked wealthy and white children into advanced classes and poor and nonwhite children into remedial classes. In some cases, teachers presumed that children in the remedial classes were not even capable of learning to read or write and held them back, year after year, until these students abandoned school altogether.

Norma avoided this trap. Probably because her family was not poor, her teachers perceived her to be a more promising student. Indeed, her background was unusual but not unique in the sense that hers was one of the few families of color—out of the thousands that migrated year in and year out to the major cities —that came to Rio with property, income, and education. Her class status counterbalanced her racial status and was probably one of the reasons she merited the attentions of her teachers. Her family also had the means to keep her in school, while many other children left to work to support their families. But alongside her favorable economic situation, she benefitted from the absence of explicit barriers and the fact that her teachers apparently did not dismiss her because of her color. Instead, her teachers made her a model for other students to follow. Anyone could be a member of the "Brazilian Race," but in the opinion of educators, few students of color matched up to expectations.

One of the ways in which Norma did meet—and indeed helped to set—standards was in her enthusiastic participation in the elements of building the "Brazilian Race," from the Villa-Lobos concerts to her school's Health Brigade. Each school had a Health Brigade composed of older students, who were responsible for instructing and overseeing the basics of hygiene that were a centerpiece of school eugenic (race improvement) programs. With her armband bearing a Maltese cross, Norma was one of the junior managers of the school programs that addressed problems that educators associated with poverty and degeneracy. Norma was responsible for ensuring that her classmates had brushed their teeth; she checked them for lice and assessed the cleanliness of their uniforms: "I demanded the most from my classmates." The Health Brigade, like other activities that helped to build the "Brazilian Race," was a progressive attempt to remedy the perceived inferiority of poor and nonwhite Brazilians, but it was also a program that reinforced stereotypes. In a similar fashion, policies for placing and advancing students as well as for selecting and training teachers were ostensibly meritocratic procedures that also suffered from assumptions about race and class. These policies relied on norms of medical and psychological fitness and dress, speech, and comportment as well as special training and preparation available only to more prosperous Brazilians.

Through her social class and her participation in school activities, Norma fit into a social category of whiteness, the color of her skin becoming one aspect among others ascribed equal or greater social weight by her peers. Consequently, although fewer than half of the students who entered the first grade finished elementary school, Norma did. And although the city offered almost no public high-school programs that bridged the elementary school to the secondary system, Norma gained admission into the Colégio Pedro II, the most prestigious high school in Brazil. Norma's mother aspired for her to study at the Institute of Education because its graduates had their careers as teachers for the city virtually guaranteed. During the Estado Novo, teaching was a relatively well-paid job and was widely seen as a gender-appropriate profession for a young woman. The Institute was a gateway to a respectable middle-class career for women, and its graduates often married military officers and cadets who also studied and worked in Rio. Still, Norma dreamed of attending the Colégio Pedro II. It was located near her home, and she saw the students coming and going and admired their khaki military-style uniforms.

In the mid-1900s uniforms conveyed a sense of privilege. A blue skirt and white blouse unmistakably meant being a normal school student at the Institute of Education. Students at the Colégio Pedro II complained bitterly when a school in Niteroi, a city across the bay from Rio de Janeiro, adopted uniforms similar to their own. These adolescents recognized that in a society in which very few individuals held most of the social, political, and economic privileges, status came from being part of recognized public institutions. The uniform conveyed that sense of status for students as it did for police or members of the military. The uniform was all the more important for a young woman such as Norma who, because of her color, would be presumed to be poor and probably a domestic servant. The uniform was a guarantee that despite the stereo-types held about Afro-Brazilians, she was part of the system. While the corporatist Vargas regime foreclosed democratic political participation, it defined paths for symbolic citizenship that Norma followed, which offered some protections from common racism.

At the Colégio Pedro II, Norma gained a rare opportunity to earn a public secondary school education. Admission was highly competitive since the school was the only federal institution providing secondary education. Five Brazilian presidents had graduated from the Colégio. Its curriculum was the national model for secondary education, and students who attended the Colégio were all but guaranteed admission to a university. Norma, for instance, enrolled in the Federal University of Rio de Janeiro after graduation. Her teachers were commonly the leaders of their fields, writing textbooks that would be adopted for use in public schools nationally.

In this rarified environment, the question of race was in some ways hardly visible. Norma recalled only one classmate of color and no teachers of color. But the question of race was present in other ways. The Colégio Pedro II's history curriculum presented a picture of Brazilian development that emphasized the achievements of whites while reinforcing stereotypes about Brazilians of color. One of the leading history texts of the period, written by a professor at the Colégio Pedro II, exemplified the ways that Afro-Brazilians were depicted. In a section on African influences in *Epítome da história brasileira* (Epitome of Brazilian History), author Jonathas Serrano first cited the *mãe preta*, or black wet nurse, and added that other African contributions to Brazilian culture included "superstition, love for music and dance, a certain 'creole negligence,' heroic resignation in the face of misery, a fatalistic and light-hearted attitude in regard to work—these are some of the more or less favorable qualities we have inherited from the blacks." Students reading this book also learned that slavery in Brazil was less harsh than elsewhere since the mostly white masters were fond of their slaves, and that the black "re-tempered" the white race that came to America. The historic race being created undeniably profited greatly from African blood.

Serrano agreed with other leading educators such as Minister of Education Capanema that the "Race" being created would be white. Following the convention established in the 1930s and expressed by Gilberto Freyre, among others, Serrano recognized an African influence in the formation of modern Brazil. But he saw this influence as being anthropological and historic. It was an encounter that took place in the past, between primitive peoples and their European masters. In Serrano's textbook as in the visions of other educators, right up to Minister of

Education Capanema, Afro-Brazilians were an artifact of Brazil's past, not partners in its present and even less participants in its future. Was Serrano's vision racist? Within his context, Serrano would have seen himself as a well-meaning progressive who championed a vision of Brazilian history that acknowledged an African presence. He also interpreted Afro-Brazilian culture through the most modern, technical, and scientific lenses available to him: anthropology and Freudian psychoanalysis. In his mind, there could be no room for racism in beliefs so firmly grounded in science—beliefs that showed a presumed trajectory of assimilation for the Afro-Brazilian population.

The racial values woven into educational practices in the years during which Norma studied constantly reinforced an impression that Afro-Brazilians were largely unfit for modern society and would gradually disappear from the social landscape. This assumption was based on the belief not that people of African descent were inherently or biologically inferior, but that the conditions under which they had historically lived had left them in a state of physical, cultural, and social atrophy. Naturally, this complex of beliefs allowed room for exceptions. Social class, education, occupation, or celebrity status could outweigh race. Once Norma entered the Colégio Pedro II, she became part of an educational and educated elite. A tiny minority of Brazilians finished high school in these years, and a miniscule portion of these gained their degree from an institution as rigorous and prestigious as the Colégio. Entering the Colégio also opened the doors to further study. Upon graduation, she completed university studies in history and embarked on a career as a high-school teacher.

Norma's experience reveals one of the particularities of race relations in Brazil. The nation's society is characterized by gapping disparities in the social status of white, racially mixed, and black citizens. Still, this gap has seldom been reinforced by outright racial segregation or exclusion. Instead, widespread but subtle barriers to social mobility operate. Leading educators of the Vargas era created educational policies that are one example of the values and practices that perpetuated the social exclusion of Afro-Brazilians. A principal feature of this subtle system of racial exclusion was its elasticity: exclusion was not absolute. Some exceptional individuals, such as Norma, were occasionally able to succeed in institutions like Rio's public schools. The combination of ostensibly scientific, meritocratic, and technical educational policies with the presence of individual exceptions to the pattern of exclusion helped to develop the impression that Brazil was a racial democracy. This perception drew attention away from the ways educators wove racial values into the school system, and the ways the school system made it harder for Afro-Brazilians to enjoy its rewards.

Norma defied the odds through her participation in the system's practices. The Health Brigade, the Villa-Lobos performances, and the uniforms of the Colégio Pedro II were elements of a symbolic citizenship made all the more significant by the dictatorship's foreclosure of the instruments of active citizenship, such as the right to vote or to form political parties. What is more, her role in these activities made her part of the "Brazilian Race" despite her color. Advocates imagined the "Brazilian Race" to be white, but this whiteness was to be achieved through participation, and Norma participated. Being part of the system neutralized many of the negative connotations associated with being a person of color in Brazil. Norma's status was conveyed by her school uniform rather than by the color of her skin. Even though the system made it hard for Norma to ever wear the uniform, once she had it, the system worked to defend her privileged status.

During the 1940s students at the Colégio were increasingly drawn into political activism in support of the war. This involvement in national political debates was nothing new for students who had long seen themselves as part of a vanguard. Norma did not participate in these movements. This does not mean that she was politically inactive. To the contrary, Norma's politics were the politics of defying the odds and the social expectations that would place her in the uniform of a maid rather than in the uniform of the Colégio. Through her accumulated educational opportunities, she began a career as a high-school history teacher. At the end of this career, as she made time in her comfortable apartment in a middle-class Rio de Janeiro neighborhood for the interviews that are the basis of this story, Norma's recollections revealed the creative ways in which she shed the subtle racial expectations and obstacles placed against her and made herself counted. Who is to say which political struggle was more heroic? They were also the politics of presence and participation. By defying the odds, Norma was a self-identified black member of the "Brazilian Race."

SOURCES

This essay is based upon interviews with Norma Fraga, Wilson Choeri, and Aloysio Barbosa conducted between 1999 and 2000. Their remarkable personal stories show us what it was like to go to school during the Estado Novo, and they also reveal ways in which individuals could, and did, defy the social expectations of this time. In a period of repressive political demobilization, Choeri and Barbosa became political activists. At a time when the school system was far more likely to judge a student of color than to educate him, Fraga gained one of the finest educations available in Brazil. Yet in order to fully appreciate the extraordinary nature of Norma's experience, one has to do more than look at the statistical improbability of her education. One has to look at the ways in which the institutions she took part in understood the meaning of her color, and how that meaning turned into everyday practices.

This essay relies, then, upon an array of fragmentary sources from the Vargas-era Rio de Janeiro school system. In most cases, individual educators or participants in educational programs kept the best-preserved records. Heitor Villa-Lobos's decade of coordinating the school system's Musical Education Service can be studied through the archive located within his Rio de Janeiro home, which has become a museum. Although Jonathas Serrano's textbooks were so widely used that they can still readily be found in used bookstores, his papers can be found at the Brazilian National Archive and contain an especially rich set of documents pertaining to his membership in a federal commission that evaluated other historians' textbooks for content and accuracy. The papers of educators Gustavo Capanema, Anísio Teixeira, and Manoel Bergstrom Lourenço Filho, who respectively served as minister of education, directed the Rio school system, and developed the psychological testing and tracking systems, are preserved at the Getúlio Vargas Foundation's Centro de Pesquisa de Documentação Histórica. The Colégio Pedro II and the Institute of Education are the only two public educational institutions in Rio that conserved a record of their own historical development. Both schools maintained impressive collections of materials pertaining to their operations in the first half of the twentieth century. A more detailed analysis of these sources, especially in regard to the patterns of racial exclusion in schools, can be found in Jerry Dávila's *Diploma of Whiteness: Race and Social Policy in Brazil, 1917–1945* (Durham: Duke University Press, 2003).

SUGGESTED READINGS

For further reading on the exclusion of Afro-Brazilians in the nineteenth and twentieth centuries, see Eduardo Silva, *Prince of the People: The Life and Times of a Brazilian Free Man of Colour* (New York: Verso Books, 1993); George Reid Andrews, *Blacks and Whites in São Paulo, 1888–1988* (Madison: University of Wisconsin Press, 1991); Hendrik Kraay, ed., *Afro-Brazilian Culture in Bahia, 1790s to 1990s* (Armonk, NY: M. E. Sharpe, 1998); Pierre Michel Fontaine, ed., *Race, Class, and Power in Brazil* (Los Angeles: CAAS, 1985); and Rebecca Reichmann, *Race in Contemporary Brazil* (University Park: Pennsylvania State University Press, 1999). Thomas Skidmore's *Black into White: Race and Nationality in Brazilian Thought* (New York: Oxford University Press, 1974) explores the concept of whitening. Kim Butler's *Freedoms Given, Freedoms Won: Afro-Brazilians in Post-Abolition São Paulo and Salvador* (New Brunswick, NJ: Rutgers University Press, 1998) offers an analysis of Afro-

Brazilian struggles for political and cultural integration. For the Afro-Brazilian experience in a comparative perspective, see Leo Spitzer, *Lives in Between: The Experience of Marginality in a Century of Emancipation* (New York: Cambridge University Press, 1989).

CHAPTER 10

Vicente Racioppi

The Local Preservationist and the National State

DARYLE WILLIAMS

Daryle Williams analyzes the life of a local citizen who fought to preserve the art, architecture, and history of one of Brazil's most beautiful colonial cities, Ouro Preto, in Minas Gerais state. Ouro Preto was at the center of what was probably the world's largest gold rush. During the eighteenth-century boom years, the town's inhabitants, including thousands of slaves, spent lavishly to create spectacular baroque-style architecture, sculpture, and art. Once the boom ended, however, the town suffered a slow decline, becoming somewhat of an economic and political backwater by the twentieth century. An unintended benefit of this decline was that although they were poorly maintained, few of Ouro Preto's important colonial buildings were demolished. Dynamic urban centers such as Rio de Janeiro and especially São Paulo emphasized modernization over preservation. Developers destroyed much of these growing cities' colonial architecture in the name of progress, and what remained was largely wedged between commercial sky-scrapers, factories, and apartment buildings that diminished the older struc-tures' once opulent dominance of the cityscape. Ouro Preto, meanwhile, remained largely untouched.

The story of Vicente Racioppi combines many themes that personify important trends in the Brazil of his day. Racioppi was the son of an Ital-ian immigrant who made good, becoming a respected middle-class lawyer. Many respectable gentlemen at the turn of the century (such as Adolfo Caminha and Cândido Rondon in Chapters 5 and 6) professed the secular creed of positivism, and expressed anticlerical views critical of the Catholic Church. Racioppi, on the other hand, maintained a profound devotion to the Church. Positivists had typically rejected the Iberian architecture of the colonial period in favor of the more fashionable modern styles popular in Europe, especially in France. This symbolized the generation's rejection of Iberia as a model for their intellectual, artistic, political, and economic projects; instead, they found their inspiration in more "modern" North Atlantic nations. After the cataclysmic violence of World War I, however, Racioppi joined other intellectuals and politicians in a reassessment of Brazil's history that began to valorize aspects of its colonial and early na-tional heritage, including colonial art and architecture. An ascendant Catholic nationalism—part of the larger Catholic hierarchy's response to the challenges of an unfettered materialism celebrated by capitalists and denounced by Communists as well as the growth of Protestant missionary work—became a powerful force in Brazilian politics and society at the time, and Vicente was an independent player in this far from monolithic movement.

Racioppi is an excellent example of how individuals play key roles in shaping larger historical trends. This mineiro *successfully brought to the attention of federal authorities the need to preserve Ouro Preto's historical heritage as a unique part of Brazil's national heritage. Racioppi's dilemma, as Daryle Williams shows, was that his very success ultimately undercut his ability to control the process of preservation in Ouro Preto.*

Daryle Williams is associate professor of history at the University of Maryland. He came across the story of Vicente Racioppi while undertaking research for his book Culture Wars in Brazil: The First Vargas Regime, 1930–1945 *(2001). He is presently researching the cooperation and conflicts that shaped the multinational historical preservation of the Jesuit-Guaraní missions in what are now the borderlands of southern Brazil, northern Argentina, and eastern Paraguay.*

Ouro Preto, a modestly sized town whose contemporary economic life is largely organized around historical tourism, sits nestled in a winding mountain valley in the southeastern state of Minas Gerais. Every month, thousands of tourists trudge up and down the town's insanely steep cobblestone streets, alternately sweating from the intense heat of the day and shivering from the night's damp chill, to stop and to marvel at works of religious and civil architecture that date from the frenetic days of a spectacular eighteenth-century gold rush. The more adventuresome visitors descend into dank mine shafts, where local guides recount the terrible working conditions endured by the thousands of slaves who produced a quantity of gold so large that the entire Portuguese empire knew of Vila Rica, or Rich Town, as Ouro Preto (literally, black gold) was originally known. The artistic and architectural heritage financed by the riches that remained in Ouro Preto is so exceptional that in 1984 the city's historic quarter won UNESCO's coveted designation of World Heritage Site.

The tourist to Ouro Preto will encounter small plaques indicating that the city's architectural treasures are protected by the Instituto do Patrimônio Histórico e Artístico Nacional (National Historical and Artistic Patrimony Institute, or IPHAN), Brazil's most important preservationist agency. Many of these plaques date from the late 1930s, when the central state first made historical preservation a top priority. These plaques have a double meaning. The first, and most self-evident, message points to the state's aggressive efforts to institute innovative preservationist projects during the authoritarian-nationalist regime known as the Estado Novo (1937–1945). The plaques are signposts to a heroic, nationalist campaign to save Brazil's cultural patrimony from oblivion. An alternative message points to a more uneasy politics of preservation, where the rescue of the past was an arena for intense conflict during a period of nationalist mobilization. In this second reading, our attention must be drawn to the sometimes amicable, sometimes tense relations between everyday citizens, regional authorities, and the central state over the right to manage the past. This essay concentrates on the second reading, where the seemingly apolitical designation of the "national historical and artistic patrimony" is a signpost to a varied cultural landscape where local preservationists and the central state struggled to give meaning to old buildings.

The essay centers upon Vicente Racioppi, a cantankerous resident of Ouro Preto who embroiled himself in a series of confrontations with federal officials over the proper way to go about saving the town. Racioppi embraced the preservationist cause with an enthusiasm equal to that of the National Historical and Artistic Patrimony Service (the IPHAN's predecessor, then known by the acronym SPHAN), which coordinated a major restoration campaign between 1936 and the mid-1940s. Sharing a common belief that the loss of Ouro Preto's cultural heritage would be a loss for all Brazil, Racioppi and the SPHAN were divided about who should manage restoration efforts and how. Racioppi agitated for strong local participation; federal agents claimed that any city designated as part of the national historical patrimony should be administered by agents of the national state. The disagreements between the local preservationist and federal officials escalated to a point where Racioppi would be forced from Ouro Preto and his personal effects mockingly paraded through the streets by rowdy students. Humiliated in a place he loved dearly, Racioppi resettled in Belo Horizonte, the state capital, where he remained a vocal defender of Ouro Preto's traditions well into his old age. Ouro Preto, in the meantime, became a major tourist destination and a site of civic pilgrimages. Racioppi's marginalization from and by the "official" keepers of Ouro Preto's past is emblematic of a larger politics of state- and nation-making that characterizes modern Brazil.

∽

Racioppi's investment in the local traditions of Ouro Preto was not preordained. His father, Vital, was Italian. When the elder Racioppi made the transatlantic passage to Brazil, he could hardly imagine that he might raise an American-born son who would dedicate his life to the impassioned defense of Brazilian history. It is more likely that Vital, like millions of other Italian immigrants who disembarked in Buenos Aires, Montevideo, and New York in the late nineteenth and early twentieth centuries, maintained hopes of one day returning to Italy after "making America." Yet like so many immigrants whose ideas of making America changed once they reached the New World, Vital Racioppi ended up staying in Brazil, first establishing himself in Rio de Janeiro and later making his way to Minas Gerais. There, Vital set aside his hopes of earning a living as a violinist and married the daughter of a local records clerk. Together, Vital and his wife Affonsina set themselves up as shopkeepers in Queluz (today's Conselheiro Lafayette) and started a family. Their son Vicente was born on October 13, 1886.

The details of Vicente's childhood are obscure, but we have clear evidence that Vital and Affonsina Racioppi succeeded in getting their son admitted to the well-regarded seminary in Mariana. There, the young Vicente studied Catholic theology, history, philosophy, and classical languages in preparation for the priesthood. But the priesthood did not suit the younger Racioppi, who set his sights on a career in law. By 1913, Vicente had moved to Belo Horizonte and earned a degree in the juridical and social sciences. Surviving a near-fatal bout of typhoid fever, which left him gray-haired at age twenty, Vicente went on to establish a small law practice, marry, and start a family.

Racioppi's formative years were exemplary of immigrant aspirations to provincial middle-class respectability. The choice to become a lawyer, rather than a priest, was emblematic of an upward social ascent under a young republican system. The distinction of having a liberal professional in its ranks afforded all Racioppis the right to claim a shared worldview with established and up-and-coming families in Minas. The income generated by Vicente's law practice provided wealth sufficient to emulate the domestic life of the regional bourgeoisie: the professional male provided for his wife and children; neither wife nor children had to engage in work outside of the home. Religious piety was an equally important component of Racioppi's social respectability, particularly in a region known for its Catholic devotion. A hybridized ethnic identification was yet another badge of honor, allowing the Racioppis the right to present themselves as Brazilians of European ancestry in a region where the cultural and ethnic legacies of chattel slavery made Africanness and miscegenation inescapable, but socially undervalued, parts of everyday life. Finally, Vicente was a proud *mineiro*—that is to say, his social identity was built around legal and cultural claims to being a citizen of Minas Gerais.

Late in life, Vicente praised his parents as people who "knew how to construct *mineiro* homes that were fundamentally Catholic and dignified by humility, hard work, circumspection, and honesty; [they made] blessed homes, where virtues reigned supreme and where domestic, spiritual, and civic beauty flourished." By all indications, Racioppi wanted nothing less for his own family.

Dividing his time between the demands of raising a large family—he and his wife had seven children—and his professional career, Vicente maintained a legal practice in Belo Horizonte and also taught Latin, philosophy, and Catholic sociology at two local secondary schools. This dual career path as lawyer and educator were consistent with earlier experiences in the seminary and law school as well as with a commitment to the defense of the Catholic faith. Racioppi's early professional choices also reflected the opportunities for social and economic advancement for an educated, middle-class white male who chose to remain in Minas Gerais, rather than seek his fortune in more cosmopolitan cities such as Rio de Janeiro and São Paulo.

The decision to remain in Belo Horizonte did not necessarily condemn the Racioppis to a life of provincial obscurity. The state capital was a city of growing importance, where economic and political decisionmakers moved in the same circles as the regional intelligentsia. Had Vicente wanted, he could have capitalized upon his educational and professional background to make a bid at joining the city's social elite. His chances for winning a position of influence in the state government were reasonably good, if we use the life histories of his contemporaries as a yardstick. If he had been especially close with the state's republican party, he might have been able to land a job in Rio, where *mineiro* politicians cycled through the presidential palace with regularity. Racioppi, however, seemed little interested in the trappings of cosmopolitan culture. When the lawyer-educator relocated his family to Ouro Preto, the prospects of winning a position of state or national influence diminished greatly. Racioppi continued to maintain professional contacts in the capital, but the move to Ouro Preto put significant distance between his daily life and the "civilized" culture of wide boulevards, public tramways, industrial parks, cinemas, professional clubs, and consumerism that were making Belo Horizonte into the modern city that is now Brazil's third largest.

If we consider Ouro Preto as Racioppi's antidote to modern "civilization"—a place where he could live and work within a urban setting that was Catholic, austere, and organically Brazilian—it is important to recognize that his disengagement with progress was never unilateral. Social status and material comfort remained dependent upon certain standards of modernity set in modern cities. So, Racioppi kept current his registry with the Brazilian Lawyers Association and the National Department of Professors, two important professional organizations headquartered in Rio. He was an active contributor to newspapers in Belo

Horizonte and occasionally published pieces in the Rio press. He participated in the state government, serving as secretary of the Council of Public Instruction in Minas. He served on the Brazilian delegation to the Panamerican Institute of History and Geography, held in Buenos Aires in 1932. Thus, Racioppi carved out a niche in a public sphere that was indeed modern, modernizing, and national. Nevertheless, the colonial and local past became Racioppi's preferred home.

Racioppi's turn to the past coincided with the coming together of a loosely knit circle of intellectuals and politicians who feared that Brazil's historic heritage had been ravaged by both the passage of time and a collective disinterest in the past. The physical decay of Ouro Preto, the colonial city that found itself in a long decline dating back to the first decade of the nineteenth century, was especially troubling to Brazil's would-be preservationists. In 1928 the members of the Brazilian Historical and Geographic Institute, the nation's most prominent historical academy, called upon the national government to do something about the deterioration that threatened to despoil Ouro Preto's colonial treasures. These efforts paid off modestly when the federal government agreed to preserve a handful of buildings associated with the Inconfidência Mineira, the proto-republican conspiracy against colonial rule that originated in Ouro Preto in 1789. Racioppi became the local agent in this early preservationist campaign. In a short time, he began to take a leading role in preservationist mobilization, joining calls for the federal government to confer some form of special status upon Ouro Preto. His efforts won the recognition and thanks of powerful figures in the national capital, including the secretary of the Brazilian Historical and Geographic Institute, who credited Racioppi with leading the charge to save Ouro Preto.

On July 12, 1933, Chief of the Provisional Government Getúlio Vargas, a reformist politician from Rio Grande do Sul who swept into power in a brief civil war in 1930, issued an executive decree designating Ouro Preto as Brazil's first National Monument. *Mineiro* politicians were pleased to see that Vargas was open to extending formal federal protection to their regional heritage. Racioppi must have been delighted to see how the regime change in 1930 appeared to open up new opportunities for local citizens living in the interior to cultivate a political engagement with national leaders even in the absence of democratic institutions.

High on the success of winning federal recognition of Ouro Preto's monumental status, Racioppi and his preservationist allies were still troubled by the town's sad state. The poverty of municipal coffers, compounded by the lack of federal monies for preservation, meant that preservation was really a moral campaign. Hopes for an increase in historical tourism were unrealized in large part because the local tourist accommodations were primitive. This depressing state of affairs did not deter Racioppi from calling his adopted city a *National* Monument, where individual citizens and public officials throughout the country had the obligation to take corrective action.

In hopes of stirring up a more broad-based social mobilization around rescuing Ouro Preto from oblivion, Racioppi made regular appearances in the press. He also took up the cause of history writing, sketching essays on local history and famous *mineiros* to be distributed through the primary school system. This historical scholarship was not especially substantive or innovative. It was, nevertheless, patriotic in its belief in the virtues of celebrating the great feats and figures of regional and national history.

Racioppi also scoured Ouro Preto and surrounding towns in search of original documents, historical artifacts, and artwork tied to the region's history. These efforts yielded some impressive finds, including papers signed by participants in the Inconfidência Mineira, as well as works of history painting, religious art, and items of everyday use that dated from the colonial period. In time, his assemblage of regional art and artifacts came to rival similar collections held by the National Historical Museum, the Catholic Church, and wealthy connoisseurs.

Racioppi's most notable achievement was the organization of a local historical academy, the Historical Institute of Ouro Preto (Instituto Histórico de Ouro Preto, or IHOP). Founded in August 1931, the Institute's mission statement, written by Racioppi in florid eighteenth-century prose, was to promote and defend local history. The motto of the IHOP was: "He who does not love the past shall not trespass." A municipal decree recognized the Institute as a "public utility" in the same year and Getúlio Vargas extended federal recognition in 1932, noting that Racioppi was serving "not only Ouro Preto, but all Brazil."

Perhaps the most impressive aspect of Racioppi's accomplishments was his keen understanding that the success of local activism, at least in Ouro Preto, hinged upon a close and collaborative relationship between local and national actors. The financial resources of the IHOP were simply too scarce to make substantive gains without outside support. So, Racioppi secured presidential authorization to install the IHOP in a colonial-era structure that had once belonged to *inconfidente* (as the participants of the 1789 conspiracy were known) poet Tomás de Gonzaga. In thanks, Racioppi designated Vargas as a honorary member of the Institute and often spoke of the president as a personal protector. He also relied upon outsiders to provide the IHOP with the social and cultural capital of intellectuals with greater national projection. The cofounders of the Historical Institute were Gastão Penalva and José Paulo Pires Brandão, two prominent intellectuals who resided in Rio and enjoyed intimate contact with members of the intelligentsia. Quickly figuring out that the success of his efforts depended upon a successful appropriation of the nationalistic discourse promoted by the Vargas state, Racioppi described all these efforts, not to mention the broader politics of historical preservation, in heroic and patriotic terms.

The high point for Racioppi came in July 1938, when the *mineiro* participated in a municipal delegation to welcome Vargas, who had become president-dictator of the Estado Novo in November 1937. Vargas, who had studied in Ouro Preto as a youth, was in the colonial city to oversee the transfers of urns containing the remains of the *inconfidentes*. An urn holding the remains of Tomás de Gonzaga was included in a ceremonial procession that described all *inconfidentes* as national heroes.

During Vargas's two-day visit, Racioppi had the privilege of offering the president and other dignitaries a personal tour of the collection of artifacts that had been installed on the Historical Institute's ground floor. (In all likelihood, he kept quiet the fact that he also used the IHOP headquarters for his law offices and residence.) The privilege of greeting the president as an unpaid local preservationist, patriotic citizen, and member of the regional intelligentsia was, indeed, quite an accomplishment for a lawyer who had abandoned hopes of circulating among the powerful when he settled in musty Ouro Preto. Racioppi was able to show Vargas that he was a dedicated defender of Ouro Preto's—and the nation's—cultural riches. His unspoken agenda was to prove to Vargas that official calls to cultural renewal empowered everyday citizens to assert their place in national cultural mobilization, even in the context of a dictatorship. Vargas personally thanked Racioppi for his efforts and later went on to deliver a speech thanking all *mineiros*, past and present, for their contributions to the national cause.

∼

Racioppi experienced a fall from grace in the decade following Vargas's visit. He initially did not perceive that his success in early preservationist efforts would contribute to his undoing. In time, however, the combination of political missteps, rising federal intervention into regional affairs, and changing rules in cultural nationalism pushed local figures such as Racioppi to the margins of national preservationist campaigns.

The changing relationships between the local and the national political actors, particularly concerning questions of cultural patrimony, began in 1934, when Vargas approved the creation of the National Monuments Inspection Service. The Service concentrated its efforts in Ouro Preto, where Epamimondas Macedo, a graduate of the city's School of

Mines, undertook a survey of local historical structures. The results of the survey guided a modest restoration plan directed at a handful of churches, fountains, and bridges exhibiting signs of advanced physical decay. After contracting a small crew of local artisans and laborers, Macedo oversaw restoration work that lasted through the end of 1936. Racioppi, apparently bristling from the prospect that these federally financed activities might result in more direct competition in determining how Ouro Preto might be restored, grumbled that the work under way had been poorly executed.

By 1937, when the National Historical and Artistic Patrimony Service had taken over full responsibilities for federally sponsored conservation in Ouro Preto, the tone and volume of Racioppi's opposition to federal agents increased. In March, Racioppi appealed to the mayor, the governor, and the minister of education to take note of the restoration work in progress at São Francisco de Assis, one of the town's most spectacular churches, which he found to be misguided. The following year, he asserted that some of the urns containing the *inconfidentes'* remains— icons of the Vargas regime's campaign to rescue neglected and imperiled symbols of national culture—contained the bones of blacks mistakenly exhumed in Africa by misinformed federal agents.

The year that the *inconfidentes'* remains were brought to Ouro Preto— 1938—was clearly a good one for Racioppi. He received Vargas in what was essentially the parlor to his house. However, his criticisms of official efforts to repatriate the *inconfidentes*, in conjunction with an ever more intransigent opposition to the SPHAN, soured considerably his relationship with the more immediate representatives of the federal government in Ouro Preto.

Federally sponsored restoration efforts continued apace after Vargas's visit. Much of the town's major monumental architecture was surveyed and registered as "national historical and artistic patrimony," a legal term codified by Decree-Law 25, issued November 30, 1937. The *inconfidentes'* remains were installed in an austere pantheon that remains one of the most sacred civic spaces in Brazil. In 1944 the federally run Inconfidência Museum opened to pay permanent homage to the heroic and creative age of the ill-fated conspiracy and its supreme hero, Joaquim José da Silva Xavier, better known as Tiradentes (literally, tooth-puller). By 1945, Ouro Preto had become the crown jewel in the SPHAN's collection of national cultural treasures. Federal publications promoted the architectural and artistic legacy of Brazil's Age of Gold to readers throughout the country and abroad. The SPHAN contracted Manuel Bandeira, a well-known poet, to write a tourist guide to Ouro Preto. Federal funds also covered the costs of the construction of a major tourist hotel, the Grande

Hotel de Ouro Preto, that was distinctive for its modern amenities as well as for its uncompromisingly modernist design executed by the up-and-coming architect Oscar Niemeyer.

Federal approval for the Grande Hotel project vexed Racioppi, who believed adamantly that a historical city of Ouro Preto's caliber should not, *could not*, be contaminated by the modernist style, with its flat roofs, right angles, reinforced concrete walls, and large glass windows. In a letter written directly to Vargas, Racioppi described the new hotel as an abominable "coffin for a dead person" that would make a poor fit in the old colonial city. Like many advocates of a revivalist style known as neo-colonialism, Racioppi thought that any new construction in Ouro Preto should harmonize with the town's existing eighteenth-century Luso-Brazilian architecture, marked by red-tile roofs, stone and adobe walls, and exterior latticework. Any attempt to modernize the city had to take place within the symbolic language of the past. To do anything less would be to defile the nation's heritage. Racioppi quickly discovered that his traditionalist vision of architecture would not carry the day, especially when Niemeyer had the protection of powerful allies in the federal government. The Niemeyer project went forward over the protests of local and national preservationists who did not subscribe to the theory that modernist and eighteenth-century architecture might complement one another.

After railing against the Grande Hotel, Racioppi was sharply rebuked by officials who were fed up with his very public charges of federal incompetence, overstepping, and high-handedness in local affairs. The rebuke came in response to the demand that the SPHAN submit to an independent oversight committee. On October 12, 1940, SPHAN director Rodrigo Melo Franco de Andrade published an editorial in the widely read Rio daily, *Diário de Notícias*, to inform the paper's readership (and Racioppi, no doubt) that federal restoration projects would not be subject to citizens' oversight. The SPHAN's Advisory Council, according to Andrade, was the sole entity legally empowered to review decisions related to properties that had been designated as part of the national historical patrimony. Since the entire core of Ouro Preto had been designated en bloc as historical patrimony in 1938, no private citizen—not even the residents of Ouro Preto—enjoyed the legal right to override decisions that had been determined to be appropriate by the Advisory Council. Like Racioppi, the SPHAN director was an ardent defender of the ideal that federally sponsored historical preservation could *and should* be the basis for a strong, participatory social movement organized around ideas of the common good and love of country. What Andrade, a fellow *mineiro*, would not accept were Racioppi's continual efforts to undermine the work of federal agents charged with guiding this movement.

Labeling Racioppi a local citizen who made himself a "gratuitous enemy" of the federal government, Andrade made Racioppi out to be persona non grata in the monumental city.

In the following half-decade, Racioppi jockeyed to maintain a voice in local preservationist projects. The results were mixed. On the one hand, he convinced the federal government to acquire 240 objects, taken from his collection of art and historical artifacts, for the permanent collection of the Inconfidência Museum. Racioppi was certainly proud to see that the fruits of his early preservationist efforts became a permanent part of the federal museum system and the national memory that it celebrated. On the other hand, Racioppi was denied the post of museum director, which he sought, and he was effectively frozen out from all of the preparatory work that went into the installation of the museum exhibit. His exclusion from any restoration projects associated with the SPHAN was a foregone conclusion.

Most troubling was the rising level of federal scrutiny toward operational irregularities at the Historical Institute. Agents questioned why the private academy, which occupied federal property rent-free, was failing to fulfill key items in its mission statement. Racioppi's antagonism with federal preservationists, who considered him poorly qualified to offer any technical advice (as well as being a thorn in their side), together with his lack of legitimacy among professional historians, further compromised his position. The single, most glaring irregularity was the conditions under which Racioppi occupied the Casa de Gonzaga, as the Institute's headquarters were known. It was no secret that Racioppi had appropriated parts of the building for his law practice. The fact that the building's upper floor had been converted into a private residence flaunted the bounds of acceptability.

A presidential decree issued in 1944 authorized a commission of inquiry to determine whether the occupation of the Casa de Gonzaga was consistent with the concession granted in 1932. The commission found that the Institute was effectively defunct, that the structure was in disrepair, and that the Institute's museum, which intermixed historical artifacts with personal items such as Racioppi's shoes, fell far short of rising standards in collection management. The commission indicated that Racioppi had to return the building to federal hands or begin to pay rent. Racioppi reportedly responded with a demand to be compensated for structural improvements made at his expense. When the property title was transferred to the School of Mines, a local institution desperate for new facilities, Racioppi stayed put.

The next four years would be extremely rough for Racioppi, who faced continual federal pressure to vacate the Casa de Gonzaga. He hunkered down, invoking the protections originally offered by Vargas.

The bloodless military coup of October 29, 1945, which ousted Vargas and ended the Estado Novo, afforded a brief respite. National and local political arrangements were restructured to conform to the ideal that Brazil's participation in the Allied defeat of Nazism meant the dismantling of authoritarian structures and practices. The expropriation of property without a proper warrant might seem antidemocratic.

Racioppi was still in a predicament. He had lost his biggest patron, Getúlio Vargas, who was sent into internal exile before returning to the national scene as a federal senator with diminished influence in areas such as historical preservation. In defending his position without Vargas (whose actual interest in the IHOP was dubious), Racioppi was forced to invoke the language of patriotic self-sacrifice and defense of tradition that had won him a place in early federal preservationist efforts. The dilemma centered on the fact that Racioppi's opponents at the SPHAN had wholly appropriated this language as their own. The nationalization of the politics of preservation, which Racioppi helped to set in motion at the local level, had basically excluded local dissent in language and most certainly in the allocation of decision-making powers.

His tragicomic downfall came unexpectedly in late August 1948, while Racioppi was away from Ouro Preto to attend the burial of his son, a decorated veteran of the Brazilian Expeditionary Force who had fought alongside American troops in Italy during World War II. On the night of August 25—four days shy of the Historical Institute's seventeenth anniversary—thirty-four students enrolled at the School of Mines, with the aid of the mayor's secretary and a local carpenter, used a crowbar to break into the Casa de Gonzaga. Racioppi soon discovered that the invaders had set up camp in his home and turned it into a *república* (republic), as the city's group houses for students were known. To add insult to injury, the rowdy students altered the plaque at the entrance to the building, which originally read "Here lived Tomás Antonio de Gonzaga, 1784–1788," by affixing a hand-written addendum, "who at least paid the rent."

Racioppi immediately called for a police inquiry, but he received little assistance. He also began a letterwriting campaign in the Minas press, in which he attributed the invasion to an executive order approved by President Eurico Dutra that improperly ceded the building to the School of Mines. Dutra, who was advised by the SPHAN on matters relating to historical patrimony, expressed no interest in reviewing Racioppi's cause.

Facing indifference in the federal capital and ridicule at the local level, Racioppi appealed to his fellow Brazilians' sense of democratic principles. In a letter published in the Belo Horizonte daily *O Diário*, Racioppi called upon "the men of government, honorable and patriotic, who act under the mantle of the Federal Constitution, to do justice by respecting liberty and the fundamental rights of all those who live in a democratic regime." The invocation of notions of democracy illustrates how desperately Racioppi wanted to find a language in which to describe how he had been done an injustice. What was originally an argument based upon an affront to the patriotic citizen whose work had been recognized by no less than Getúlio Vargas shifted to language about the violation of property rights. In another instance, Racioppi described the occupation of the Casa de Gonzaga as "Communist barbarism," thus pandering to the rising tide of anticommunism that was putting Cold War limits on the nature of democracy in the Americas. These rhetorical acrobatics yielded little. Nor did any attempts to win sympathy for the injustice of an attack upon the grieving father of a decorated war hero. The Racioppis reluctantly took up residence in Belo Horizonte, where Vicente prepared a lawsuit to win, at a minimum, the return of his personal belongings that remained locked up in the Casa de Gonzaga.

For a brief moment in 1949, the lawsuit appeared to work. *Cruzeiro*, the most influential newsweekly read by Brazil's growing urban middle classes, devoted a feature story to Racioppi's plight. Unfortunately, the article cast an unflattering light on his long history of conflicts with municipal and federal officials. Racioppi came off as an ill-tempered eccentric rather than as an everyday patriot who had been wronged by big government and local politics. The case received some positive press in Belo Horizonte, but in the end, Vicente and his wife had to content themselves with the restitution of their belongings, which university students paraded through the streets of Ouro Preto in a carnivalesque slap to the scorned historian, and with the prospects of a new life in the state capital.

In June 1951, Racioppi once again turned to Vargas, who had returned to the presidential palace as the constitutionally elected president. This cry for help from an old friend was an act of desperation. But Vargas, who had offered some kind words to Racioppi when he signed the authorization for the Historical Institute to occupy the Casa de Gonzaga in 1932, demonstrated no interest in the plight of the Institute or its beleaguered director. Vargas's dramatic death by suicide in August 1954 ended all hopes that somehow, some way, Vargas might see personally to the restoration of Racioppi's honor.

For the remainder of his life, Racioppi busied himself with the project of rebuilding the legitimacy lost in 1948. He proceeded without the support of the president or any other federal official. He did manage to organize a new historical museum, again in his home, in a quiet neighborhood of Belo Horizonte. The new museum displayed items related to the Inconfidência Mineira as well as the Brazilian Expeditionary Force, sacred art, and historical artifacts. The bitterness remained, however. In

1952, Racioppi told one reporter who visited his new home that the "republic" established in the usurped Casa de Gonzaga was far from the republic dreamed up by the *inconfidentes* in 1789.

In 1958 he published the first volume in a self-named series of books "on a variety of themes, studies, and items of interest relating to the religious art, tradition, and civilization of Minas Gerais." The series had limited distribution and remained incomplete. A decade later, he complained that the Inconfidência Museum had failed to properly display all of the objects that he had "ceded" in 1944. Museum director Orlandino Seitas Fernandes issued a report that the objects in question had been sold, not ceded. Fernandes dismissed Racioppi's curatorial criticisms.

Racioppi's last-known publication, a collection of brief essays about historical themes related to Minas Gerais, appeared in 1970. Published to commemorate the thirty-ninth anniversary of the founding of the IHOP, Racioppi dedicated the book to his family, a handful of *mineiro* politicians, the cofounders of the IHOP, and Vargas. The book includes a profile of Holy Week processions in his beloved Ouro Preto. Racioppi must have been terribly disappointed to see that Ouro Preto had became one of Brazil's most important tourist destinations and the object of tremendous interest by historians and art critics, while he remained on the sidelines.

∽

Aside from the brief mention of the acquisition of portions of his art and artifact collection for the Inconfidência Museum, Vicente Racioppi has been wholly expunged from official memories of the restoration of Ouro Preto. The two most important federal institutions that manage Ouro Preto's magnificent historical and artistic treasures, the IPHAN and the Inconfidência Museum, tell their stories without crediting the influence of this local citizen who shared, at least in his emotion, the same commitment to celebrating Ouro Preto. The few locals who play a prominent role in these national narratives are historical figures associated with Ouro Preto's past and federal employees. Any outsider who visits one of Brazil's premier World Heritage Sites would have no idea of the dramatic and comic history of the Casa de Gonzaga.

Much of the silences surrounding Racioppi were of his own making. He was ill-tempered and arrogant. His allegations of federal incompetence were poorly substantiated. His efforts to curry favor with powerful figures, especially Vargas, were crass. His misappropriation of public property was ill advised. Vicente Racioppi conquered by his own hand a place in the history of the conservation of Ouro Preto—a place located far from the celebratory history that tells us how it was that Brazil and the world came to share Ouro Preto.

There are, of course, other narratives to be told surrounding Racioppi's near-disappearance from the historical record, the most important of which is the narrative of an everyday citizen who lived very much in a local place, and his relationship to an expanding, interventionist, and often authoritarian state. The language of cultural nationalism, the celebration of the national past, and the call to patriotic collective action united local citizen and central state in a common cause. But the terms of this association were not egalitarian. The politics of preservation empowered different national actors unequally. The recovery of the history of this process—which gives us wonderful eighteenth-century vistas and unsettling historical erasures—helps us to see the dynamic and contested nature of nationalism and its cultural artifacts in modern Brazil.

SUGGESTED READINGS

Racioppi's writings are not easy to come by, and none has been translated into English. The principal source materials consulted for this chapter were found in the institutional archives of Racioppi's adversaries. Publications about Minas Gerais, from the colonial period through the Vargas era, are more readily available. See C. R. Boxer, *The Golden Age of Brazil, 1695–1750* (1962); Kenneth Maxwell, *Conflicts and Conspiracies: Brazil and Portugal, 1750–1808* (1973); Helena Morley, *The Diary of Helena Morley* (1957); and John D. Wirth, *Minas Gerais in the Brazilian Federation, 1889–1937* (1977). For more reading on the complex relationships between Getúlio Vargas and everyday Brazilians, see Robert M. Levine, *Father of the Poor? Vargas and His Era* (1998), and R. S. Rose, *One of the Forgotten Things: Getúlio Vargas and Brazilian Social Control, 1930–1954* (2000). The Instituto do Patrimônio Histórico e Artístico Nacional maintains a website about Ouro Preto at <http://www.iphan.gov.br/bens/Mundial/p2.htm>. Travel guides will provide additional information on this World Heritage Site.

PART IV

THE GENERATIONS OF AUTHORITARIAN MILITARY RULE AND NEOLIBERALISM
(1960 TO THE TWENTY-FIRST CENTURY)

*A*fter the 1959 Cuban Revolution, U.S. foreign policymakers feared that Brazil would become the next country in Latin America to succumb to leftist insurgency. Before 1959, Washington's Communist containment policy had focused on Europe, Asia, and the Middle East, but the Cuban Revolution moved Latin America from the margins to the front lines of the Cold War. Because Brazil bordered on nearly every South American nation, it was a potential nightmare for U.S. Cold War strategists. A central tenet of Communist containment policy, known as the "domino theory," posited that if one nation fell to Communist subversion, then it would not be long before its neighbors would do so. Like a line of dominos, governments sympathetic to the Western capitalist-bloc countries would fall into the Soviet sphere of influence. In retrospect, these fears were overblown, but at the height of the Cold War, fear-mongering often drove U.S. policy. While the United States had officially voiced support for democracy in the hemisphere, in the early 1960s its new policy held that Latin American democracies were fragile and that rightwing anti-Communist dictatorships would be better able to thwart leftist rebellions.

To many outside and local observers and actors, Brazil seemed ripe for leftist agitation. While industrial development had created great wealth, it was extremely unevenly distributed. Poverty stalked urban areas where many rural workers displaced by the modernization of agriculture looked for a better life, but instead they found unemployment, hardship, and exploitation in fetid slums. Many Brazilians had good reason to be discontent. The state-organized labor unions had been largely run by corrupt leaders (*pelegos*), who had kept down the rank and file for the most part, but in the early 1960s urban laborers became more outspoken in their demands for better wages and conditions. Even rural laborers had in some areas begun to organize to pressure large landowners for fair wages and the government for land reform. Some activists worked to organize military enlisted personnel and noncommissioned officers, to the chagrin of the high command. The rising expectations of Brazil's laborers and soldiers came just as the import-substitution model of industrial development began to slow down.

199

Amid rising labor activism and economic downturn, Brazil's political institutions experienced gridlock and instability. Congress was divided almost evenly between three major political parties: one conservative, one moderate, and the other leftist. While Juselino Kubitschek had managed compromises to bring factions together across party lines, harder economic times made passage of meaningful legislation difficult. Kubitschek's successor, President Jânio Quadros, was a maverick with loose ties to the major political parties that had won election by pledging to fight government corruption. The mercurial Quadros quickly tired of the legislative battles that thwarted his reform agenda, and he unexpectedly tendered his resignation. While Quadros had been a moderate, many feared that Vice President João Goulart was too far to the left. Goulart's succession almost provoked a military coup, but a compromise allowed him to assume office with diminished powers. The compromise ultimately proved untenable because Goulart, like any good populist politician, sought to develop and integrate a new electoral base of support during his mandate: rural workers. When a group of military enlisted men and noncommissioned officers mutinied, even more moderate military officers joined a cadre of conservative officers who had been plotting to overthrow Goulart's government. In alliance with conservative civilian politicians and with the support of many disillusioned members of the middle class, the military staged a coup in 1964. The U.S. government quickly recognized this regime that had illegally deposed a democratically elected president. Washington was reassured by the anti-Communist and pro-U.S. credentials of the new military dictatorship.

From 1964 to 1985 military officers allied with civilian experts (technocrats) dominated Brazil's politics. The military government maintained a facade of democratic institutions. Five different military presidents served as chief executives of the so-called bureaucratic authoritarian regime. When strikes and protests against military rule reached their height in 1968, the government responded with heavy-handed repression. While populist politicians had mobilized workers through state-organized labor unions, the military regime squelched union activism and supported policies that compressed the wages of industrial workers. Now, the government courted the favor of foreign investors and multinational corporations. It intensified the use of repression and cancelled many political freedoms the following year when small bands of leftist insurgents, many of them inspired by the Cuban Revolution, began to rob banks, kidnap foreign diplomats and businessmen, and employ urban guerrilla tactics.

The military responded with mass arrests of suspected terrorists, torture, and assassinations. With these harsh methods they soon eliminated the guerrilla combatants who had not managed to escape into exile. In an attempt to cover up these activities, the government censored the media and used intimidation, arrests, exile, and assassination to silence critical voices. One group of voices that the military government found difficult to mute, however, was a growing community of Catholic priests who spoke out against the human rights abuses. Some of these activist priests were arrested and tortured, but their efforts drew even more international attention and criticism of the military government's abuse of power. Many Brazilian priests became radicalized during the 1960s and 1970s when they began working more and more with the poor. They soon discovered that it was not possible to minister to the spiritual needs of people who were malnourished, in need of health care, and mostly uneducated. Some of these priests helped to develop Liberation Theology, one of Catholicism's most significant world movements in the twentieth century. Liberation Theologians combined the teachings of Christianity with Marxist critiques of the inhumanity of what some referred to as Brazil's savage capitalism.

Why did many Brazilians support such a repressive military regime? Much of its legitimacy came from its success in fostering a period of fantastic economic growth from 1968 to 1974. During these years of the "economic miracle," the gross national product grew at fantastically high rates of 10 percent or more per year. This growth created new opportunities for a rising urban middle class, but once again the distribution of this wealth was skewed toward higher-income groups. The industrial working class and the majority of Brazilians with even lower pay and fewer protections and benefits enjoyed a disproportionately small share of this economic bounty. Those who stuck their necks out to protest conditions, however, rightfully feared that they might lose what little security they had, if not their freedom and life.

This heady period of growth that saw Brazil become a major exporter of industrial goods had been funded largely by foreign investment and loans that mostly state-owned corporations made from foreign banks. The miraculous model of development began to unravel in the midst of the oil crises of 1973 and 1979. Brazil's industrial machine depended heavily on imported oil to run, and state-led attempts to tap alternative energy sources (for example, nuclear, hydroelectric, and ethanol) could not overcome the need for imported petroleum. Suddenly, Brazilians were paying three times as much for petroleum imports, but instead of slowing down plans for development, as South Korea did at the time, the state continued to borrow. Profits from petroleum-producing nations began to be deposited in European and U.S. banks, whose loan officers were eager to find borrowers in growing economies such as Brazil. By the mid-1970s, the incredible growth rates that Brazil had known came to an end. When the second oil shock hit in the late

1970s, the country was deep in debt just at the moment when international interest rates tripled. The 1980s would be known as the lost decade in Latin America because regional economies experienced little, if any, growth and many countries defaulted on international loans.

As their legitimacy became tarnished by the faltering economy, military officers began a slow and painful process to extricate themselves from political leadership roles. As the repressive police state allowed for more freedoms, Brazilians organized and joined myriad political action groups that advocated many causes, some old, others new: black consciousness, human rights, women's rights, gay and lesbian rights, indigenous rights, land reform, environmentalism, independent labor unions, and consumer protection, among many others. Almost all of these groups felt some sense of unity in their opposition to military rule, and their ebullition in the late 1970s and early 1980s reflected a pent-up desire on the part of the populace for an active role in political organizations, movements, and debate. Significantly, many of these emerging movements and organizations were international in scope, identity, membership, and affiliation. Their members often looked beyond the nation-state and national territory for an imagined common community, and some even questioned the utility of nationalist sentiments. The globalization of identity and politics took off before the fall of the Soviet Union in 1989 brought an end to the Cold War.

In popular youth culture, some of Brazil's rock 'n' roll groups, which often took flack for adopting foreign, even imperialistic music, expressed their disillusionment with the nationalist visions of the previous generation. As Hermano Vianna observed, the rock group Titãs expressed this frustration in a 1987 song "Nowhere at All," which reworded a vulgar insult ("*puta que pariu*," the prostitute who gave birth to you, or, roughly, son of a bitch) to "*nenhuma pátria me pariu*" (no fatherland or nation gave birth to me).* This disillusionment with nationalism does not mean that all Brazilians have abandoned national pride, including many who harshly criticize their country. Conversely, many who condemn jingoistic nationalism also fear that globalization will overwhelm local cultures and lead to a dreary homogenization—that is, Americanization—of world cultures. Still, the heady nationalism of the mid-1900s no longer seemed fashionable in youth culture, as it did in the school days of Norma Fraga.

In 1985, Brazil returned to civilian rule with great hopes that an open government would work to resolve the many social and economic

---

*Hermano Vianna, *The Mystery of Samba: Popular Music and National Identity in Brazil*, trans. John C. Chasteen (Chapel Hill: University of North Carolina Press, 1999), 100.

problems that remained in the wake of the military government's failed policies. A constitutional assembly drafted a progressive Constitution that laid the ground rules for the new political order, which included a much-expanded electorate that admitted illiterates and those age sixteen and older. The Brazilian electoral system has never been more open than it is now, and voters were soon just as critical of their civilian leaders as they had been of their military forebears. President José Sarney vacillated when unpopular economic decisions were needed to fight inflation and balance budgets, and political corruption scandals sullied his administration. He was soon outdone in both these arenas by his successor and the first directly elected president since 1960, Fernando Collor de Mello. Collor's presidency (1990–1992) ended in ignominy when corruption scandals led to his impeachment, and most of his efforts to fight inflation and reorient Brazil's market economy faltered. Collor's drab vice president, Itamar Franco, took office, but the uninspired Franco empowered a flashy former leftist sociology professor, Fernando Henrique Cardoso, as finance minister to come up with a workable plan to fight inflation. Cardoso's "Real Plan" imitated the strategy that Argentina had pursued by pegging the value of the national currency to the U.S. dollar. While the plan created problems for sectors of Brazil's economy, overall it proved to be popular because it brought chronic inflation down to bearable levels. The Real Plan's success helped Cardoso win election as president in 1994.

By the 1990s, Cardoso had turned his back on the socialist views of his earlier days when the military government had exiled him. Instead, like many center left chief executives of his day, he sought to implement moderate neoliberal economic policies or to reduce the size and scope of state participation and interference in the marketplace. He hoped to balance aggressive free-market economic growth strategies with government investment and spending on Brazil's less-advantaged populace to give free markets a more human character. This endeavor has proved to be a difficult balancing act. At the end of the twentieth century, United Nations researchers declared Brazil the nation with the most uneven wealth distribution in the world.

The Real Plan largely came undone in the late 1990s after Russia's President Boris Yeltsin was forced to devaluate the ruble, a move that panicked currency markets around the world. Cardoso's government began to allow the value of Brazil's currency to float, and while this move led to fears of a return to hyperinflation and recession and while growth was slow, Brazil's economy remained surprisingly resilient. Cardoso used much of his political capital to amend the 1988 Constitution to allow him to run for reelection in 1998. While some observers questioned the legality of this amendment and others accused him of suborning congressional representatives to win their votes, Cardoso ultimately won a second four-year term.

By the end of his term in 2002, Cardoso's neoliberal policies had alienated much of the electorate, and many opted for a new direction by voting for the four-time presidential candidate for the leftist Partido dos Trabalhadores (PT, or Workers' Party), Luiz Inácio Lula da Silva, more popularly known as Lula. In order to win the election, however, this former metalworker and trade union representative toned down his radical socialist rhetoric and embraced free-market economics, something that the PT had been loath to do in the past. He also had to ally his party with many of the same conservative leaders he had criticized Cardoso for incorporating in his administration. Thus far, Lula has maintained most of the economic and political initiatives he inherited from the Cardoso administration, and Wall Street has praised his restraint in the area of economic policy: stimulating foreign investment and easing speculative pressure that had devalued the national currency during the elections. Lula has remained outspoken in his criticism of George W. Bush's handling of the war in Iraq, and he maintains that international law and the United Nations have to be strengthened.

Cardoso's government had sold many of Brazil's state-owned industries (some profitable, others not) to national and international investors. Many nationalists accused their president of auctioning off the national patrimony to foreigners. But times had changed since the mid-1900s, and many believed that the foundering of state-led development strategies in the 1980s indicated the need for new policies in the microelectronic era. The free-market and freer trade philosophies of neoliberalism were the vogue after the collapse of the Soviet Union. Brazil's government loosened up many trade restrictions to encourage its manufacturers to become more competitive and efficient, but in certain sectors, vulnerable national industries remain protected by tariffs. Brazil joined with Argentina, Uruguay, Paraguay, Bolivia, and Chile to form Mercosul (Mercosur in Spanish), a NAFTA-like trade organization that lowers tariffs on most goods sold between these nations.

Cardoso and Lula, however, have been wary of American pressure to form a free-trade zone throughout the Western Hemisphere. Now that President Bush has received fast-track negotiating powers from the U.S. Congress, the issue of a free-trade zone for the Americas will undoubtedly be revived as an issue on the agenda of hemispheric relations. Lula's government and Brazilians more generally will play a crucial role in these negotiations as the largest economy and most populous nation in Latin America. Argentina's recent economic meltdown has had a harmful impact on Brazil's economy, and it is difficult to foresee whether this crisis will envelop Brazil and the nations of the Southern Cone. It is perhaps more difficult to speculate how it might affect the way most Brazilians think about international trade pacts and globalization over-all. Up to now, the nationalist community that Vargas had struggled to construct has given way to a greater sense of cosmopolitanism in the late twentieth and early twenty-first centuries that many argue is a natural outcome of globalization.

$\sim$

The vignettes in Part IV tell us how individuals responded to the important trends and events outlined above. Jôfre Corrêa Netto was an army sergeant during the World War II era who, after being dishonor-ably discharged, returned to an itinerant rural life until he suddenly be-came the charismatic leader of a widely publicized sharecroppers' strike in western Brazil. Jôfre's humble background, exposure to nationalist culture in the military, heartfelt anti-Americanism, and later claims to affiliation with the Communist Party reveal the tide of influences that washed over rural Brazilians in the tumultuous years of the 1960s. Caro-lina Maria de Jesus became even more famous than Jôfre at a time when world leaders worried about where the loyalties of the Third World's poor resided: with the capitalist or Communist-bloc nations. Her best-selling diary of the harrowing life of a ragpicker in a São Paulo slum drew attention to those who had been left behind by the state-led drive for industrialization in Brazil and, by extension, in other Third World nations. Her indomitable independent spirit made her unwilling to show the deference that most educated Brazilians expected from a poor black woman. Carolina's rise to notoriety and slide back into obscurity reveal much about the anxieties over development in the early 1960s. Her struggles with social mobility reveal how persistent and difficult it re-mained to overcome compounded prejudices related to gender, class, race, birth status, and geographic origins.

Dom Hélder Câmara's biography illuminates the changing roles of the Catholic Church and the priesthood in twentieth-century Brazil. Young priests such as Dom Hélder espoused Conservative ideas that were broadly supportive of the state during the Vargas era. Under the military regime (1964–1985), however, the venerated and ascetic Dom Hélder became an outspoken critic who called attention to the government's human rights abuses and the suffering of Brazil's poor. The concerted efforts of Pope John Paul II to remove Church leaders and punish activ-ist priests who advocated Liberation Theology in the 1980s in Latin America brought a more conservative tone to the clergy.

Madame Satã (Satan) was one of Rio de Janeiro's most colorful un-derground figures from the Vargas era. A well-known street tough, he often dressed openly as a woman and did not try to hide his sexual preference for men at a time when this behavior was considered scandalous. His various street brawls were often provoked by insults to his manhood and sometimes ended in homicides that landed him long stretches in jail. In the 1960s and 1970s, Brazilian youths interested in protesting the abuses of the military police state interviewed the by-then elderly Madame Satã. They identified with his uncompromising resistance to government authority, even though they did not relate to his sexuality. An emerging gay and lesbian community, however, identified with Madame Satã's inflexible pride in his sexual orientation and his unwillingness to tolerate the abuse so often directed at gays and lesbians.

Finally, Mario Juruna's intriguing life story reveals how a Xavante Indian navigated his way from life as a hunter-gatherer to a federal deputy in Brazil's Congress. He demonstrates the creativity that many indigenous persons cultivated to survive the loss of tribal lands and independence. Many learned how to manipulate concepts of nationalism that portrayed the indigenous peoples as the first Brazilians. They also astutely cultivated alliances with elements in state institutions, the Church, and international organizations (especially environmental and human rights groups) to defend their rights. Like Mario Juruna, the struggles of all the individuals in this volume reflect changes and continuities in their relationship to different, sometimes competing ideas of community that are a central part of the human tradition.

CHAPTER II

Jôfre Corrêa Netto

The Fidel Castro of Brazil

CLIFF WELCH

Brazil had been the U.S. government's strongest Latin American ally during World War II, but Washington quickly lost interest in Latin America after the fighting stopped. As the Cold War developed, the United States worked to contain communism by reforming and developing the economies of Western Europe, Korea, and Japan. It invested prodigious sums of money in these nations and even pressured leaders in Korea and Japan to redistribute land to peasants to bolster political stability, weaken rural oligarchs, and create broader-based rural consumer markets. Latin America, in the meantime, received little in the way of U.S aid. Indeed, American policymakers worked to scuttle moderate programs of wealth redistribution, such as land reform, in Latin America, sometimes through military intervention, in part because many U.S.-based corporations in the region had become large landowners whose properties might be affected by these reforms.

Many nationalists in Brazil and other Latin American nations began to resent the arrogance and negligence of U.S. government policy toward the region. Even those Latin American nationalists who had little sympathy for socialism admired the way that Fidel Castro appropriated properties owned by U.S. corporations and investors to promote "national" development in Cuba. Castro's example soon inspired similar efforts to bring greater equality and justice to national economies where the gaps between the overwhelmingly poor majority and the tiny wealthy minority seemed obscene. One of these settings was Brazil, where wealthy and powerful landowners and speculators pushed small farmers and squatters off lands they had cleared and developed. Ranchers, plantation owners, and farmers exploited a growing population of rural workers who now had to earn wages or sharecrop to survive, and many of these workers migrated to large urban centers with few resources where they were forced to live in burgeoning unsanitary slums. The misery of Brazil's urban and rural poor made its population ripe for Communist agitation in the view of U.S. Cold War pundits. It is no accident that President John F. Kennedy emphasized the Brazilian situation when he called for a version of the Marshall Plan (the policy that rebuilt Western Europe after World War II) for Latin Americans as a means of winning their support for the capitalist-

bloc nations. Lamentably, the United States spent most of its money to equip and train Latin American militaries and police forces to conduct counterinsurgency operations against militant leftist groups. This same hardware and training was also used to intimidate moderate reformers and disband progressive organizations that sought to change Latin American societies by nonviolent means.

Most of Brazil's agricultural workers had not benefited from new labor legislation first put in place by President Getúlio Vargas that provided basic protections for urban industrial workers. But during the 1950s rural workers began to organize, and some populist politicians eager to attract a rural base of loyal voters began to speak out against the abuse of farm workers and peasants. These conditions provided opportunities for charismatic figures who seemed to come out of nowhere, such as Jôfre Corrêa Netto, to start a rural uprising that attracted international interest. Here was a modest individual who shaped a significant chapter of Brazilian history during the Cold War.

Professor Cliff Welch's biography of Jôfre demonstrates how, like nations and ethnic groups, all individuals create certain myths about their origins. These memories often give greater coherence to our lives and help us to make sense of our place in the social and material world around us. They are a part of the human tradition that historians must analyze and corroborate in their attempts to create an accurate portrait of the past. Pay attention to how over time Jôfre shifts his birth year, attributes great significance to his birthplace, and exaggerates his military career and Communist Party credentials. As Welch shows here, memories are imperfect, but even these imperfections can be significant for understanding history. As you read the chapter, ask yourself if Jôfre's penchant for embellishing his past diminishes in any way his achievements as a labor organizer. While Jôfre's enemies attempted to use his past to discredit him (and they did some rewriting of his biography on their own), most of his supporters were unperturbed by these efforts.

Cliff Welch is associate professor of history at Grand Valley State University and coordinator of its Latin American Studies Program. His biography of Jôfre Corrêa Netto sprang from his broader study of rural labor union organization and struggle in the fertile northern region of the state of São Paulo: The Seed Was Planted: The São Paulo Roots of Brazil's Rural Labor Movement *(1999).*

Shortly after the Cuban Revolution of January 1959, Jôfre Corrêa Netto became famous as a peasant leader in Brazil. This transformation was surprising for a man who had worked as a teamster and served his country as a soldier during World War II before taking up the roving life of a traveling salesman (*mascate*) and herbal healer (*herbanário*). Like most

Brazilians of the era, he grew up in the countryside and knew the life of peasants and rural workers, but this life was not one he chose to follow. He was too gregarious, undisciplined, and rebellious to spend his years watching vegetables grow. His charismatic qualities and not a green thumb caused the press to turn him into Brazil's "Backlands Fidel Castro." They saw in him a colorful and willing advocate for thousands of threatened tenant farmers in a frontier region of São Paulo state where he had gone to sell pots and pans. Overnight, Jôfre became a peasant leader linked to the Brazilian Communist Party, and it proved to be an identity suited to his personality and an appropriate fit for the moment.

In 1959, Brazil entered the final stage of its Populist Republic, a period marked by the dramatic appearance of peasants and rural workers in the mass media and politics. With everyone from the president to peons calling for agrarian reform, it was as if Jôfre had responded to a second call to national service after the war. Without the slightest sense of contradiction, he blended his war service as a soldier with his service as a peasant leader by adopting the name "Captain Jôfre." By fighting for the rights of rural workers, he saw himself as continuing the World War II fight for democracy, despite undergoing constant persecution by the military police and several arrests and incarcerations for threatening national security. The 1964 military overthrow of the civilian government ended his career as a Communist peasant leader and returned him to a life of wandering, odd jobs, and eventually a military pension for his war service. Jôfre's biography—a story of personality shaped by class, party, regional, ethnic, and national identities—helps to illustrate significant aspects of Brazil's Populist era and its aftermath. It also shows how, when the moment is right, individuals can rise above their conditions and join with others to influence history.

The complications in recounting Jôfre's life begin with his birth. Like most poor Brazilians living in remote areas before the 1950s, Jôfre's birth went unrecorded. Until the late 1980s, when scholars and journalists demonstrated an interest in his story, Jôfre gave his birth date as April 3, 1921. With growing interest in his life as a Communist militant, however, Jôfre began to assert that this date was incorrect and that he had really been born in 1917, a date seemingly chosen to link his birth to the Bolshevik Revolution and the birth of the Soviet Union. He became all the more emphatic about this date as the Soviet Union collapsed, a process that left him angry and dismayed. Identifying with diverse struggles against the imperialist United States, he dressed himself like Palestinian leader Yasir Arafat and then like Iraqi leader Saddam Hussein and scrawled "Communist Party Base No. 1" on the front of his house in large, runny red paint. Although the records confirm neither 1921 nor 1917 as his birth year, Jôfre's determination to sustain his rebellious profile suggests the earlier date was chosen to impress and that 1921 is a sounder starting point.

Rebellion and turmoil marked Jôfre's youth. Political rivalries and dramatic socioeconomic change set off rebellions around Brazil in the 1920s and 1930s. The state where Jôfre says he was born, Rio Grande do Sul, initiated some of the revolts and participated in all of them. As Brazil's southernmost state, the historian Joseph Love explains, Rio Grande developed a bellicose tradition of defending Portuguese America against its Spanish-American rivals, Argentina and Uruguay. Its rolling pasture lands gave rise to the *gaúcho*, the Brazilian cowboy, known for his independence, loyalty, and ferocity. Where cowboys in the United States mastered the .45 caliber six-shooter, the *gaúcho* defended himself with a *facão*, a sword-like knife kept stuck in the belt of his blowsy pants. He enlisted in rebellions that seemed to be about power but actually reflected growing conflict between the traditional landed oligarchy and a rising conglomeration of urban, modernizing groups that favored industrial development and professional government.

Determining where Jôfre stood in the midst of this upheaval is not an easy task. The lack of a birth certificate and baptismal record makes his claims of parentage impossible to confirm. He has consistently reported his parents to be Pedro Corrêa Netto and Joana de Figueiredo da Silva and his birthplace as Santo Angelo das Missões. Jôfre's sense of origin as a *gaúcho* from Santo Angelo formed a strong part of his identity, and yet it seems certain that he was not born in Santo Angelo. And if he was born in Rio Grande do Sul, he spent very little time there before moving upriver to the state of Mato Grosso. In a 1989 interview, for example, Jôfre says that he was born in Rio Grande do Sul but that his mother raised him in Mato Grosso from the time he was three years old.

Santo Angelo sits close to Rio Grande do Sul's northwestern border with Argentina. There, dividing the two countries, is the wide Uruguay River, used by shippers to carry goods from rivers farther inland to ports downriver, including the Atlantic Ocean port at Montevideo on the River Plate. Jôfre remembers nothing about his time here, but a half-sister he never knew, Olga Alves Godoy, says that their father, Pedro, operated a crude barge on the river, hauling firewood and lumber from Mato Grosso to Rio Grande. Olga and Jôfre never met because they each had different mothers. While Jôfre does not remember his father, the younger Olga recounts talk of their father having a second family. Since Jôfre is certain that his mother was from Mato Grosso and recalls growing up with her father and brothers, it seems possible that Pedro formed a family with Joana in Mato Grosso during his travels to gather lumber there. In this scenario, Jôfre loses his claim to being a *gaúcho*.

In matters of identity, facts often matter less than feelings. In this case, Jôfre expresses an uncanny identity with a father who abandoned him and a place he cannot remember and may never have seen. In this way, Jôfre is both representative and exceptional, for until the midtwentieth century many Brazilians had little more than family lore to document their origins, and yet few were as driven as Jôfre to give life a sense of purpose and direction by building a strong sense of identity. Jôfre not only came to celebrate his *gaúcho* origins as a badge of freedom and strength, but he also found in the father he cannot remember a model of manly behavior.

Jôfre's father was known as a doctor because people came to him for herbal cures. Until 1932, health care specialists in Rio Grande could practice without formal training or license. Those who in other contexts might have been called snake-oil salesmen could earn the prestigious title of "doctor" in Rio Grande if their cures did the trick more often than not. It seems that Pedro knew his trade and impressed his neighbors and his son, for this was a trade that Jôfre pursued later, at a time when health care standards and the law were not quite so lax.

In his work as healer and barge operator, Jôfre's father traveled a lot, establishing a peripatetic life that his son would later adopt. João Pires Netto, Pedro's nephew and Jôfre's cousin, speculates that the elder Corrêa Netto abandoned Jôfre in 1924 when he and João's father joined a barracks revolt initiated in Santo Angelo and led by Captain Luís Carlos Prestes. The rebellious soldiers, tired of ill treatment in the ranks and frustrated by the backward policies of Brazil's landed oligarchy, converged on Santo Angelo to demonstrate their solidarity with a similar army revolt in São Paulo state. By October, historian Neill Macaulay reports, several hundred troops and civilians followed Prestes and other commanders on an epic, 2,000-mile march through the backlands of Brazil before withdrawing to Bolivia in 1927. Due to his medicinal skills, Pedro left with the troops, João claims. Another rebellion of national importance started in Santo Angelo in October 1930 when a local, Lt. Col. Pedro Góes Monteiro, became the leader of the conspiracy that ended the First Republic and brought to power Rio Grande do Sul's governor, Getúlio Vargas. Both Olga and João believe that Pedro participated in this movement, claiming that he was an especially courageous man.

Jôfre, who did not know these particular stories, nevertheless grew up with the impression that his father was not only brave but also a "Communist." This is improbable. Although Captain Prestes eventually became the Brazilian Communist Party's general secretary, he did not join the party until 1931. The party had been founded by a group of intellectuals and artisans in Rio de Janeiro in 1922, and its links to Rio Grande do Sul were limited to a few radicals in Pôrto Alegre, the state capital. The timing and distance of these events from Santo Angelo make it unlikely that Pedro's worldview was significantly influenced by Communist ideology. But there does seem to be something to the idea that Pedro was a man of action who enthusiastically took part in the rebellion, a tendency said to be characteristic of *gaúchos*. Whatever the truth, Jôfre's identity has been shaped by the notion that his father was brave and willing to challenge authority, and this idea left a family heritage of militancy for his son to emulate.

Pedro's behavior also seems to have left his son with the idea that it was manly to be a womanizer and dead-beat dad. Pedro may have had as many as four children with Jôfre's mother, five with Olga's mother, and untold numbers with other women, for he seems to have spent very little time with either of these two known families. In Brazil in that period (and to this day), Pedro's way with women conveyed socially appealing values of virility, dominance, and freedom. Jôfre followed in his father's footsteps. In 1949 he had at least one child with a common-law wife, and in 1961 he married Jandirá Freitas Campos, a student activist, with whom he had three children. There was a third common-law wife, too, with whom he had two children. He spent almost no time with his various families, has no stories to tell about his children, and proudly reveals to his male listeners that he has had many additional liaisons and untold numbers of illegitimate children. By the 1990s, his extended family included a second and third generation of fatherless families and troubled children, many of them debilitated and marginalized by the modern scourge of drug abuse and trafficking.

One woman seems to have had a significant impact on Jôfre's life: his mother. "She was everything to me," Jôfre told the author in 1997. "She taught me everything. She taught me about character and how to be a cultured person. As a seamstress, she was a master craftswoman." The support of Joana's family enabled Jôfre to attend school for three years, probably in the late 1920s, an opportunity few in his class then enjoyed. His ability to read and write placed him a notch above the average backlander. As Jôfre remembers it, his mother and father had another son before him—Ney Corrêa Netto—and after him, a daughter of forgotten name who soon died. Jôfre and Ney grew up together but had little contact after the elder son left home in the mid-1930s; the brothers have not had any contact at all since 1961. With Pedro gone, Joana earned money to raise her sons by sewing. Eventually, Jôfre dropped out of school and began work as a helper to an ox-cart driver, spending as many as two to three months away from home to follow the teamster's life. Until he was thirteen years old, Jôfre walked in front of the oxen, leading them down miles of dirt track and setting up camp along the roadside, where he remembers roasting such wild game as snakes and fowl. Thereafter, the family migrated to São Paulo state, where they moved from place to place, with Joana sewing and Jôfre pursuing odd jobs and eventually developing some skills as an electrician.

Tired of wandering and underemployment, Jôfre eventually followed the advice of his mother and joined the army. "She told me," he said, "that poor people never become more than corporals or sergeants but that the army still offered more support than she could." Moreover, in 1939, Vargas instituted a mandatory military service law. Those men who lacked a card documenting their service could not apply for government jobs or benefits and could not register to vote; once caught, those without cards had to pay hefty fines. Jofre's mother may have recommended the army to him in these circumstances, but he put off enlistment until October 1940. On the fourth day of the month, he presented himself to the Fourth Infantry battalion in Quitauna, São Paulo, and was enlisted as a healthy, single, literate white male with brown hair and clear brown eyes who worked as an electrician and knew how to swim. Toward the end of his life, Jôfre made much of his army days. When he was not reminiscing about his activities as a Communist peasant leader, Jôfre's core identity was as a veteran of World War II.

World War II was a transitional moment in the history of Brazil's armed forces, as historians José Murilo de Carvalho and Peter Beattie have shown. Since the rebellion of 1930, the army had grown in status, and people began to see it less in its traditional role as a destination for social outcasts and more as a professional, nation-building institution. It was this idea of the army that must have caught Joana's attention. Although it was still in transition during the 1930s, the army had become respectable in the 1940s and its soldiers were increasingly seen as men of honor and guardians of the nation. The soldiers of the World War II Brazilian Expeditionary Force (*febianos*) were the first to earn this stature. As veterans, they eventually gained public support for an unprecedented level of old-age benefits, including a pension, medical care, and free housing.

Jôfre's identification with the army seems in sharp contrast to his life as a Communist militant, yet this normal if somewhat complicated contradiction was the kind of commingling of opposites that typifies Brazil. Long-time Communist leader Luís Carlos Prestes, for example, began his radical journey as a disgruntled army captain. Although Prestes's ideology and partisanship alienated the army hierarchy and he was jailed from 1935 to 1945, many officers and soldiers respected him for his intelligence, rigor, and nationalism. All the same, the army among all the armed forces of Brazil introduced a program of ideological indoctrination as early as 1934 that aimed to eradicate Communist thought in the ranks. Jôfre claims, however, that he was introduced to the Brazilian Communist Party (PCB) while in the army. This claim was common due in part to the Western alliance with the Soviet Union during the war. Under Prestes and especially after 1945, the PCB shared with the army a hierarchical structure, regimentation, and social leveling based on merit as well as dedication to defining and advocating solutions to national problems. These consistencies, rather than the stark contrasts between them, contributed to Jôfre's ability to feel patriotic and at home in both organizations. In his mind, he worked to build and defend the fatherland in both the army and the party.

Nothing in Jôfre's service record supports his contention that clandestine Communists helped to awaken his political consciousness while in the army. He remembers his time there as one of constantly challenging authority. During the first two years of his enlisted service, his activities were so predictable that they filled only a page or two in the record books kept by army scribes. By the end of 1942, he had reached the pinnacle his mother had envisioned for him by first being promoted to corporal and then to third sergeant. But he never wore three stripes, and he certainly never attained the officer status that his "Captain Jôfre" nickname later suggested.

Something happened in the last quarter of 1942 that completely changed his relationship with the army. From then on, the record books recount a perplexing history of repeated bad conduct, desertion, insubordination, and, consequently, months in the brig, including many days of solitary confinement. What had happened? Jôfre explains that a dramatic shift in his attitude came when he learned that his mother had died toward the end of the year. "There was this mean sergeant who decided not to tell me my mother was sick and dying until she'd already passed away," Jôfre recounts. The withholding of such crucial information about this most valued person in his life struck him as high treason, and he rebelled against this stern paternalism with barely a pause until he was dishonorably expelled nearly three years later.

When looking at this record and comparing it to Jôfre's later conversion to proud World War II veteran, one cannot help but marvel at his inventive regeneration. He appears as a quintessential Brazilian *malandro*, a clever manipulator who, because of Brazil's oppressive social structure, is seen as heroic in popular culture. The *malandro* is honored, argues anthropologist Roberto da Matta, because he is someone who turns weaknesses into strengths, who defies class boundaries and paternalist strictures to build for himself, his friends, and his family a life of greater comfort and autonomy. He is someone with few privileges who turns inside out the exclusive, hierarchical Brazilian system to make it work for him.

Jôfre saw active duty only from July 13 to August 6, 1943, when he was sent to help guard a power plant, one year before the Brazilian Expeditionary Force invaded Italy. Both before and after this three-week period of active duty, Jôfre spent most of his time imprisoned. And yet, to meet him fifty years later at the veterans' compound in Brasília, the federal capital, one would think that he had led the final assault in Italy on the German stronghold at Monte Castello (a battle where Brazilian troops defeated Nazi forces). As he aged, Jôfre increasingly identified himself as a war veteran despite his shabby service record. In 1981 he successfully petitioned the army to change his dishonorable discharge status and gradually accumulated government benefits reserved for former combatants. By the mid-1990s, Jôfre typically sported a military beret and kept his veterans' identity card in full view as a badge of honor and privilege. In June 2002 he died at the army hospital in Brasília.

After his expulsion in January 1945, Jôfre followed an obscure path, working at odd jobs, selling pots and pans, prescribing herbal remedies, running numbers, writing letters for illiterates, and falling afoul of the law. He was arrested in 1953 for battery and in 1956 for knifing a man, and served several months in jail each time. After the Grass War broke out in Santa Fé do Sul in the late 1950s, the conservative press made much of Jôfre's criminal record in order to diminish him and weaken his leadership. They added to the above list two detentions in 1950 for "identity verification," one in 1952 for a beating, one in 1953 for vagrancy, one in 1954 for gambling, and a "background check" in 1955, but none of these appears in Jôfre's official police record; perhaps the authorities thought they needed to feed these added charges to the press to secure their collaboration in discrediting Jôfre. In any event, he seems to have spent much of the 1950s living on the margins of mainstream society, bouncing around country towns in an effort to make a living and avoid police attention. The rap sheet indicates that the former soldier encountered a rough life as a civilian but nevertheless was able to thumb his nose at Brazil's elitist social structure.

Around 1957, Jôfre arrived in the Santa Fé do Sul region of São Paulo for the first time. In 1988 he told historian Nazareth dos Reis that he moved to the area to find farmland. In a 1989 interview, he told sociologist Vera Chaia that he had been invited there by an army buddy, a "discharged captain named Guiné," to invest in some land on Grand Island at the confluence of the Grand and Paranaíba rivers. In his 1997 interview with the author, however, he said that the São Paulo state central committee of the PCB had sent him to the region to agitate among peasants under the cover of traveling salesman. He told all three that at first he lived among some fifty families who farmed disputed land in the flood zone of the river bank and that at some point in 1957, while he was away, the man who claimed to own the land had had their makeshift homes burnt down and their crops destroyed. "By the time I came back from my travels," Jôfre recalled, "they'd burnt down forty-five homes, lean-tos, burnt down with what little money each family had saved over the whole year, burnt down with their harvests stored inside." Jôfre and the others blamed this attack on José de Carvalho (Zico) Diniz, the area's largest private landholder.

The fiery attack proved to be the first battle in a confrontation between Jôfre and his peasant allies, and Zico Diniz, his business partners, and their retainers in what escalated into the so-called Grass War. This prolonged conflict turned Jôfre from a backlands wanderer into someone whom people called the "Backlands Fidel Castro," an honorable moniker for almost any Latin American in the context of Cuba's daring revolution. It raised Jôfre from a man with few to no connections, not even family, to someone with a rich and varied web of relationships. As Roberto da Matta has explained, relationships, more than any other single factor, define who you are in Brazil. By simply asking the question, "Do you know who you are talking to?" a man immediately conveys a sense of power through his relationship to others. Jôfre—this orphaned, demoted, dishonored, much-persecuted roamer—was suddenly mixing with powerful politicians, union leaders, journalists, and foreigners. Out of respect for his leadership capacities and his military service, he became "Captain Jôfre." All his years of travel, diverse occupations, fitful soldiering, confrontations with authority, and living by his wits suddenly became the stuff of priceless skill and charisma. "God gave me an instinct for leadership," he said in a 2001 documentary about the Grass War.

In the late 1950s, Brazil was entering a unique period in which doors opened for people such as Jôfre. As the world economy realigned following the war, Brazil enjoyed increased demand for commodities such as coffee and increased foreign investment as U.S. businesses sought opportunities abroad. "Economic development" and "modernization" were bywords of the era. President Juscelino Kubitschek promised "fifty years of progress in five" and started construction of Brasília, a new capital designed to signal the country's modernity and advancement. Brazil's 1958 World Cup soccer victory, its first ever, demonstrated to many that it was indeed "the country of the future." Part and parcel of these changes was an awakening of mass society, particularly in the countryside, where political movements began to engage the rural underclass. While acclaimed novels and movies in Brazil's burgeoning cultural industry mined backlands folklore for a sense of national identity, rural workers and peasants themselves insisted on being included in the modernization process. They wanted electricity, household appliances, motorized transportation, hospitals, schools, unions, fair wages and prices, and the chance to prosper with the rest of the country and the world. A body of laws grew to offer rural workers rights and duties like other working-class Brazilians. In December 1958, for example, Law 3,494 gave tenants the right to have their occupancy prolonged by up to two years so long as they notified their landlords in advance. Such laws inspired peasants to fight for broader social and political participation. Jôfre's emergence as a peasant leader on the frontier of São Paulo, Brazil's wealthiest agricultural and most industrialized state, coincided with this set of changes.

Santa Fé do Sul was founded in 1948, and the events that took place there had roots in its development process. A colonization and immigration company known as CAIC had purchased much of the region's land in 1946. The company, which was controlled by some of the state's richest and most established growers, represented the transformation of São Paulo's agriculture away from its traditional strength in coffee and toward greater diversity. CAIC sold or leased land mostly to middling family farmers who intended to grow a variety of crops. In the case of Santa Fé do Sul, however, one landlord—Zico Diniz—bought two extremely large sections of territory amounting to more than one-fifth of the original CAIC purchase. These holdings were known as the Fazenda Mariana and the Fazenda São João do Bosque.

Diniz represented an expanding force in Brazilian agriculture, the cattleman. As the urban population grew, especially in industrial centers, the market for beef expanded. Diniz intended to capitalize on this market by clearing the forests off his Santa Fé land and turning it into pasture. To do this economically, in an era before the widespread availability of machines such as bulldozers, he employed a subletting system. By written contract, he rented large parcels of his land to a couple of tenant contractors (José Lira Marim rented the Fazenda Mariana and Joaquim Nogueira rented the Fazenda São João), who then sublet it through oral agreements to hundreds of migrant families. As tenant farmers, the migrants' job was to clear the land of dense, tangled woods, cultivate it, and then plant *capim-colonino*, a vigorous pasture grass. They were supposed to make a living by selling surplus food from their crops and by earning a little money for each acre of grass they planted. Tenant-contractors Marim and Nogueira made money by selling the cleared timber for firewood, lumber, and railroad ties. Zico Diniz claimed half the sales profits from the timber and, after three to five years, stood to gain more than 18,000 acres of new pasture for his cattle herds at virtually no cost. This was how it was supposed to work, at any rate.

This tried and true method of exploiting both natural and human resources ran aground in April 1959 when Jôfre inspired some of the tenant farmers to uproot the grass they themselves had planted in their crops at the behest of Nogueira and Marim. The threat to the established order posed by Jôfre's activities had been under observation by São Paulo's secretive "political and social order" police for several months. In early March an agent reported Jôfre's participation at a neighborhood meeting organized in São Paulo to protest the high cost of living, and a spy at a meeting of the PCB's rural labor-organizing front (ULTAB) noted the presence of this "Communist and leader of the Santa Fé farmers' association." The spy reported that Jôfre denounced Zico Diniz for treating "long-resident peasant families in Santa Fé like animals." Earlier intelligence showed that Jôfre had earned some clout in the region by campaigning in 1958 for Santa Fé do Sul mayoral candidate Deraldo da Silva Prado. Inaugurated on January 1, 1959, Mayor Prado warmly received a petition from "thousands" of farmers living in the county who asked for his help in providing for their medical and schooling needs. The petition requested that the mayor and city council support the peasants in "creating an association of farmers" so that the farmers and municipal government could "work together more easily and less painfully to help Santa Fé grow and to promote a better standard of living for the greatness" of the state and the "pride" of the nation.

The list of those who signed the petition has not surfaced, so it is difficult to confirm that Jôfre was responsible for it. It is clear, however, that by March the police had identified Jôfre as a leader of the Santa Fé peasant movement. By June, when a large assembly of more than 1,000 peasants formally founded the association, Jôfre was elected president by acclamation. His apparent connections in São Paulo, his role in the April grass uprooting, and his charisma propelled him to leadership.

What caused his involvement in the first place? Although the sources are plentiful for this period of his life, they are silent or ambiguous about his sudden appearance as a full-fledged political activist. It should be said that Jôfre's recollection of this period rejects the notion of transition. He argues that his father was a Communist, that he became a Communist in the army, and that the PCB sent him to Santa Fé do Sul to organize the peasants. But this version is almost certainly false. Although the authorities persistently assumed that he was a Communist, PCB leaders deny it to this day. In 1994 the PCB's chief rural labor organizer, Lindolfo Silva, said in an interview with Vera Chaia that "Jôfre had nothing to do with us, nothing more than a similar outlook in his head. Jôfre was just making the most of the situation, to defend those people." After the grass uprooting, the PCB sent Pedro Renaux Duarte, acting president of ULTAB, to Santa Fé to help settle the situation. "I don't know if he was a member of the party," Duarte told the author. "He was a natural leader from the area." The police said that he was called Captain Jôfre because he had violent tendencies and was "militant," but all other sources contend that his charisma earned him this title. Accoding to Duarte, "He was the darling of all the peasants." "It's a name I got from the people," Jôfre said in 1989. They admired him, he says, for his aggressive response to the 1957 incident in which their riverside farms were burnt down. He claims to have pursued outside support for the peasants in São Paulo and Rio de Janeiro. This claim is possible but unlikely unless he had relationships established for him by someone else, given his evident lack of connections.

There were Communists in the region, and at least two became connected to the association. Arlindo Quiozini, a tenant farmer on the Fazenda Mariana who owned a small rice-processing machine, and Olimpio Pereira Machado, a peasant poet whom Jôfre claims to have befriended in 1957. It is possible that these two men influenced Jôfre to get involved and that they came up with the idea of seeking alliances and founding an association. Readers of PCB newspapers also knew that since 1954, the party had pursued a strategy of founding associations in order to enhance the rights of rural workers and peasants. By 1959, dozens had been formed in the state of São Paulo, and, despite their questionable legal standing, they often helped the rural working classes defend themselves and gain political experience. More than likely, then, Jôfre simply got caught up in local circumstances, learned from his friends, and found in the association a stage for his storehouse of skills.

As the grass began to grow and stifle the farmers' crops in March, Jôfre stepped up his activities. Before the uprooting took place, he threatened the action in several confrontations with the tenant-contractors Marim and Nogueira. Contacts with lawyers seem to have encouraged him. Roberto Valle Rollemberg, a politically connected lawyer from Jales, the region's judicial and administrative center, spoke for the nascent association at Mayor Prado's inauguration, and a Santa Fé lawyer and publisher, Nuno Lobo Gama D'Eça, donated his services to the association and its members. In conversations with these attorneys, association leaders developed the argument that Law 3,494 gave tenants the right to prolong their stay on the land. Moreover, a wave of agrarian reform measures from Cuba to northeast Brazil, where a sugar plantation was being considered for expropriation and distribution to resident workers, led Jôfre and the others to argue that if the tenant farmers held on long enough, they might be able to permanently keep the land they had cleared and planted. Jôfre promoted these ideas and claimed that the law supported the association's position. In a society where the law always seemed to favor the powerful and the wealthy, most people appreciated its power. The supposed legality of the plan to stay on the land and the morality (or justice) of uprooting the grass to restore the crops gave Jôfre's arguments considerable weight. To have the law on *their* side meant turning the world upside down, a social revolution of sorts. And it was just the idea of this turnabout that made Jôfre so threatening.

Anticipating the tenant farmers' resistance early in April, Diniz appealed in court for an injunction against Jôfre and the association. The court asked the police to open an investigation. The authorities concluded that the association was subversive, which allowed them to close it down by confiscating its belongings: basically some leaflets, legal papers, and a desk located in a boardinghouse in the village of Rubineia. But these measures did not stop Jôfre's plans. Rather than be intimidated, he took the lead in organizing an uprooting of 60 to 240 acres on the Fazenda Mariana. "The peasants set off with Jôfre leading them on horseback," said Benedito da Silva, an area resident. And according to Laurindo Novaes Netto, Rollemberg's law partner, "it was Jôfre's way of implanting his leadership."

The sources agree that Jôfre Corrêa Netto inspired the tenant farmers to resist being expelled from their farms and instigated the Grass War. By April 1959, the expulsion of some 800 families—perhaps as many as 5,000 people—was imminent. Diniz's contracts with Marim and Nogueira obliged them to return one-half of the land they had rented by September 1959 and the rest by September 1961. The first half, where the majority of the peasants lived, was to be delivered as pasture by the end of January 1959. Some accounts argue that Nogueira and Marim misled many peasants, promising them that their tenancy would be for five years. Others had arrived recently and when their first crops began to grow, the overseers ordered them to plant grass and leave.

Newspaper reports speak of their hardship and misery. The grass stifled their food crops and some tenants were reduced to starvation. Many were lucky to eat meals of roasted *capivara*, a giant rodent, and boiled roots. There was an increase in the death of infants. One family still living in the area in 1999 reported the tragic loss of five babies during this period. They protested that poor migrants were enticed to the region with promises of great opportunity, only to be kicked out just as they had succeeded in turning the wilderness into productive farmland. Reluctantly, some began to plant the *capim* in their fields. But Jôfre and his comrades in the association understood the tenant farmers' misery and seized on their complaints and needs to resist expulsion. They adopted an ancient method of resistance by destroying the result of their labor in order to take control of the situation. Some tore up the grass and declared their intention to stay put. Intuitively, Jôfre grasped the core injustice. "My friends," Jôfre said to them, "let's treat these grass clods well so that we can send them to Diniz and the governor to eat!" Speaking for many of the tenants, he said no to the idea that the farmers passively give up their crops and livelihoods so that cattle could be grazed for a meat market that few of them could afford.

This audacious act attracted considerable attention from authorities, the media, and politicians. Naturally, one of the first reactions came from Diniz and his agents. Soon after the April 16th uprooting, the landlord filed a complaint against Jôfre and the association as well as a list of nineteen named and other unnamed tenant farmers, appealing to the court to block them from further uprooting activities and demanding indemnity payments. The Fazenda Mariana swarmed with police and Jôfre sought refuge on the Fazenda São João, where he soon organized another uprooting. In May and June, reporters from São Paulo's two leading papers, *Ultima Hora* and *O Estado de São Paulo*, arrived to cover the story. The Rio de Janeiro-based news magazine, *O Cruzeiro*, also sent a reporter, and a crew arrived from São Paulo's nascent television industry, TV Tupi. The press questioned the behavior of authorities and the duties of the state, pressuring politicians and bureaucrats to get involved in settling the dispute. Jôfre enjoyed the attention. He had always demonstrated an unusual flair for fashion by wearing peculiar hats and boots, but now he adopted revolutionary-chic by cultivating a beard and sporting a beret. Jokingly, his associates started to call him Fidel, and the allusion found its way into police reports and the popular press. On May 16, as one of a nine-part series on the events in Santa Fé do Sul, *Ultima Hora* ran a cover story about Jôfre's role titled "Backlands 'Fidel Castro'!"

The name itself propelled Jôfre to national attention. From its start, stories about the revolution in Cuba appeared regularly on the front pages of Brazilian newspapers. The dark, bearded faces of Fidel Castro and Ernesto "Che" Guevara became readily recognizable images, ones associated with proud nationalism, militancy, and working-class rights. Jôfre's military background together with his height, dark beard, and backlands peasant-organizing activities gave people enough reason to imagine the comparison. For authorities, the similarities were more than skin deep. They worried that Santa Fé, with its river access and links to three states, was strategically located and that Jôfre had the motivational skills to set off a rebellion among what they assumed to be a group of illiterate, ignorant, desperate, and easily manipulated peasants. While Castro had a tendentious relationship with Cuban Communists, the network of Cold War military and police agencies in the Americas assumed that he was a Red. Since Jôfre worked closely with known PCB activists in Santa Fé, his "Fidel Castro" nickname gave authorities pause. But they never expressed doubts that they could contain the Grass War, and there is no reason to question their confidence. No one spoke of revolution: both Silva and Duarte of the PCB saw in the event and in Jôfre a chance to enhance their image and usefulness as power brokers of the working classes to government authorities, not as revolutionary leaders of the masses. In 1997, Jôfre insisted that he had never intended to model himself on Castro, either in appearance or in behavior. "I take off my hat to Fidel and Guevara but if I'd followed their line in Santa Fé, needless bloodletting would have resulted," he said. "I never followed Fidel's approach, I followed the PCB's."

The party's approach was oriented by a "popular front" strategy. It sought alliances with the "progressive bourgeoisie" to fight against the "feudal lords" and those willing to sell out to "imperialists." In its thinking, a democratic, national capitalist system had to precede the socialist "stage of history." The Brazilian Communist Party, like the Communist Cuban Popular Socialist Party, was not a revolutionary party. And Brazilians, like Cubans, were not revolutionary people. The Communist parties of both nations had trouble with Fidel and Jôfre because they refused to take orders. Backed by wealthy parents, a rigorous Jesuit education, and a law degree, Castro imposed discipline on himself and his followers, but his independence and "adventurism" scared the Communists. Jôfre's background differed entirely from Fidel's, but he, too, irritated the Communists with his independence and lack of discipline. If Jôfre had been a trusted party operative, the Grass War would never have happened because the party eschewed this sort of provocation.

Jôfre's behavior served the party by grabbing headlines and drawing attention to the problems of the rural poor, a constituency that the PCB had been trying to make its own since the mid-1940s. But Jôfre's behavior also produced the Grass War's only bloody encounter, something the Communists wanted to avoid. On the morning of August 5, Jôfre stopped at a bar on his way to catch a train to São Paulo when a gunman shot him in the face and leg with a .38 caliber revolver. The first bullet, fired point-blank, smashed through his teeth and lodged miraculously in his jaw. The second bullet, fired at his gut, missed its mark when Jôfre reacted to the first shot. The shooter, later identified as a man named Silva Preto, fled the scene, and bystanders are said to have run about town yelling, "They've killed Jôfre! They've killed Jôfre!"

But "they" had not killed Jôfre. By the next morning he had been sent by plane to a São Paulo hospital for treatment of his wounds. Duarte argues that Jôfre brought the shooting on himself by refusing to follow party restrictions against speaking out, drinking, and chasing women. Jôfre could not be silenced. The more he spoke out against Zico Diniz and his allies, the more Duarte worried about his safety and the image of the party. Jôfre spent lots of time in bars and relished the attention that his new fame brought him. Some alleged that Silva Preto shot him in a dispute over "a blonde whore." Predictably, Jôfre's opponents dismissed the shooting as a "personal matter," but this is doubtful. Although Silva disappeared and the state never tried or convicted anyone for the crime, many fingers pointed at the Fazenda São João tenant-contractor, Joaquim Nogueira, who admitted that the shooter worked for him and that he wanted to see Jôfre dead. After the shooting, the police suggested that Jôfre leave the area until tensions relaxed. In 1987 he told historian Nazareth dos Reis that he challenged Silva to shoot Jôfre "as a joke." But naturally, Nogueira stopped short of admitting that he had hired an assassin. Like Jôfre's supporters at the time, most analysts agree that it was a political crime, designed by Diniz or Nogueira to silence an agitator in hopes of reestablishing control in the region.

After Jôfre's departure, the state government gradually took control. The governor sent a versatile biologist named Paulo Vanzolini as a troubleshooter with special powers to contain and settle the dispute. The PCB assisted him in a clever way. While the party condemned the shooting and threatened violence, it also worked to find a compromise. The PCB put out the order that if any other peasant were shot, they would "burn down the *fazendas*, not leaving a single tree standing. It will be violence against violence." In this way, the party used the incident to gain some leverage and convince the governor to take the conflict seriously. Duarte then worked closely with Vanzolini to persuade the tenant farmers to accept a one-year extension on their tenure. By the end of September, they convinced Diniz and his men to allow most of the others to stay on until July 1961. Lawyers for both sides wrote a model contract and Vanzolini attended mass meetings organized by the association to get it signed; they also rode horseback around the vast property to get the reluctant ones to accept the deal. Foreshadowing future trouble, some worried that by signing the contract they were giving up on the possibility of owning the land, as Jôfre had proposed. The party presented the contract deal as a great victory. A weekly PCB tabloid ran an article titled "Landlord Loses the Grass War." It featured a photograph of Jôfre, with a caption that described him as the "leader of the Santa Fé do Sul peasants." In the photo, Jôfre projected an image of great confidence. He sported a mustache and stood in a relaxed pose with his left hand in his coat pocket.

Jôfre had been on his way to a São Paulo rally organized by the PCB when Silva shot him. When he was finally released from the hospital in mid-September—with one of the bullets still embedded in his mouth—he found that party officials had more work for him to do. For a few weeks, they put him through training in Communist ideology and clandestine organizing methods. His notoriety after the shooting seemed to enhance his value as a peasant spokesman, and the party directed him to speak at various protest rallies and to "preside" over the founding of rural labor associations and unions. In this populist period, when political leaders and parties vied with one another to be the legitimate voice of the so-called masses, Jôfre served to strengthen the Communists' claim to leadership of the rural working classes. This image mattered to the party because more and more politicians and groups sought rural constituents, and the PCB had its role to defend alongside rival groups such as the Peasant Leagues, which had been founded by a Socialist party politician from northeast Brazil named Francisco Julino. Jôfre's effectiveness in this role was acknowledged in a 1970 English-language publication when he was described as one of "two authentic peasant leaders of national reputation" whom the PCB counted among its ranks. Ironically, Jôfre had few credentials as a peasant, but he certainly knew how to motivate them.

In November 1959, Jôfre was back in Santa Fé do Sul. From his São Paulo hospital bed in August, he had declared his intention to return to the fight in Santa Fé. "I'm going back," he told a reporter. "Threats don't mean anything to me. The peasants need me to carry the movement forward." The police ridiculed his presence, describing his failed attempts to revive the movement by bragging about his travels and meetings with the São Paulo governor and President Kubitschek. But on November 19 he helped organize a public celebration around the laying of the founding stone of the association's new building near downtown Santa Fé. The success of the event inspired a new attitude of concern among the police. Later secret police reports noted that peasants doffed their hats to him on the street, called him Captain Jôfre, and treated him "like a god." According to an informant, "a greater rural agitator than Jôfre can't possibly exist."

Jôfre worked at another level during his second appearance in the region. Using techniques he had learned during his postoperative tutelage with the São Paulo Communists, Jôfre held clandestine meetings to convince the tenant farmers to defy their contracts by not planting grass in December and January. When outsiders hired by Nogueira and Marim planted grass in the tenants' fields, some acted quickly to uproot it. In December a group of merchants sent a petition to government officials requesting more protection from the militants in order to avoid a repetition of 1959. Paradoxically, some of these same merchants had supported Jôfre and the association previously, calculating that peasants would be more reliable consumers than cattle. Tensions flared as more police were sent to the area. In February 1960 the police raided the homes of peasant militants and arrested a group of twenty-nine on vague charges, intimidating them before being forced to release them. In March the news that a decadent sugar plantation in the northeast state of Pernambuco had been expropriated and distributed to Peasant League members revived expectations of Jôfre's land-reform vision coming true in Santa Fé. In April, Jôfre traveled to São Paulo to attend a conference of union leaders, thanking them for their support and appealing for their continued solidarity. In May he presided over a "roundtable" discussion in Santa Fé with political leaders and agricultural experts that "hundreds of tenants and their families, including their little children," attended. Speakers called for prolonging tenancy once again in order to await the governor's decision on distributing the land.

But Zico Diniz and his associates opposed land reform and new negotiations. To fight back, they repeated some of the violent tactics of 1957. His henchmen burnt down a number of farms and planted grass in the peasants' crops. But as the cool fall breezes of the high, dry plains blew in, the situation suddenly changed with Jôfre's arrest and imprisonment. On May 23, Jôfre was indicted; and on June 2, some six weeks before an expected showdown over the expiring contracts, he was arrested and detained in Jales under the provisions of the National Security Law. Jôfre was held in jail for three months before being convicted. Aimed at Communists, the 1953 law allowed for the "preventive imprisonment" of individuals deemed a threat to the "social order." On July 18 a judge invoked the law to charge Jôfre with threatening order by "inciting the Santa Fé do Sul farmers to act against a judicial decision" barring further grass uprooting. The police hoped that Jôfre's confinement would reduce the chance of trouble in the region since without him, they concluded, the "farmers have no leader."

Police hopes were dashed by subsequent events. The association and its officers survived Jôfre's arrest, and the jailing itself seemed to intensify rather than relieve the struggle. In June, association vice president Olimpio Pereira Machado published a poem celebrating the inspiration of "fearless Jôfre" and the importance of the peasant organization in resisting the violent actions of "big sharks" such as Diniz. Association lawyers Rollemberg and Novaes Netto went to work appealing for Jôfre's release, and petitions from politicians and union leaders began to arrive at the Jales court. In July, Olimpio expressed "indignation" toward authorities for the charges of subversion leveled against Jôfre and concluded that the peasants "know perfectly well that Jôfre was no agitator but a man who cried out against injustice." The real agitators, he wrote, were Diniz and the Jales judge. Later in the month, fifteen tenants were arrested after they uprooted nearly 60 acres of grass in protest against Jôfre's imprisonment. Another large tenant family then tore up more than 100 acres in protest over the arrest of their neighbors. Realizing how little had been gained by Jôfre's arrest, the governor sent Vanzolini back to the region in August.

Vanzolini found a difficult situation. The police refused to follow his orders and Diniz's gunmen had the run of the place. They terrorized resistant tenant farmers by filling their water wells with dirt and burning down their shacks. Vanzolini befriended Olimpio, telling the secret police that he was useful and that it was better not to arrest him until calm had been restored. With Olimpio's help and the backing of the governor, Vanzolini began to regain control. With the help of assistants, he reassigned belligerent policemen, confiscated Diniz's gun, and arrested his henchmen. Then he worked on the tenants, dividing them to conquer them. He concluded that if he let some of the 600 remaining families stay, he could entice most of them to leave. For these he offered no financial aid but several sacks of rice and transportation to government land where they could start new farms all over again. Belligerent tenants used the association to sue Diniz for damages against their personal property and the destruction of their farm buildings. Vanzolini tried to buy them off while Diniz, now disarmed, used cattle as a weapon, letting 500 loose on the Fazenda Mariana and 1,000 on the Fazenda São João. The back of the movement was broken. At the end of the month, when Vanzolini thought that he had settled the conflict, the secret police arrested Olimpio and other association leaders and confiscated all their possessions. The Grass War was over, but Jôfre's peasant struggle continued.

Jôfre waited in jail until September, when he was tried with Olimpio and other association leaders. On September 4 the court convicted them of trespassing and of threatening national security by inciting violent class struggle. It sentenced Jôfre to three years and the others to sixteen months' jail time. Releasing these "political prisoners" became a cause célèbre for the Communist Party and one that succeeded at the end of the year when the Supreme Court overturned the convictions. The Court unanimously supported the defendants' argument that using hoes to uproot grass on land they had rented constituted neither a violent act nor a private property invasion. By the first of the year, Jôfre was free again. He spent the next twenty months in liberty, traveling from town to town, speaking out against "feudal landlords," organizing rural workers, serving as a peasant delegate at state and national conferences, and celebrating the Cuban Revolution. He told Brazilians in January 1961 that they should "imitate the Cuban Revolution which, even though it was small, demonstrated great strength in overthrowing North American trusts." In November 1961 a play written about the events in Santa Fé with the protagonist based on Jôfre premiered at the first national congress of rural workers, where President João Goulart made an appearance.

Arrested again in September 1962 for threatening national security, Jôfre spent the remainder of the populist era in jail. During his imprisonment, he continued to serve the rural labor movement as a symbol. Communist organizers and publications exploited him to document the injustices faced by the rural working classes. In May 1964, almost two months after the Brazilian armed forces had toppled the presidency and cracked down on social movements, especially those tied to the Communist Party, Jôfre returned to society. Interrogated by the secret police upon his release, he denied affiliation with the Communist Party and the Peasant Leagues. He must have known that the times and power relationships had changed. The new military regime had declared war on the left wing. The Fidel Castro of Brazil had lost his canvas, and he became a near ghost until historical researchers began to paint his portrait in the 1980s.

Jôfre's identification with Fidel Castro offers insights about Brazilian society in the early 1960s. As we have seen, very little in Jôfre's background, character, and behavior supported the comparison. The police accused him of seeking this identity by growing a beard in the spring of 1959, but within a month they also reported that he had cut it off and was now "wearing a moustache like Joseph Stalin." Clearly, this Cold War speculation reveals nothing about Jôfre's sense of self. The daily newspaper *Ultima Hora* coined the "Backlands Fidel Castro" image and used it whether or not Jôfre had facial hair. Its publisher, Samuel Wainer, was well known as a supporter of the Brazilian Labor Party (PTB), which was founded by Getúlio Vargas in 1945. This party promoted working-class organization through government-sanctioned unions, associations, and leagues. Its political candidates sought the support of organized workers by promising better wages, lower prices, and more social services such as schools and clinics. As a typical populist party, a nationalist platform was fundamental. For many Latin Americans, Castro was a brave nationalist, someone who stood up against a dictator-puppet of foreign interests to reclaim Cuba for the benefit of Cubans. For Wainer, describing Jôfre as Fidel meant linking the Brazilian experience to the Cuban experience, and the PTB to what appeared to be the triumph of a popular nationalist cause. While Jôfre stood in for Fidel, the landlord Zico Diniz played the role of the dictator who would not let the rural working classes advance. By attaching the Fidel Castro of Brazil handle to Jôfre, Wainer must have also hoped to sell more newspapers to his largely working-class readership. The name said more about Brazil at the time than it did about Jôfre.

As an individual, Jôfre was transformed by the Grass War of Santa Fé do Sul. We cannot know for certain what triggered his transformation from a *malandro* to a militant, but whatever it was, it changed his life. He was almost forty years old in 1959, and he discovered a calling in the Grass War that took him far beyond his own concerns and made him into someone who mattered. Psychologists might emphasize the influence of a fatherless upbringing in shaping Jôfre's rebellious character. Jôfre himself prefers to emphasize his origins in the combative state of Rio Grande do Sul and argues that he descended from a long line of Communists. But Communist ideology rarely broached his lips and played a very small part in the Grass War. It is just as easy to find Christian origins for the most typical PCB phrase of the era: "The land belongs to those who work it." Among the multiple sources for his awakening one must list his army service, the actions of his peasant comrades, the support of Communists, and the context of Brazilian populism.

As the 1950s unfolded, equal rights for rural workers and promises of land reform sprang from the campaign baggage of Brazilian politicians. The link between the nation's success and the well-being of peasants was still tenuous by 1959 but, inspired by populist rhetoric, the tenant farmers of Santa Fé do Sul latched on to the idea. Among them, the itinerant nonconformist former soldier and self-proclaimed *gaúcho* named Jôfre Corrêa Netto proved himself adept at merging his own identity with this emerging national identity. Elaborating on his World War II role in the struggle against fascism, he encouraged his colleagues to call him Captain Jôfre and associated with Communists in building an organization to fight for the peasants' right to participate in the country's progress. He seems to have started this campaign haphazardly, without fully understanding its significance. At first, it may have seemed like another road adventure in a life already full of detours. But the attempted assassination made it clear that the stakes were high. The shooting and his education among professional Communist activists in São Paulo turned him into a serious militant. He could have disappeared from the scene, but he rose instead to confront his assailants and continue the fight in a far more disciplined fashion. On one level, he ceased to be an individual and became a social being, a historical agent. While events in Santa Fé made him, he made them, too.

SUGGESTED READINGS

For an excellent documentary companion to this article, including archival footage and interviews with participants such as Jôfre, see Cliff Welch and Toni Perrine, *Grass War! Peasant Struggle in Brazil*, 2001 (VHS 34 mins.), distributed by The Cinema Guild, New York. For a concise overview of Brazil's rural labor movements in Jôfre's era, see Clodomir Santos de Moraes,

"Peasant Leagues of Brazil," in *Agrarian Problems and Peasant Movements in Latin America*, ed. Rodolfo Stavenhagen (New York: Doubleday, 1970), 453–501. On São Paulo's central role in Brazil's mid-1900s rural labor movement, see Cliff Welch, *The Seed Was Planted: The São Paulo Roots of Brazil's Rural Labor Movement* (University Park: Pennsylvania State University Press, 1999). For perspectives on the attempt to kill Jôfre in 1959, see Cliff Welch, "The Shooting of Jôfre Corrêa Netto: Writing the Individual Back into Historical Memory," *Radical History Review* 75 (Fall 1999): 28–55.

To better understand why Jôfre may have been both attracted to and repulsed by his military service, see Peter M. Beattie, *The Tribute of Blood: Army, Honor, Race, and Nation in Brazil, 1864–1945* (Durham: Duke University Press, 2001). On the *malandro*, see Roberto da Matta, *Carnivals, Rogues, and Heroes· An Interpretation of the Brazilian Dilemma*, trans. John Drury (Notre Dame, IN: University of Notre Dame Press, 1991). On Rio Grande do Sul and the image of the *gaúcho*, see Joseph Love, *Rio Grande do Sul and Brazilian Regionalism, 1889–1930* (Stanford, CA: Stanford University Press, 1971).

CHAPTER 12

Carolina Maria de Jesus

From Ragpicker to Best-Selling Author and Back Again

ROBERT M. LEVINE

Carolina Maria de Jesus's life story demonstrates the hardships confronted by even some of the most talented descendants of slaves in Brazil, but, more than just racial prejudice, her humble origins subjected her to compounded bigotry. Born a poor illegitimate black girl in a small town in mountainous Minas Gerais, Carolina also suffered the discrimination commonly experienced by women, the poor, bastards, and rustics both before and after she migrated to the burgeoning industrial urban center of São Paulo as a young woman. While she felt close to and admired her grandfather, whose father had been a slave, she found intolerance even within her own family, where lighter-skinned relatives shunned her and her mother because of their dark skin. Despite these strikes against her, Carolina parlayed her meager education, personal dignity, and harsh past into temporary celebrity when her diary about her life in a São Paulo slum became an international best-seller in the early 1960s. Her grit, independence, and lack of deference, however, ultimately alienated many of the middle- and upper-class white Brazilians who had initially supported her. Like all of us, Carolina had contradictory views that made some advocates for the poor who lavished praise on her work uncomfortable. While she railed against the prejudice of whites and browns, she also at times disparaged blacks and poor migrants from the Northeast as lazy and irresponsible. After briefly climbing into the ranks of Brazil's middle class through her book sales, Carolina slipped back into a precarious lower-class lifestyle before she died in relative obscurity in the late 1970s.

Carolina's voice gave rare insight into the lives of those millions of rural Brazilians who migrated to the cities in the twentieth century. São Paulo, Brazil's largest urban center and its industrial and financial heart, remains dotted with makeshift slums. After Carolina's day, crime rings that made their money from narcotrafficking maintained order and paid for local improvements with drug profits. The police only entered these neighborhoods in large numbers to make arrests. Even though the favelas *were less threatening in Carolina's day, crime, deadly disputes between neighbors, and squalid conditions were common. Still, some of São Paulo's most powerful politicians came to know the outspoken Carolina during their campaign swings through the shantytowns. Although many ordinary workers lived in the slums,* favela *dwellers were stereotyped as vagrants, criminals, and prostitutes.*

As a nineteen-year-old exchange student in Mendoza, Argentina, Robert M. Levine read in the newspaper that a black Brazilian writer, Carolina Maria de Jesus, would be appearing at a bookstore to autograph the Spanish edition of her newly published diary about slum life in São Paulo. When Levine mentioned it to some Argentine friends, they replied that no macaco *("monkey," insulting Argentine slang for blacks as well as their Brazilian neighbors) could have written a book, an argument that many educated Brazilians believed as well. Levine never managed to visit the bookstore, but he used the English translation of Carolina's diary when he started teaching in 1966 and continued to do so until his death on April 1, 2003. In addition, an oral history project initiated by Levine in collaboration with José Carlos Sebe Bom Meihy and Juliano Spyer led to the publication of nine books on Carolina, including* The Life and Death of Carolina Maria de Jesus *(1995). Royalties from their books and documentaries made about Carolina go to her grandchildren. In 1981 the University of Miami recruited Bob to develop one of the most successful Ph.D. programs in Latin American history in the United States.*

From 1989 until the beginning of 2003, Levine directed the Center for Latin American Studies in Miami. He published more than two dozen books on subjects ranging from Brazilian social and political history to Cuban history and the use of historical photographs as documents. He was one of the most productive and generous historians of Brazil, and his legacy lives on in his colleges, students, and publications.

Carolina Maria de Jesus, the great-grandchild of Brazilian slaves, was born in 1915 in poverty to an unmarried mother in Sacramento, a lethargic rural town in the dairy state of Minas Gerais.[1] A harsh childhood burdened by poverty and discrimination marked her for life, but it also gave her the motivation to struggle to improve herself. She had become literate largely on her own after attending for a scant two years a private school paid for by a benefactress, the wife of a local landowner. As a young girl, she developed a passion for reading. She shocked her mother by reading aloud the labels in shop windows and the names on storefronts. Her peers mocked her and claimed that a black girl enamored of reading must be a creature of the devil. By then she had developed a feisty personality; and rather than groveling in shame, as she claimed her mother did, she soldiered on, unperturbed.

When her mother died, Carolina, by then a young woman, migrated to the industrializing city of São Paulo in search of work. She became determined to write down her feelings and to tell her story. Starting in 1955, she began to keep a diary in notebooks fashioned from scraps of paper she found while foraging for her living in garbage. Her diary entries, written with a powerfully personal narrative force, reflected a mixture of hope and ruefulness. She captured moments of poignancy in a touching manner: once, when she ran out of things to eat, her daughter Vera asked Carolina to sell her to her godmother, Dona Julita, "because she has delicious food." Whether or not all diaries are subconsciously written for others, Carolina's handwritten fragments conveyed a richly felt sense of her personal life. She was, as feminist scholars say, "constructing a self."

Carolina's initial success resulted in large part from fortuitous timing. Brazil had reached a crest of national optimism over economic development and populist reform in the late 1950s. Economic development, however, had left many Brazilians behind as rural migrants, such as Carolina, crowded into unhealthy urban slums. Many people saw hope in Carolina's rags-to-riches story. To them, she embodied the possibility that with help, *favela* residents could rise out of poverty and transform themselves. Carolina's personal honesty and her unwillingness to fall into despair contributed to the popular view of most slum dwellers as "poor but honest."

During the 1950s, Carolina, who had always dreamed of being a writer despite her two meager years of schooling, tried to find publishers while working as a maid for wealthy *paulista* families. She sent a short poem to a newspaper, which was printed, but publishers rejected other submissions of stories, plays, poems, and novels. Interviewed on Brazilian television after the success of her diary made her a celebrity, she said on camera, "If I weren't so happy I would cry. When I first gave my manuscript to Brazilian editors they laughed at this poor Negro woman with calloused hands who wore rags and only had two years of schooling. They told me I should write on toilet paper." She concluded the interview by saying: "Today I had lunch in a wonderful restaurant and a photographer took my picture. I told him: 'Write under the photo that Carolina who used to eat from trashcans now eats in restaurants. That she has come back into the human race and out of the garbage dump.' "

In April 1958, São Paulo newspaper reporter Audálio Dantas discovered that Carolina had written a diary about her hard life; he managed to edit it and published some of the entries in his paper. In August 1960, Dantas had the edited diary printed under the title *Quarto de despejo* (literally, Garbage room, but translated into English as *Child of the Dark*). It became the best-selling book in Brazilian history and brought its author worldwide fame.

Child of the Dark would not likely have been published at all if Carolina's diaries had been discovered before 1958 or after 1961. President Juscelino Kubitschek's successor in office in 1960 was the mercurial

Jânio Quadros. He resigned abruptly in 1961 and fled the country when his government became paralyzed in the midst of economic stagnation and political polarization. His successor, João Goulart, advocated leftist reforms that further polarized Brazilian politics and heightened ideological rhetoric in the tense Cold War climate that pervaded Latin America after the 1959 Cuban Revolution. In this climate, Carolina's diary would have been dismissed as being too naive. The right-wing military dictatorship that seized power in 1964 by overthrowing Goulart was little interested in social reforms. It initiated an era of Chicago School economic development that greatly increased the disparity between rich and poor and left many Brazilians feeling helpless and angry.

Brazilian society had become more divided than ever between an affluent world of mostly whites and a marginalized world of poor blacks and persons of mixed racial ancestry. Women fared much less well than men in this world. Until 1988, Brazil's civil laws discriminated against women. For instance, before a battered wife could press charges against her husband, he had to give his written permission. Carolina, a poor black woman, possessed an iron will and a strong sense of what she wanted. She was aware of the legacies of racism, gender prejudice, and political neglect of the poor, but she dealt with these burdens only as they directly affected her.

Carolina thought herself rich when Dantas opened a bank account for her in the amount of 858 U.S. dollars. The fact that she had to cash bills for 1,000 cruzeiros ($4.88) to make change amazed her and her children. She earned the equivalent of 20,000 or 30,000 dollars (in 1996 value) and a few thousand more from American and French royalties, for her an undreamed-of fortune. On her earnings she was able to afford a maid. When she wanted to withdraw money from her bank account, she had to take the bus downtown and wait for Dantas, who then walked with her to the bank to sign for her. Her wealth disappeared quickly, however; she was besieged by requests for money, and she doled it out generously. She paid for an unsuccessful samba record featuring her voice, and she likely subsidized the poorly received editions of her later books.

Carolina Maria de Jesus died in 1977 not in utter poverty but in austere circumstances, a strange fate for the author who had sold more books than any other Brazilian. As a poor black woman, she faced unceasing prejudice. Given Carolina's unprecedented recognition worldwide for her insights about the lives of the social underclass, it is difficult to understand why so few women rose to her defense when attacks began after the first, flush days of her fame. Female Brazilian journalists generally treated her as harshly, or more harshly, than did their male counterparts. If Carolina had been a man, she likely would not have ended up in the *favela*. Most upper-class families preferred live-in maids, and they routinely fired their female servants if they became pregnant. They did not want the child living in their home and their employee distracted with child care. The disdain directed at Carolina after her publishing success was perhaps a predictable response to an unconstrained, outspoken black female.

When Carolina died in 1977 she was a recluse. Her diary remained out of print for nearly two decades until it was reissued in a limited edition. *Casa de alvenaria* (Brick house) remained out of print and ignored. The generation who became adults in the early 1990s—born during the military dictatorship with its antipathy to social questions—had no way of knowing who she was when older scholars and intellectuals revived the debate over her significance following the "discovery" of her surviving children and the controversy over whether or not she merited recognition.

In all, she produced three autobiographical volumes. One of them, *Bitita's Diary*, about her early years (Bitita was her nickname), was published in France after her death and in Brazil only years later. Her autobiographical writing reflected her bitterness, although she fought against despair, often ending the description of a harrowing day with something that had made her happy—the sunset, or the lights of the city at night. She wrote of death and of watching restaurant employees spill acid on garbage so that the poor could not rummage for food. She wrote about excrement, drunkenness, sons who beat their parents, prostitution, undernourishment, and hopelessness. "Black is our life," she said, "everything is black around us." She wrote about race, about how she had always been discriminated against, about how she disliked idle people, about how she disliked most of her fellow blacks, whom she considered lazy. No revolutionary, she believed that if people worked hard, within the system, they could aspire to a better life.

On November 27, 1960, she returned to Brazil from Argentina for the publication of *Casa de alvenaria* in Rio de Janeiro. When her Argentine editor visited her a week later in São Paulo, she asked him for 20,000 cruzeiros to buy a suit for her son João. On December 12 she flew to Montevideo. As in Buenos Aires she was received warmly and asked hard but respectful questions about society and about her opinions and philosophy. She confessed that she had never expected her writings to be published, that she wrote to forget the bitterness of her life. She was struck by how clean the streets were; there were no beggars, and the Uruguayans dressed well and showed that they were cultured. She was taken to visit a neighborhood of *cantegriles*, a kind of slum, where she noted that the government was constructing permanent housing, with running water and bathrooms, to replace the shanties. There was a government school in the slum, although many men and youths were without work. She advised the poor Uruguayans who came to see her to plant gardens and raise chickens.

In Montevideo, when she left the slum, Carolina was taken to visit the president of Uruguay, Victor Haedo, in his palace, where he embraced her and presided over a luncheon of Brazilian *feijoada* (bean stew). The next day, he and Carolina rode in a motorcade down the streets of the capital to the airport, where they flew to Salto to dedicate a monument. The archbishop was present as well as the governor and the chief of the president's military staff. She spent much of the day with Haedo. The reception given to Carolina less than a year removed from a São Paulo slum was stunning, although it was only sparsely reported back home in Brazil. Her reception in Argentina and Chile was similar. On January 16, 1961, she addressed a filled lecture hall at an international conference attended by Nobel Prize winners, Columbia University professor Frank Tannenbaum, and the Mexican and Cuban writers Carlos Fuentes and Alejo Carpentier.

In the United States and Canada, Western Europe, Japan, Cuba, and the Soviet-bloc nations, critics hailed Carolina as a heroine, a lone voice expressing the cry for help from the underprivileged classes. But fortune's pendulum swung back as soon as she returned from her second publicity trip to Chile, the last of her tours. The flood of requests for interviews and radio and television appearances stopped, although journalists continued to consider her fair game and dropped in, if now sporadically, at any time. Her royalties diminished abruptly. Although *Child of the Dark* became an international sensation, translated into more than a dozen languages, her publisher never anticipated the degree of its success and therefore sold the rights to foreign literary agents, who then assumed the bulk of the royalties. She would receive some meager payments from publishers in the United States, Holland, and France, but not a single royalty check from any other country. There were a few payments for movie rights, but except for a documentary made in Germany and another by TV Globo, little came of the projects to film her life story. Her last two books, issued while she was alive, *Pedaços de fome* (Pieces of hunger) and *Provérbios* (Proverbs), were commercial failures.

Brazilian intellectuals on the left rejected Carolina because she was not, in the words of one, a "typical proletariat." Her beliefs and attitudes did not fit the image of the heroic poor whom leftists imagined inhabited Brazil's fetid slums. She was not a revolutionary; her quest was personal, to fend for and protect her family. Nor did conservatives recognize her, even though she advocated a deeply felt work ethic, did not drink, and in later years gave statements to the press that seemed to support the military dictatorship. Her political views, in fact, were very much like those of O. J. Simpson in the United States, who declined to support the Olympics boycott by African Americans in 1968 for the same reason that Carolina gave for her lack of political activism: "you can't change the world until you change yourself." Some Brazilians considered her, according to one university professor, a *palhaço* (clown).

The social reformism that had been prominent in 1960 when her diary was published had been replaced by a polarization of attitudes by the time of her death. At one end of the political spectrum stood right-wing backers of the military, who favored economic development over social change, and at the other end, a small group of leftists, mostly driven underground, who ignored Carolina because she was not revolutionary enough for them. The 1977 obituary published in Rio de Janeiro's *Jornal do Brasil* illustrates this ambivalence:

> Carolina Maria de Jesus, the author of *Quarto de despejo*, died yesterday . . . as poor as she had been when she began to write the diary which would turn into the major best-seller in Brazil of all time. . . . In 1961 her book royalties allowed Carolina to purchase a brick house, a symbol—as she often pointed out—of her personal victory over hunger and misery. But her second book failed to attain the popularity of the first, and she began to quarrel with her friends and supporters, including the journalist Audálio Dantas, who had discovered her scavenging for paper on which to write her diary, and who had acted as her agent. Little by little, Carolina dissipated the resources that her book had brought her. She purchased everything in sight: she visited the famous, frequented the salons of the rich—but in time she began to irritate her hosts. . . . Her inability to adjust to success cost her dearly. . . . Forced to sell her brick house for nonpayment of debts, she relocated her family to a rural shack along the Parelheiros road. There she raised chickens and pigs and lived in poverty, refusing, however, to become a burden on her now grown children. It was in this place that she was found yesterday, dead of an attack of acute asthma. When her body was discovered, the mayor of nearby Embú-Guaçú offered a valedictory. She was buried in the cemetery at Vila Cipó, a polluted industrial suburb near Parelheiros, the place to which she had escaped in search of fresh air and seclusion.

Some educated Brazilians disliked Carolina because they considered her a traitor to their idealized image of the working class. Instead of wearing modest clothes, Carolina wobbled in stylish high-heeled shoes, and she talked back to wealthier and better-educated Brazilians who expected deference from a poor black woman. She also clashed with their stereotypes about race. Although she expressed pride in being black, she preferred romantic relationships with white men; each of her children had been fathered by a white man from a different country. In the 1960s, a decade in which black pride became an international movement, Carolina's preference for white lovers came to be seen as out of step to many leftist and black Brazilian activists. Although she wrote that she thanked God for making her a Brazilian, she also castigated her fellow countrymen for their shortcomings.

In many ways, Carolina explored the nuances of Brazilian life as if she were a foreign traveler because her status as an outcast made her almost an alien among her own people. Like Alexis de Tocqueville, the French visitor to the United States in the 1830s, Carolina brilliantly described social contradictions and singular secrets.[2] She casually described little things about daily life that most people did not see or write about because they were considered taboo, trivial, or in bad taste. In *Bitita's Diary*, she meets a woman named Nair who is so depressed at being black that she does not go to "dances for blacks," a cogent reference to the segregated lives of blacks and whites in her country and especially in São Paulo. Carolina quietly hoped for racial harmony, but her observations of Nair and other everyday realities unmasked the national myth of racial democracy—that Brazil was uniquely blessed among nations because of its heritage of racial harmony and cooperation. When she saw whites and blacks together, she commented on how good this made her feel, just as she was glad when she visited her black friend Ivete and found that she lived in a house that was comfortable and well furnished. Her comments about her disappointment in the lack of traditional May Day commemorations (an international holiday celebrating workers) in 1961 reveals sympathy with working-class concerns. Her observations about a black youth who lost the use of his hand in an industrial accident, but for whom President Getúlio Vargas's new labor legislation did nothing, divulged much about the legacy of this popular political figure. (Vargas committed suicide before he was to be ousted as president in 1954, but he left nostalgic memories among the poor for his populist rhetoric on behalf of ordinary Brazilians.)

No one in Brazil spoke out against the cruel insinuations that journalists made about Carolina's person. Nor did most Brazilian scholars believe that the conditions that Carolina had exposed merited greater national debate. No one acknowledged that it was perfectly understandable for a former slum dweller to have difficulty in adjusting to a world that reviled people like her. By emphasizing her brusqueness, eccentricities, and faux pas the media deflected attention from her social critique of society's many injustices.

Throughout her life, Carolina was weighed down by the scorn heaped upon her by society. Even though she shielded herself and her children from the squalid aspects of slum life, these conditions took their toll. By the time she was liberated from the *favela* by a stroke of fate, it was too late. She was exhausted, too beaten down to learn middle-class manners, to censor her thoughts, to remove the layers of suffering from her psyche, or to prescribe solutions for society's ills.

Hostility to her blackness also plagued Carolina. Most educated Brazilians accepted the myth of Brazilian racial democracy despite the obvious evidence of racism surrounding them, especially discrimination against people of very dark skin. Carolina's writings describe racist incidents constantly, almost matter-of-factly, long before other Brazilians acknowledged racial prejudice. Foreigners less influenced by this racial mythology often recognized race prejudice when they visited Brazil. For example, Hollywood film director Orson Welles, invited in 1941 to participate in a birthday celebration broadcast for dictator Getúlio Vargas, was told that he could not bring a black friend with him into the studio. Welles's attempts to film *It's All True*, an anthology with segments about Carnival and the plight of northeastern raft fishermen, was criticized in a secret letter from his Brazilian production manager to the police complaining about Welles's "insistence on emphasizing the unsavory Negro element and mixture of the races."

❧

In 1996, Vera Eunice de Jesus Lima, Carolina's daughter, revealed that she possessed thirty-seven of her mother's handwritten notebooks. Some had been copied by Carolina from the originals, in some cases with changes. Most of the more than 4,500 pages had been written after Carolina moved to Parelheiros, then on the outskirts of São Paulo. There she fell back into poverty but recouped enough economic stability to send her children to school.

Her unedited diary entries offer two kinds of insight into Carolina Maria de Jesus. First, they show her to be more complex than the two-dimensional woman depicted by Dantas. He knew that Carolina's lack of tact would irritate readers who expected lower-class celebrities to know their place; as a good journalist, moreover, he also knew the importance of simple, straightforward writing and aimed, through deletions in her text, to simplify her message. The problem is that Dantas's editing muted her personality, which was more feisty and angry than readers of her published diaries encountered. Readers of her diaries wondered why Carolina seemed so docile. In truth, she was angry and frustrated much of the time. She had a much deeper insight into how Brazilian society functioned, and she was willing to name names. She may not have always been accurate—she was entirely dependent on her own resources—but her perceptions were tenaciously held. Her experience shows us that indigents were capable of engaging the system that trapped them, and that if that system produced individuals whom society considered loose cannons, there were many reasons for it.

The second contribution of her unedited writing is the welter of new information it offers about Carolina's life and, by extension, the lives of the poor, especially in the entries that continued after her two diaries were published. We also have additional detail about the periods covered by the entries. This information is especially valuable for the insight it offers into Carolina's new role as a consequence of her celebrity. Brazilian society was not accustomed to indigent black single mothers talking to reporters, or being interviewed on television, or writing about their lives. We should not be surprised at how she reacted. The woeful circumstances of her early life had steeled her to rejection and had given her a tough coat of psychological armor. Carolina was always an outsider, yet unlike many outsiders, she craved acceptance and fame; she wanted to be recognized as a writer, to achieve upward mobility.

Not surprisingly, her observations sometimes confused her readers; some found her contradictory; others, elusive and inconsistent. Not only was she a self-taught writer, but she was also tormented by hunger and by the frequent crises that afflicted slum dwellers. When the rainy season came to São Paulo, her shack, along with the others in her riverfront slum, was flooded, and her family had to find other housing. They might have to live in doorways or under bridges until the waters subsided. Once she was hospitalized after a woman in the slum stabbed her. Her routine frequently was disrupted by the need to protect her children from threatened violence, or by her inability to find enough junk in garbage to sell and then buy food. She had to spend hours each day in line at the *favela's* single spigot to draw water. With these hardships, she underwent mercurial mood shifts from despair to joy to hope to dejection. At the height of her fame, her writing style became reflective. She never shed her depression, however, although she had an astonishing ability to rise to the occasion when she had to fend for her children and keep her family afloat.

Her diary entries reveal a homespun philosophy that demands honesty in relationships between men and women. Carolina, whether she knew it or not, was a practicing feminist in a society that was overwhelmingly dominated by males. She refused offers of marriage because she knew that the men would not respect her and would treat her as their servant. "I have loved," she wrote, but "I have never been in love." She defied the Catholic Church's insistence on marriage as the basis for having children and raising them, and she insisted on choosing her own sexual partners. Even living amid garbage and sometimes covered with sores, she found herself sexually attractive to white men from higher social classes, yet she never betrayed her independence to exploit this advantage, even for the benefit of her children.

She decried the suffering of undernourished and illiterate children and preached basic family values that she held as guiding principles both before and after she became famous. Mothers, she believed, were duty bound to observe their children, care for them and protect them from danger, and discipline them when they were in error. Other *favela* parents shrugged when their children stole or cursed or acted irresponsibly; Carolina thrashed hers when they misbehaved. In a society in which the poor for centuries had drowned their pain in *cachaça*, she refused alcohol and tried (ultimately in vain) to keep her sons from liquor as well.

She lashed out at sycophants, playboys, perverts, unfaithful husbands, drunks, layabouts, and people who refused to work and who lived on the dole. She excoriated politicians who cynically promised poor voters what they never intended to deliver. She demanded that society show responsibility in providing education, health care, and housing for the poor, but she showed no sympathy to those who called for radical reform. She criticized Brazil out of her love for her country. She never alienated herself from the law or from political authorities, some of whom she cultivated to obtain favors. She once convinced São Paulo's popular mayor, Adhemar de Barros, to pay for a hospital stay. Her verses took landowners and arrogant politicians to task. Her statements to the press gave her entry into the offices (but not the hearts) of local officials, publishers, the media, and some members of the elite. Despite her generally favorable disposition toward the have-nots in society, she knew that people perceived her as a dirty black woman to be scorned.

As soon as her diaries were serialized by Dantas's newspaper before the first edition was published, she guided not only Dantas through her *favela* but also other newspapermen and photographers. Even after her celebrity had faded, she served as a conduit into the slums for filmmakers, journalists, and politicians. When the Finnish writer Eva Vastari came to her house, Carolina turned over her children's bedroom to the visitor. Eva paid her nothing but did buy some food for her host; Carolina acted as her personal escort. These visits must have been difficult for Carolina because reporters often criticized her clothing and the way she kept house. Once, Eva accused Carolina's children of stealing money from her purse. Although Carolina defended her children tooth and nail, she pulled her son José Carlos aside and told him that if he was guilty she would feed him poison.

The unedited diary entries provide invaluable details about the changing composition of the *favelas* in São Paulo as migrants from Brazil's North and Northeast poured into the slums of the industrialized cities of the South. Blunt and opinionated, Carolina looked down on these migrants, in part because she herself was from the interior of Minas Gerais—a place of higher status than the Northeast—but mostly because the hapless migrants seemed to her to have given up. They lacked her burning work ethic and her sense of civic duty. Carolina's frequent calls from a pay phone to the radio patrol—the Brazilian equivalent of dialing 911—and to the police document her determination to rid the *favelas* of troublemakers and law breakers. Foreigners—namely, Portuguese but also some Japanese—were also changing the character of the slum population. Carolina was astonished by a Japanese woman who claimed that children were "worse than the devil," and in her diaries she berated the woman for "engaging her mouth before engaging her brain." On the other hand, she admired Japanese men, whom she considered hardworking, eager to better themselves, and not disdainful like the northeasterners.

She wrote about calling the police to stop fights in the *favela*, about her conversations in the street, about her appeals for medical assistance. All were aimed at dispelling what she considered the elite's contempt for those forced to live in slums and shantytowns. This goal is significant given that Carolina wrote during a period of peak interest in Brazil in social reform, when public sentiment (and real estate speculation) focused on *favela* removal as a leading solution for the expanding urban center. After she became a celebrity, she was always aware of the tenuousness of her fame, and she flailed away at social ills as if she knew that she had little time left before she would fade from public attention.

Carolina reveled in the prominence that came to her in 1960 and was susceptible to notice and flattery, especially from men of higher social status. She was receptive to journalists and other promoters of her talents, and she often confided in them, a trust which they often betrayed. She was quick to report instances of hypocritical behavior or attitudes that she saw as demeaning or derogatory toward the poor, especially blacks. She recorded her horror at hearing a socially prominent Argentine claim that the rich were the descendants of Abel and the poor the descendants of Cain. Once, she tried to learn to drive a car. Perhaps this goal was part of her yearning for middle-class status; perhaps she thought that being seen behind the wheel of an automobile would bring her respect. Instead, it had the opposite effect: when she steered the driving school's automobile down her street, her neighbors, who had been hostile to her from the first day she moved in, stared at her as if, in her words, she came from another planet.

Her assumed role as spokeswoman for the downtrodden empowered her to maintain her stoicism and not let insults get her down. She sat quietly outside the offices of would-be publishers to speak with people whom she knew were inside, although their secretaries had assured her that they had not returned from lunch. It irked her that her desire to purchase a new house in the countryside and pay the installments from the rent of her present house was repudiated by her sponsors and publishers. Still, she persisted, resisting affronts to her social status, her skin color, and her gender. She refused to be defeated by people who inwardly snubbed her while they outwardly accorded her her due. She shocked and charmed, cajoled and flirted. At the height of her popularity as a public figure she threatened to cancel her publicity trip to Argentina and Chile if her sponsors did not guarantee that in her absence they would buy food for her children, who stayed behind in São Paulo. She knew that despite the clamor about her diary, no one really cared about her. She was and always would be a loner, the sole responsible person in her life and the lives of her children while they were still young.

∽

Carolina wrote almost every night after she put her children to bed. She began most of her diary entries in the same way, telling when she woke up in the morning and what chores she set out to do, and then following the day's activities hour by hour. Some of her entries, however, were brief; others went on for pages. For the published versions of *Quarto de despejo* and *Casa de alvenaria*, Audálio Dantas shortened most of the entries and cut out enormous sections that he considered repetitious or otherwise unnecessary. He deleted details of her morning wakeup, her daily routine, her repetitive comments about neighbors, repaying loans, or paying off bills to local merchants. For some reason, Dantas switched around dates, adding sections to entries from other days and taking small liberties with the diaries to enhance their readability. He did not, however, write a single word that was not hers. He edited by selective cutting, not by adding or by making changes.

As a result, the first diary, *Quarto de despejo*, ran only 181 pages with fairly large type and wide margins. More than two-thirds of the entries written by Carolina for the period of the published diary were deleted. Yet this is not to say that *Quarto* suffered because of its length; its simple brevity, in fact, contributed to its power as a social document and testimony. But the edited *Quarto* as well as the edited *Casa de alvenaria* projected an image of their author that shortchanged her personality, simplifying it and robbing it of the contradictory elements that made Carolina more human than the packaged diaries suggested.

The Carolina Maria de Jesus of the edited diaries, then, comes through as a desperately poor, black single mother and shantytown dweller who is observant, aware of her surroundings, dutiful toward her children, and judgmental toward *favela* neighbors of whom she disapproved. The unedited diaries, however, show her in a far less restrictive way. The questions that fly off the pages of her published diaries—why she was always so docile, so single-minded, so patient—emerge more clear-cut. Instead of being resigned, her personality flares up unpredictably and then subsides. Sometimes she seems manically agitated; at other times she lapses into depression. She not only records her observations but also offers them in great detail, believing the common stereotype that marginalized victims of society did not have complex explanations for their plight. She is astute and politically savvy in her criticisms, so much so that Dantas thought that he had to sanitize them lest her militant tone compromise her promoters and those who sympathized with her.

Carolina's two published diaries appeared in 1960 and 1961, at the height of national and local political reformism in Brazil. But this was reformism held in check—not the leftism of militants, but a measured set of demands that stopped well short of calling for structural social change. By packaging Carolina as a simple woman whose complaints seemed poetic in their innocence, Dantas managed to create diaries that neither threatened readers nor motivated them to demand political reform. What she really said in her diaries would not have ingratiated her with the authorities in São Paulo. Had Dantas's cuts not been made, it is likely that the editors at Francisco Alves would not have risked publishing them.

Few people understood the thickness of the protective shell that Carolina had been forced to construct around herself in response to decades of fierce adversity. Audálio Dantas did not remain her patron for long. Carolina, he insisted, would not accept the relationship he needed to impose on her as her agent. She never asked to be defended or cared for—she was too independent for that. Dantas explained that he could not deal with what he considered Carolina's petulance and irascibility. His opinion is consistent with that of other journalists and intellectuals who gave up on her. Perhaps it is understandable that her diary continued to sell well outside of Brazil, where readers wanted to find in her words an expression of rage against poverty and suffering that Brazilians grew tired of because they considered her attitudes simplistic and self-serving. She was the product of a society that tolerated the most glaring maldistribution of income in the world, yet she did not lend her voice to calls for massive social change. She simply wanted to escape from poverty with her children and to become a famous writer.

Carolina's diary entries, on the other hand, record a wealth of new detail that opens our eyes to the realities of poverty in underdeveloped societies. The exactness of her charges shatters our preconceptions about how marginalized people relate to the system that overwhelms them. Dantas's editing retains some of the shocking revelations, but on the whole it obscures the extent to which *favelados* such as Carolina struggled to engage the system. Carolina recorded people's reactions to what they perceived as unjust prices and fare increases; she reacted to measures taken by São Paulo's corrupt populist mayor, Adhemar de Barros, to police the streets as well as trains and buses. She demanded accountability for public figures, particularly in those actions that affected the poor. In so doing, she was advocating active political citizenship for people denied voices by a system that gave them the vote but then paternalistically doled out to them empty rewards—for example, the playground equipment donated to Carolina's *favela* on the eve of the 1958 mayoral election, an act that, ironically, made it possible for Dantas to meet Carolina and bring to light her diaries. These diaries show us that even *favelados* wanted to be informed, wanted to be consulted, wanted explanations for urban renewal, fare increases, the unavailability of hospital beds in emergency wards. An outspoken nobody, she risked arrest for her militancy. How sad it was that after she was discovered, she was showcased as a sideshow freak—an illegitimate black scavenger who dreamed about Heaven—while her courage was ignored and her prescriptions for needed social change were brushed aside.

While *Quarto de despejo* offered details, Dantas balanced Carolina's criticisms carefully with passages of idealism and hope. Taken as a whole, Carolina's written output swings the balance to the darker side. Her unedited words provide invaluable new evidence about the way poor people related to their world and how they coped with it.

As a nontraditional author whose untutored works lacked polish and who spoke about matters considered banal by most intellectuals, Carolina's writings have been excluded from the Brazilian literary canon. Irving Stern's 400-page *Dictionary of Brazilian Literature* devotes only two lines to her. Carolina has never been included in a standard anthology. Only a single Brazilian critic, Marisa Lajolo, publicly acknowledged in 1995 when the Brazilian version of *The Life and Death of Carolina Maria de Jesus* was published, that her story contained a valuable lesson. Carolina had died, Lajolo noted, in 1977, the same year that José Louzeiro's novel on the evils of street life was published.[3] Louzeiro's book inspired Hector Babenco to make his stunning film, *Pixote, the Law of the Weakest* (1981), whose principal real-life child actor, Fernando Ramos da Silva, was assassinated by the São Paulo police in 1987 as the blight of urban poverty and violence depicted by Carolina Maria de Jesus in 1960 continued.

Brazilian critics have continued to berate Carolina and to denigrate her significance. In November 1993, following the publication of the new Ática edition of her diary, literary scholar Wilson Martins wrote in his syndicated column, which appeared in more than forty newspapers across Brazil, a savage and ignorant dismissal of *Quarto de despejo* as a "literary mystification" and a fake. He attacked the book's "precious" language. He commented on Carolina's "casual lovers," as if her personal behavior canceled her right to be respected for her achievement. Dantas's outraged reply was published only six weeks later in the same newspaper, buried on an inside page. This author wrote to Martins in Curitiba, respectfully explaining that there was hard written evidence to prove that Dantas had not put words in her mouth, and mailed him a prepublication copy of the manuscript of *The Life and Death of Carolina Maria de Jesus*. Although Martins perfunctorily acknowledged receipt of the letter and manuscript, he did not change his mind. In a subsequent review of the Brazilian version of the study about Carolina published in Rio de Janeiro in April 1995, he repeated the charge that Carolina's diary was a "literary mystification" and called foreign academics who assign it for classroom reading "naïve" and "ingenuous."

For some Brazilian intellectuals it remains easier to dismiss the legitimacy of Carolina's message than to confront the harsh realities of desperate urban poverty and the sexism, racism, and class prejudice that her life story and writings reveal. After Carolina's death, *favelas* have become dominated by well-armed gangs who thrive on the drug trade in cocaine, which swept urban centers in the economically sluggish decade of the 1980s when the military loosened its grip on repressive government power. Recently, jailed drug kingpins have demonstrated their ability to conduct their affairs via cell phone: ordering terrorist attacks and assassinations, and forcing merchants to close their businesses to demonstrate their power to state authorities and a frightened public. It would seem that the luxury of ignoring the many problems of urban slums that Carolina laid bare is one that politicians, scholars, and an informed public can no longer afford.

NOTES

1. Some of the text for this essay first appeared in Robert M. Levine and José Carlos Sebe Bom Meihy, *The Life and Death of Carolina Maria de Jesus* (Albuquerque: University of New Mexico Press, 1995); José Carlos Sebe Bom Meihy, *Cinderela Negra: A Saga de Carolina Maria de Jesus* (Rio de Janeiro: Editoria UFRJ, 1994); Robert M. Levine and Melvin S. Arrington Jr., *I'm Going to Have a Little House* (Lincoln: University of Nebraska Press, 1997); Robert M. Levine, ed., *Bitita's Diary* (New York: M. E. Sharpe, 1998); José Carlos Sebe Bom Meihy and Robert M. Levine, orgs., *Meu Estranho Diário* (São Paulo: Editora Xama, 1997); and Robert M. Levine and José Carlos Sebe Bom Meihy, *The Unedited Diaries of Carolina Maria de Jesus* (New Brunswick, NJ: Rutgers University Press, 1999).

2. See George Wilson Pierson, *Tocqueville in America* (Baltimore: Johns Hopkins University Press, 1996).

3. Marisa Lajolo, Preface to Meihy, *Cinderela Negra*, i–ii.

SUGGESTED READINGS

On life in Brazil's *favelas* or slums see, for example, Nancy Scheper-Hughes, *Death without Weeping: The Violence of Everyday Life in Brazil* (Berkeley, 1992); and Janice E. Perlman, *Rio's Favelados and the Myths of Marginality* (Berkeley, 1973). For more views from Brazilian women of various backgrounds see *Brazilian Women Speak: Contemporary Life Stories*, interviews edited and translated by Daphne Patai (New Brunswick, 1988); on poor women and respectability see Sueann Caulfield, *In Defense of Honor: Sexual Morality, Modernity, and Nation in Early Twentieth Century Brazil* (Durham, 2000); and on race and racism in twentieth-century Brazil see George Reid Andrews, *Blacks and Whites in São Paulo, Brazil, 1888–1988* (Madison, 1991). For an overview of populist politics and society in the era of Getúlio Vargas see Robert M. Levine, *Father of the Poor? Vargas and His Era* (Cambridge, 1998).

F

CHAPTER 13

Dom Hélder Câmara

The Father of the Church of the Poor

KENNETH P. SERBIN*

Brazil is currently the nation with the largest population of self-identified followers of the Roman Catholic faith. The Catholic Church played an important role in the foundation and development of Portuguese America, but because of the Portuguese crown's control of appointments of high-ranking clergy, the Church was never as powerful and independent as it was in Spanish America. The founding of the Republic in 1889 led to a definitive separation of Church and state in Brazil and freedom of religious observance. Still, the Church establishment continued to support the status quo that favored the interests of the wealthy and powerful. The twentieth century brought a series of new challenges to the Church that had serious repercussions for this venerable institution's role in Brazilian society. These challenges included the rise of Communist ideology and its critique of capitalism's injustices and religion's role in mystifying the exploitation of the poor, and competition from growing Protestant sects that aggressively proselytized Brazil's Catholic faithful to win converts. In nations such as Brazil where the Church had had a virtual monopoly on official religious practice, the influence of these competing institutions and ideologies made Church leaders more aware of the need to concern themselves with the hearts and minds of their parishioners. These and other pressures spurred the Church's leadership in Rome to promulgate the major reforms in the 1950s that came to be known as Vatican II. The intent was to make the Church and its clergy more effective in communicating the faith and more responsive to the needs of its members. For instance, the Mass, which had traditionally been celebrated in Latin, would now be celebrated in Portuguese or the local vernacular so that less-educated parishioners would understand the liturgy. Priests and nuns also became more active in the communities that they served and as a result became more aware of the need to improve the lives of their brethren, particularly the most vulnerable.

Professor Kenneth P. Serbin illuminates the dramatic shifts in Church-state relations during the twentieth century by focusing on the story of a

*The author thanks Peter Beattie, John Burdick, Rafael Ioris, and Zildo Rocha for their helpful comments on earlier versions of this chapter.

man of relatively modest origins who became one of Catholicism's most admired and influential leaders. Dom Hélder Câmara lived the big changes of the twentieth century with intensity as a dedicated clergyman. He began his career as a priest supporting conservative political movements that drew inspiration from fascism, but would later go on to become one of the most outspoken leaders of the Catholic left. His leadership brought about dramatic transformations in the Brazilian Church's organization, theology, and practices. Under his influence, members of the Catholic clergy and laity became activists, some of whom contributed to the development of Liberation Theology, which sought to square Christianity with socialist critiques of the excesses of capitalism that left the poor subject to "institutional violence." Conservatives saw Liberation Theology as, at worst, outright Communist subversion and, at best, a school of thought that lent legitimacy to Marxist ideology and the violent leftist guerrilla movements that flourished in Latin America after the Cuban Revolution. Leaders such as Dom Hélder, however, held a peaceful vision of Christian social transformation that would bring about greater equality.

Professor Serbin's research has focused on the history of Catholicism and society in Brazil. His book Secret Dialogues: Church-State Relations, Torture, and Social Justice in Authoritarian Brazil *(2000) explores the behind-the-scenes negotiations between representatives of the military government and the Catholic Church during the military dictatorship (1964–1985). These "secret dialogues" sought to ease tensions between the military and the Catholic Church. The regime's censorship and savage repression created conditions that made the Church one of the few Brazilian institutions whose members could speak out against the torture and assassination of suspected leftists and the grinding poverty that continued to brutalize the country's poor. Dom Hélder was one of the most outspoken critics of the military regime, and, as Professor Serbin shows, he gave up his chances to be a cardinal in order to speak his conscience during a dark chapter of the Cold War. Kenneth Serbin earned his Ph.D. from the University of California at San Diego in 1993 and is currently associate professor of history at San Diego University.*

Dom Hélder Pessôa Câmara, the archbishop of Olinda and Recife, was one of the great leaders of the twentieth century. Profoundly dedicated to social justice through nonviolence, he was a Latin American version of Mahatma Gandhi and Martin Luther King. In striving to reform the Roman Catholic Church, Dom Hélder helped to change the course of one of Latin America's—and the world's—oldest and most important institutions.

The diminutive but fiery bishop from Ceará pioneered the implementation of a Catholic ideal known as the "Church of the Poor." Once a pillar of conservatism, in the 1960s and 1970s the Church in Latin America began to strive for social justice through the profound transformation of society. Dom Hélder and the Brazilian Church played a decisive role in this shift. He and other leaders of the Church of the Poor preached Christian salvation not as an abstract afterlife but as a just society built in the present on Earth. The Church of the Poor defended human rights and socioeconomic equality, and it preached a "preferential option for the poor" over other social classes, urging common people to participate actively in politics, unions, and social movements such as neighborhood groups seeking better schools. (Some followers were self-avowed socialists.) In terms of international relations and economic policy the Church of the Poor espoused the most nationalistic ideas in Brazilian Catholicism. It strongly supported economic development, and it stressed the Brazilian and Latin American aspects of Catholicism as opposed to the European tradition.

As Dom Hélder's life demonstrates, faith and politics are intertwined in Latin America. Along with military officers, the clergy carried great weight in the region's politics throughout the twentieth century. Priests and bishops exerted even greater influence in the sphere of religion, which played a significant role in the daily lives of most people.

Dom Hélder personified how religion both participated in and was changed by Brazil's political and social modernization. His path was long, arduous, and complex. Dom Hélder, who died in 1999, reached the age of ninety in a strife-filled era. His theological and political development both reflected and reinforced many of the major themes of a century in which Brazil and other Latin American countries strived but often failed to establish democratic systems, industrialize their economies, and alleviate wrenching poverty. The Church's involvement in this process deepened and led to its religious and political transformation. The modernization of Catholicism came with a price. Dom Hélder received widespread praise and extended his influence to all of Latin America and to the United States, Europe, and elsewhere, but he also received much criticism for denouncing human rights abuses and the social injustices practiced by strong nations against the weak. He and his followers suffered violent persecution by an anti-Communist Brazilian military regime that was supported by the U.S. government.

A deep and unwavering religious faith was the key to Dom Hélder's perseverance. He was born in 1909 into a large and humble family in Fortaleza, the capital of Ceará and an important port on northeastern Brazil's Atlantic coast. Like many Brazilians, Hélder's first examples of piety came from his mother, a primary school teacher. She wanted him to be a priest. Hélder's father, a bookkeeper, ignored the antireligious aspects of the Masonic lodge to which he belonged and fervently practiced the faith. Ceará had one of the strongest Catholic traditions in Brazil. Father Cícero, Brazil's most revered priest, whom many in the northeast considered a saint, established a popular pilgrimage site in the backlands of Ceará in the late 1800s, and he later became the state's governor. As a young seminarian in 1927, Dom Hélder met Father Cícero and witnessed the profound respect that poor people still showed for the 85-year-old priest.

Dom Hélder studied under the French and Dutch Vincentian fathers, a religious order that had unique rules, tasks, and spirituality with the atmosphere of a tightly knit brotherhood. These strict disciplinarians played a major part in the Romanization, or conservative modernization, of Brazilian Catholicism between the 1850s and the 1960s. During this era the Church vastly augmented its political and social influence by carefully reorganizing itself, emphasizing morality, and bringing people's everyday, sometimes unorthodox religious practices into line with official Church teachings. From the Vincentians, Dom Hélder learned obedience to the Church hierarchy, but he also questioned the institution's arbitrary stifling of creativity. Like most Brazilian priests, Dom Hélder left the seminary with a superior education—he learned French and Latin, for example—yet he lacked knowledge of current events and his country's reality. In 1931, Dom Hélder was ordained as a diocesan priest and as such came under the authority of the Archdiocese of Fortaleza and its archbishop.

Dom Hélder developed a remarkable spiritual discipline and dedication to God. He renounced physical pleasures, offered up to God his feelings of attraction to women, and once fasted so rigorously that he fainted. He wore his cassock daily, even long after most priests had abandoned theirs. The long, white robe accented his image as a simple, holy, and kind man. Throughout his adult life, Dom Hélder would awaken each morning at two o'clock and for the next three hours would pray, read his breviary (prayerbook), answer correspondence, meditate on the challenges of the previous day, and write poetry. In all, during these nightly vigils, Dom Hélder composed more than 7,000 poems, known as the "Meditations of Padre José."

The renunciation of physical comfort impressed people. "It was impossible not to be attracted to him," remembered the prominent Catholic intellectual Rose Marie Muraro, who worked with Padre Hélder in the 1940s. "And we all knew that he was a man who practically didn't eat or drink, who prayed all the time, who didn't sleep, and who expressed such a deep love!" Dom Hélder drew his greatest inspiration from the teachings and life of Francis, his favorite saint, whose self-abnegation both resembled and softened the harsh penitential aspects of the northeastern backlands. "Brother Francisco" was one of Dom Hélder's favorite nicknames. With his tenderness, tolerance, and captivating smile, he was perhaps the closest approximation to a Brazilian Saint Francis. Dom Hélder's profound spirituality and asceticism later provided him with the strength to overcome the adversities of his public and political life.

Dom Hélder developed a substantial political career and underwent a profound ideological shift before becoming a militant for peace and social justice. As a seminarian he already had demonstrated a strong inclination for politics and particularly admired the ideas of Jackson de Figueiredo, a fervent convert to Catholicism. Jackson was a follower of French integralism, an archconservative, corporativist form of Catholicism that resonated with elements of fascism. He founded the newspaper *A Ordem* and the important Centro Dom Vital, both of which deeply influenced many Brazilian intellectuals. In the early 1930s, Dom Hélder became deeply involved in Ação Integralista Brasileira (AIB, or Brazilian Integralist Action), first in Ceará, where he successfully promoted the movement, and then in Rio de Janeiro, where he served as a secret member of AIB's supreme council at the behest of Dom Sebastião Leme da Silveira Cintra, the cardinal-archbishop of Rio de Janeiro.

The most influential bishop of his time, Dom Leme lent the Church's support to the regime of President Getúlio Vargas, who had seized power in the revolution of 1930. In return for privileges and subsidies, the Church gave the increasingly nationalistic and authoritarian Vargas moral support and a Catholic ideological framework that lent legitimacy to his government. Dom Leme also felt the need to bet discreetly on the Integralistas in case they came to power. Many other churchmen joined or sympathized with AIB because of its opposition to both communism and liberal capitalism. Communism, of course, was atheistic, and the unsuccessful 1935 revolt by its followers against the Vargas government polarized society. Capitalism was too individualistic and did not recognize the need for the social safety net and political unity of the integralist model. Significantly, young Padre Hélder's embrace of Integralismo led him to defend the use of violence for political ends. Wary of Integralismo's potential as a political competitor, however, Vargas crushed the organization in 1938.

Like several other important Integralista intellectuals, Dom Hélder ultimately rejected the movement for its association with violence and European fascism in the period before World War II. When political opponents later tried to use his authoritarian past against him, Dom Hélder readily admitted his mistake. Significantly, however, many former Integralistas retained the movement's nationalistic fervor. Among them were the great intellectuals San Tiago Dantas, who would become the minister of foreign relations for leftist president João Goulart (1961–1964), and Alceu Amoroso Lima. Alceu introduced Dom Hélder to the work of the French Catholic philosopher Jacques Maritain, whose anti-authoritarian "integral humanism," support for democracy, and acceptance of religious pluralism influenced an entire generation of Brazilian clergymen and intellectuals who later became proponents of the Church of the Poor and Liberation Theology.

Starting in the late 1940s, Dom Hélder gradually shifted to the political left. In order to keep the Church in step with the rapidly changing world of the postwar era, he undertook efforts to modernize it and increase its sensitivity to social questions. In the process he became the most dynamic and original leader in the recent history of the Brazilian Church.

Dom Hélder began by reorganizing Ação Católica (Catholic Action), the most important movement for the laity within the Church. The laity were those members of the Church who were not clergy (ordained priests or nuns). In spiritual matters, the Catholic laity was expected to follow the dictates of the Church hierarchy. In the 1900s, however, the Church's fear of losing its flock to growing and aggressive Protestant churches and the atheistic tenets of Marxism convinced its leaders to involve the laity more actively in the life of the institution. Catholic Action arrived in Brazil in the 1930s. As its national director from 1952 to 1962, Dom Hélder shifted its emphasis from spirituality and organizational questions. He criticized the clergy's paternalistic treatment of the laity and transformed Catholic Action into a vibrant array of groups that became involved in adult literacy training (for example, in the Movimento de Educação de Base, or MEB), union organization, and other kinds of political and social work. The most influential Catholic Action group was the Juventude Universitária Católica (JUC, or Catholic University Youth). The JUC grew rapidly in political importance and advocated cultural and economic nationalism. In 1959 the JUC developed "a Christian historical ideal for the Brazilian people." This platform focused on Brazil's economic underdevelopment, criticized capitalism for its anti-Christian abuses, and accepted socialism as a viable option. In the early 1960s the JUC supplied leadership to the radical student movement, many of whose members came to embrace Marxism in the wake of the 1959 Cuban Revolution.

By stimulating the search for a socially relevant faith, Dom Hélder helped to provoke a major shift in the basic values and practices of Catholicism. He wanted the Church to break away from its exclusive emphasis on traditional morals and the afterlife and instead focus on people's daily concerns and needs. One key example was his advocacy of agrarian reform, the redistribution of unused land owned by the wealthy few to poor landless Brazilians to farm. Along with other clergymen, Dom Hélder stimulated some of the first serious discussions of the issue. In

1950, while still a priest, he wrote a famous pastoral letter on the topic published under the name of a bishop. The Church believed that redistributing the property of large landowners among the poor would stop the flow of migrants to the cities, thus solving the problem of the burgeoning *favelas* (urban shantytowns) and preserving the Church's traditional base in the countryside.

The demand for agrarian reform became a trademark of the Church of the Poor and eventually led to the founding of its Pastoral Land Commission in 1975. This commission has defended small rural property owners and landless agricultural workers in their struggles against violent land speculators, large landowners, and oppressive government actions. The work of the Church in this area contributed significantly to the establishment of the Movement of the Landless (Movimento Sem Terra, or MST; see also Chapter 11). The MST is perhaps the liveliest and most innovative initiative for the poor to emerge in all of Latin America in the 1980s and 1990s. Its activists frequently occupy unused private property and public lands in order to grow subsistence crops. Dom Hélder and the Church of the Poor's efforts pressured the Brazilian government to implement full-fledged agrarian reform. Until now, land reform has been piecemeal, but the MST has helped to accelerate government land-reform programs.

Dom Hélder also modernized the Church by founding the Conferência Nacional dos Bispos do Brasil (CNBB, or National Conference of the Bishops of Brazil) in 1952. One of the first such organizations in the Catholic world, the CNBB revitalized the institution, increased the bishops' interest in social and economic problems, and laid the groundwork for programs such as the Pastoral Land Commission. Dom Hélder served as secretary general from the start until 1964. The CNBB has consistently pressured Brazilian leaders on issues of social justice.

Dom Hélder also sought religious modernization by employing the mass media to transmit his message. He contributed frequently to newspapers and other publications, appeared on a prime-time weekly television program called "On God's Paths," and spoke on a nightly radio program. In 1959, Dom Hélder organized a "demonstration of faith" on Good Friday that filled the Maracanã soccer stadium with 200,000 people and was broadcast on television and a nationwide radio network of 300 stations. Dom Hélder's television popularity caused some conservative Brazilians to label him a show-off.

The year 1955 marked a decisive moment in Dom Hélder's religious and political quest when he reached a new height of ecclesiastical prestige by becoming an archbishop. He also organized the 36th International Eucharistic Congress (IEC). Held in Rio with government support, this event united the state, the armed forces, business, the tourist industry, the working classes, and the Church in the campaign for economic development and anticommunism. It marked the pinnacle of the triumphalistic, corporativistic neo-Christendom model of Catholicism first introduced by the Vincentians and fulfilled by Dom Leme. The IEC highlighted Dom Hélder's extraordinary (though often forgotten) organizational skills. By boosting his appeal among Brazil's entrepreneurial and social elite, it projected him as the country's most dynamic, most beloved bishop. But the IEC had the added effect of forcing Dom Hélder to reflect on the growing gap between rich and poor generated by the Brazilian development model. Pierre Cardinal Gerlier, one of the attending dignitaries from Europe, urged Dom Hélder to "use this organizing talent that the Lord has given you in the service of the poor. You must know that although Rio de Janeiro is one of the most beautiful cities in the world, it is also one of the most hideous, because all these *favelas* in such a beautiful setting are an insult to the Lord." With this revelation, Dom Hélder later recalled, "I was thrown to the ground like Saul on the road to Damascus."

After the IEC, Dom Hélder intensified his efforts for the poor. He took part in the formation of the Conselho Episcopal Latino-Americano (CELAM, or Council of Latin American Bishops). The CELAM increased awareness of the region's importance in the Catholic Church and provided support for the emerging Church of the Poor. In Rio, Dom Hélder inaugurated a housing project for *favela* dwellers and set up an ongoing charitable drive for the needy. He soon gained international renown as "the bishop of the *favelas*." Dom Hélder also lobbied the government for development programs to assist the masses. His prestige and growing political influence enabled him to become one of the principal advisers to President Juscelino Kubitschek (1956–1961), who promoted rapid industrial development through foreign investment, government stimulus, and the transfer of the national capital from Rio to newly built Brasília. Dom Hélder and the CNBB assisted Kubitschek in the effort to spread the benefits of development. For example, the bishops were instrumental in the foundation of an ambitious government program to bring industry and progress to the impoverished northeast.

Dom Hélder drew spiritual inspiration from groups that identified with the experience of poverty—for example, the French worker-priests, who sought to attract the working class to the Church by earning a living in factories. Dom Hélder and other clergymen of his time adopted a spirituality of poverty and literally sought to live like the poor. In Recife he abandoned the archiepiscopal palace to reside in a small parish house behind a modest church.

More than anything else, Dom Hélder's profound faith in the Brazilian people shaped his support for social justice. Although as an archbishop he represented the central power of the world's quintessential multinational and multicultural religious organization, headquartered in Rome, he believed in the self-determination of nations and individuals. Consummately loyal to the institution, he also favored the administrative decentralization—and even democratization—of the extremely hierarchical and male-dominated Church. He believed that only by respecting the dignity of all followers could Catholicism become truly modern. As the leader of Catholic Action, Dom Hélder encouraged the laity to assert itself within the Church and to focus on questions of national importance. He demonstrated these ideals through his willingness to delegate responsibility—especially to women.

A host of female members of Catholic Action, volunteers, and Church employees assisted Dom Hélder throughout his career. One of them was the young Rose Marie Muraro, the future feminist intellectual and author. She belonged to a group of young female followers known as "Hélder's Girls." "Dom Hélder was really one of the first men to value women," she recalled. "He had great female friends, but everybody accepted that as something human and important, including the quite deep spiritual conviviality he shared with women." Rose Marie and some of the other women came to hold important jobs in the Church. These women assistants were especially instrumental during Dom Hélder's leadership of the CNBB. Dom Hélder's relationship with women contrasted sharply with the exploitation of nuns and other women in many sectors of the Church. To this day his trust in women and the people has yet to find its equal in the Church, which, like numerous other Brazilian institutions, continues as an outmoded patriarchal structure hindered in its effectiveness by its refusal to tap the professional and leadership potential of women.

Dom Hélder transcended Brazilian issues to become a spokesman for the underdeveloped world. Some of his greatest achievements took place at the Second Vatican Council. In this series of momentous meetings some 2,000 bishops from around the world came together in Rome between 1962 and 1965 to discuss how the Church might be modernized. Vatican II resulted in the greatest reform in the history of the institution. At the Council, Dom Hélder successfully propagated the ideas of the emerging Church of the Poor. He pointed out the need to address the injustices of the world economy through dialogue between rich and poor countries and through international cooperation for development. Setting up informal meetings of reform-minded bishops, Dom Hélder worked behind the scenes to change the hierarchical, Eurocentric organization of the Church and to encourage greater lay participation. He also worked for the Council's adoption of ecumenical relations with other religions (such as Judaism and Protestantism) and dialogue with other ideologies, including atheistic Marxism. Vatican II revealed the new influence of Latin American ideas in world Catholicism and projected Dom Hélder as one of the great international leaders of the Church.

In 1963 and 1964, Brazilian politics became extremely polarized between left and right. Dom Hélder swung further left, signaling a clear break with Brazil's elite. He declared that the wealthy had caused the failure of the Alliance for Progress, a Cold War program started by President John F. Kennedy to stop the spread of communism in Latin America after the 1959 Cuban Revolution through financial assistance and social reform to help the poor. Brazil became a focus of this and other U.S. programs because it bordered every nation in South America except Ecuador and Chile. It was feared that if Brazil became a Communist nation like Cuba, then all of South America would follow suit.

At the urging of Dom Hélder the CNBB issued one of the most radical pronouncements in the history of the Brazilian Church. This document supported the expropriation of land for transfer to the poor. Dom Hélder became ever more deeply involved in President João Goulart's controversial efforts to implement land redistribution and other basic reforms. Conservatives attacked Dom Hélder because of his support of literacy and other programs for the poor that some observers feared were inspired by communism. He refused to back the brewing military conspiracy against President Goulart's government, which further disenchanted many of his old friends among the elite.

Meanwhile, at Vatican II, Dom Hélder angered conservative and traditionalist bishops with his progressive positions. In early 1964 ecclesiastical jealousy of Dom Hélder's success and suspicions about his politics led to his transfer to the obscure archdiocese of São Luís do Maranhão. The sudden death of another archbishop, however, caused the Church to return Dom Hélder to Olinda and Recife. Radical politics and cultural movements had flourished in Recife for years, making it one of the most important cities of the Third World and drawing the attention of U.S. government officials worried about revolutionary upheaval in Latin America. On March 31, 1964, the Brazilian army overthrew President Goulart, thus beginning twenty-one years of repressive martial rule. The U.S. government quickly recognized the military officers who came to power by deposing a democratically elected government as Brazil's legitimate political representatives. Later in the year the Brazilian bishops voted to replace Dom Hélder's faction in the CNBB with a more conservative leadership.

At first, Dom Hélder took a wait-and-see approach toward the military regime, hoping to keep open channels of dialogue and possible collaboration. Unlike many on the left, Dom Hélder did not have prejudices against the military. He considered himself a pastor to all people. General Humberto de Alencar Castelo Branco, the first military president of the new regime, liked his fellow *cearense* Dom Hélder and even after 1964 went to hear some of his sermons. Although Dom Hélder accepted dialogue with Marxism and defended the rights of political prisoners held by the regime, he continued to oppose communism—but never in the truculent, intolerant manner of the right. He wanted to pre-empt communism with a nonviolent, Catholic, and humanistic social revolution in which the government would promote the well-being of all its citizens, effect the radical transformation of society, and maintain Brazil's independence from foreign powers such as the United States and the Soviet Union. At the same time, Dom Hélder was well aware that the Church itself was not capable of creating or leading a socialist regime. Socialism could develop only through the efforts of politics and civil society, and it had to maintain its independence of the superpowers. The Church should not trade neo-Christendom for a socialist Christendom.

Yet Cold War fears and hatred blinded both members of the left and right to the peaceful political middle ground offered by Dom Hélder. The growing conflict between Catholic progressivism and the military regime's oppressive anti-Communist national security policy seriously undermined Church-state relations. Military officers and conservatives now branded Dom Hélder a "Communist," the "Red bishop." In the northeast, especially around Recife, the army unleashed the worst repression of the immediate post-coup period. Dom Hélder aided the persecuted while continuing to speak out against injustice. President Castelo Branco and other moderates tried to reduce tensions with the Church, but many military hard-liners disliked the activist clergy and stepped up their attacks against the Church of the Poor and Dom Hélder. Conservatives frequently accused him of encouraging violence in his critiques of inequality. The popularity of Cuban revolutionary leader Ernesto "Che" Guevara who died organizing Bolivian guerrillas, the revolutionary Colombian priest Camilo Torres, and others increased the appeal of violence as a solution to the political and developmental impasse of the Third World.

Dom Hélder recognized the violence present in Latin America, yet he increasingly emphasized nonviolence as the solution. Some on the left criticized his "pacifist" attitude toward the military regime. Perhaps naively, in 1967 he outlined a plan to form a third political party—the Partido do Desenvolvimento Integral (Party of Total Development)—as an alternative to the two official parties allowed by the military to function after it abolished all traditional ones in 1965. In 1968, Dom Hélder officially launched a movement called "Action, Justice, and Peace," partially modeled on the work of Gandhi and Martin Luther King. The movement foundered, however, because of deepening political polarization and military censorship.

In mid-1968 the Latin American Church made its clearest, most mature statement about the kind of society it envisioned for the region. Bishops representing the area met in Medellín, Colombia, to study how Vatican II's conclusions might be applied locally. Dom Hélder led the other delegates in forging a proposition for radical but peaceful social transformation in the region. They denounced the "institutionalized violence" inherent in social inequality and the oppressive social structures of Latin American nations that victimized the poor. They also promoted the creation of Comunidades Eclesiais de Base, or Grassroots Church Communities. In these small groups humble Catholics came together to reflect on the importance of the faith in their daily lives and political struggles. This methodology became known throughout Latin America as *conscientização*, or consciousness-raising. The Medellín conference marked the birth of Liberation Theology, which became the ideological foundation of the Church of the Poor. The Medellín statement led many priests, nuns, and lay volunteers across Latin America to become activists for the poor and to oppose authoritarianism. The Brazilian military regime considered the document to be susceptible to manipulation by Communist revolutionaries. Yet the generals failed to understand that Church leaders held the Medellín meeting as part of its own strategy to contain communism and encourage social reform rather than violent revolution. In line with Dom Hélder's own beliefs, the declaration emphasized nonviolence.

In December 1968 the Brazilian generals decreed full dictatorship by suspending civil liberties and freedom of the press, closing the National Congress, and allowing the security forces free rein against not only the growing antigovernment guerrilla movement but against peaceful opponents of the regime as well. Again, Dom Hélder tried to give the military a chance to prove its good intentions. But torture had become routine at military interrogation centers. Dom Hélder himself came under intense scrutiny by military and police intelligence. His home was riddled with machine-gun fire, and in May 1969 a right-wing death squad brutally murdered one of his young priests. In November 1969 the security forces assassinated Carlos Marighella, a violent revolutionary considered Public Enemy No. 1 by the regime. In the process they jailed and tortured Dominican friars and other priests accused of collaborating

with Marighella, who wanted to overthrow the military and install a socialist government. Among the detainees was Father Marcelo Carvalheira,
one of Dom Hélder's assistants and today the vice president of the CNBB.
The intelligence community unsuccessfully tried to use the incident to
link Dom Hélder to the violence.

In May 1970, Dom Hélder attacked the government by denouncing
the existence of torture to the world in a public speech in Paris. The
decision to speak out was perhaps the most controversial of his life. Since
1964, Dom Hélder had worked for the release of political prisoners and
had visited them in jail. In Recife he publicly denounced torture by the
political police. Yet at no time had he commented on torture abroad,
where he was well known. Dom Hélder specifically mentioned the case
of Tito de Alencar Lima, one of the imprisoned Dominicans. Friar Tito
was brutally tortured by the security forces and, unable to recover psy-
chologically, later committed suicide.

The Paris speech was unthinkable for Brazil's military leaders. Proud
of an "economic miracle" that made their nation one of the world's fast-
est growing, they dismissed critics as "bad Brazilians" and adapted the
propaganda phrase used by conservatives in the United States: "Brazil:
Love it or leave it." The generals became locked in a battle with the
Church over Brazil's foreign image and the redefinition of patriotism as
the country became an industrial power. The generals increasingly considered defense of human rights to be subversion.

Dom Hélder's denunciation of torture was one of his biggest contributions to peace and social justice. It helped to solidify the Church's new
position in favor of human rights and made the theme an issue in international politics and diplomacy. But it also infuriated the generals and
wrecked his ecclesiastical career. The Paris speech brought down a rain
of criticism in Brazil. The press and conservative intellectuals engaged
in an intensive smear campaign against Dom Hélder. Then the dictators
prohibited any further mention of the archbishop in the media. They
also used diplomatic channels to prevent him from winning the Nobel
Peace Prize. It was as if Dom Hélder no longer existed. Bureaucrats of
the Vatican, the central authority of Church government in Rome, also
tried to restrict Dom Hélder's movements. By now he was far too controversial to become a cardinal, a high post he surely deserved but which
the military regime opposed. Dom Hélder strategically retreated from
internal Brazilian politics and concentrated on making speeches abroad,
where he continued to draw attention for his support of peace and justice. At a meeting of Church leaders in São Paulo he passed the mantle
of defender of human rights to Archbishop Paulo Evaristo Arns, who in
the 1970s became the most outspoken critic within Brazil of the regime's

violations of human rights. Only in 1977, after the regime began to relax censorship, did a Brazilian newspaper once again interview Dom Hélder.

Despite fears of assassination, Dom Hélder maintained his calm during the difficult 1970s by remaining a man of simplicity, peace, and deep spirituality. His quest for peace relied on the daily exercise of basic values not always easy for human beings to practice: kindness, patience, respect, humility, humor, willingness to learn from young people and the poor, and, when necessary, silence. Dom Hélder symbolized the Christian, nonviolent face of the Brazilian left as many students and activists in the 1960s and early 1970s lost patience and turned to armed struggle as a way to fight the military and transform society. The atheistic revolutionary left nevertheless admired Dom Hélder for his courage in criticizing the military regime.

Many of the innovations anticipated in Dom Hélder's earlier work came to fruition in the 1970s. These were the heroic years of the Church of the Poor. The CNBB and many individual bishops outspokenly defended human rights and advocated socioeconomic equality. Inspired by Catholic Action and reinforced by the Medellín declaration, the Grassroots Church Communities multiplied, and Brazilian Liberation Theologians published prolifically. Liberation Theology became one of the most important religious schools of thought in twentieth-century world Catholicism. In addition to the Pastoral Land Commission, the Church established the Indigenous Missionary Council to protect Brazil's native peoples from exploitation. The Church gave key support to the development of a labor movement independent of the government-controlled unions first set up in the 1930s and emasculated of all significant leadership after the coup of 1964. As a result of these and other initiatives, the Church became a primary force in the broad opposition front that gained strength in the late 1970s and helped to speed the return to civilian rule. Dom Hélder's faith and ethics contributed to other important developments—for example, the fight for women's equality, the trend toward religious diversity and plurality, and the growth of nongovernmental advocacy groups, many of them staffed by Catholic activists.

As archbishop of Olinda and Recife, Dom Hélder presided over important experiments in ecclesial democracy. He maintained his delegative style of governance, relying greatly on a council of laity and priests to run the archdiocese. These and other activists organized a network of grassroots communities known as the Encontro de Irmãos, or Brotherly Meetings. Dom Hélder also set up the Peace and Justice Commission to examine human rights issues.

In seminary training, Dom Hélder oversaw the implementation of one of the most radical experiments in the post-Vatican II Church. He and other bishops established the Seminário Regional do Nordeste II (SERENE II, or Regional Seminary of the Northeast II sector of the CNBB). Instead of living in a large and traditional seminary shut off from the world, SERENE II students were divided up into small residences in the metropolitan area's poor neighborhoods and shantytowns. Some did pastoral work in the vast sugarcane-growing region, where powerful landowners still ruled with an iron fist not unlike the slaveowners of Brazil's colonial era. Others took part in a program called "the theology of the hoe," which trained priests for work among the poor of the backlands. The SERENE II students and other seminarians from the northeast did their academic work at the Instituto Teológico do Recife (ITER, or Theological Institute of Recife).

ITER developed an extraordinarily ecumenical staff who aroused suspicion among more traditional Catholics. It included priests who had left the ministry to marry, radical Church activists, and female professors such as the North American nun Janis Jordan, who lived in a *favela*, and the controversial Brazilian sister and liberationist-feminist writer Ivone Gebara, punished by the Church in the 1990s for her views. ITER had few resources and functioned in a decrepit building, but its teaching staff showed remarkable intellectual productivity. ITER broadened its program to include special classes for lay activists and poor Catholics who wished to study theology and apply its principles in their communities. Thus, in his archdiocese, Dom Hélder and the ITER staff ended the monopoly on theology held by ordained males and chipped away at the stern clericalism that had ruled the Church for centuries.

In 1985 the military left power and Dom Hélder retired as archbishop. The Brazilian Church now felt less need to play its denunciatory role as "the voice of the voiceless" in defense of the poor and victims of human rights abuses. The Church retreated to a more conservative position. This shift occurred partly under pressure from Pope John Paul II, an ardent anti-Communist fearful of leftist influence in the Latin American Church. John Paul II, who became pope in 1978, focused on winning the Cold War for the West and rejected radical approaches to ending Latin America's social ills. The fall of the Berlin Wall in 1989 especially muted the arguments of those in the Church of the Poor who advocated socialism. Another factor was the rise of new political parties, unions, and a plethora of nongovernmental organizations and grassroots groups in a democratic system now free of the violent repression and censorship earlier employed by the military. These movements had largely grown under the protective wing of the Church, but they now took over the role of speaking for the people. The political climate had changed and the Church of the Poor began to lose steam.

Although he respected Dom Hélder, John Paul II worked to roll back many of the innovations introduced by his Brazilian colleague at Vatican II and in the 1970s. The Vatican's most direct attack on the Church of the Poor came precisely in the archdiocese of Olinda and Recife, where Dom Hélder's conservative replacement, Dom José Cardoso Sobrinho, dismantled many of his programs and punished or suspended a number of progressive priests. In a move that at best can only be termed insensitive in light of the recent dictatorial era, Dom José called out the police on several occasions to enforce his ecclesiastical policies against groups of Catholics who protested. In addition, in 1989 the Vatican ordered the closing of SERENE II and ITER. It was one of the most painful moments for Dom Hélder and the history of the Church of the Poor in all of Latin America. Throughout these incidents, Dom Hélder once again remained calm and, unlike his time of conflict with the military regime, spoke little about them. He continued his simple, unassuming lifestyle until his death in 1999.

Dom Hélder was a major Latin American religious figure and leader of great popularity. He captured the hearts of the people through his charisma and piety. Like most bishops, Dom Hélder was a politician who built links to the rich and powerful, yet he had the rare gift of appealing to all groups, including students, revolutionaries, and the press. Until 1964 even conservatives liked Dom Hélder. He ultimately renounced the seductive temptations of power and ecclesiastical honors. Had he played the game, Dom Hélder could have become a cardinal, and, had he danced with the military, perhaps even archbishop of Rio de Janeiro or São Paulo. He rejected these possibilities in order to side with the poor.

More than any other bishop, Dom Hélder was responsible for the modernization and political transformation of the Brazilian Church. Catholic values changed. They kept in step not only with a rapidly growing Brazil but also with the moral and social concerns that arose out of economic progress. Even after the conservative reaction of the 1980s and 1990s, the Church remained sensitive to social issues and unafraid to criticize the government when it failed to show concern for the national interest or the fate of the poor.

In a century filled with international conflict and ideological polarization, Dom Hélder made the transition from advocate of violence to peacemaker. His struggle for economic development, social progress, human rights, and greater equality among nations largely defined the Church of the Poor and had an impact on Catholics around the world. Dom Hélder embodied human humility and fraternity. Yet he helped

Brazil and other Third World nations assert themselves within the great human community by giving a voice to the poor.

SUGGESTED READINGS

In Portuguese the best work is Nelson Piletti and Walter Praxedes, *Dom Hélder Câmara: Entre o poder e a profecia* (São Paulo: Editora Ática, 1997). It is one of the few sources based on his personal papers, which are still held by private individuals. A good set of essays is Zildo Rocha, ed., *Hélder, o Dom: Uma vida que marcou os rumos da Igreja no Brasil*, 3d ed. (Petrópolis: Vozes, 2000). Other data are in Rose Marie Muraro, *Memórias de uma mulher impossível* (Rio de Janeiro: Editora Rosa dos Tempos, 1999); Marcos Cirano, *Os caminhos de Dom Hélder: Perseguições e censura (1964–1980)* (Recife: Editora Guararapes, 1983); Sebastião Antonio Ferrarini, *A imprensa e o arcebispo vermelho (1964–1984)* (São Paulo: Edições Paulinas, 1992); Frei Betto, *Batismo de sangue: A luta clandestina contra a ditadura militar: Dossiês Carlos Marighella e Frei Tito*, 11th (first revised) edition (São Paulo: Casa Amarela, 2000); José Cayuela, *Hélder Câmara. Brasil: ¿Un Vietnam católico?* (Barcelona: Editorial Pomaire, 1969); and Gustavo do Passo Castro, *As comunidades do Dom: Um estudo de CEBs no Recife* (Recife: Fundação Joaquim Nabuco; Editora Massangana, 1987). Dom Hélder's testimony on the Integralistas is in Dom Hélder Câmara, "Minha passagem pela Ação Integralista Brasileira," CNBB, Instituto Nacional de Pastoral, document 02143. The files of the extinct political police of Rio, held at the Arquivo Público do Estado do Rio de Janeiro, contain an extensive dossier on the bishop. Two churchmen provided key interviews: Raimundo Caramuru de Barros, Brasília, February 7, 1990 (by the author), and Dom Waldyr Calheiros, Volta Redonda, December 28, 1998 (by the author and Célia Costa).

The top work in English is Hélder Câmara, *The Conversions of a Bishop: An Interview with José de Broucker*, trans. Hilary Davies (New York: Collins, 1979). For a fine earlier synthesis, see Patrick J. Leonard, "Dom Hélder Câmara: A Study in Polarity" (Ph.D. diss., St. Louis University, 1974), which has an excellent bibliography. Also see Margaret Todaro, "Pastors, Prophets, and Politicians: A Study of the Brazilian Catholic Church, 1916–1945" (Ph.D. diss., Columbia University, 1971); and Kenneth P. Serbin, "Church-State Reciprocity in Contemporary Brazil: The Convening of the International Eucharistic Congress of 1955 in Rio de Janeiro," *Hispanic American Historical Review* 76:4 (November 1996): 721–51. On Recife, see Robin Nagle, *Claiming the Virgin: The Broken Promise of Liberation Theology in Brazil* (New York: Routledge, 1997). A good study of John Paul II is Carl Bernstein and Marco Politi, *His Holiness, John Paul II and the Hidden History of Our Time* (New York: Doubleday, 1996).

Good overviews of the Brazilian Church are in Thomas C. Bruneau, *The Political Transformation of the Brazilian Catholic Church* (Cambridge, Eng.:

Cambridge University Press, 1974); Scott Mainwaring, *The Catholic Church and Politics in Brazil, 1916–1985* (Stanford: Stanford University Press, 1986); and Jeffrey Klaiber, S.J., *The Church, Dictatorships, and Democracy in Latin America* (Maryknoll, NY: Orbis Books, 1998). For recent critical interpretations of Catholic progressivism, see Anthony Gill, *Rendering unto Caesar: The Catholic Church and the State in Latin America* (Chicago: University of Chicago Press, 1998); Manuel A. Vásquez, *The Brazilian Popular Church and the Crisis of Modernity* (Cambridge, Eng.: Cambridge University Press, 1998); John Burdick, *Looking for God in Brazil* (Berkeley and Los Angeles: University of California Press, 1993); Cecília Mariz, *Coping with Poverty in Brazil* (Philadelphia: Temple University Press, 1994); and Kenneth P. Serbin, *Secret Dialogues: Church-State Relations, Torture, and Social Justice in Authoritarian Brazil* (Pittsburgh: University of Pittsburgh Press, 2000).

CHAPTER 14

Madame Satã (Satan)

The Black "Queen" of Rio's Bohemia

JAMES N. GREEN

The reader briefly met Madame Satã in Chapter 7. He was the cross-dressing malandro (streetwise hustler) who landed the punch that killed his fellow malandro and samba composer Geraldo Pereira in a street altercation. Who was this cross-dressing thug? Madame Satã often dressed and behaved like a woman to proclaim his sexual tastes and his public rejection of respectable norms. For Satã, the title "Madame" had an ironic twist that associated his black masculinity with the tawdry world of prostitution, where French women traditionally provided the high-priced intimacy prized by many Brazilian men of means. Even Madame Satã lashed out when others first began to call him this name. Despite stereotypes that we might have about cross-dressing men, Madame Satã was far from sissified. He could strike fear even in the burly hearts of Rio's sadistic cops, who sometimes brutalized other men who dressed as women on the streets of Rio's downtown neighborhood and nighttime hotspot of Lapa, where Madame Satã, when not in jail, preferred to hang out.

Professor James N. Green's analysis highlights the changing sensibilities and nostalgia that later made Madame Satã into a celebrated figura (character) of Rio's nightlife and underworld in ways that would have been hard to imagine when Madame was a younger man. In the 1960s and 1970s the youth of Brazil, as in other parts of the world, became disillusioned with traditional ideas of patriotism and conformity to protest government indifference to many of the injustices of the day. While many young people in the United States focused their protests around the civil rights struggle and the war in Vietnam, in Brazil they protested an authoritarian military regime that came to power in 1964 after overthrowing an elected democratic government. Under Brazil's twenty-year military dictatorship, censorship, the suspension of civil rights, the violent suppression of public protests, and the incarceration, torture, and murder of suspected Communist subversives angered many young Brazilians who sought to criticize military rule. Well-heeled young people more generally joined prohibited acts of protest where they became subject to the police brutality usually reserved for Brazil's poor. In the 1970s the hip, upper-middle-class journalists of the counterculture newspaper Pasquim *fought government censorship with biting parody to offer alternative views in a stilted media environment. When they interviewed the by-then elderly Madame Satã,* Pasquim's *journalists found in him a countercultural hero from a previous generation, even if they saw his sexuality as unsavory or, at best, eccentric; they, too, considered themselves "Bohemians" and, in a chauvinistic heterosexual sense, favored sexual liberation. Most of all, Madame Satã stood up to the abuses of government officials and spent years in jail because of his defiance of authority and cultural norms.*

The protest movements of the 1960s and 1970s also gave rise to feminist, black consciousness, gay and lesbian, and other organizations in Brazil that fought for an end to military rule and for the rights, opportunities, health, and safety of their constituents. Before the emergence of gay and lesbian political activism, most Brazilians condemned those who exclusively sought out sex with their own gender as victims of social pathology or psychological instability, as did the novelist Adolfo Ferreira Caminha in the 1890s (see Chapter 5). The broad-based civil struggle to oust an oppressive military regime that legitimated its rule with jingoistic appeals to nationalism opened new spaces for underground groups to challenge traditional ideas of propriety and to refashion their identities. Gay and lesbian leaders who advocated pride in themselves and their lifestyle also found a countercultural hero in Madame Satã. Here was a man who flaunted his preference for sex with men, but who would not let others humiliate him because of his sexuality. Madame Satã's life story indicates how historical memory can shift to accommodate the needs of new politicized groups within a national community. In the first case, one such community was based largely around an age cohort, such as the youthful journalists of Pasquim *and their hip countercultural readership; in the second, they coalesced around alternative sexual preferences and lifestyles. Both of these unconventional, nonconformist groups challenged the conventional, homogenizing nationalist ideals that the military regime embraced as essential to promote Brazilian unity and national security, as President Getúlio Vargas had in the 1930s and 1940s. These groups clamored for tolerance of their diverse views and lifestyles amid political repression that demanded obedience and uniformity.*

James N. Green's research has explored the intersection of sexuality, politics, and community. His Beyond Carnival: Male Homosexuality in Twentieth-Century Brazil *(1999) examines the emergence of self-identified communities of men who prefer romance and sex with other men in the cities of Rio and São Paulo. He is currently focusing on the response of U.S. academics who study Brazil to the military regime that ruled from 1964 to 1985. In another project, he is researching Tiradentes Square in Rio, famous as a site for popular protests, for a nightlife of theaters, bars, and dancehalls, and as a point of nocturnal same-sex male cruising. Professor Green is associate professor of history at California State University, Long Beach, and is currently the president of the Brazilian Studies Association.*

Pasquim *Editors*: Are you a homosexual?
Madame Satã: I always have been, and I always will be.[1]

𝒥n 1938 some of his friends convinced João Francisco dos Santos to enter the Fantasy Costume Contest during the Carnival Ball held at the Teatro República in downtown Rio de Janeiro. The event, promoted by the Carnival street group Caçadores de Veados (deer [or faggot] hunters), was an opportunity for homosexuals to dress up in fancy drag for Carnival revelry. Remembering the event many years later, João Francisco commented, "It was really a contest that attracted tourists from all parts of Brazil and foreign countries. Everyone applauded a lot, and the *bichas* (effeminate gay men) who participated won good prizes and got their photos in some newspapers and became famous."[2]

João Francisco created a sequined-decorated costume inspired by a bat from northeastern Brazil and won first prize— an Emerson radio and a rug wall hanging. Several weeks later, he was arrested with several other *bichas* while strolling in the Passeio Público, a downtown park where homosexuals cruised. When the booking officer at the police station asked all of the *bichas* to give their nicknames, João Francisco stated that he did not have one. He feared that the arresting officer would recognize him because he was constantly in and out of jail and give him a hard time. Indeed, the policeman remembered that he had seen João Francisco at the Fantasy Costume Contest during Carnival. Associating the costume with the principal actress in a recently released American film with the Brazilian title, *Madame Satã* (Madame Satan), that was having a successful run in Rio de Janeiro at the time, he inquired: "Weren't you the one who dressed as Madame Satã and won the *bichas'* contest at the República this year?" Unwittingly, the police officer had just rebaptized João Francisco.

As soon as the *bichas* arrested with João Francisco were released, the story spread throughout the city. The nickname stuck, although at first João Francisco was not sure he liked it: "I didn't want to have the nickname of a *bicha* because I thought it would be too much of an announcement of who I was, and I got into a lot of trouble. I even hit some of the first people who called me Madame Satã. But this only made things worse. . . . And so slowly I got used to it. Later, comparing my nickname to those of others, I saw that mine was much more beautiful. It was distinguished."[3]

HEROES AND MYTHS

Forty years later, in 1978, during the twilight years of the military regime that ruled Brazil from 1964 to 1985, small clusters of lesbian and gay activists invented a new social movement. They gathered in semiclandestine meetings, organized consciousness-raising groups, articulated tenuous links with the feminist and black-consciousness movements, and cautiously participated in mobilizations against the dictatorship. Over the last decade in Brazil a massive movement of lesbians, gay men, and transvestites has burst onto the political scene demanding same-sex domestic partner benefits, legal protections against discrimination based on sexual orientation, and an end to violence and murders. In June 1991 more than 200,000 people marched down Paulista avenue, the center of the country's financial district, for São Paulo's annual Gay Pride Parade. Currently, a plethora of web sites, myriad interest groups, and a visible, organized national movement challenge long-standing notions of homosexuality as immoral, indecent, and an inappropriate topic for polite conversation. No longer can politicians, comedians, and other public figures make gratuitous jokes about effeminate men or masculine women without running the risk of being denounced for their prejudiced and homophobic comments. A significant cultural transformation has taken place in Brazil.

Indicative of these changes has been an increase in intellectual and cultural production about homosexuality that treats the subject in a positive way. Academics in the fields of anthropology, literary studies, psychology, film studies, communications, and sociology are reexamining long-held stereotypes about people engaged in same-sex romantic and sexual relationships, rereading Brazilian fiction and poetry to uncover homoerotic subtexts, and "queering" interpretations of contemporary Brazilian culture and society. Research into the social history of homosexuality has lagged behind work in other disciplines, although scholars have begun to write the history of sodomites and transgressive women during the colonial times, and stories of *mulheres-homens* (women-men), *frescos* (faggots), and men and women who lived beyond heteronormativity in the late nineteenth and twentieth centuries.

Parallel to this scholarly attention to the social history of homosexuality has been the search by activists and academics alike for prominent figures who may have engaged in same-sex eroticism. The hunt for historical "homosexuals" is not unique to Brazil and reflects a moment in the history of national movements when discovering icons from the past plays a part in formulating contemporary lesbian and gay identities. Finding what are thought of as positive historical role models offers a link with previous generations, a sense of continuity, and a notion of the universal and transhistorical nature of homosexuality. If we are and have been everyone, so the logic goes, we have the right to equality and respect in the present. At times, scant documentation does not discourage imposing late twentieth-century sexual identities on women and men of the near or distant past.

One can readily point to prominent Brazilians such as writers João do Rio and Mário de Andrade, or singer Chico Alves, who all engaged in same-sex relations but shrouded their private affairs in mystery and secrecy, leaving historians with few clues with which to reconstruct this aspect of their personal lives. Ironically, the thousands of ordinary men and women who lived openly with people of the same sex remain "hidden from history" because until recently no one bothered to record or document their stories. There are noted exceptions. Some "infamous" homosexuals, who have engaged in their own self-promotion or have participated in the myth-making by others, have come to the fore as "emblematic" of self-affirming individuals.

This article examines one such figure, João Francisco dos Santos, popularly known as Madame Satã, and the ways in which he shaped his own identity and forged the myths that surrounded his own persona. In certain aspects, he was a representative of poor, lower-class *bichas* (still a pejorative expression for effeminate men who have sex with other men) who circulated in the social milieu of Bohemian Rio de Janeiro of the 1930 and 1940s. At the same time, Madame Satã confounded prevalent social stereotypes about those same *bichas*. He might have slipped into historical obscurity if he had not been resurrected by another generation of Carioca (resident of Rio de Janeiro city) Bohemians in the 1960s who promoted his image in the counterculture weekly newspaper, *Pasquim*. The dialogue between 1960s Bohemian intellectuals and the ambiguous and fluid self-identity of Madame Satã reveals an intriguing dialectical refashioning of his life narrative. More recently, Brazilian film director Karim Anöuz has reclaimed Madame Satã in his full-length cinematographic debut, *Madame Satã*, as larger than life, worthy of projection as a Brazilian mythic figure onto the international silver screen in a new incarnation.

BROTHELS, BARS, AND BOHEMIANS

Madame Satã was born João Francisco dos Santos on February 25, 1900, one of seventeen children, in the town of Glória do Goitá in the hinterlands of the northeastern state of Pernambuco. His mother, a descendant of slaves, came from a humble family. João Francisco's father, the result of a union between a former slave and a son of the local landed elite, died when João Francisco was seven. The next year, with seventeen mouths to feed, his mother swapped the boy to a horse trader in exchange for a mare. Within six months, João Francisco had managed to escape from this harsh apprenticeship by running away with a woman who offered him work as a helper in a boardinghouse she planned to set up in Rio de Janeiro. Madame Satã later summed up the change: "I stayed with her from 1908 to 1913, and the difference between Dona Felicidade and Lareano [the horse trader] is that I took care of the horses for him the whole day long and for her I washed dishes and cleaned the kitchen, carried the prepared meals and did the shopping at the São José market . . . It was a full day's work. I had no rest. I didn't earn anything. I didn't go to school, and I received no affection. I was a slave just the same without anything a child needs."[4]

At age thirteen, João Francisco left the boardinghouse to live on the streets and sleep on the steps of the tenement houses in the downtown Lapa neighborhood. For six years he worked at odd jobs in and around the neighborhood, earning a meager existence through menial chores ranging from carrying grocery bags from the market to selling pots and pans door to door. At age eighteen he was hired as a waiter at a brothel, Pensão Lapa. Madames of brothels commonly hired young homosexuals to work for them as waiters, cooks, housekeepers, and even as part-time prostitutes if a client so desired. Since many of these young men had taken on certain traditional feminine mannerisms, it was assumed that they could easily and efficiently perform domestic chores and live among prostitutes without creating sexual tension. Their marginalized, anomalously gendered identity comfortably coexisted with the *francesas* (French prostitutes), *polacas* (Eastern European Jewish prostitutes), and *mulatas* (women of mixed European and African descent) who worked at the many bordellos that operated in Lapa.

In the 1920s and 1930s the Lapa district of Rio de Janeiro was a crisscross of winding streets, one- and two-story buildings with their large portals opening onto a honeycomb of rooms and apartments, and corner bars where men gathered to drink beer and *cachaça*. In boardinghouses, tenement buildings, brothels, and rooms that could be rented by the hour, Lapa offered private spaces for intimate interactions, both heterosexual and homosexual. Lapa's bars and cabarets were also sites frequented by men who were looking for "fast" women and a good time as well as by those desirous of sex with other men. Public employees, journalists, middle-class professionals, Bohemian intellectuals, and adventurous young men from traditional families mixed freely with small-time crooks, thieves, gamblers, pimps, *bichas*, and whores. Literary figures from the modernist movement, artists, and rising stars in intellectual circles, such as Jorge Amado, Cândido Portinari, Sérgio Buarque de Holanda, and Mário de Andrade, came to the bars and cabarets of Lapa to mingle with important names in popular music—Noel Rosa, Cartola, Nelson do Cavaquinho, Chico Alves—and hear their latest compositions.

Amid the confusion of brothels, bars, and Bohemia, many poor Cariocas survived as hustlers, rogues, and thieves. The prototype petty crook or con man, known as the *malandro* (rogue), offered a gendered model of virility and cunning. With his slick, polished manner he radiated easy success, especially for young men of Afro-Brazilian origins who had been relegated to the margins of society in the aftermath of the abolition of slavery and the massive influx of Portuguese and other European immigrants to the Brazilian capital in the late nineteenth and early twentieth centuries. The *malandro's* masculinity was predicated not only on his skill at survival in a hostile environment, but also on his ability to project a image of sartorial style and sophistication that communicated an effortless access to money. An expensive white Panama hat, a silk shirt with rhinestone buttons, a white tie, and fingers covered with rings proclaimed success, even though it may have been the result of shady dealings. João Francisco himself defined a *malandro* as "a person who joined in the singing, frequented the bars and cabarets, did not run away from a fight, even when it is with the police, did not turn anyone in, respected others, and used a knife."[5] In Rio de Janeiro, where unemployment was high and poverty widespread among the lower classes, the *malandro* survived by gambling, hustling, pimping, stealing, composing samba songs, or running some small-time racket. His weapon, the knife, was ever ready to seal the fate of anyone who had offended his honor, cheated him in cards, or betrayed his trust.

BEACH BOHEMIA OF THE 1960S AND 1970S, MASCULINITY, AND MADAME SATÃ

When the freewheeling editors of *Pasquim* catapulted Madame Satã to countercultural cultdom through their 1971 collective interview with him, the aging Bohemian seemed to take special pleasure in fashioning his history to establish early credentials as an authentic Lapa *malandro*. At the time, a featured interview in *Pasquim* was the ticket to national fame, although not necessarily fortune. Indeed, Madame Satã died five years later of lung cancer, famous but penniless.

Pasquim, a weekly tabloid, was styled along the lines of the foreign underground youth publications of the 1960s that articulated the aspirations of a rebellious generation. It also reflected and promoted the hypermasculinized culture of "beach life, beer, and beautiful women" prevalent among middle- and upper-middle-class young men of the trendy Ipanema beach-front neighborhood in Rio's comfortable Zona Sur (southern zone). The satirical undercurrent in the publication, its sexualized humor, and its often direct and open criticism of the military regime subjected *Pasquim* to continual government censorship. The tabloid's coverage of cutting-edge Carioca culture and government harassment also won it a devoted nationwide readership that closely followed its columnists, cartoonists, and popular interviews with national and international figures. The self-styled Bohemian editors of *Pasquim* found a counterpart in Madame Satã, a remnant of 1930s Lapa who had survived the knife fights and bravado that had cut down most *malandros* of his generation. At seventy-one, Madame Satã remained a colorful figure with his white hair and dark skin that sharply contrasted with his bright silk shirts and flashy jewelry. He could still spin tales of cocaine consumption, cabarets, and casinos that revived the decaying Lapa district of the early 1970s in the imagination of Carioca Bohemian intellectuals and youth. *Pasquim*'s promotion of a link to a by-gone era of nightlife, prostitution, gambling, and the criminal underworld endowed its editors with additional Bohemian credentials through their association with Madame Satã. It also suggested that they shared insiders' knowledge of the history and culture of the Lapa of the 1930s. Madame Satã offered *Pasquim*'s corps of writers the opportunity to prove that even though they were privileged intellectuals of the Zona Sur, they nevertheless identified with and could easily communicate with Brazil's popular classes, or at least emblematic symbols of those classes.

There was, however, one glitch in Madame Satã's image that might clash with these purveyors of the Brazilian counterculture current in the 1960s. Madame Satã was a *bicha*, a faggot, a fairy, and did not mince words in referring to himself as such. *Pasquim* had an uneven track record when it came to dealing with homosexuality. The editors' use of sexual innuendoes, irreverent criticism of traditional middle-class conventions, and prolific display of photographs of semi-nude women placed them squarely among those Brazilian men whose anxiety about homosexuality led them to reaffirm their masculinity through pejorative jokes about effeminate men. *Pasquim*'s cartoons and columns were riddled with such allusions. To be fair, *Pasquim* did not always undercut coverage of overt transgressive sexual or gender behavior with negative commentary. The journal, for example, published several interviews with Rogéria, a Brazilian cross-dressing performer who made his way to the Parisian stage. In these interviews, the journalists effusively admired the beauty, grace, and talent of this international entertainer. Rogéria's performance as the epitome of femininity, however, merely reinforced traditional gender norms, and in this regard the conventional heterocentric and male-dominated discourse of the journal remained secure. On the other hand, *bichas*, as effeminate homosexuals who did not aspire to imitate beauty queens and screen stars, suffered harsh lampooning by *Pasquim*'s staff. In fact, *Pasquim* historian José Luiz Braga argues that the journal popularized the expression *bicha* throughout the country. The headline on the cover of one issue, for example, announced in large type: "TODO PAULISTA É BICHA" (All Paulistas Are Faggots). In small type squeezed in between the phrase "All Paulistas" and "Are Faggots" was the modifier, "who don't like women."[6] In an inside article, humorist Millôr Fernandes explained that sales of the journal had dropped, and so the editors had come up with the inflammatory banner to attract readers' attention.

At the time of the 1971 *Pasquim* interview of Madame Satã, the issue of masculinity and public performance was an essential component of the pervasive (and until recently hegemonic) notions of who was and was not considered a *bicha*. Since at least the late nineteenth century, if not earlier, Brazil's predominant gendered construction of homosexuality has been (and, to a great extent, remains) hierarchical and role-based. Men who engage in same-sex activities fall into two categories, the *homem* ("real" man) and the *bicha*. This binary opposition mirrors the dominant heterosexually defined gender categories of *homem* (man) and *mulher* (woman) in which the male is considered the "active" partner in a sexual encounter and the woman, in being penetrated, is "passive." As anthropologist Richard G. Parker has pointed out,

> The physical reality of the body itself thus divides the sexual universe in two. Perceived anatomical differences begin to be transformed, through language, into the hierarchically related categories of socially and culturally defined gender: into the classes of *masculino* (masculine) and *feminino* (feminine). . . . Building upon the perception of anatomical differences, it is this distinction between activity and passivity that most clearly structures Brazilian notions of masculinity and femininity and that has traditionally served as the organizing principle for a much wider world of sexual classifications in day-to-day Brazilian life.[7]

Thus, in same-sex activities, the *homem* takes the "active" role in the sexual act and anally penetrates his partner. The *bicha* is "passive" and is anally penetrated. His sexual "passivity" ascribes to him the socially inferior status of the "woman." While the sexually penetrated "passive" male is socially stigmatized, the male who assumes the public (and presumably private) role of the penetrating *homem* is much less so. As long as he maintains the sexual role attributed to a "real" man, he may engage in sex with other men with much less risk of losing social status.

VIRILE *BICHAS* AND THE DISRUPTION OF GENDER CODES

Why, then, did *Pasquim*'s editors embrace such a self-affirming *bicha* who readily admitted taking the passive role in same-sex activities? Why was Madame Satã's homosexuality worthy of respect while the journal consistently poked fun at effeminate men who did not totally embrace a traditional feminine performance? The answer lies in part in the way that Madame Satã constructed and recounted his life story, which deserves attention to understand how his self-narrative compelled sympathy among *Pasquim*'s writers as well as among its wider readership.

According to the 1971 *Pasquim* interview, the pivotal turn of events in Madame Satã's life was the 1928 shooting of a night patrolman who had offended his honor by calling him a *viado*. In the interview, Madame Satã then went on to assert that he had also been unjustly accused of killing the famous samba composer, Geraldo Pereira. *Pasquim*'s editors, fascinated by his criminal record, encouraged him to tell other tales of how he put up a fight, attacked policemen, and defended himself. Each additional story seemed to reconfirm his image as an audacious combatant who stood up to anyone who crossed his path. In Madame Satã's memoirs, as recounted to Sylvan Paezzo and published in a slim volume a year later, he retells with dramatic detail the same story of his murder of the night patrolman. The journalist is clearly speaking through the voice of João Francisco, creating details about what was going on in João Francisco's mind in 1928 during the incident that first sent him to jail.

In spite of his lasting image as a hard-hitting *malandro*, which was memorialized by *Pasquim*, on closer inspection the João Francisco of 1928 seems to have been a somewhat different person. That year he found employment as a cook's helper in another boardinghouse, where he met a young actress who enjoyed his imitations of other female stars. Through connections, she got him a job in a show at Praça Tiradentes, where many musical revues were staged. He had a small part where he sang and danced, wearing a red dress with his long hair falling down over his shoulders. One evening after the show João Francisco, according to his retelling of this epiphany in his life, returned to his room in Lapa. It was late at night, and on the way he decided to eat at the corner bar. While drinking *cachaça* and waiting for his meal, a local policeman came into the bar. Noticing João Francisco dressed in a fine silk shirt and stylish pants and sandals, the night patrolman confronted him aggressively. "*Viado*," he called out. João Francisco ignored this epithet, so the man repeated it. "Is it Carnival time, faggot?" Again there was no reply from João Francisco. "Well, is it or isn't it Carnival, faggot?" João Francisco remained silent, and so the officer approached him and shouted: "*Viado vagabundo*" (Shiftless faggot). "I just came from work," João Francisco finally replied. The night patrolman retorted: "Only if your work was getting fucked or robbing others." The name-calling escalated into an altercation. João Francisco went to his room nearby and returned with a gun.

"So the faggot has returned?" the night guard challenged. "Your mother!" shot back João Francisco. "I'll hit you for that," the guard threatened. "Try it," sneered João Francisco. "And you are going to sleep in the police station." "With your mother," answered João Francisco.[8] As they fought, João Francisco pulled his gun and shot the night patrolman dead. Sentenced to sixteen years in prison, he was released after serving two years based on an appeal that he had fired in self-defense. According to the Madame Satã of the 1970s, the incident and his time in jail launched him on his career as a *malandro*. His fame as a tough, no-nonsense cop killer enabled him to "protect" local bars for a fee when he was not serving time in prison for some major or minor offense.[9] His reputation also provoked many confrontations with the police, who hauled him into the precinct station more than once, allegedly in retaliation for the shooting of a fellow officer of the law. Between 1928 and 1965 he spent more than twenty-seven years in prison.

Although Madame Satã projected a tough-guy image, his assumed name undercut the traditional association of *malandro* with manliness. Rather, it evoked a mysterious, somewhat androgynous, and sinister figure. And it is precisely this violent and sinster persona that seems to have captured the imagination of the *Pasquim* journalists as they interviewed him in 1971. No limp-wristed fairy, no effeminate hairdresser, no artist of "questionable" sexual proclivities, the Madame Satã of mythic proportions was masculine, virile, and violent, as all *malandros* were supposed to be. Just as Rogéria gained the nod of *Pasquim's* editorial board and its avid national readership for being a model of femininity, even though he was biologically male, so, too, did this paragon of masculinity win approval from *Pasquim's* journalists because, even though he was a *bicha*, he represented the supposed raw masculinity of the criminal lower class. Madame Satã's homosexuality made him an intriguing figure, a *bicho raro* (strange beast) or, should we say, *bicha rara* (strange faggot), who defied the stereotypes and destabilized what was supposed to be the proper comportment of Brazilian homosexuals. His enigmatic mixture of the masculine and feminine seemed appealing to the editors of *Pasquim*, just as the immaculately constructed transvestite, male genitals intact, seems alluring to many Brazilian men who self-identify as heterosexual. Madame Satã's willingness to fight, thus affirming a virile masculinity on the streets, set him apart from other *bichas* and endeared him to his promoters at *Pasquim*.

The stories that Satã generated about his life in the early 1970s emphasize these indicators of masculinity, especially his ability to wield a knife and win a fight, two marks of a *malandro's* bravery and virility. The popular respect usually afforded a *malandro* was linked to his potency, masculinity, and willingness to die for his honor. However, Madame Satã also provoked the stereotype and caused anxiety, especially among the men who picked fights with him:

> They couldn't get used to my bravery because I was a known homosexual. They thought that they wouldn't lose [a fight] with me, and that is why they were always trying to provoke me and beat me up. On the other hand, the newspapers always emphasized my exploits precisely because I was a homosexual. What was I supposed to do? Become a coward just to satisfy these people? Let them do with me what they do to all of the other *bichas* who are beat up all the time and are arrested every week only because the police believed that *bichas* should be hit and should do the cleaning in the police stations? And for free. No, I couldn't go along with that vexatious situation. I thought that there was nothing wrong with being a *bicha*. I was one because I wanted to be, but that didn't make me any less a man because of it. And I became a *bicha* willingly; others did not force me.[10]

Madame Satã clearly identified as a *bicha*, a man who "performed" in bed as a woman: "I began my sex life at age thirteen when the women of Lapa organized bacchanals in which men, women, and *bichas* participated . . . I was invited to some and functioned as a man and as a *bicha*. I liked being a *bicha* more and that is why I became a *bicha*."[11] He not only identified with being a *bicha*, but he was also proud of it. It was common practice for the police in Rio de Janeiro and São Paulo to round up homosexuals in the downtown areas and detain them for several weeks so that they could be made to clean the precinct stations. Unlike other *bichas*, who would be routinely arrested for allegedly violating the Criminal Code's Article 282 (public assault on decency) or Article 399 (vagrancy) so that the police could force them to work as domestics at the stations, Madame Satã refused to submit to such humiliation and abuse. His rebellious attitude outraged the police and his enemies and made good copy in the press precisely because he did not conform to the standard stereotype of the homosexual.

Masculine bravado mixed with same-sex sexual behavior that undercut notions of "appropriate" homosexual comportment, however, explain only part of *Pasquim's* fascination with Madame Satã. Race cannot be ignored as an element in these journalists' interest in the black Bohemian as a living legacy of the 1930s. In the popular Brazilian imagination, a *malandro* is invariably of Afro-Brazilian descent. Dressed in the white suits, Panama hats, and brightly colored shirts that are essential to every Samba School parade, these men are associated with Afro-Brazilian festivities and traditions. *Malandros* with their petty criminal personas are thus conflated with Afro-Brazilians. Indeed, when criminologists studied homosexuality in Rio de Janeiro in the 1930s, one of the subtexts in their articles linked race to sexual transgression as well as pathological, even murderous behavior.[12] Febrônio Índio do Brasil, a man of mixed race accused of sexually molesting young boys and then murdering them, personified the dark, black, menacing pederast (a common term used in the period) who captured and raped children.

The figure of Febrônio lived on as a sort of bogeyman invoked by parents to discipline their children. Interestingly enough, in the 1971 *Pasquim* collective interview with Madame Satã, Sérgio Cabral repeated these adult-induced children's nightmares. But instead of referring to Febrônio, he links them to Madame Satã:

> *Sérgio*: Satã, tell me something: this story that you would take boys by force, is it true?
> *Satã*: It's something that I never did in my life because it was something that I didn't need to do. You must understand since you live a modern life that that is something that one doesn't need to use force [to do].
> *Sérgio*: Ever since I was a child I used to hear that when I passed through Lapa, they would say: "Be careful, Madame Sata is going to get you."
> *Satã*: Nonsense, I wasn't that kinky.[13]

Madame Satã, not Febrônio, becomes the bogeyman, the predator, ready to pounce and snatch away little white boys who misbehave. One cannot know if Sérgio Cabral's memory served him correctly. Perhaps in the 1940s, middle-class parents or residents of Lapa themselves (it is not clear which from the interview) associated the crimes of Febronio Índio do Brasil with the exploits of Madame Satã. Nevertheless, the dark and sinister image of this "bogeyman"—that is, his African origins— is the unstated, yet underlying metaphor that serves to engender trepidation in white middle-class children. Ironically, later in the same interview, when Madame Satã recalls the famous people he had known in the Lapa of the 1930s, he himself referred to Febrônio and repeated the legends surrounding his alleged murders of Carioca youth: "When he [Febrônio] committed those crimes he lived at 115 Gomes Freire avenue. He was a dentist. I got along really well with him. . . . It seems that he killed ten or twelve boys. He killed them, buried them, and then ate [or sexually penetrated] them until they rotted. When one rotted, he would kill another. He went to the Mental Hospital for the Criminally Insane."[14]

This mention of Febrônio Índio do Brasil in the interview may have been triggered by Sérgio Cabral's earlier reference to Madame Satã as a bogeyman, or simply another of his own tales about "the famous *malandros*, criminals, and celebrities whom I have known." Regardless, the fact that Madame Satã replicated the urban legend about the cannibalistic nature of Febrônio reveals the pervasiveness of the myths about the alleged murderer of little boys. Afro-Brazilians were not immune from believing stories that reinforced stereotypical ideas about the potentially "savage" aspects of their own beings.

In the early 1970s, *Pasquim* and Sylvan Paezzo were not the only journalists involved in circulating tales that presented Madame Satã as a powerhouse of manliness. In another story about him, one memorialist, remembering the Bohemian life of Lapa, portrayed Madame Satã as an indomitable superhero unwilling to submit to police control:

> It was said that five cars from the emergency unit went to Lapa just to arrest Madame Satã. The minute they saw him, one of the officers shouted: "Madame, get into the car and don't even scratch or you will take lead." To which he calmly replied: "You can have them send more cars. Five isn't enough to pick me up." And they had to ask for help and three more cars. And even then they had to tie him to a handcart in order to take him off to jail.[15]

Madame Satã's public display of virility, however, may not have been so masculine in his real day-to-day life on the streets of Rio de Janeiro in the periods between serving time in jail. In a 1946 court case when he was arrested for disorderly conduct after he had been refused entrance to a cabaret because he was improperly dressed, the police commissioner painted a detailed description:

> He is a person of above average height, rather robust and black; he dresses modestly and appears to be in good health. He is very well known in the jurisdiction of this police station, since he frequents the Lapa Plaza and its surroundings. He is a passive pederast; he shaves his eyebrows and adopts feminine ways, even altering his own voice. Nevertheless, he is an extremely dangerous person since he doesn't even respect the police authorities. He has no religion. He smokes, gambles, and gets drunk. His education is rudimentary. He is single and has no progeny. He is always seen with pederasts, prostitutes, and other people of low social status.[16]

While Madame Satã did not wear rice powder makeup and rouge like so many other *bichas* in the 1930s and 1940s, he did arch his eyebrows. And, although the police commissioner was wrong about his gambling habits, he did note Madame Satã's identification with the street life of Carioca "queens," as he could easily slip in and out of their banter with his "altered" voice. Yet it was his capacity for violence, in spite of his feminine demeanor, and his projection as a dangerous criminal that caught the attention of Lapa memorialists, police commissioners, and the journalists of *Pasquim*. In the second article about Madame Satã that appeared in the pages of *Pasquim* soon after his death, his obituary prominently listed his criminal record from the Instituto Felix Pacheco:

27 years and 8 months in prison
13 counts of aggravated assault (Article 129 of the Criminal Code)
4 counts of resisting arrest (Article 329)
2 counts of receiving stolen goods (Article 180)
1 count of public indecency (Article 233)
1 count of illegal arms possession (Article 19)[17]

Ultimately, his legacy seemed to be a roster of crimes committed and a willingness to fight back against police and those who called him a faggot—the latter being a laudable trait if one looked to the international gay and lesbian movement as a new political response to the homophobia that Madame Satã combated with his fist, a knife, or a gun.

Pasquim's editors, however, showed no such facile predisposition toward the emerging gay liberation movement when it touched ground in Brazil. In 1977, Winston Leyland, the editor of the San Francisco-based publication *Gay Sunshine*, visited Brazil as part of a continental tour in search of material for an anthology on Latin American literature. A friend, João Antônio Mascarenhas, organized an interview with *Pasquim* where one of the journal's best-known cartoonists joined several gay intellectuals in interviewing Leyland. The interview turned into an interesting debate about whether Brazilian gays suffered social discrimination or if economic disparity was the country's principal problem. The issue's cover and inside cartoons, however, reproduced all of the pervasive stereotypes that confused gay men with transvestites and linked Nazism to homosexuality. This journalist's projection in the country's leading alternative newspaper was to be expected. *Pasquim*'s writers held nothing sacred in their humorous attacks on middle-class Brazilian life, politics, and the military, but homosexuals and early feminists, such as Betty Friedan, who visited Brazil in 1971, were easy targets for this haven of countercultural male chauvinists. Although *Pasquim* remained a symbol for criticism of the social status quo, the journal only reluctantly changed its coverage after the feminist and gay movements had marked their place on the cultural and political landscape in the late 1970s.

COOL, QUEER, AND BEYOND

The internationalization of U.S.- and European-generated gay culture in the last decade has contributed to the reshaping of Brazilian sexual identities and comportment. Whereas twenty years ago the only hypermasculine men on the stretches of Copacabana's and Ipanema's beaches where gay men congregated were a handful of hustlers and body-builders, today pumped-up muscled "Barbies" proliferate. After all, so the joke goes, "Isn't a perfect Barbie doll body all a 'girl' ever wanted?" Gay macho—masculine, stylish, and cool—predicated on middle-class consumption has become a norm, peddled in soft-porn publications and more high-brow printed endeavors alike. Although most Brazilian gay men are far from having the resources to acquire the sartorial and other accoutrements linked to this sexual lifestyle that reaches far beyond the bed, a new standard of performative masculinity is creeping toward a norm in the country's largest urban centers.

Concurrently with the masculinization of the self-image of many gay men has been the emergence of a curious new term to describe the ubiquitous nature of the hip-gay lifestyles of Rio and São Paulo. Bars, restaurants, and other public spaces frequented by gay men and lesbians have been redubbed GLS (*gay, lésbica e simpatizantes*). The third term in this trilogy is a play on words that refers to the supporter of a political party or cause. The expression, used at times to reflect a proliferation of commercial venues where gays and lesbians are welcome, also implies a category of people who, while not having intercourse with someone of the same sex, remain comfortable in their company. Still others use the term GLS to imply a new identity that goes beyond the categories of heterosexual and homosexual, gay or straight. "GLS" is even the title of an ongoing column in *Folha de São Paulo*, Brazil's largest circulating news-paper, that reports on gossip, events, and politics of interest to the gay consumer culture. Although GLS can encompass those who are not *praticantes* (practitioners), it has not taken on the significance that the word "queer" has assumed in the United States. That expression is itself loaded with multiple meanings when employed by literary critics and political activists. One would imagine that Madame Satã, who defied easy classification as he revealed himself to the editors of *Pasquim* in the early 1970s, would fit nicely into the post-identitarian politics promoted by proponents of queer theory.

Part of the power of the persona that Madame Satã projected onto Rio's self-styled Bohemian intellectuals of the 1960s and 1970s was the way in which it did not neatly fit into either category of *bicha* or *homem*. Madame Satã seemed to be both, and for the macho beach culture of *Pasquim* and its devotees, his masculine potency as a fighting *malandro* in some way made him a safe and sympathetic figure. Although his some-what allusive gendered behavior unsettled neat notions of what was appropriate for a *malandro* and made him queer in the sense of being strange or different, as well as someone who defied easy typecasting, Madame

Satã's masculine bravado, or at least the myths about it, kept him within the comfortable framework of traditional gendered roles.

The influence of U.S. and European gay culture in present-day Brazil has been one of many factors that have strengthened the consolidation of gay identities as fixed sexual and social constructions among many activists and the hundreds of thousands more who interact in ever widening realms of "gay culture." Within Brazil's urban gay milieu, some intellectuals argue for a post-gay and post-identitarian way of thinking about same-sex eroticism. It seems possible that the international release of Karim Anöuz's film version of the life of Madame Satã will encourage resurgence of an interest in the black "queen" of Carioca Bohemia and the ways in which his ambiguities have resonance today.

NOTES

1. Sérgio Cabral et al., "Madame Satã," *Pasquim* (Rio de Janeiro) 95 (April 29–May 5, 1971): 7.

2. Sylvan Paezzo, *Memórias de Madame Satã: Conforme narração a Sylvan Paezzo* (Rio de Janeiro: Lidador, 1972), 59.

3. Ibid., 64.

4. Elmar Machado, "Madame Satã para o *Pasquim*: 'Enquanto eu viver, a Lapa viverá,' " *Pasquim* 7:357 (April 30, 1976): 9.

5. Paezzo, *Memórias de Madame Satã*, 17.

6. A *paulista* is a native of the state of São Paulo. "Todo paulista que não gosta de mulher é bicha," *Pasquim* 3:105 (July 8, 1971): 3.

7. Richard G. Parker, *Bodies, Pleasures, and Passions: Sexual Culture in Contempo rary Brazil* (Boston: Beacon Press, 1991), 41.

8. Paezzo, *Memórias de Madame Satã*, 23–26. I have reduced Paezzo's retelling of this event without modifying the essence of the exchange between João Francisco and the night patrolman. Paezzo himself recreated the incident from interviews he conducted with Satã in preparing his book. I have also changed the spelling of *veado* to *viado* to reflect the popular use of the term.

9. Antônio Correa Dias, former owner of Colosso Café, where Satã spent much of his time, insisted that while Satã kept order in the bars he frequented, he did not extort protection money and insisted on paying his bills. Machado, "Madame Satã," 9. However, Satã himself admitted that he protected bars. "I gave protection to the bars and had a lot of money, and a lot of them [boys] were after me because they knew that if they were with me they would be with a king." Cabral et al., "Madame Satã," 3.

10. Paezzo, *Memórias de Madame Satã*, 115–16.

11. Ibid., 116.

12. James N. Green, *Beyond Carnival: Male Homosexuality in Twentieth-Century Brazil* (Chicago: University of Chicago Press), 121–26.

13. Cabral et al., "Madame Satã," 3.

14. Nestor de Holanda, *Memórias do Café Nice: Subterrâneos de música popular e da vida boêmia do Rio de Janeiro* (Rio de Janeiro: Conquista, 1970), 171.

15. Ibid.

16. Cabral et al., "Madame Satã," 3.

17. Machado, "Madame Satã," 6.

SOURCES

Most of the information about and citations of Madame Satã and his contemporaries comes from four sources in Portuguese: Sylvan Paezzo, *Memórias de Madame Satã: Conforme narração a Sylvan Paezzo* (Lidador, 1972); Sérgio Cabral et al., "Madame Satã," *Pasquim* (Rio de Janeiro) 95 (April 29–May 5, 1971); Rogério Durst, *Madame Satã: Com o diabo no corpo* (Brasiliense, 1985); and Elmar Machado, "Madame Satã para o *Pasquim*: 'Enquanto eu viver, a Lapa viverá,' " *Pasquim* 357 (April 30, 1976). I also consulted Madame Satã's arrest and trial records from the 1940s in Rio's Arquivo Nacional; see, for example: Processo no. 6262, Delito 29/10/46, 14º Vara Criminal; Processo no. 2230, Delito 04/12/48, 15º Vara Criminal; and Processo no. 481, Delito 24/09/49. I thank Karim Aïnouz for sharing these trial documents with me.

SUGGESTED READINGS

On the emergence of homosexual identity and politics, see James N. Green, *Beyond Carnival: Male Homosexuality in Twentieth-Century Brazil* (University of Chicago Press, 1999). For a more focused history of Brazilian gay and lesbian movements, see James N. Green, "More Love and More Desire: The Building of the Brazilian Movement," in *The Global Emergence of Gay and Lesbian Politics: National Imprints of a Worldwide Movement*, ed. Barry Adam, Jan Willem Duyvendak, and André Krouwel (Temple University Press, 1998), 91–109. On violence against homosexuals, see Luiz Roberto Mott, *Epidemic of Hate: Violations of the Human Rights of Gay Men, Lesbians, and Transvestites in Brazil* (Grupo Gay da Bahia/International Gay and Lesbian Human Rights Commission, 1996). On the vicissitudes of sexual identity, history, and politics, see James N. Green, "Challenging National Heroes and Myths: Male Homosexuality and Brazilian History," *Estudios Interdisciplinarios de América Latina y el Caribe* 11:2 (June 2001). On sexual positions and gender identity, see Richard G. Parker, *Bodies, Pleasures, and Passions: Sexual Culture in Contemporary Brazil* (Beacon Press, 1991); Peter Fry, *Para inglês ver: Identidade e política na cultura brasileira* (Zahar, 1982); and Michel Misse, *O estigma do passivo sexual: Um símbolo de estigma no discurso cotidiano* (Achiamé, 1979).

On representations of the Brazilian transvestite, see Fernanda Farias de Albuquerque and Maruizio Jannelli, *A princesa*, trans. Elisa Byington (Nova

Fronteira, 1995); Don Kulick, *Travesti: Sex, Gender, and Culture among Brazilian Transgendered Prostitutes* (University of Chicago Press, 1998); Hélio R. S. Silva, *Travesti: A invenção do feminino* (Relume Dumará, 1993); and Andrea Cornwall, "Gendered Identities and Gender Ambiguity among *Travestis* in Salvador, Brazil," in *Dislocating Masculinity: Comparative Ethnographies*, ed. Andrea Cornwall and Nancy Lindisfarne (London: Routledge, 1994), 111–32. For references to *mulheres-homens*, see Sueann Caulfield, "Getting into Trouble: Dishonest Women, Modern Girls, and Women-Men in the Conceptual Language of *Vida Policial*, 1925–1927," *Signs: Journal of Women in Culture and Society* 19:11 (Autumn 1993): 146–76. For an analysis of the publication *Pasquim*, see José Luiz Braga, *O Pasquim e os anos 70: Mais pra epa que para oba* (Editora Universidade de Brasília, 1991). For the interview with San Francisco's *Gay Sunshine* editor, see "Os gays estão se conscientizando—Entrevista com Winston Leyland," *Pasquim* 436 (November 4–10, 1977). Keep an eye out for the forthcoming biographical film "Madame Satã," directed by Karim Aïnouz. On the history of Lapa, see Luís Martins, *Noturno da Lapa* (Editora Brasileira, 1964); and Hernâni de Irajá, *Adeus! Lapa* (Gráfica Récord Editora, 1967).

CHAPTER 15

ℳario Juruna

Brazil's First Indigenous Congressman

Seth Garfield

It is fitting that this volume's final chapter returns to consider Brazil's aboriginal inhabitants and how they responded to the dizzying change of contemporary times. It would be hard to invent a more revealing example of the diversity of Brazil's population, land, environment, and culture than Mario Juruna, a Xavante (pronounced Sha-von'-teh) hunter-gatherer who went on to became a federal congressman in 1982. In Chapter 6 of this volume, the reader learned about Cândido Rondon, the army officer who championed the establishment of the Indian Protection Service at the turn of the twentieth century and who advocated contacting and peacefully assimilating Brazil's Indians into the national culture. What remains less clear in the preceding vignettes is how indigenous peoples themselves responded to these efforts by agents of the federal government and others. Frontier landowners and developers resented outside interference in local disputes with native peoples, and government agencies were often too weak or too corrupt to provide meaningful protection to Indians. For most of the 1900s, Mario's village of Xavante Indians preferred to pursue a strategy of isolating themselves from white Brazilians. They and other Xavante sometimes violently attacked whites who made forays into their territory or made peaceful attempts to contact them, and they earned a reputation for fierceness that for a time worked to ward off settlement near their territory. As Professor Seth Garfield shows, this strategy of resistance had become untenable for Mario and his fellow villagers by 1958, when they sought protection on a frontier Catholic mission in Mato Grosso from the attacks of settlers.

Mario had been raised to adulthood as a hunter and warrior according to the traditions of the Xavante, but then missionaries attempted to acculturate him to Brazilian society. The missionaries' attitudes about the cultural assimilation of Indians (except for the religious factor) shared many similarities with those advocated by General Rondon. In the second half of the twentieth century, however, homogenizing models of national cultural assimilation policies came under increasing attack in the West. What many have come to refer to as a "multicultural" model for national communities that favored greater tolerance of and respect for cultural differences and rights began to arise out of the ashes of the ethnic and racial intolerance

*that fueled genocidal violence during World War II. Mario would take
full advantage of these shifting attitudes.*

*As a young man, Mario perceived the need to ally the interests of his
village and indigenous peoples more generally with powerful whites to maxi-
mize their chances for survival. He became a masterful strategist at playing Church and government officials against one another and at using the
media and foreign organizations to pressure officials to better protect and
provide for its indigenous citizens. He even used the nationalist myths
developed by Brazilian intellectuals in the 1800s to chastise the government for its neglect and abuse of the "true" Brazilians or those peoples who
had first inhabited the sacred national territory. Mario developed hybrid
strategies that combined his Xavante traditions with what he knew of
modern culture and technology to become a political activist. He then parlayed his celebrity into a successful political career representing not his home
state of Mato Grosso but one of Brazil's most developed industrial coastal
states, Rio de Janeiro. Mario and his political allies played on popular
perceptions of Indians as noble savages incapable of the deceptions commonly practiced by white politicians, but, as Professor Garfield shows, he
too was human, not a stereotype.*

*Seth Garfield is assistant professor of history at the University of Texas
at Austin. His biography of Mario Juruna originated in his broader research on the Xavante Indians found in* Indigenous Struggle at the
Heart of Brazil: State Policy, Frontier Expansion, and the Xavante
Indians, 1937–1988 *(2001). His current focus is on the* "soldados de
borracha" *(soldiers of rubber), or workers sent to the Amazon region to
tap rubber trees during the World War II era.*

In 1958, when he was just about seventeen—an age when many middle-
class Brazilians were first entering college—Mario Juruna, a Xavante
Indian from central Brazil, was facing a far greater form of culture shock.
After nearly a century of autonomous rule and unmitigated hostility toward outsiders, his community, battered by settlers' attacks, had been
compelled to leave their ancestral land and seek assistance from Salesian
missionaries. Like other young Xavante men, Mario had been well trained
by village elders in the art of hunting and warfare. Indeed, it was the
mastery of the former that had allowed Xavante communities to subsist
on the abundant wild game that thrived in the *cerrado*, or tropical savanna, of central Brazil, while expertise in the latter kept covetous ranchers
and homesteaders at bay and earned the Indians a fearsome reputation.

These defenses were no longer adequate. As white settlement increased on the western frontier in the 1950s, and land values along with
land speculation increased, Mario's village, and perhaps a dozen other
Xavante villages in the region between the Culuene and Couto Magalhães

rivers in the central-western state of Mato Grosso, came increasingly under siege. Indians were murdered by armed bands, houses were burned down, poisoned meat was offered to famished Xavante refugees, and, in an act of biological warfare, ranchers deposited contaminated clothing to infect Indian communities lacking immunity from diseases. A local rancher who took pity on the Indians shepherded Mario's village to safety hundreds of miles away to the south at a mission run by the Salesians in Merure, Mato Grosso.

The Catholic mission, along with its longtime residents, the Bororo Indians, had once been a target of raids by the semi-nomadic Xavante, who had roamed the countryside to hunt and gather food. But now, in a trail of tears, the Xavante had been forced to seek refuge among the Salesians, whose "kindness," to be sure, had been secured at the expense of subordination and suppression of indigenous lifestyles. And so a bewildered and besieged Mario had entered that day a different type of "school," one in which his "teachers" sought, through both persuasion and force, to eradicate "objectionable" cultural mores; to instill in the Indians "proper" notions of sexual morality; to teach the Indians the meaning of "work"; to instruct them in Portuguese and civics lessons; and, of course, to save their souls from the "devil." How strange or intriguing must have seemed these white lifestyles, and how frustrating their stringent rules and regulations to a people proud of their own cultural traditions and embittered by a history of persecution.

Slightly less than one-quarter of a century later, Mario Juruna, who had not been one of the Salesians' most diligent or cooperative students, was only semi conversant in Portuguese and failed to fully acquire literacy in either Portuguese or the Xavante language. Yet he had attained through observation, determination, and ingenuity a savvy understanding of power dynamics in Brazilian society and the importance of political mobilization to secure the rights and entitlements of indigenous communities. In fact, he had achieved a national and international renown that few of his college-educated peers would ever know: in 1982, he was elected to Brazil's national congress, the first and only indigenous person in that country ever to achieve such an honor. Two years earlier, he had symbolically presided over an international tribunal in Rotterdam, Holland, in which the Brazilian government was put on trial for its violations of the rights of indigenous peoples. Mario Juruna, in more ways than one, had come a long way.

How did this Xavante man find the wherewithal to challenge the policies of the Brazilian government, then under the iron-fisted control of the armed forces? How did a member of a small ethnic minority—from an indigenous group numbering only several thousand in a nation of more than one hundred million—summon the courage to denounce abuses perpetrated by the government's Indian agency? How did this onetime hunter-gatherer—who knew little of "Brazil" for much of the youth that he spent trekking in the thickets of the Mato Grosso savanna— find himself in the national and international spotlight? And why did his star fade less than a decade later?

To unravel this mystery, we must analyze the radical transformations triggered by the process of western frontier expansion in twentieth-century Brazil. This process was marked by much of the violence, inter-ethnic conflict, territorial usurpation, and consolidation of state power that occurred in the American West; but in Brazil, western frontier ex-pansion took place nearly a century later, in an age of mass media, high-speed technology, international human rights movements, and worldwide decolonization. Therefore, we need to explore the ways in which indig-enous peoples in Brazil, victimized by the shocking assault on their com-munities, lands, and ancestral traditions, have struggled to defend their rights in the national and international arenas and to clamor for cultural respect. To understand Juruna's career, we must explore the larger state policies that shaped the life of an indigenous leader and his people; the political dynamics within Xavante villages through which such dramatic changes were filtered and engaged; and the efforts of one individual— however constrained by overwhelming historical circumstances—to re-shape the world around him, armed with both traditional tactics and the legal defenses and political opportunities provided by Brazilian society. The story of Mario Juruna's transformation from hunter-gatherer to political leader is rather unique: few Brazilians, irrespective of ethnic background, become national political figures. Yet the larger trends that fueled and that are reflected in Juruna's dramatic personal trajectory— the political mobilization of indigenous leaders to defend their commu-nities against territorial loss and social marginalization—characterize the experience of many leaders of Brazil's nearly 180 different indigenous groups.

In 1940, around the time that Mario was born, Brazil was led by Getúlio Vargas, a nationalist dictator who sought to transform the pre-dominantly rural, agro-exporting nation into a modern, independent, industrial power. Vargas had inherited a nation riven by sharp socioeco-nomic and regional disparities—a nation in which many residents of the backlands, such as Juruna and his people, had little or no contact with the market or ties to the state. Indeed, the lopsided nature of Brazil's socioeconomic development and demographic profile gravely concerned Vargas, his military supporters, and nationalist ideologues. Despite Brazil's immense national territory—larger than that of the continental United States—over 90 percent of its population cleaved to the coastal regions, with the other 10 percent dispersed over the remaining two-thirds of the country. The state of Mato Grosso (home to the Xavante) and the entire region of the central-west (home to numerous other indigenous peoples) was one such sparsely populated area whose purportedly untold economic potential beckoned to state planners. After all, government officials reasoned, why should Brazil fail to make use of the legendary mines, extensive land, and abundant natural resources in its heartland? Why not allocate "unoccupied" frontier land to small farmers who were denied such access under Brazil's grossly inequitable pattern of land distribution, thereby ensuring cheaper food for the rapidly growing urban populations? How could a modern nation, military officers clamored, allow its vast hinterland to remain a backwater and its international borders unfortified? Should not the Brazilian nation-state contact and assimilate indigenous populations and convert these "noble" but "primitive" peoples into full-blooded Brazilian citizens?

Thus, under Vargas's dictatorship (1937–1945), western expansion became a nationalist crusade planned, funded, and propagandized by the state and ceremoniously christened the "March to the West." The regime organized an expedition to penetrate the backlands of Mato Grosso through the Xingu region of the Amazon and entrusted the team members with constructing roads and airstrips for future transportation and settlement. Vargas endorsed the creation of agrarian colonies in the west, where the poor would be resettled on cooperatives. Indigenous populations would be converted into small farmers and regimented rural laborers working on their small reservations, whose demarcation was mandated by the federal constitution.

Vargas officials accorded both a protective mission to the state and a special role to indigenous peoples in the process of western frontier expansion that, incidentally, they often contrasted with the belligerent tactics of the U.S. government in its conquest of the West. Indigenous peoples were to be treated with benevolence, faithfully instructed in agricultural cultivation and animal husbandry, and, due to their legal status as minors and wards of the state, fully safeguarded by the Indian Protection Service. State officials proclaimed that this was a debt owed to the indigenous population, who had assisted the early Portuguese settlers in colonizing Brazil and whose biological and cultural contributions accounted for the nation's grandeur. As Cândido Rondon, director of the state's National Council for the Protection of Indians, stated in a speech in 1940, "Of all the precious things that befall us in this new march to the West, all relevant to the greatness of Brazil, none surpasses the Indian." For, as Rondon asserted, "they have given us the base of our national character: resistance, bravery, generosity, and modesty, contributed by the Indian to the formation of our people, is what we consider precious, as much in the past as it still is in the present."[1]

The Vargas regime did not invent these stereotypes. The image of the "noble savage"—the inherently peaceful, benevolent, and persevering Native American—dates back to the earliest accounts produced by Europeans following their encounter with the New World. Of course, Europeans and their descendants in Brazil and other regions of the Americas also harbored a countervailing image of the bloodthirsty, sanguinary, barbaric Indian—an image that often served to justify genocidal warfare against Native Americans. Thus, it is significant (if not entirely original) that the ideologues of the Vargas regime embraced the former tradition, disseminating a "kinder"—if not necessarily wholly accurate—image of native peoples. Indeed, Vargas's touting of the indigenous contribution to the nation's biocultural makeup conformed to the larger ideological directives of his populist-nationalist regime, which celebrated the importance of racial mixture (*mestiçagem*) and racial democracy as a hallmark of Brazilian exceptionalism. In 1943 he decreed April 19 the "Day of the Indian," a national civic commemoration in which all Brazilians were to pay homage to the nation's aboriginal inhabitants (and, of course, to the benevolent state that protected them). Through the radio, newspapers, and other forms of mass media, Vargas sought to beam his nationalist message to far-flung corners of the country.

Mario Juruna was about three years old when expeditionaries from the March to the West resolved to tramp through as well as fly over his people's ancestral homeland in northern Mato Grosso. Juruna's family did not own a radio, or clothing, for that matter; they had never heard of Vargas or Rondon, nor did they probably care to; and their attitude toward their non-Xavante Brazilian brethren (whom they referred to as *waradzu*) was about as brotherly as Cain's toward Abel. The Xavante correctly understood that even if outsiders might be able to provide steadier access to industrial goods (some of which appealed to the Indians on utilitarian grounds), the tradeoff was far too great: drastic reduction in their access to the plant foods and wild game of the *cerrado* that assured their nutritional mainstay, the curtailment of their political and cultural autonomy, and the spread of devastating diseases. Brazilian officials—who never really moved beyond their romanticized or condescending notions to comprehend or value the complexity of indigenous peoples' social structures, political economies, and historical memories—tended to dismiss any resistance to assimilation as naiveté or childish stubbornness. Indeed, by law, indigenous peoples were defined as "relatively incapable" in civil matters (as were married women and minors), and were assigned to the guardianship of the Indian Protection Service to shield them from fraud, abuse, and exploitation.

Within Xavante society, which was structured by a strict division of labor based on gender and age, members of each hierarchically ordered age-set were considered supremely capable in their specific tasks and responsibilities. Villagers pooled labor and shared natural resources and knowledge to ensure successful mastery over the forbidding natural environment; goods were bartered and acquisitiveness repudiated. Moreover, unlike Brazil itself, Xavante society was not ruled by a dictator, but rather governed by a council comprised of all elder men, who met each night to discuss and plan community affairs. Yet Xavante villages were not the communitarian utopias celebrated by government ideologues and romantic intellectuals. Instead, they were settlements prone to constant rifts and reconfigurations and racked by factionalism and warfare. These feuds stemmed from accusations of sorcery (which usually arose in the aftermath of the death of an individual and were levelled by one male against a male of an opposing faction), competition over natural resources (and, increasingly, access to western goods), and historical grudges and vendettas. Xavante "chiefs" were more accurately leaders of factions, and since various factions existed within a single village, at any time several chiefs might vie for power. In short, Xavante society was sociopolitically complex and defied the simple stereotypes of Brazilian officials.

To be sure, the Xavante had not made it easy for the Vargas regime during the March to the West. In 1941, six members of the Indian Protection Service were bludgeoned to death by Xavante warriors in an abortive attempt to achieve peaceful contact with the Indians. Five years later, the government did succeed in "pacifying" one Xavante village, an episode celebrated with great hoopla and media coverage. Nevertheless, because Xavante society lacked political centralization, with villages vying with each other for resources and prizing their autonomy, other villages did not immediately follow suit. Juruna's community, living farther to the west of the territory traversed by government officials, resisted peaceful contact with *waradzu* for more than a decade. Yet although they withstood submission to state control longer than their fellow Xavante to the east, the ultimate fate of Juruna's community was far more traumatic. Although the Indian Protection Service was enjoined to secure the protection of indigenous communities within their ancestral territories, such assistance often failed to materialize because of inadequate state funding, overburdened bureaucracies, opposition from local elites, and resistance from uncontacted Indians. The booming real estate market in Mato Grosso, for example, offered tremendous personal and political advantages to local state officials, who were wont to violate federal laws protecting indigenous territory. Consequently, as settlers, ranchers, and land surveyors intensified their onslaught on indigenous villages, encroached upon their land, and depleted their supply of wild game, Juruna's community could not count on the support of the Indian Protection Service. Their only recourse was to abandon their traditional territory and seek the assistance of the Salesian missionaries.

The Xavante stayed only briefly at the mission at Merure as constant friction with the resident Bororo Indians proved unbearable, and the Salesians resolved to create another mission for the Xavante nearby at São Marcos. Pedro Sbardelotto, an Italian Salesian who helped to establish the new mission, was met by a brutal attack by a local landowner, who sought to indicate, in no uncertain terms, that neither the missionaries nor their indigenous charges were welcome in the region. Sbardelotto survived, and the Xavante remained at São Marcos, but the conflict did not bode well for the Xavante's future relations with their neighbors.

While at São Marcos, Juruna would witness the dramatic changes that befell his people. A measles epidemic killed a great number of children as well as adults at the mission. Whooping cough and pneumonia also took the lives of many Xavante children, with an apparent overall rise in infant mortality after contact. Various visitors to the missions noted the Indians' dependence on the Salesians for medicine and health care; as one noted, "The Indians appreciate our medicines a lot, including the application of injections, even faking being sick just to take injections."[2] In fact, the geographic dispersal historically practiced by Xavante communities probably served as a better strategy to deal with infectious diseases, but now with settlement at the mission and limited mobility, such options were untenable.

Salesian accounts emphasize the great personal sacrifices that the missionaries endured in their efforts to redeem the Xavante, including a fatal attack by the Indians in 1934 that claimed the lives of two priests. Undoubtedly, missionaries (as well as Indian Protection Service officials) who toiled in rural Mato Grosso amid a contrary indigenous group did not live in the lap of luxury or comfort. Yet it is also undeniable that they exploited the Indians' enforced dependence to engineer drastic socioeconomic and cultural changes within the Xavante community. Missionaries insisted that such "improvements" were necessary to groom diligent workers, loyal citizens, and good Christians, although they, like government officials, rarely consulted the Indians.

The Salesians separated Xavante children from their families and placed them in a mission-run boarding school, or *internato*, where they were taught Portuguese, Latin for the liturgy, and civics. Xavante girls were trained in domestic service, sewing, and animal husbandry, while boys were apprenticed as carpenters, shoemakers, machine operators, and agriculturalists. Indian youths were discouraged from accompanying elders on hunting and gathering treks, a position that directly challenged the subsistence strategies and age-based hierarchies that had historically ordered Xavante society. To acclimate the Indians to their future lives as rural workers and market consumers, the Salesians instituted a remunerative system under which Xavante men and women received vouchers of various colors that corresponded to the value of the services they had performed. Thus, for, say, tending to the mission's orchard, an Indian received a piece of yellow scrip which he or she could redeem at the mission store for goods (fishing hooks, hunting supplies, sewing equipment) or cooking supplies (salt, sugar, oil) on which the Xavante had become increasingly reliant. In 1966 a government official who visited the Salesian mission marveled, "The work carried out by the Xavante with the assistance of the missionaries is really notable: large plots planted, a brickyard, diverse wooden buildings. All demonstrate work, order, and the spirit of organization."[3] While the missionaries took credit for transforming the Indians more fully into agriculturalists and regimented laborers, they also noted that such compliance stemmed from "insufficient [land] for hunting, fishing, and gathering of wild fruits."[4]

In the cultural and religious realm, the Xavante also faced constant surveillance and restrictions, which led to the suppression or alteration of traditional beliefs and practices. Indigenous sexual mores, such as polygyny, for example, which had been a prerogative of elder men, suffered clerical condemnation. Whereas prior to contact, Xavante women went about naked and adult men covered themselves only with a penis sheath, missionaries clothed the Indians and sought to inculcate Christian notions of shame and modesty. Clearly, religious indoctrination, educational training, and labor discipline all served to constrain communal ceremonies and endeavors that required broader participation.

External signs of religious observance or social compliance did not necessarily entail abject submission to missionary hegemony. As the Indians struggled to temper the sociocultural effects of enforced dependence, they engaged in various acts of defiance: malingering, dissembling, working sloppily or contrarily, and relocating. For example, one visitor noted that notwithstanding the Salesian efforts to convey proper notions of modesty, "When far from the priests, in the natural life of the village, men and women do not use, in general, even feathers as a covering. They go about entirely naked."[5] The Xavante, moreover, retained their age-set system, exogamous marriage patterns, communal institutions, and numerous rituals. Through these ceremonies, the Indians fostered a sense of cultural resilience in the midst of such wrenching historical change. Because certain communal ceremonies apparently bore little connection to theistic beliefs, they did not clash head-on with missionary doctrine.

Xavante testimonies and life stories display a great deal of ambivalence toward the Salesians. Among the converted, the Salesians represented divine messengers who redeemed the Indians from a life of darkness and sin and blessed them with the eternal grace of Jesus Christ. Even among the less zealous, many Xavante recognized the historic refuge that the Salesians provided, the ongoing medical care, the valuable apprenticeship that trained them in the ways of civilization, and the more modern amenities that the mission offered in comparison to the state-run Indian posts. Indeed, the Xavante undoubtedly saw that their physical and cultural survival no longer depended on martial prowess but rather on new skills—acquisition of Portuguese, apprehension of legal rights, understanding of Brazil's political and socioeconomic system, and alliances with sympathetic *waradzu*. They recognized that the Salesians could offer such remedies, however painful and disagreeable the dose.

Critics, however, recount with great bitterness the heavy-handed methods employed by the missionaries. Physical abuse of Xavante children, a practice unheard of among the Indians, was used to discipline supposedly uncooperative or wayward students. Other Xavante resented the missionaries' exploitation of their labor, the mission-run "company store" that drained their "wages," and the Salesians' efforts to restrict access to outsiders and straitjacket the Indians. Yet others found the intrusive tactics, strict regimentation, and relentless surveillance of the missionaries to be utterly insufferable.

Mario Juruna belonged unequivocally to the camp of malcontents. Perhaps because he was already seventeen when he arrived at the mission, he chafed under its rules and restrictions. Or perhaps, to the contrary, he was too ambitious and wished to engage the world around him at his own pace, rather than bow to the intermediation of the Salesians. As he stated in one interview, "We have to learn how to live, to think, how whites act. Staying inside the village at São Marcos, one is worse off."[6] In any event, in 1964, Juruna left the mission to work as a farmhand on various ranches in the vicinity, with meager pay and under exploitative conditions, but he broke free of the Salesians' control. Five years later, he returned to the mission to live among his people, although he remained unremitting in his hostility toward the missionaries. In 1975 he led 230 members of his community in seceding from the mission to create a new village named Namunkurá within the territorial confines of São Marcos. In Xavante society, such fissures had been historically common in response to cultural tensions or demographic pressures and probably were at play here as well; nevertheless, the Salesians rightfully interpreted the founding of this village miles away from the mission as a major rebuff. Indeed, Juruna became an outspoken critic of the Salesians, denouncing their educational system for deculturating Xavante youths and lambasting the mission's labor regimen and remunerative systems as forms of semi-servitude. Juruna also deployed his combative skills to confront and harry the Brazilian government—then under military rule—for its violation of indigenous land rights. Like other Xavante leaders, he faced formidable obstacles, for the northern region of Mato Grosso had become a favorite among government planners, corporate investors, and real estate speculators committed to the development of the region.

Since 1964, when the military seized power, the Brazilian government had shown a steadfast commitment to the settlement and economic growth of northern Mato Grosso and other parts of Legal Amazonia—the vast western and northern hinterland of the country that continued to remain sparsely populated and economically underdeveloped decades after the March to the West. The military constructed a network of roads through the region to link economic markets and facilitate transportation and communication with more economically dynamic regions. Through generous tax breaks, fiscal subsidies, and sweetheart deals, corporate investors were encouraged by the military government to establish cattle ranches in Mato Grosso, while large-scale immigration was also sponsored in an attempt to increase the population on the frontier and to protect national security. Most of these landowners failed to use their plots productively; instead, they found that razing the vegetation, clearing the land, and reselling their property proved easier and far more lucrative in a booming real estate market. For the Xavante, the developmental model endorsed by the military government triggered increased settlement by outsiders, social marginalization, and alarming deforestation of their territory. As a result of such conflict, violence mounted in the area.

The military government sought to resolve the "Indian problem" by reserving small plots of land for indigenous communities, thereby allowing for outlying areas to be sold off and developed while ensuring social peace and safeguarding its image in the international community. In 1967 it replaced the Indian Protection Service with the National Foundation of the Indian (FUNAI), entrusted with the demarcation of reserves and providing assistance to indigenous communities. Yet over the course of the 1970s, FUNAI found that its goals were stymied on two fronts: landowners objected when reserves encroached on what they considered "their" territory, while indigenous communities insisted that the state create larger reserves and evict all invaders. In Mato Grosso, such tension reached a boiling point in 1976, when landowners who objected to the demarcation of a reserve at Merure murdered Rodolfo Lunkenbein, the director of the Salesian mission at Merure as well as a Bororo Indian. Like most murders in Brazil committed by large landowners, the assassins were acquitted, in this case on the grounds of self-defense. At São

Marcos the Xavante did succeed in removing landowners and squatters from the reserve after they raided several local ranches, slaughtered cattle, interdicted road traffic, and threatened to blow up bridges; still, it took more than three years after official demarcation of the reserve by the government to secure their territory. Throughout the struggle, the Xavante were quite aware that because they were outnumbered and outgunned by their neighbors, they depended ultimately on FUNAI and the missionaries to defend their communities. Thus, Xavante leaders parlayed the aggressive tactics traditionally used in armed warfare into political mobilization, now the key to demarcating their territories and retaining access to industrial goods.

Xavante leaders regularly trekked now to the nation's capital, Brasília, to pressure government officials. Indignant and resolute—and often daubed with war paint—they would show up at FUNAI to demand the creation of larger reserves, the eviction of interlopers from their territories, the dismissal of corrupt government officials, and greater material resources and social services for their communities. Competition among Xavante chiefs and communities further served to fuel this aggressive lobbying, as the success of an actual or potential leader increasingly derived from his ability to attain the backing of influential *waradzu* for community (and factional) struggles and to net consumer goods. To publicize their struggles and spotlight bureaucratic stonewalling, the Xavante made highly effective use of the media, which during the later years of military dictatorship had seen a relaxation of state censorship. And perhaps none was more creative on this account than Mario Juruna, who had already mastered the art of playing off missionary against bureaucrat to gain leverage for his community. Juruna now sought to document the empty promises and double-talk of FUNAI leaders toward the Xavante with a hidden tape recorder and to replay them—to the officials' mortification—to the press. As he succinctly stated, "I bought the tape recorder because whites make many promises, and then forget them."[7]

Juruna's publicity stunt catapulted him to national fame. For Brazilians who held that Indians were inherently more moral than whites, Juruna's tape recorder, revealing the duplicity of government officials, only confirmed their beliefs. For opponents of the military regime, here was a brave soul who challenged authoritarianism and corruption in the government. Indeed, even for government officials, Juruna symbolized what they had long preached: Indians could benefit from technology like everyone else—and even use it for higher ends. And still for others, Juruna was an exotic or amusing diversion: a curious hybrid sporting the traditional long hair and pierced earlobes of adult Xavante men, but dressed in western clothes, toting a tape recorder, and speaking heavily accented and grammatically incorrect Portuguese. In fact, Juruna's crafty

use of the tape recorder was only another example of the Xavante's appropriation of white symbols, slogans, and accoutrements for indigenous
ends. From missionaries, government officials, and the media, he cobbled
together elements of the dominant discourse that had defined Indians as
protopatriots and noble savages but fired them back in protest. "We are
truer Brazilians than the whites," he proclaimed; "FUNAI has the obligation to pay for our things . . . all Brazilians have an obligation because
they took everything that was ours. Formerly, during the time of our
grandfathers, all the land was ours."[8] Such appeals sought to pressure
government officials to enforce the protective legal measures safeguarding indigenous lands and communities.

By 1980, many indigenous communities throughout Brazil had become politically mobilized. Assisted by the Catholic Church—which
helped to organize pan-Indian meetings and to defend native rights—by
sympathetic members of the press and civil society, and by international
pressure, indigenous leaders took FUNAI and the Brazilian government
to task for countless wrongs. The Indian bureau, staffed by military officials, systematically rode roughshod over indigenous concerns, abusing
rather than honoring its legal guardianship of Indians; large-scale state
projects, such as roads and hydroelectric dams, violently displaced and
prejudiced indigenous communities; the government, favoring investors
over Indians, authorized the exploration of minerals on native territory
and overlooked the invasion and deforestation of Indian lands; corruption permeated FUNAI, while social services for indigenous communities lagged; and the government's assimilationist policies and
condescending attitudes devalued indigenous cultures.

Thus, abundant evidence implicated Brazil when the Fourth International Russell Tribunal convened in Holland in 1980 to judge various
governments and missionary groups in the Americas for their violation
of indigenous rights, with indigenous leaders and anthropologists acting
as the jury. In a symbolic example of the sociocultural and political
shakeups that have marked the postcolonial world, Mario Juruna, whose
youth had been spent in the thickets of the Mato Grosso *cerrado*, was
invited to Europe by the Russell Tribunal to serve on the jury. Outraged,
the Ministry of the Interior exploited the state's statutory guardianship
of indigenous peoples to deny Juruna travel authorization, alleging that
he was unqualified to deliberate on behalf of other Indian groups before
a tribunal unrecognized by the Brazilian government. The military also
sought to exploit the historic rivalries among the Xavante, mobilizing
other leaders to discredit Juruna as illegitimate or unrepresentative.

The case generated substantial domestic controversy, and the
Xavante's supporters vowed to make a legal appeal on behalf of Juruna,
who had become a symbol of resistance to military rule. When the

Federal Court of Appeals struck down the travel ban, the FUNAI president admonished Juruna that he was not to defame Brazil abroad and that if he did not like Brazil, "[he should] go to Bolivia."[9] In November 1980, Juruna took his seat as the honorary president of the Russell Tribunal (having since been upgraded by its organizers to pressure the military government to grant travel authorization), which, to the chagrin of military officials, condemned the deleterious effects of the government's developmental policies on the Yanomami and Nambiquara Indians.

Shortly after Juruna returned from Europe, he began to speak publicly of his intention to enter Brazilian politics, which boasted a competitive party system in the final years of the military dictatorship. It was certainly difficult to return to São Marcos, given the opposition on his home turf from the Salesians, FUNAI, and other Xavante leaders, who accused him—either out of moral indignation, jealousy, or both—of abandoning his community and spending too much time among whites. Juruna was assiduously courted by Leonel Brizola, a populist politician who had returned to Brazil from exile to lead a left-of-center political party and to campaign for governor of the state of Rio de Janeiro. Affiliating with Brizola's party, Juruna moved to Rio to run for the federal congress, since he knew he stood little chance of being elected from his native state of Mato Grosso. In his campaign, Juruna defended the rights not only of the Indians but also of all of Brazil's poor and disadvantaged. Appearing together with Brizola at political rallies, Juruna was sure to draw a crowd of curious city dwellers either eager to hear his chastening discourse, show their irreverent disregard for the military and traditional Brazilian politics, or simply be entertained by an "exotic" candidate. It proved to be a winning ticket: Juruna was elected as congressman from Rio, and Brizola as governor.

As Brazil's first Indian elected to the national congress, Juruna faced constant surveillance, earning both praise and ridicule. Indeed, his checkered record during his term in office (1983–1987) would provide ammunition to both supporters and detractors. Juruna successfully presided over the creation of a congressional commission on indigenous affairs and met with native groups from throughout Brazil. He vowed to root out malfeasance in FUNAI and to restructure the agency to grant to Indians a greater role in its administration. Juruna denounced the leasing out of indigenous land by FUNAI for commercial purposes and the invasion of Yanomami land by gold miners, and he accused the government of fomenting or failing to prevent violence against indigenous leaders. His diatribes against economic austerity measures and corruption in the government—asserting that "every Minister is a thief"[10]—riled military officials, who demanded his removal from office for lack of decorum, but ultimately they were satisfied with a formal apology. In 1984 he spoke before the human rights commission of the United Nations in Geneva, denouncing the invasion of indigenous territory, while calling for "greater access to the channels of power in Brazil and the world for indigenous populations."[11]

Yet, Juruna was also constantly taunted for being an acculturated exotic or an inauthentic Indian by those who could or would only view "real" Indians as those still living uncontacted in the forest according to traditional ways. And notwithstanding Juruna's pan-Indian discourse and platform, Brazil's indigenous population was too small and too diverse—divided by language, culture, religion, geography, historical experiences, and traditional rivalries—to coalesce into a formidable power bloc. As a token ethnic leader, Juruna faced intense social pressure; as a national politician, he faced the temptation of illicit self-enrichment. In 1984, Juruna buckled. Reversing a position he had held since assuming office, he stunned his supporters by proclaiming that the land claims of the Pataxó Indians of Bahia—engaged in a bitter and long-standing struggle with large landowners to reclaim ancestral territory—were unfounded since the Pataxó were too acculturated to be "real" Indians. Juruna, accompanied to the area by three conservative Bahian congressmen and seduced by financial incentives offered by the landowners, had proposed that the Pataxó be relocated. Indigenous leaders and advocacy groups were outraged by Juruna's betrayal, couched in the racist stereotypes about indigenous authenticity historically used to discredit land claims (and, ironically, to impugn Juruna himself). Subsequently, Juruna was involved in another bribery scandal in the national congress.

Juruna was not reelected to office. While he would serve as an adviser on indigenous affairs and obtain a sinecure from FUNAI, he essentially faded into oblivion. Embittered by his foray into the Brazilian political system, Juruna declared: "I was used here by the whites, who are very evil, cheap, and envious. In 1982, when the PDT [the acronym of Brizola's party] was small, I was presented as an attraction at rallies, the way a street vendor uses a domesticated snake to attract a clientele to sell his knickknacks. Now that the party [PDT] is strong, a party I helped to found, they got rid of me."[12] Juruna was, in part, correct: his ethnicity had been exploited by more savvy and opportunistic politicians to attract curious onlookers and independent-minded voters. Because he was an Indian, he had been endlessly scrutinized while in office, lionized or lampooned as he deviated from or conformed to the socially constructed (and unrealistic) notions that Brazilians held regarding indigenous peoples. But whether through political miscalculation, unbearable pressure, or personal greed, he ultimately squandered a promising electoral mandate and an opportunity to strengthen a fledgling pan-Indian movement.

Mario Juruna's life, like those of other Indian leaders, was shaped by the larger socioeconomic forces that have rocked indigenous communities over the last half century with the expansion of the Brazilian frontier and the consolidation of state power: the loss of traditional lands and autonomy, the penetration of the market economy, increased socioeconomic marginalization, and painful apprenticeship and exploitation in the white world. The dismal health conditions, inadequate schools, endemic poverty, ongoing social discrimination, and pervasive invasion of indigenous lands are all grim reminders of the precarious status of Brazil's Indians. Yet Juruna's life also demonstrates the innovative ways in which indigenous peoples have sought to engage the Brazilian legal and political systems in a desperate attempt to safeguard their communities and ensure cultural respect. Manipulating societal images about noble savages, marshalling traditional warrior skills, and appealing to domestic and international allies, Juruna succeeded in becoming, against all odds, a political leader of national renown. He soon learned that such saintly images are impossible to fulfill, particularly for beleaguered communities and their leaders; that Brazilian politics offers a range of options calibrated to legislators' moral barometer; and that political allies and the media can be fickle. And perhaps Brazilians had learned that indigenous communities are complex, varied, and multifaceted; and that these communities face inordinate social pressure, racial discrimination, and internal conflict in adapting to that externally imposed reality to which they strive to belong: the Brazilian nation.

NOTES

1. Cândido Mariano da Silva Rondon, *Rumo ao Oeste* (Rio de Janeiro: Laemmert, 1942), 21–22.

2. J. R. do Amaral Lapa, *Missão do Sangradouro* (Rio de Janeiro: Coleção Saraiva, 1963), 121.

3. Ismael da Silva Leitão, "Relatório da viagem de inspeção feita a Missão Salesiana São Marcos," *Goiâna*, 21 September 1966, Museu do Índio, Sector de Documentação [hereafter MI, SEDOC], Film 273, Fot837-39.

4. Pe. Bartolomeu Giaccaria to Fundação Nacional do Índio (FUNAI), 10 July 1971, MI, SEDOC, Film 237, Fot1294-1308.

5. Lapa, *Missão do Sangradouro*, 102–3.

6. Juruna, quoted in Edilson Martins, *Nossos Índios, Nossos Mortos* (Rio de Janeiro: CODERCI, 1978), 205.

7. Ibid., 207.

8. Alvaro Pereira and Armando Rollemberg, "Entrevista: Dzururan (Mario), Cacique/Em Busca de Sobrevivência," *Veja*, 20 November 1974.

9. FUNAI President João Nobre da Veiga, quoted in "Juruna advertido para 'não atacar o Brasil,' " *Folha de São Paulo*, 1 November 1980.

10. "Ministros de Figueiredo pedem a punição de Juruna," *Jornal do Brasil*, 29 September 1983.

11. "Juruna denuncia na ONU que o maior inimigo Índio é o avanço da sociedade," *Estado de Minas*, 1 August 1984.

12. "Juruna, agora derrotado, volta à selva," *O Globo*, 21 November 1986.

SUGGESTED READINGS

On the life of Mario Juruna, see Mario Juruna, Antonio Hohlfeldt, and Assis Hoffmann, *O gravador do Juruna* (Pôrto Alegre: Mercado Aberto, 1982); for penetrating analyses of his meteoric rise and fall, see the discussion in Beth L. Conklin and Laura R. Graham, "The Shifting Middle Ground: Amazonian Indians and Eco-Politics," *American Anthropologist* 97 (1995): 695–710; and Alcida Rita Ramos, *Indigenism: Ethnic Politics in Brazil* (Madison: University of Wisconsin Press, 1998). The speeches he delivered while serving as a congressman are reprinted in Mario Juruna, *Discursos de liberdade, 1983–86* (Brasília: Câmara dos Deputados, 1986).

On the Xavante Indians, there are several enlightening ethnographies and ethnohistories: David Maybury-Lewis, *Akwe-Shavante Society* (New York: Oxford University Press, 1974); Maybury-Lewis, *The Savage and the Innocent* (Boston: Beacon Press, 1988); Laura R. Graham, *Performing Dreams: Discourses of Immortality among the Xavante of Central Brazil* (Austin: University of Texas Press, 1995); Aracy Lopes da Silva, "Dois séculos e meio de história Xavante," in Manuela Carneiro da Cunha, ed., *História dos índios no Brasil* (São Paulo: Companhia das Letras, Fundação de Amparo à Pesquisa no Estado de São Paulo, Secretaria Municipal de Cultura, 1992); and Nancy Flowers, "Forager-Farmers: The Xavante Indians of Central Brazil" (Ph.D. diss., City University of New York, 1983).

On Brazilian indigenous policy, see Seth Garfield, *Indigenous Struggle at the Heart of Brazil: State Policy, Frontier Expansion, and the Xavante Indians, 1937–1988* (Durham: Duke University Press, 2001); Ramos, *Indigenism: Ethnic Politics in Brazil*; Darcy Ribeiro, *Os índios e a civilização* (Rio de Janeiro: Civilização Brasileira, 1970); Shelton H. Davis, *Victims of the Miracle: Development and the Indians of Brazil* (Cambridge: Cambridge University Press, 1986); Mércio Pereira Gomes, *The Indians and Brazil*, trans. John W. Moon (Gainesville: University of Florida Press, 2000); Antonio Carlos de Souza Lima, *Um grande cerco de paz: Poder tutelar, indianidade e formação de Estado no Brasil* (Petrópolis: Vozes, 1995); John Hemming, *Red Gold: The Conquest of the Brazilian Indians* (Cambridge: Harvard University Press, 1978); and Hemming, *Amazon Frontier: The Defeat of the Brazilian Indians* (London: Macmillan, 1987).

On frontier expansion in Amazonia and its deleterious effects on native populations and the environment, see Susanna B. Hecht and Alexander Cockburn, *The Fate of the Forest: Developers, Destroyers, and Defenders of the Amazon* (London: Verso, 1989); Dennis J. Mahar, *Frontier Development Policy in Brazil: A Study of Amazonia* (New York: Praeger, 1979); Sue Branford and Oriel Glock, *The Last Frontier: Fighting over Land in the Amazon* (London: Zed Books, 1985); Marianne Schmink and Charles H. Wood, eds., *Frontier Expansion in Amazonia* (Gainesville: University Press of Florida, 1984); Schmink and Wood, *Contested Frontiers in Amazonia* (New York: Columbia University Press, 1992); Linda Rabben, *Unnatural Selection: The Yanomami, the Kayapó, and the Onslaught of Civilization* (Seattle: University of Washington Press, 1998); and David Price, *Before the Bulldozer: The Nambiquara Indians and the World Bank* (Cabin John, MD: Seven Locks Press, 1989).